THE SOVIET UNION

The Soviet Union
A GEOGRAPHICAL SURVEY

G. Melvyn Howe
MSc, PhD, DSc, FRSE
Professor and Head of Department of Geography,
University of Strathclyde, Glasgow.
Formerly Reader in Geography,
University College of Wales, Aberystwyth.

Second edition

Longman
Scientific &
Technical

Copublished in the United States with
John Wiley & Sons, Inc., New York

Longman Scientific & Technical
Longman Group UK Limited
Longman House, Burnt Mill, Harlow
Essex CM20 2JE, England
and Associated Companies throughout the world

Copublished in the United States with
John Wiley & Sons, Inc., 605 Third Avenue, New York, NY 10158

First published 1968
Reprinted by Longman Scientific & Technical 1986

British Library Cataloguing in Publication Data

Howe, G. Melvyn
    The Soviet Union: A geographical survey – 2nd ed
    1. Soviet Union – Description and travel – 1970
    I. Title
    914.7   DK29

ISBN 0-582-30172-6

Library of Congress Cataloging-in-Publication Data

Howe, G. Melvyn (George Melvyn)
    The Soviet Union: a geographical survey.

    Reprint. Originally published: 2nd ed. Estover,
Plymouth: Macdonald and Evans, 1983.
    Bibliography: p.
    Includes index.
    1. Soviet Union – Economic conditions – 1976–
2. Geography, Economic.   I. Title.
HC336.25.H68   1986   330.947   86-13363
ISBN 0-470-20674-8 (USA Only)

Produced by Longman Group (FE) Ltd
Printed in Hong Kong

Preface to the Second Edition

A second edition of this book has long been called for, and my delay in producing it has been due only to my commitments in other fields. I must thank my publishers for their understanding and patience.

Data from the most recent (1979) census of population, from the Eleventh Five-year Plan (1981-85) and information on new developments in the ever-expanding Soviet economy have been taken into account in this edition. Cognisance has also been taken of Soviet achievements in space flight, of the nuclear capability of the USSR and of the Strategic Arms Limitation Treaty (SALT 2) which, though signed in June 1979 by President Breshnev of the USSR and President Carter of the USA, has not as yet been ratified by the US Senate. Every effort has been made to ensure that all the information — environmental, social, political and economic — is as up to date as possible; it will be understood, however, that the USSR is a very large country, and it is not always possible to make definitive statements on every aspect. The *News Notes* sections in *Soviet Geography: Review and Translation,* prepared regularly by Theodore Shabad, and *Soviet News* published by the Soviet Embassy in London have proved invaluable in revising and updating details of aspects of the Soviet economy. I gladly acknowledge my indebtedness to these two sources.

It would burden the book unnecessarily to give sources for all statements of fact. I have done so, nevertheless, when tables of statistics are involved, and my list of further reading points to other major sources.

The updating of the book has involved an almost complete rewriting. The overview presented in Parts One, Two and Three demonstrates not only the highly centralised political, economic and social system of the country but also the great variety of physical conditions within its boundaries. Appropriate consideration

is given to physical environmental conditions but historical, economic and social aspects receive a somewhat more extended treatment.

The detailed region-by-region survey of the country in Part Four has been completely restructured. It now takes as its framework the officially designated eighteen economic regions, together with Moldavia SSR. Regional analysis on this basis is considered justifiable since Soviet geographers believe, on grounds of Marxist and Leninist dialectic materialism, that these regions exist because their functional characteristics are created and fashioned by State planning decisions. Whatever changes may have occurred, the present economic regions have remained fairly constant during the last two decades and have been used by the Soviets for statistical reporting and purposes of planning. The basic economic regions have been further grouped into seven economic macro-regions, following the scheme devised by Aleksandrov, Kistanov, and Ephshteyn of the State Planning Commission (GOSPLAN) in 1974.

The purpose of the book is, quite simply, to be informative. Ideological reasons apart, the fact remains that in little over sixty years the Soviet Union has developed from a position of international insignificance to that of a major power in our known planet. It seems to me that this is not sufficiently realised in western democracies, and if this book contributes to a differentiation between vague ideas and substantial fact, its purpose will, for the meantime, have been fulfilled.

The English version of certain commonly used names (such as Moscow instead of Moskva) has been adopted, otherwise place names have been transliterated according to *Transliteration of Cyrillic and Greek Characters* (British Standard 2979: 1958, British Standards Institution). The second edition of M.S. Bodnarskii's *Slovar geograficheskikh nazvanii* (Dictionary of Geographical Names), Moscow, 1958, has been used as source for most of the place-names. Distances, heights, areas, temperatures and precipitation are expressed in the metric system; a conversion to non-metric equivalent is given in Appendix IV. The Great Patriotic War of Soviet usage is referred to, throughout, as the Second World War.

Even if he were permitted to travel widely within the country, no foreigner is capable of describing adequately the Soviet scene. For this reason frequent use is made of literary quotations from Russian sources. For the few with some reading ability in the language, the quotations draw attention to Russian writings which may be followed up. For others, bibliographical material has been restricted to books, articles and atlases in the English language. Further references will be found in the works listed.

Acknowledgments are due, and are gratefully made, to Miss

A. Laing, Mrs J. Simpson and Mrs M. MacLeod for preparing a clear typescript from my often almost indecipherable, multi-inked, and much-altered manuscript; to Mrs S. Alford, Photograph Librarian, for allowing me to make a selection of half-tone illustrations from the extensive collection of photographs of the USSR held by Novosti Press in London; to Dr Leslie Symons of University College, Swansea, and Messrs Bell and Hyman Limited for permission to reproduce Figs. 75 and 76, Dr Russell B. Adams of the University of Minnesota for Fig. 66 and Dr E.B. Bridges of University College, Swansea, and Cambridge University Press for Figs. 30, 32 and 33 and Dr H.D. Foth and John Wiley & Sons Inc. for Fig. 34.

I wish to record my thanks to the cartographic and editorial staff of Macdonald & Evans, and in particular to Mr Peter Williams, who, with great efficiency, have guided this book through the various stages of production.

My final and greatest acknowledgment is to my wife, Patricia, and youngest daughter, Clare, who have gladly and willingly given me support and encouragement, and have cheerfully tolerated the encroachment on our normal domestic life.

1983 G. Melvyn Howe

Contents

PART FIVE: CONCLUSION

APPENDIXES

CHAPTER I

Size, Location and Space Relationships

The Soviet Union, heir to the Russian Empire and world superpower, is an immense country, covering approximately 22,400,000 km² (*see* Fig. 1). It contains almost one-sixth of the land area of the world (excluding Antarctica), extending from eastern Europe across northern Asia. Africa (30,400,000 km²) and Anglo-America (24,600,000 km²) exceed it in area, but Latin America (20,700,000 km²) is smaller. It is over ninety times the size of the United Kingdom, nearly three times that of the United States (*see* Fig. 2), three times the size of Antarctica, and two-and-a-half times that of Australia. In form, this vast area may be likened to a wide amphitheatre facing and sloping towards the Arctic Ocean. Broad plains and lowlands occupy the western and central part of the country, and an almost unbroken chain of high mountains and rugged plateaux stretches along its southern, south-eastern and eastern frontiers.

For those familiar only with distances within Britain or Western Europe, it is difficult to comprehend the size of this sub-continental Euro-Asiatic landmass. The 10,000 or more kilometres distance between the Soviet Union's westernmost point, the city of Kaliningrad, to its easternmost point, the Ratmanov Island on the Pacific coast, is roughly equivalent to that between London and Peking, or between Edinburgh and Cape Town. Rail journeys in the USSR are often measured in days rather than in hours, as may be illustrated by the average train times for 1980 shown below.

Moscow to Riga (922 km)   14-15 hours
Moscow to Leningrad (650 km)   6-8 hours (depending on
                                 the train)
Moscow to Kiev (872 km)   12-13 hours

Fig. 1. The Soviet Union in its world setting.

Moscow to Baku (2,475 km)	43 hours	
Moscow to Sverdlovsk (1,818 km)	27 hours	
Moscow to Samarkand (3,723 km)	3 days	
Moscow to Novosibirsk (3,343 km)	2 days	
Moscow to Irkutsk (5,191 km)	3 days and 9 hours	
Moscow to Vladivostok (9,297 km)	6 days and 7 hours	

The journey by air from Moscow to Novosibirsk takes only 5 hours, that from Moscow to Khabarovsk 7½ hours, from Moscow to Tashkent 4 hours, and from Moscow to Irkutsk 5¾ hours. Air travel is the obvious answer for fast passenger movement within the Soviet Union.

The northernmost point of the USSR is Rudolf Island in Franz Josef Land (82° N), though on the Soviet mainland the most northerly point is Cape Chelyuskin on the Taymyr Peninsula (78° N) (*see* Fig. 3). More than half of the Soviet Arctic coast lies north of 70° N; four-fifths of the country is north of 60° N.

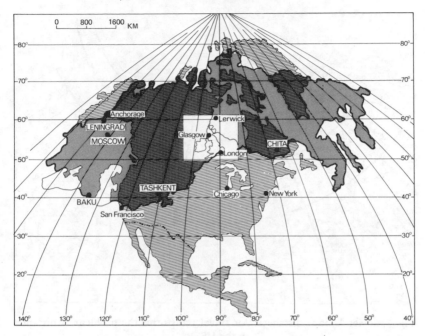

Fig. 2. A comparison of areas and latitudes: Soviet Union – North America –
British Isles.

The most southerly point of the USSR is near the town of Kushka
(35° N) in Soviet Central Asia, where the boundaries of the Turkmen
SSR project towards Afghanistan. The parallel 40° N latitude marks
the approximate southern boundary of the western half of the Union,
and the 50° N parallel the eastern half. At most, the mainland
territory of the USSR extends through 34° of latitude (just over
3,900 km); usually it ranges between 25° and 30° of latitude (2,500-
3,400 km). Moscow, capital of the USSR, is at a latitude similar to
that of Glasgow (Scotland) and Edmonton (Canada). Cape Horn,
the most southerly point of Latin America, is a latitudinal equivalent
in the southern hemisphere. Leningrad, the second largest city, lies
close to the same latitudes as Lerwick (Shetland Islands) and
Anchorage (Alaska). Chita in eastern Siberia is at about the same
latitude as London (England) (*see* Fig. 2) and Dushanbe, capital of
Tadzhik SSR is at a similar latitude to Washington DC in the USA.
    The longitudinal extent of the country is more than twice its
maximum north-south extent and embraces eleven of the world's
twenty-four time zones (*see* Fig. 4). When the clock in the Spasskaya
(Saviour's) Tower in Red Square, Moscow, tolls midnight, the people
of Vladivostok have already breakfasted. On the Kuril Islands day
breaks even earlier. From its most westerly point near Kaliningrad on

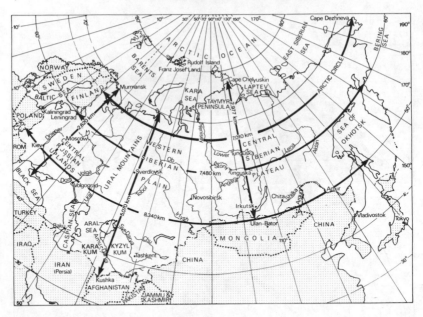

Fig. 3. Soviet Union: distances. Air travel transforms the problem of distance in the USSR.

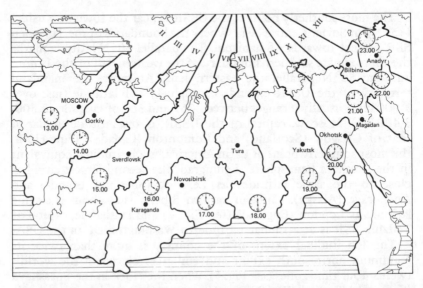

Fig. 4. Soviet Union: time zone chart. Standard time is advanced one hour the year round in the Soviet Union. The symbol in each zone shows local time when it is noon at Greenwich.

the Gulf of Danzig (20° E) to Cape Dezhneva (East Cape, 170° W) on the Bering Strait, the Great Circle (i.e. the shortest) distance is over North Polar regions and is about 6,500 km. A comparable distance in the Western Hemisphere would be that of the Great Circle route from France westwards to Georgia, USA. The Arctic and Pacific island possessions excepted, the Soviet Union forms a single continuous territorial block. Shaped somewhat like a curved or spherical parallelogram, with very irregular and indented sides, it is the world's greatest uninterrupted expanse of territory under one political system.

Statements of physical extent are impressive, but what really matters is the proportion of land that is suitable for human settlement and its true economic potential. In this respect the position is not so impressive. The Soviet Union controls abundant space, but the nature of this space and its potential for human settlement vary considerably from place to place. There are vast areas which are unsuitable for human settlement and the bulk of the population of the country inhabits only a fraction of the territory. Over 2½ million km² are desert and semi-arid steppe, 9 million km² are underlain by permafrost (permanently frozen ground) (*see* p. 20 *et seq.*, and Fig. 14), with all the Arctic and many Pacific shores and many of the large rivers frozen over for much of the year.

The immensity of the physical background is the primary and the most significant geographical fact about the country. It was this vastness and relative inaccessibility of the oceans, with corollaries of defence in depth and relative invulnerability, that provided the corner-stone for the concept of the Heartland of the Old World Island propounded in 1904 by the British political geographer, Sir Halford Mackinder. In Mackinder's time, three-quarters of a century ago, sea power was considered to be decisive in world affairs. Mackinder's hypothesis was that the Old World Island, comprising Europe-Africa-Asia, has a sub-continental Heartland, or pivot area, in the region lying generally east of the Volga in what is now Soviet territory (*see* Figs. 5 and 6). The Heartland was considered to be strategically placed to command interior lines of communication within Eurasia, with the potential to become a power base. In Mackinder's view, the state which controlled the Heartland was in an almost unchallengeable position to attempt military and, subsequently, political mastery of the World Island, since he "who rules the World Island commands the world".

The physical environment decreed that much of Mackinder's Heartland would have been more aptly described as "dead heartland", particularly the deserts and semi-deserts of Soviet Central Asia, and the icy and forested wastes of northern Siberia. In recent years, however, in the wake of technological change, the Soviets

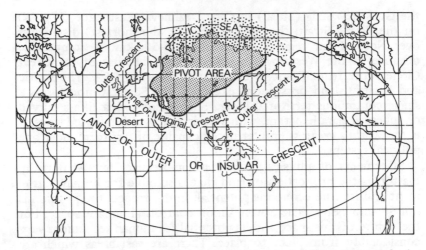

(After J.R. Fernstrom in *Principles of Political Geography* by
Hans W. Weigert *et al.*, New York, 1957.)

Fig. 5. Mackinder's Heartland (1904) shown on the Mercator projection.

have implemented and are implementing ambitious plans to develop
vast gas, oil, water, ferrous and non-ferrous metal reserves and
resources of timber in these same regions. The rapidly expanding
coal-mining areas of Ekibastuz and Karaganda in Kazakhstan, new
developments in the Achinsk-Kansk and Kuznetsk coal basins, the
highly significant natural gas finds in Western Siberia (e.g. the sub-
arctic Punga-Ingrim fields), in Turkmenistan (e.g. Achak) and
Uzbekistan (e.g. Gazli), important new oil-producing fields in the
middle reaches of the River Ob (Tyumen Oblast) and at Mangyshlak,
in the deserts of western Kazakhstan, the active construction of the
long-projected Baykal-Amur Mainline (BAM) railway to open up
the copper, aluminium and timber reserves of eastern Siberia and
the Far East, etc., all testify to the very considerable importance
the Soviets attach to these Heartland regions.

RUSSIAN ISOLATION

High mountains and deserts in the east and south cut off what was
then Russia from the ancient civilisations of China and India. The
religious barrier of Polish Catholicism prevented free intercourse
with Western Europe, while the partly frozen Arctic shores in the
north of the country proved "the sealed lips of Russia". Russia was,
in consequence, isolated from the outside world throughout much
of her history. Road and railway construction under the Soviet
regime and the forging of new air links are combining to break
down this isolation. Regular Aeroflot air services now link the

(After J.R. Fernstrom in *Principles of Political Geography* by
Hans W. Weigert *et al.*, New York, 1957.)

Fig. 6. The relationship of the Heartland and North America, shown on the azimuthal polar projection.

Soviet Union with sixty or more countries in Europe, Asia, Africa, North America and Cuba.

The shores of the Arctic and Pacific have been made accessible to convoys of ships during a few short summer months by the use of nuclear-powered and modern conventional ice-breakers following the Northern Sea Route between Vladivostok, Petropavlovsk-Kamchatskiy, Arkhangelsk and Murmansk. In Eastern Europe, the religious barrier of Polish Catholicism has long since disappeared and, after the wholesale shift of German and Polish populations and boundaries after the Second World War (the Great Patriotic War), the Soviet boundary now follows approximately the Curzon Line (a line which had been drawn on ethnographic grounds in 1919 as the eastern frontier of Poland). Even so, the isolation is still perpetuated by the

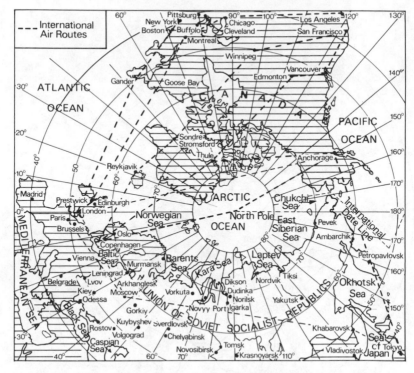

Fig. 7. Arctic neighbours of the USSR.

Communist political system, which continues to maintain an "Iron Curtain" as effective as any natural or religious barrier.

In terms of military strategy, however, the isolation is far from complete. The sheer bulk of the country and the adverse physical factors which proved a stumbling block to Napoleon in the nineteenth century and to Hitler in the first half of the twentieth century have little or no bearing in the closing decades of the twentieth century. The world is now in the air and space age, the age of space satellites and inter-continental ballistic missiles (ICBMs) armed with multiple nuclear warheads. The very heart of the Soviet Union is under constant surveillance by the space satellites of possible future adversaries and it is as exposed and vulnerable to attack by IBMs as are its boundary regions. A real or perceived threat to its security has led the Soviet Union to engage in a massive build up of its military strength, to implement an extensive civil defence system within the country, and to lauch innumerable orbital space satellites and space laboratories (e.g. *Salyut 6-Soyuz* complex*) for information surveil-

*In this complex two Soviet cosmonauts spent 140 days (5th June to 2nd November 1978) in weightlessness, two further cosmonauts completed 175 days (25th February to 19th August 1979) and on the 26th May 1981 cosmonauts Popov and Ryumin completed

lance on likely future enemies. The USSR of the 1980s is a nuclear superpower. It has long-range rocket missiles (e.g. SS20s with triple or more MIRVed* warheads) either mobile or set in steel and concrete silos scattered across the country, and a formidable front-line airforce and air transport fleet. Its merchant fleet has undergone spectacular growth and now ranks sixth in the world, while Soviet

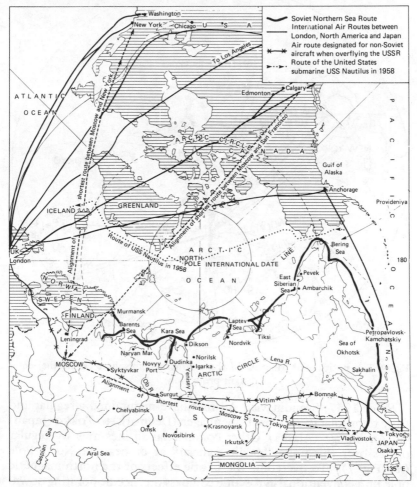

Fig. 8. Air route across the USSR for non-Soviet aircraft (e.g. British Airways) flying between London and Tokyo, the Soviet Northern Sea Route, and the route of the USS *Nautilus* (1958).

an even longer space mission of 185 days. On 10th December 1982, two other cosmonauts, Anatoly Berezovoi and Valentin Lebedev, the crew of Salyut 7 space station, returned to earth after completing a record 211 days in orbit.

*MIRV—Multiple independently-targetable re-entry vehicle.

nuclear-propelled submarines armed with SLBMs* roam the oceans. Furthermore, the country's conventional landforces greatly exceed those of any other country except China. The time when the Arctic Ocean presented a formidable obstacle has also long since passed.

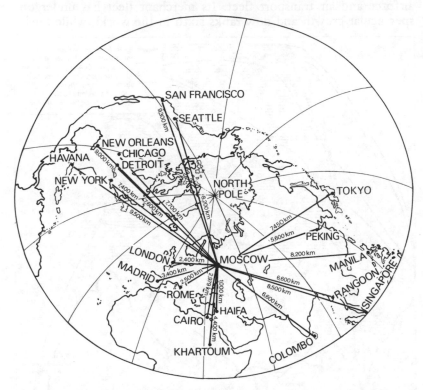

Fig. 9. The position of Moscow in the northern hemisphere (azimuthal equidistant projection).

Since 1957, Scandinavian Airlines have maintained a regular and truly transpolar route from Copenhagen (Denmark) to Tokyo (Japan) via Anchorage (Alaska). Other commercial airlines now fly regular routes over this polar "mediterranean" at or near the North Pole (see Fig. 7). (To overcome the exotic effects of the north magnetic pole on a conventional gyroscope compass (i.e. needle pointing downwards toward the ground in its vicinity) modern aircraft flying in polar latitudes employ a system called inertial navigation (INS) based on an onboard computer.) More recently, the Soviet Government has granted permission to non-Soviet aircraft to fly through its air space along a prescribed route between the Occident and the

*SLBM—Submarine launched ballistic missiles.

Orient (*see* Figs. 8 and 9) (e.g. British Airways, Air France, Japanese Airlines and Lufthansa German Airlines fly non-stop across the USSR between Moscow and Tokyo). In 1958, the United States nuclear-powered submarine *Nautilus* made history by making a successful traverse of the North Polar Sea from the Bering Strait to the Greenland Sea (*see* Fig. 7). Several other submarines have since followed this route. On 17th March 1959 the nuclear submarine *Skate* of the US Navy surfaced through the ice precisely at the North Pole. The first surface ship to reach the North Pole was the nuclear-powered Soviet icebreaker *Arktika* in August 1977.

With the northward shift of resource development in the USSR the Soviets have focussed increased attention on the Northern Sea Route and on Arctic shipping operations generally. The future may yet see nuclear-powered merchant submarines using this North Polar Sea, saving thereby almost 8,000 km on a voyage between Japan and Europe.

The Soviet Union is contained within 60,000 km of frontier. About two-thirds is a sea frontier along the coastlines of the Baltic Sea, the Arctic Ocean, the Pacific Ocean and the Black Sea. About 3,200 km of the total of 16,100 km of land frontiers delimit Soviet territory in Europe against six neighbours: Romania, Hungary, Czechoslovakia, Poland, Finland and Norway. In the Middle East the Soviet Union borders on Turkey, Iran and Afghanistan. Contact in Asia is with Pakistan and China, the Mongolian People's Republic and Korea (*see* Fig. 3).

CHAPTER II

Tectonic Structure, Drainage, Glaciation, Permafrost and Relief

TECTONIC STRUCTURE

A pattern of lowland and plain, surrounded by high mountains, characterises the Russian scene, but this belies a complex geological history. The territory at present occupied by the Soviet Union comprises two very ancient continental platforms: the Russian (East European) Platform in the west, and the Siberian Platform in the east. Both platforms are composed of crystalline rocks of Pre-Cambrian age (*see* Fig. 10) and lie at varying depths below geologically more recent deposits. The basal complexes have proved, in general, to have been resistant to the forces of folding and mountain building, and overlying deposits are consequently only slightly disturbed. They are disposed more or less horizontally. Occasionally the ancient foundations outcrop at the surface, the larger exposures giving rise to "crystalline shields", e.g. the Podolsk-Azov Shield in the Ukraine.

Two further regions of the USSR territory have a base of ancient folded strata: (*a*) the Ural-Altay-Sayan region, underlain by strata of Palaeozoic age, and (*b*) a vast area embracing the greater part of north-eastern Siberia, eastern Trans-Baykal and the Soviet Far East (Primorye-Chukotsk), underlain by Mesozoic strata.

Together the Pre-Cambrian, Palaeozoic and Mesozoic tectonic zones form the base of the greater part of the territory of the Soviet Union. In the south they are bordered by part of the great belt of Cainozoic (Tertiary, Alpine) folding which extends from Gibraltar and the Alps to the islands of Indonesia, which lay on the northern border of the ancient Tethys geosyncline. Within Soviet territory this belt includes a small section of the eastern Carpathians, the Crimea, the Caucasus, the mountains of the Kopet-Dag and the Pamirs. Here volcanic activity belongs to the recent geological past, and extinct volcanoes (e.g. Mount Elbrus, 5,642 m) and earth movements are

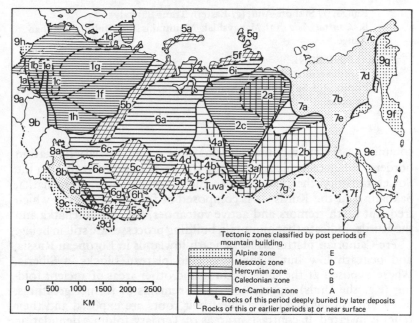

(Adapted from Plate 90 V in Vol. I of the *Great Soviet World Atlas*.)

Fig. 10. Soviet Union: tectonic zones.

A. PRE-CAMBRIAN ZONE

1. *East European Platform:* (a) Baltic Shield; (b) Ukraine Shield; (c) Voronezh Block; (d) Black Sea Basin; (e) North Ukranian Basin; (f) East Russian Basin; (g) Moscow Basin; (h) Caspian Basin.

2. *Siberian Platform:* (a) Anabar Shield; (b) Aldan Shield; (c) Tungus Basin.

B. CALEDONIAN ZONE

3. *Eastern Section:* (a) Pre-Baykalya; (b) Western Trans-Baykalya.

4. *Western Section:* (a) Yenisey Range; (b) Sayan Mountains; (c) Minusinsk Basin; (d) Kuznetsk Basin.

C. HERCYNIAN ZONE

5. *Uplands:* (a) Novaya Zemlya; (b) Ural Mountains; (c) Central Kazakhstan; (d) Altai; (e) Tyan-Shan; (f) Taymyr Peninsula; (g) Severnaya Zemlya.

6. *Lowlands:* (a) Ural-Siberian Depression; (b) Irtysh Basin; (c) Turgay Depression; (d) Amu-Darya Basin; (e) Syr-Darya Basin; (f) Fergana Basin; (g) Chu Basin; (h) Balkhash Basin; (i) Khatanga Depression.

D. MESOZOIC ZONE

7. *Siberia and Maritime Country:* (a) Verkhoyansk Range; (b) Cherskiy Range; (c) Anadyr Range; (d) Kolyma Range; (e) Dzhugdzhur

Range; (f) Sikhote-Alin; (g) Eastern Trans-Baykalya.
8. *Central Asia:* (a) Mangyshlak Mountains; (b) Bolshoi Balkhan Range.

E. ALPINE ZONE
9. *Mountain Border:* (a) Crimea; (b) Caucasus; (c) Kopet-Dag; (d) Pamirs; (e) Sakhalin; (f) Kamchatka; (g) Koryak Range; (h) Carpathians.

common. A second mountain belt of more recent Tertiary formation borders earlier tectonic zones along the Pacific seaboard. Within the Soviet territory the belt includes the Koryak ranges, Kamchatka, Sakhalin and the Kurils. It is composed of fold mountains in which frequent earth tremors and active volcanoes, e.g. in Kamchatka and the Kurils, indicate that mountain building processes are still in being.

Pre-Cambrian platforms lie beneath lowlands in European Russia, and beneath low but highly dissected plateau blocks in Siberia. Where exposed at the surface, these and other areas of ancient folding (e.g. the Urals) represent vestigial remains of former greatness. They are usually low in altitude, their roots are exposed and their relief is inverted. In contrast, in areas of Tertiary folding, denudation has had only a relatively short time in which to work, tectonic structures are conformable and landscapes youthful. Slopes are steep and mountain peaks high and jagged. Upfolds continue to form the mountain summits, and downfolds the intervening valleys.

Past periods of mountain building are of undoubted importance in the geological history of the Soviet territory. Possibly of greater significance, however, were the frequent alternations of marine transgression and regression which occurred particularly west of the Urals in the European part of the USSR. Such advances of the sea — accompanied by the laying down of sedimentary strata — and withdrawals led to a great extent to the variety in age and character of the surface deposits over much of the USSR.

DRAINAGE

Surface waters from Soviet territory find their way into three oceans: the Arctic, Atlantic and Pacific, and into a vast area of inland drainage centring on the Aral-Caspian Basin and Lake Balkhash (*see* Fig. 11).

More than half the country (*see* Table 1), embracing the whole of the north Russian Lowland and Siberia, from the western part of the Kola Peninsula and Karelia to the Kolyma River, drains into the Arctic Ocean. The Northern Dvina (1,290 km with the Sukhona) and Pechora (1,780 km) are the chief rivers of the north Russian

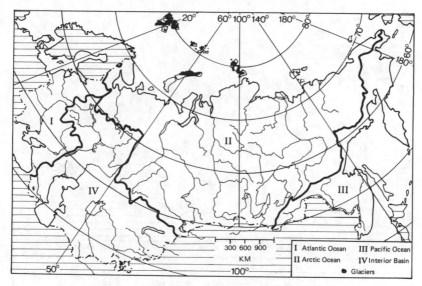

Fig. 11. Soviet Union: major drainage basins.

TABLE 1. DRAINAGE OF THE USSR

Drainage to	Drainage area of USSR million km²	
	million km²	per cent
Arctic Ocean	11.39	51.0
Atlantic Ocean	2.58	11.5
Pacific Ocean	2.33	10.5
Aral-Caspian-Balkhash region of inland drainage	5.95	27.0

Lowland flowing to the Arctic. They rise in glacial morainic hills, flow gently across almost level plains through extensive forested areas, and frequently follow courses that have been altered by glacial action. The Valday glaciation (*see* p. 18) was, geologically speaking, so recent here that the rivers have had insufficient time in which to develop the asymmetric transverse profiles (high right bank, low left bank) which characterise long sections of many other Russian rivers (e.g. the Dnieper and Don in European Russia and the Yenisey in Siberia). The rivers of north European Russia rely on melting snow as the main source of their water. Melting snow gives rise to high water in the spring, although extensive forests and low evaporation rates help maintain a full volume of flow in summer (*see* Fig. 12). In this context it may be noted that by comparison rivers in Britain

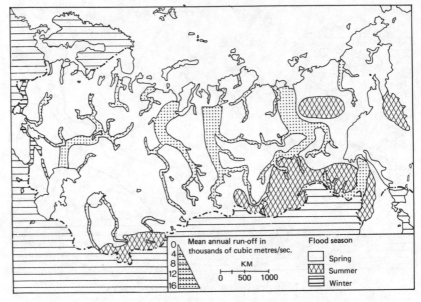

Fig. 12. Soviet Union: run-off and flood seasons.

are rain-fed, their regimes controlled by seasonal evaporation rates, and winter flooding is not unusual.

In western Siberia, the sources of such rivers as the Ob (with Katun, 5,410 km), Irtysh (2,962 km) and Yenisey (4,092 km) are glaciers and snowfields in the Altay, Sayans and in the mountains of pre-Baykalya. Gradients across the lowlands are very gentle and watersheds exceptionally low. River flow through the zones of steppe, forest and tundra is sluggish. Here, too, snow-melt gives rise to high water in the spring. Because the thaw progresses from source to mouth, i.e. is earlier in the upper, more southerly reaches, up-stream melt-water tends to overflow the river banks in the lower reaches and inundates vast areas which are still frozen and under-lain by permafrost, and mouths that are ice-blocked. The resulting flood-marsh and swamp harbour mosquitoes and other blood-sucking insects which make life intolerable for man and beast. Because the greater part of its catchment is underlain by permafrost, run-off in the Lena system in eastern Siberia (4,440 km) is faster than in the Ob-Irtysh system, and with rainwater supplementing snow-melt, high water occurs in the period May-June.

Just over 11 per cent of the rivers in the Soviet Union drain into the Atlantic via the Baltic and the Black-Azov Seas. The Baltic receives the waters of the Neva (70 km), Narva (77 km), Western Dvina (1,015 km) and Neman (885 km); the Black-Azov Seas receive run-off waters from the Dniester (1,411 km), Dnieper (2,200 km), Don (1,960 km), Kuban (937 km), Rioni (290 km) and Danube (2,816 km), though only the lower reaches of the Danube flow through Soviet territory. High water in these rivers generally comes in spring from the melting of a considerable snow cover, and is often accompanied by floods and waterlogging.

The Aral-Caspian-Balkhash region of inland drainage accounts for drainage from over a quarter of the USSR. The Volga (3,530 km) and its tributaries form the greatest drainage system of this region, and it is the longest river in Europe. Its source in the Valday Hills is no more than 200 m above sea-level, and its gradient to the Caspian Sea (26 m below sea-level) is slight throughout its length. Spring floods are usual, but during the excessive heat of the summer, evaporation so reduces run-off that shallows and sand-bars are formed. To counteract this reduction in flow and at the same time improve navigation, huge barriers and multi-purpose reservoirs have been constructed (e.g. at Kuybyshev and Volgograd). Unfortunately, vast open stretches of water along the Volga suffer serious loss through intense evaporation and the level of the Caspian is being appreciably reduced.

The Amu-Darya (Oxus, 2,600 km) and Syr-Darya (Iaxartes, 2,990 km) rise in the Pamirs and Tyan-Shan, and discharge into the enclosed Aral Sea, the fourth largest lake in the world (66,500 km^2). Fed by ground-water, glaciers and snow, these are perennial rivers which flood in the spring and summer. Flow diminishes markedly downstream, where the rivers cross the deserts (Karakum and Kyzylkum). The Ili (1,384 km) and Chu (1,126 km) centering on Lake Balkhash are similar, except that the Chu loses itself in the desert before reaching Balkhash.

Ten and a half per cent of the surface area of the Soviet Union drains to the Pacific. The basin of the Amur (formed by the confluence of the Shilka and Argun rivers) and its tributaries account for practically 60 per cent of these waters. Most of the feed water of the Amur (4,416 km), the longest river of the Soviet Union, comes from the summer monsoon rains of Eastern Asia, and it is during this season that high-water stage is reached in the Amur.

Rivers are the product of the climate which determines their volume and regime. The sub-freezing temperatures which persist throughout the greater part of the Soviet Union in winter cause most rivers to freeze up. In Siberia the middle and upper reaches of the Ob, Yenisey and Lena are frozen for five to six months and their lower reaches for practically eight months in the year. In European Russia, the Pechora is frozen for six and a half months, and the Northern Dvina for five and a half months. In the south and southwest the Don, Dnieper, Bug and Dniester are frozen for between three and four months. The rivers of Central Asia freeze for two to four months. The Rioni, Kura and Araks in Trans-Caucasia do not freeze. The annual freeze up of most rivers in the Soviet Union constitutes a major obstacle to waterborne traffic and an economic inconvenience for several parts of the country.

GLACIATION

During the Pleistocene period, large ice sheets moved outwards from centres in Scandinavia, northern Karelia, Novaya Zemlya, the northern Urals, the Altay, Sayan and Pamirs and the Caucasus. The growth of these ice sheets was initiated by very low temperatures and not, as was once thought, by any increase in precipitation. Three major glacial stages have been recognised in European Russia and another earlier stage surmised. In order of decreasing age these are:

 (a) early glacial stage;
 (b) Oka glacial stage;
 (c) Dnieper glacial stage, with a younger Moscow sub-stage;
 (d) Valday glacial stage.

The discovery in the Baltic and Belorussia regions of glacial deposits older than the Oka glacial stage (lying within deep erosional troughs and separated from Oka deposits by others containing an interglacial flora) lends support for the view that there was an earlier pre-Oka glacial stage.*

The second, or Oka, glaciation spread out from an ice centre in Novaya Zemlya and was the most extensive of the glaciations in European Russia (not the Dnieper glaciation as was previously thought). It penetrated to the edge of the Central Russian Upland, sent a great lobe down the basin of the Don, and extended to the middle Volga and the basins of the Ob and Yenisey rivers. In Siberia it is called the Demianka glaciation (see Fig. 13). Here, further away from the principal nourishment source, the glaciation was thinner and less extensive than in what is now European Russia. Whereas the ice mantle was as much as 2,000 m thick in the west, it was little more than 700 m thick in Siberia.

A third, or Dnieper glaciation, followed by a Moscow sub-stage, was separated from the Oka glaciation by two or more interglacial periods (one called the Likhin Interglacial). Scandinavian sources played a leading role in supplying the snow for this glaciation and lying further west and nearer its source accounts for the penetration of an ice lobe deep into the Dnieper valley.

Revaluation of the glaciations in the USSR is still in progress,

*The modifications on previously accepted views which are contained in this section are based on the article "Soviet glaciers were late developers" by A.A. Velitchko of the Institute of Geography of the USSR Academy of Sciences (Geog. Mag., April 1979, pp. 472-8).

(Novosti)

Fig. 13. Landscape scene in the valley of the Khouvaksyn, Yenisey basin. This region was glaciated by the earliest ice advance to affect Siberia. This, known as the Demianka glaciation, corresponds to the Oka glaciation in European USSR.

but the Samarovo glaciation of Western Siberia is now thought to be contemporaneous with the Dnieper glaciation and the Taz with the Moscow sub-stage.

The last, or Valday, glaciation which reached its maximum 18,000 to 20,000 years ago extended only as far south as a line through present-day Vilnyus and Smolensk, thence northwards through Vologda and Velsk. The polar Urals were the source of some of this ice and of part of the contemporary West Siberian Plain ice. Because it was the last glaciation, the Valday glaciation (Zyrianka glaciation in Siberia) has left the most evident traces and accounts for many of the existing landscape features in the areas it affected. Near the ice centres, e.g. Kola-Karelia, the effects were mainly erosive. Surface soils were removed and rocks bared, smoothed and rounded. In-numerable irregular shallow hollows scooped out by the ice are now occupied by myriads of lakes, and long low sandy ridges (eskers) cross the region. Beyond, in the northern part of the Russian Low-land and southwards to the limit of the ice sheets, is a region of glacial deposition. Here chains of terminal moraines with broken hilly relief, gently sloping ground moraines, eskers, drumlins, boulder clay, fluvio-glacial deposits, peat bogs, marshes and lakes abound. The Lithuanian-Belorussian-Valday Hills Ridge, a terminal moraine, is perhaps the most significant relief feature of the Russian Lowland. It also constitutes the main water divide separating north- and south-flowing drainage.

South of the terminal moraine belt of the maximum glaciation is a broad region of water-eroded relief. Here sandy and clayey plains were formed by melt-water flowing southwards from the limits of

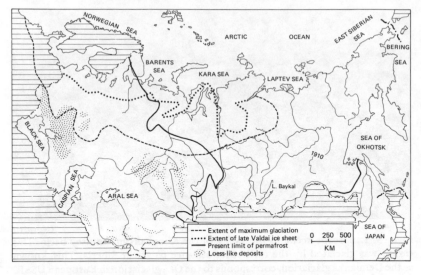

Fig. 14. Soviet Union: limits of glaciation and permafrost.

the ice sheet. Southwards again, and beyond the area of glacial cover, are extensive deposits of thick loess (*see* Fig. 14). These completely mask the underlying relief. The loess was probably formed from fine-grained silt and sand which, having been washed southwards by melt-water accompanying the final retreat of the ice, were dried out and then transported still farther south by wind.

Remnants of shrunken Quaternary icefields and glaciers persist in the mountains of Middle Asia (Pamirs), southern Siberia (Sayans and Altay) and the Caucasus.

PERMAFROST

Perennially frozen ground (permafrost — *vechnaya merzlota*) underlies more than 9 million km^2, or 47 per cent, of the territory of the USSR (*see* Fig. 14). (The term permafrost, which was coined only in 1945, stood for permanently frozen ground. It is better to substitute "perennially" for "permanently" because the phenomenon can thaw and disappear (Armstrong *et al.* 1978). Many landforms and processes owe their origin to permafrost, e.g. patterned ground, pingos, frost boils, icings, and thermokarst topography in general.)

In the extreme north-east of Siberia permafrost extends as a continuous zone, but southwards and westwards it forms islands of permanently frozen ground within areas of unfrozen ground. The thickness of the layer of permafrost varies locally. At Yakutsk the thickness is about 140 m, while at Nordvik it is about 600 m, but it can be more than 1,000 m thick; in other areas permafrost may reach no more than a few metres. Below the lower surface of the permafrost temperatures are above freezing point.

Opinions differ as to the origin of the permafrost. Discoveries of mastodon and mammoth remains, refrigerated since the Pleistocene period (see Fig. 238), tend to support an origin during the glacial period. On the other hand, a layer of perennially frozen ground has developed in relatively recent mining dumps in the Kolyma goldfield. Seemingly both viewpoints are correct in that some of the permafrost is of recent origin and some has been preserved since Quaternary times.

The upper layer of the permafrost — the so-called active layer — thaws every summer to a varying depth depending on latitude, vegetation cover, orientation to sun and other factors. In peat bogs the thaw extends to a depth of about ½ m, in marshy areas to about 1 m, and to about 2 m beneath the coniferous forest. The frozen layer beneath the thaw acts as an impervious bed. This, together with the cool summers, means that the very meagre precipitation of northern Siberia is conserved and the surface soil remains moist. Herbaceous vegetation, shrubs and small trees with shallow root systems grow readily, but waterlogging of the soil is widespread. Black and white spruce, larch and birch (not aspen) are capable of existing where the active layer is 30 cm or more deep, though the soil must be reasonably well drained. Pines, with their deep roots, will flourish only in well-drained sandy soils. It is the shortness of the summer and its lack of warmth, rather than the permafrost or cold of winter, which restrict agriculture in the higher latitudes of the USSR.

The heat reserve of surface and ground-waters is often sufficient to keep large areas adjacent to watercourses, lakes, estuaries and the seas free of permafrost. It also hastens their seasonal thawing.

The summer thaw of the surface layers causes appreciable soil movement in the form of solifluction and landslides, which, in turn, creates both technical and financial problems for economic development. Special so-called "active" method of construction and engineering techniques have been devised to protect buildings, roads, railways, bridges, dams, airfields, water and sewer pipes, etc. Heated structures settle or heave if the upper layers of permafrost are thawed by conduction. In consequence many lightweight buildings are constructed on floating foundations which move as a whole, rather than in parts, should settling or heaving take place. Substantial buildings are built on reinforced concrete piles. The piles are inserted into the permafrost layer after it has been temporarily thawed to a quagmire state by the use of superheated steam; thereafter it is allowed to refreeze. More usually, "passive" methods of construction are used. These endeavour to preserve the natural permafrost table. Sewage disposal, the piping of domestic water supplies, the protection of ground-water supplies from contamination, and even soil fertilisation, present serious difficulties in areas of permafrost.

RELIEF

The broad relief regions of the Soviet Union are on such an immense scale that the same scenery tends to occur again and again over vast areas (*see* Fig. 15). The general pattern of broad plains and lowlands, surrounded by an almost unbroken chain of high mountains, is relatively simple, yet in detail there is a surprising variety of scene. This is the result of a long and complex geological history, unremitting sub-aerial erosion, age-long erosion and deposition by rivers, and during Quaternary times, also by ice. Only a brief statement of the main relief divisions is given at this stage: details are provided in the regional sections (Chs. XII-XVIII).

The *Russian Lowland* (or *East European Plain*) forms almost the whole of the European part of the Soviet Union. Its general elevation is between 100 and 150 m above sea-level, though there parts where altitudes of over 300 m are attained. The Lowland rises almost imperceptibly eastwards towards the Ural Mountains, but such is the scale that the impression is that of a monotonously rolling countryside. The sedimentary rocks which make up the greater part of the Lowland are the result of alternating transgressions and regressions of the sea over the Russian Platform between Silurian and Tertiary times. They are largely undisturbed. Typically disposed in broad swelling upfolds and downfolds, these rocks tend to mask the irregularities of the foundation structures, except where the latter are exposed, as the Khibiny Mountains in the Kola Peninsula in Karelia, in the Podolsk-Azov Uplands and in the Donetsk Heights.

The present continental form was assumed at the beginning of the Quaternary period and followed an isostatic movement, either of a slight uplift of the land or subsidence of the sea. That this occurrence was so recent geologically helps to explain the comparatively small amount of stream dissection and erosion that is evident in much of the Lowland. Quaternary glacial deposits account for many of the details of the present relief.

The *Ural Mountains* comprise a composite and much denuded north-south mountain system which reveals itself as a gentle swelling within the broad Russian-West Siberian Lowland. They are relatively low (300-800 m) and do not form a mountain range of conventional

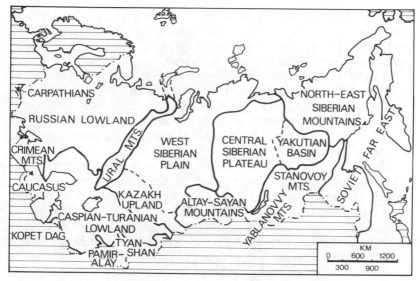

Fig. 15. Soviet Union: major relief regions.

aspect. Consequently their use to delimit Europe in the East is often rejected by geographers. In its central and most densely populated part, the Urals are neither a barrier to communications nor a climatic divide.

Siberia occupies a large part of northern Asia. It extends from the eastern edge of the Urals to the mountain ranges of the Pacific water-shed, and from the shores of the Arctic Ocean to the arid Kazakh steppes and the frontiers of the Mongolian People's Republic. It falls into three distinct regions — the West Siberian Plain (or Lowland), the Central Siberian Plateau and the North-East Siberian Mountains.

The *West Siberian Plain* lies lower than the Russian Lowland. It is only insignificantly above sea level; its highest points are mostly below 200 m and most parts are less than 100 m. It has been described as the perfect plain and has long been considered the world's finest example of a peneplain. This, the largest area of level land on the Earth, stretches 2,000 km from the Urals eastwards to the Yenisey and is drained by the Ob, Irtysh and Yenisey rivers. Slopes northward are very slight and the great rivers are sluggish, braided and tortuous. The spring thaw and high water are invariably accompanied by extensive flooding and in the north there are vast areas of swamp and marsh.

An abrupt change in the landscape takes place east of the Yenisey River. Here the greater part of the countryside is plateau-like, extensively dissected and thickly forested. This is the *Central*

Siberian Plateau at heights of 400 to 1,000 m above sea level. Drainage is either westwards into the Yenisey, or southwards to the and Lena Rivers. The trough-like valleys of the Lena and Vilyuy mark the eastern boundary of the Plateau.

Beyond the Lena in north-eastern Siberia, the character of the landscape changes yet again. Here there is an irregular surface of mountains, plateau blocks and rifts which are extremely difficult of access. In the north-east, mountains such as the Verkhoyansk and Kolyma Mountains attain 3,000 m and form a great semicircle facing the Arctic.

The *Soviet Far East* is that comparatively narrow part of the USSR separated from Siberia proper by the Dzhugdzhur Range and similar mountains which traverse the Pacific seaboard in a south-west and north-east direction. The predominant landscape is mountainous; plains are small and comparatively insignificant. The lengthy coast fronting the Arctic and Pacific Oceans is most inhospitable. It is generally mountainous in character, and its climate, accentuated by the cold offshore Bering-Okhotsk current and by summer fogs, is most unfavourable. Kamchatka and the Kuril Islands are part of the arcuate system which runs the length of the east coast of Asia to form a section of the "fiery girdle of the Pacific", i.e. the great belt of composite volcanoes extending from the Andes in South America, through the Cascades of North America and the Aleutians, into Japan; thence south into Indonesia and New Zealand.

Soviet Central Asia is essentially the *Caspian-Turanian Lowland* of the Caspian-Aral-Balkhash Basin. It is an extensive desert area of low plateaux, eroded hills, expansive sand dunes and basins of inland drainage. The two principal rivers, the Amu-Darya and the Syr-Darya (the ancient Oxus and Iaxartes respectively), drain into the Aral Sea.

The mountain border encircling the Russian Lowland, Soviet Central Asia and West Siberian Plain in the south and east is a series of Alpine-type fold mountains and associated plateaux. In the south-west the Ukrainian *Carpathians* reach heights of 1,800 m. In the *Crimean Mountains* elevations of 1,500 m are attained. The *Great Caucasus Mountains*, with peaks reaching 5,640 m, and without any low passes, present a definite barrier which can be crossed only with difficulty at a few points. East of the Caspian, the *Kopet-Dag* attains 800 m in Soviet territory, but it lies mainly in Iran, where the greatest elevations are attained. The *Pamir-Alay* Mountains and the *Tyan-Shan*, with summits rising to over 6,000 m (Mount Communism, 7,495 m, 360 km south-east of Tashkent), are some of the highest mountains in the Soviet Union (*see* Fig. 16). Between the Tyan-Shan and the Altay Mountains lies the relatively low Dzhungarian Gate, the historic highway from China across Mongolia

(*Fotokhronika Tass*)

Fig. 16. Some of the higher ranges of the Pamir and eastern Tyan-Shan have crests continuously rising above the snowline for tens of kilometres, with some important areas of glacier formation.

to the Kazakh steppes and thence to the Volga. The Altay are followed eastwards by the *Salair* and *Kuznetskiy Ala-Tau*, the *Sayans*, the mountains of Tuva and those of the Pre-Baykal and Trans-Baykal regions bordering the Mongolian People's Republic and China. The high mountain barrier girdling the Soviet Union hampers economic and cultural links with China, India, Pakistan, Bangladesh, Burma and other countries of South Asia.

CHAPTER III

Weather and Climate

The vast expanse of Soviet territory, positioned in middle and high latitudes, exerts a dominant influence on the atmosphere and climate of the country. The high mountain ranges along the south and eastern border exclude warm moist tropical air masses and only parts of the Soviet Far East experience maritime influences from off the Pacific. Distance limits the ameliorating influences of the Atlantic to the western part of the country although bleak polar air masses enjoy an uninterrupted flow to all parts except Trans-Caucasia and the south-east of Crimea. The climate of the greater part of the USSR is continental, and characterised by a large annual range of air temperature (hot summers and cold winters), considerable diurnal variations in air temperature and slight precipitation, with the maximum occurring in the summer half of the year. Continentality increases eastwards from moderate in the European part of the country to severe in eastern Siberia. A narrow strip along the south coast of Crimea protected from cold, northerly winds enjoys a warm Mediterranean-type climate. Trans-Caucasia, similarly protected by the Great Caucasus Mountains, is generally sub-tropical. The Soviet Far East is monsoonal, coming under the influence of continental air masses in winter and maritime air masses in summer.

SEASONAL CONDITIONS

In winter, in the high latitudes of the USSR, outgoing terrestrial radiation exceeds incoming solar radiation and there is a net heat loss from the land, i.e. there is a negative radiation balance (*see* Fig. 17 — January). Air temperatures are low at the surface and atmospheric pressure is high. The Siberian anticyclone (Asiatic maximum, *see* Fig. 18 — winter) establishes itself and calm, sunny and steadily cold weather is experienced. The cold dry continental polar air masses (cP) blow out in a clockwise direction to affect most parts of the country. The north-west winter monsoon in eastern Siberia and in the Soviet Far East is part of this circulation.

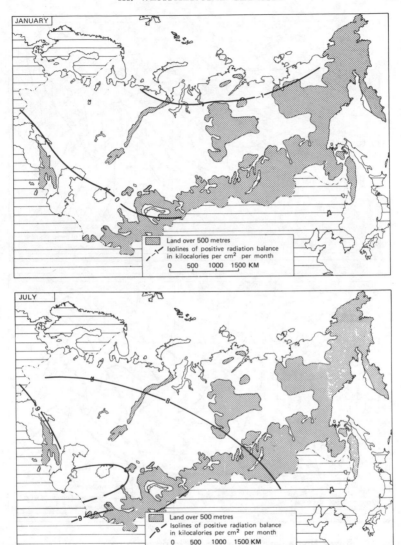

(Based on Barashkova *et al.*, 1961.)

Fig. 17. Soviet Union: mean radiation balance (Kcal/cm^2) at the earth's surface in January and July. Radiation balance is the balance of incoming solar radiation and outgoing terrestrial radiation at the surface of the earth.

In the European part of the USSR, a ridge of high pressure, the "baric barrier" which extends westwards along 50° N latitude from the Siberian high, acts as an effective wind divide. To the south of the ridge bitter cold winds blow out from the anticyclone over central Asia and the Ukraine; to the north, westerlies from the Atlantic

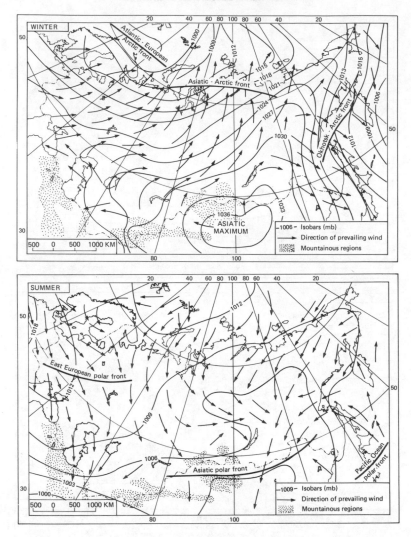

Fig. 18. Soviet Union: average atmospheric pressure patterns and associated winds in winter and summer.

bring maritime polar air masses (mP) and their accompanying moderating influences. Such influences, not least the precipitation, extend into north European USSR and western Siberia.

The prevailing stationary winter anticyclone is accompanied by clear weather with cloud amounts nearly as low as those of tropical deserts. But the winter days are so short and nocturnal radiation so excessive that air masses coming from the Atlantic — with its positive anomaly of 11 °C in its north-eastern part — provide a greater source

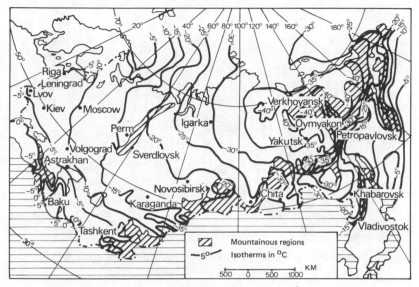

Fig. 19. Soviet Union: mean air temperatures in °C for January.

of heat for northern USSR than does direct insolation, much of which is reflected from snow-covered surfaces. In fact, much of European USSR has a positive temperature anomaly in winter and is abnormally warm for its latitude. However, the latitude is high so that winters are still quite severe. Winter (January) isotherms are aligned north-west/south-east in European USSR and into Siberia as far east as 130° E (*see* Fig. 19). Beyond this longitude Atlantic influences disappear and isotherms in Siberia are more latitudinal in alignment. Until about December, Lake Baykal provides a local source of heat and isotherms in its immediate vicinity are deflected northwards around it. Thereafter, the frozen surface of the lake provides less heat and the effect on the orientation of the isotherms disappears.

Almost the whole of the Soviet Union has a January mean temperature below freezing point and Siberia, with the exception of the south of the Pacific coast, has a January mean below −18 °C. Winter temperatures decrease until "a pole of cold" is reached in the vicinity of Verkhoyansk-Oymyakon in north-eastern Siberia, where an average January temperature of −48 °C to −50 °C is attained. The minimum recorded temperature at Verkhoyansk was −67.8 °C in January 1885; −67.7 °C has been recorded in Oymyakon (February 1933). Siberian (Yakutia) temperatures are the lowest in the world. It is worthy of note, however, that although absolute temperatures are lower in the interior of the country than elsewhere, the cold is probably more keenly felt along the Arctic and Pacific coasts where

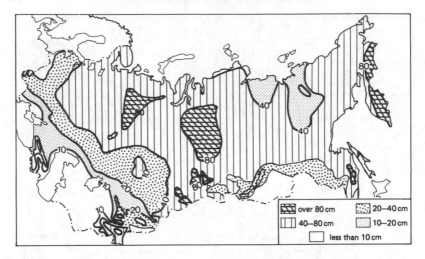

Fig. 20. Soviet Union: depth of snow cover, showing mean maximum ten-day snow-cover thickness.

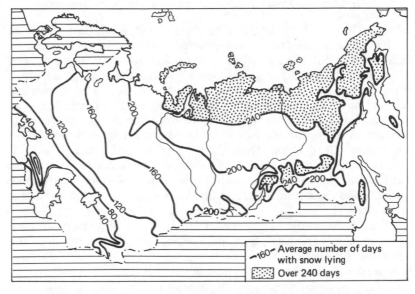

Fig. 21. Soviet Union: average number of days a year with snow lying.

strong winds blow for much of the year. The combination of low temperatures in winter and strong winds result in wind-chill factors of enormous magnitude in some places along the Arctic coast.

The winds blowing out from the continental anticyclone are inimical to precipitation and, in general, winter in the Soviet Union is the season of least precipitation. Even so, some precipitation does occur in winter, practically all in the form of snow (*see* Figs. 20 and 21). Within the westerly circulation north of the barometric divide (*see* p. 26) most of the annual precipitation occurs in autumn and comes from depressions moving westwards along the polar front. Such depressions skirt the Siberian high-pressure cell and are usually dissipated along the Arctic coast of western Siberia. Other depressions, moving along a more southerly route by way of the Mediterranean low pressure region and the southern fringes of the Siberian high, bring maximum precipitation in winter to the south coast of the Crimea and the east coast of the Black Sea.

During the Siberian winter the air is generally bracing and calm and furs afford adequate protection for individual. There is, however, a serious climatic hazard — the *buran* or *purga* of the tundra. This is a snowstorm in which freshly fallen snow is whipped up by strong and bitterly cold winds. It is a serious danger to man and beast, dreaded throughout Siberia.

The European part of the Soviet Union also experiences *burany* and sudden and violent cold spells, but the settled conditions that typify the Siberian winter are generally absent. In northern and central parts the winter cold is occasionally broken by temporary thaws (*ottepeli*) which follow invasions of moist Atlantic air. Such thaws make the ground sodden, free rivers from ice for a short time and cause disastrous floods.

In summer, incoming solar radiation exceeds outgoing terrestrial radiation and there is a net heat gain (positive radiation balance) over the USSR (*see* Fig. 17 — July). There is considerable heating of the land and a region of steady low barometric pressure extends from Afghanistan and north-western India into Soviet Central Asia and the Trans-Caucasus region (*see* Fig. 16 — summer). Warm dry tropical continental air masses (cT) dominate although the slight barometric gradients allow western oceanic influences to spread over a far wider area than in the winter. The longer hours of daylight during the summertime make for temperature uniformity; isotherms in this season are aligned more nearly latitudinally (*see* Fig. 22). In summer Lake Baykal provides a limited and local cooling influence and in its immediate vicinity isotherms are displaced to the south. In eastern Siberia and in the Soviet Far East, under the cooling influence of the south-west monsoon, isotherms turn southwards.

Summer temperatures attain mean values in excess of 26 °C in Soviet Central Asia (an extreme maximum of 50 °C has been recorded at Chu Adzhi in Turkmen), but northwards there is a slow gradation to less than 8 °C along the Arctic coast. It is really the length of the summer, rather than its intensity, which is of greatest significance to man in the USSR (*see* Fig. 23). The average length of the frost-

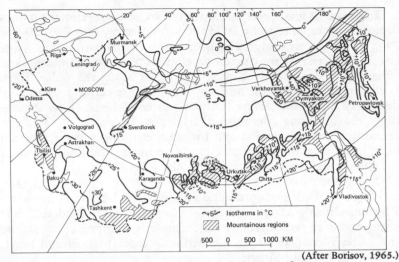

(After Borisov, 1965.)

Fig. 22. Soviet Union: mean air temperatures in °C for July.

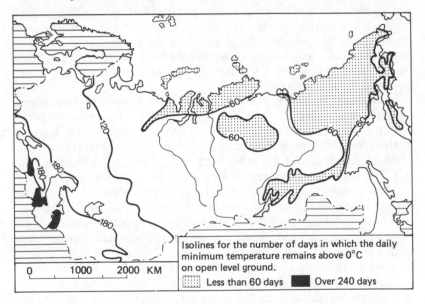

Fig. 23. Soviet Union: average frost-free period.

free season is 200 days along the Black Sea but dimishes to less than 45 days in the uplands of eastern Siberia and the Soviet Far East. There are, nevertheless, appreciable fluctuations in the length of the frost-free period from year to year. Frost is a possibility even in the summertime throughout much of the agricultural land of the Soviet Union.

The long winters and short though peaked summers in the Soviet Union are strongly marked and differentiated by a large annual range of temperature. The rigours of the continental winter give way to tropical heat within the space of a few months (*see* Table 2).

TABLE 2. TEMPERATURE AND PRECIPITATION
DATA FOR SELECTED STATIONS IN THE USSR

Station	Location	Temperature °C Jan.	July	Mean annual temperature range	Mean annual precipitation (mm)
Arkhangelsk	North-West Russia	−13	+15	28	539
Leningrad	North-West Russia	− 8	+17	25	475
Moscow	Central Russia	−10	+18	28	533
Kiev	Ukraine	− 6	+19	25	615
Odessa	South Ukraine	− 4	+22	26	409
Sevastopol	South Ukraine	+ 3	+24	21	528
Astrakhan	Lower Volga	− 7	+25	32	196
Batumi	Trans-Caucasia	+ 5	+23	18	2,367
Baku	Trans-Caucasia	+ 3	+25	22	241
Ashkabad	Central Asia	0	+30	30	210
Mary	Central Asia	+ 1	+30	29	200
Tashkent	Central Asia	− 1	+27	28	417
Sverdlovsk	Ural Mountains	−16	+17	33	462
Dudinka	Western Siberia	−30	+13	43	267
Novosibirsk	Western Siberia	−19	+19	38	425
Semipalatinsk	Kazakhstan	−16	+22	38	185
Irkutsk	Eastern Siberia	−21	+17	38	390
Chita	Eastern Siberia	−27	+19	46	343
Vladivostok	Far East	−14	+21	35	600
Yakutsk	Far East	−44	+19	63	348
Verkhoyansk	Far East	−50	+15	65	102
Anadyr	Far East	−23	+10	33	250

The transitional seasons of spring and autumn are brief and almost non-existent. In Moscow, for instance, the mean monthly temperature rises 8 °C between April and May (comparable with the mean annual range in parts of western Britain), while at Verkhoyansk there is a drop of 23 °C in the mean temperature between October and November. The suddenness of such temperature changes is no less striking than their magnitude and it further emphasises the continental character of the climate of the USSR. In spring — which does not usually begin before April — the *rasputitsa* (or thaw, literally "slush") is a hazard. The snow melts and floods the streams, there is an excess of surface water, the soil thaws and "all Russia is an epic of mud".

Low pressures over the land in summer mean indraughts of air from neighbouring areas. The Atlantic is too remote to provide any generous supply of water vapour and the Baltic, Black and Caspian Seas are too small to make any appreciable contribution to the rainfall. The high mountain barriers in Central Asia and Siberia prevent entry of water vapour from the Indian Ocean and restrict to coastal areas that from the Pacific Ocean. The temperature of the Arctic Ocean is too low to allow much evaporation, and few moisture-bearing winds from this source reach the continental interior. Even so, late summer is the season of maximum precipitation in European USSR and in Siberia. It is the result of convective activity and comes from thunderstorms or hailstorms in July and August at a time when evaporation is at its greatest. Consequently, the effectiveness of the precipitation is considerably reduced. It is unfortunate also that the meagre precipitation in the better agricultural areas is concentrated in the middle or late summer rather than in early summer. Crops often suffer from drought during early periods when they are undergoing most rapid growth and development. The intensity and general character of the rainfall, the speedy run-off, considerable soil erosion and gullying, particularly in the steppelands of the southern part of the European USSR often lead to crop damage. The added wetness during the short harvest season causes difficult conditions that often reduce crop yields by as much as 25 per cent. Rainfall is unreliable in time and place and, in areas where the annual totals are less than 400 m, droughts are common. An additional climatic hazard for the farmer of the steppelands is the dry wind known as the *sukhovey* which blows from the Turanian area. This wind has the effect of speeding up transpiration rates in crops, causing them to wither.

Annual precipitation throughout the greater part of the Soviet Union is scanty (*see* Fig. 24). Aggregates are 500-600 mm in the west, little more than 500 mm in Western Siberia and 380-400 mm in Eastern Siberia. South-eastern European USSR gets less than 400 mm per annum. Annual aggregates are below 150 mm in the Aralo-Caspian region. The south coast of the Crimea, with its "mediterranean-type" climate, receives most of its 250-500 mm from winter depressions passing eastwards along the Mediterranean Sea. The moist and cheerless climate of the Soviet Far East provides 600-1,000 mm per annum, most of it in association with the summer monsoon. There are only two areas of the Soviet Union which have a generous supply of precipitation and both are in Trans-Caucasia. They are the Kolkhida Lowland, fronting the Black Sea, and the Lenkoran Lowland alongside the Caspian Sea. Each has an annual aggregate in excess of 1,500 mm. The effectiveness of precipitation is shown in Fig. 25.

The presence of mountain ranges and plateaux, of large bodies of

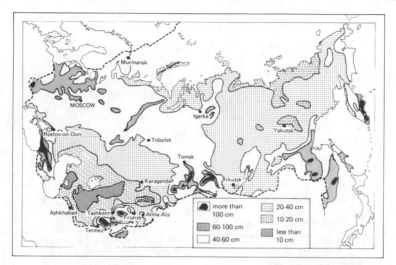

(After Pokshishevsky, 1974.)

Fig. 24. Soviet Union: mean annual precipitation (in mm).

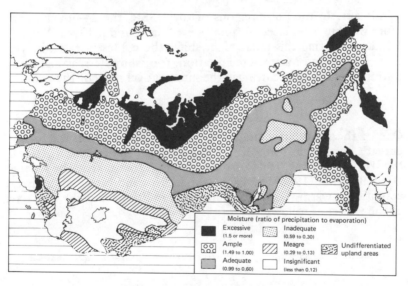

Fig. 25. Soviet Union: moisture zones.

water in large inland lakes and seas, and the varying distances of the different parts of the country from the sea, give rise to appreciable local climatic variations, but on the whole the continental character of the climate is remarkably uniform over vast areas. It is the diurnal and seasonal rhythms of climatic phenomena which are biologically

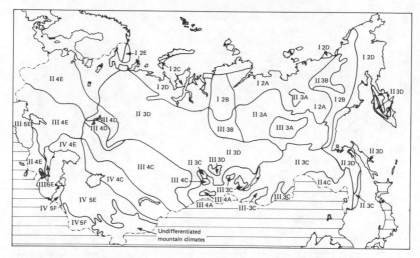

Fig. 26. Soviet Union: climatic regions (for key, *see* text below).

significant. In the polar regions of the USSR, the 24-hour temperature rhythm is replaced by a half-year "day" and half-year "night". Radiation during this polar night shifts the coldest part of the year to February and March. Precipitation, too, shows a seasonal distribution, maximum occurring in the summer over most of the country.

CLIMATIC REGIONS

One of the many attempts to regionalise the USSR on the basis of climate is given in Plate 203 of the *Physical-Geographical Atlas of the World* (Moscow, 1964), from which Fig. 26 is taken. The scheme, after Budyko (1966), is based on indices indicative of moisture conditions, warm-season temperature conditions and the character of the winter as follows:

	Moisture characteristics	*Dryness index*	*Geographical conditions*
I	Excess moisture	less than 0.45	Arctic desert, tundra, wooded tundra, alpine meadow
II	Humid	0.45-1.00	Forest
III	Inadequate moisture	1.00-3.00	Wooded steppe, steppe, dry sub-tropics
IV	Dry	over 3.00	Desert

The dryness index is the ratio of evaporability (related to radiation balance, temperature and humidity) and precipitation.

Thermal conditions of warm season	Sum of temperatures of earth's surface during period in which the air temperature remains above 10°C (50°F)	Geographical conditions
1	Very cold	Air temperature below 10°C the year round	Arctic desert
2	Cold	less than 1,000°C	Tundra, wooded tundra
3	Moderately warm	1,000°-2,200°C	Coniferous forest, alpine meadow, mountain steppe and steppe of Siberia
4	Warm	2,200°-4,400°C	Mixed and broadleaf forest, wooded steppe, steppe, northern desert
5	Very warm	more than 4,400°C	Sub-tropics, desert

The sum of the temperatures at the earth's surface is, as a rule, greater than the sum of air temperatures in the same period.

		Climatic indicators	
	Winter characteristics	Mean January temperature in °C	Maximum day-to-day snow cover
A	Severe, little snow	below −32	less than 50 cm
B	Severe, snowy	below −32	more than 50 cm
C	Moderately severe, little snow	−13 to −32	less than 50 cm
D	Moderately severe, snowy	−13 to −32	more than 50 cm
E	Moderately mild	0 to −13	
F	Mild	above 0	

By using these criteria and their corresponding number and letter designations, the climatic conditions of each region are designated by a combination of three quantitatively-defined symbols. For example, II 4 D refers to a humid climate with warm summers and a moderately severe, snowy winter.

A static approach to the classification of the climate of the USSR such as this fails to take into account seasonal variations of the elements and the general variability of climate. A more dynamic approach based on the frequency with which air masses from different sources affect the country, either singly or in conflict, has much to commend it. Borisov (1965) used the frequency of cyclonic and anticyclonic days and the associated air masses to differentiate eight climatic regions (see Fig. 27). What is described as "continental air of temperate latitudes" (the term "polar" is universally used

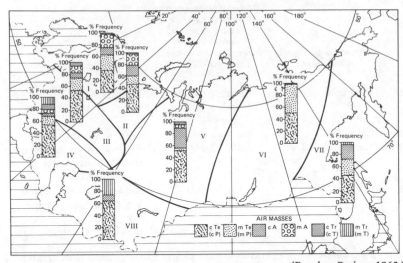

(Based on Borisov, 1965.)

Fig. 27. Soviet Union: climatic regions (for key, *see* Table 3).

TABLE 3. OUTLINE AND CHARACTERISTICS OF CLIMATIC
REGIONS OF THE USSR

Region	Circulation type	(Sub) dominant air masses	Prevailing winds	Characteristic climatic phenomena
I European north-west	Cyclonic	Maritime air of temperate latitudes (mT)	SW, N	Winter thaws
II European north-east	Anticyclonic	Continental arctic (cA)	NE, S	Cold waves
III European centre	Anticyclonic	Continental air of temperate latitudes (cT)	SW	Occlusions
IV European south	Anticyclonic	Maritime tropical (mT)	NE	Pre-winter droughts and dry winds
V West Siberia	Anticyclonic	Continental arctic (cA)	W, N	Heavy snowfalls
VI East Siberia	Anticyclonic	Continental air of temperate latitudes (cT)	NW, SE	Permafrost, frosts and fogs
VII Far East	Monsoonal	–	NW, SE	Periodicity in the annual march of precipitation, typhoons
VIII Turan-Kazakh	Anticyclonic	Continental tropical (cT)	NE, NW	Hazes and harmsili

Source: Based on Borisov (1965) and according to data for 1930-39.

outside the USSR) tends to dominate the whole country. For this reason the frequency of this particular air mass type is ignored in the climatic differentiations of the different regions of the USSR and only the frequencies of other air mass types are considered (*see* Table 3).

CHAPTER IV

Soils, Vegetation and Rural Land-use Patterns

Within the Soviet Union the progressive rise in summer temperatures, the decrease in average annual precipitation and increase in evaporation from north-west to south-east have largely determined the nature of the soil cover. The growth and decay of vegetation, the action of burrowing animals and bacteria together with the effects of man's action through crop and animal husbandry (though sometimes counterbalanced by various agricultural malpractices which lead to soil erosion) have contributed further to soil-forming processes. That there is a relationship between the distribution of climate, zonal soils, natural vegetation and rural land use is evident from a study of Figs. 26, 28 and 29.

Humus, produced from decaying vegetation, determines not only soil cover but is important also for its water-holding property. In suitable conditions, the humus or organic content of the soil is rapidly reduced by bacteria to salts or inorganic forms which then become available for new plant growth. These salts are normally dissolved in the soil water and carried to the lower soil layers. In this way is produced the soil profile which, in a well-developed soil, consists of three major horizons: the upper of A horizon, usually loose in texture and generally robbed of its mineral content by the soil water; the B horizon, more compact and containing most of the salts leached by the soil water from the A horizon; and the C horizon which consists mainly of fragments of the underlying bedrock. This, of course, applies to unglaciated areas only. In arid regions soils naturally contain little humus. The excessive evaporation of arid regions brings soil water to the surface where it leaves behind its dissolved mineral content. Extreme cold, in association with either high latitudes or high altitudes, and the check such extremes place on plant growth and on bacterial activity, limit or prevent soil development. In mountain areas altitude, aspect and steepness of slope cause soil to vary greatly within short distances,

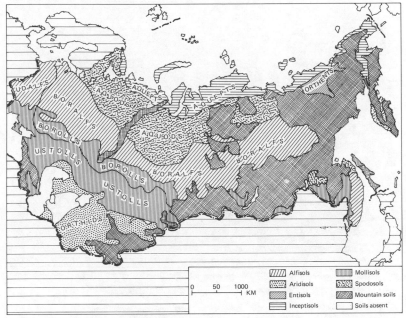

(Simplified after US Dept. Agriculture, Soil Conservation
Service, 1960, 1967.)
Fig. 28. Soviet Union: zonal soils.

and vertical zonation is common. Soils are absent in many mountainous areas.

The zonal soils of the Soviet Union (based here on the comprehensive *Soil Taxonomy* of the Soil Survey Staff, US Department of
Agriculture (1975)) fall into the major orders and sub-orders shown
in Table 4. The order names have a common ending *sol* from the
Latin *solum* meaning soil (the letter *s* is added for the plural form).

1. Inceptisols
The most northerly group of soils, these are found in a belt between
the northern margin of the coniferous or boreal forest zone and the
shores of the Arctic Ocean. Intensely cold long winters cause soil
moisture to be frozen during many months of the year. Under such
conditions chemical alteration of the minerals is slow, bacterial
activity is limited and much of the parent material of the soil consists of mechanically broken particles. Soil acidity and permafrost
prevent earthworms from carrying on their beneficial work. The
slow rate of plant decomposition results in the presence of much
raw humus or peat.

Inceptisols lack simple, distinctive soil profiles. They are slate-
blue in colour and of low fertility. The sub-order *aquepts* refers to

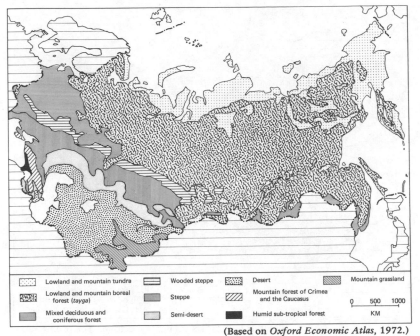

Lowland and mountain tundra		Wooded steppe		Desert		Mountain grassland	
Lowland and mountain boreal forest (*tayga*)		Steppe		Mountain forest of Crimea and the Caucasus			
Mixed deciduous and coniferous forest		Semi-desert		Humid sub-tropical forest		0 500 1000 KM	

(Based on *Oxford Economic Atlas*, 1972.)

Fig. 29. Soviet Union: natural vegetation and rural land use.

TABLE 4. ZONAL SOILS OF THE SOVIET UNION

Order	Examples of sub-orders
1. *Inceptisols:* moderately developed soils	*Aquepts:* seasonally or perennially wet
2. *Spodosols:* podzols of high latitudes	*Aquods:* wet
3. *Alfisols:* podzolic soils of middle latitudes and degraded grassland soils	(a) *Boralfs:* cool (b) *Udalfs:* temperate to hot and usually moist
4. *Mollisols:* brown forest, chernozem or chestnut soils	(a) *Borolls:* cool or cold (b) *Ustolls:* temperate to hot; dry more than 90 cumulative days a year
5. *Aridisols:* desert or saline soils	*Argids:* clayey
6. *Entisols:* weakly developed soils	*Orthents:* clayey or loamy texture; often shallow to bedrock

Source: US Dept. of Agric., 1975.

the poorly drained or perenially wet characteristic of the inceptisols of the USSR. Most of the ground in the inceptisols belt is permanently frozen. In consequence the ground is impervious below the few centimetres of "active layer" near the surface which thaw out during the short summer. Although precipitation is slight and summer temperatures low, there is very little evaporation and waterlogging is widespread.

The *tundra* and *wooded tundra* vegetation, found in association with inceptisols, occupy about 16 per cent (345 million hectares) of the USSR. This sub-polar expanse is treeless and marshy except for the occasional wooded "island". It comprises a sod of lichens, mosses and low-growing herbaceous shrubs. Agriculture is impossible within the tundra and the few inhabitants are pastoral nomads dependent on their reindeer herds, summer fishing and winter hunting on the forest fringe.

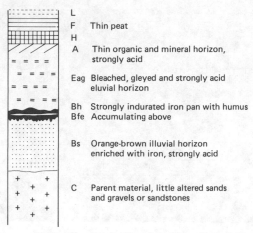

(After Fig. 7.4 in *World Soils* by E.M. Bridges, Cambridge Univeristy Press, London, 2nd ed., 1978.)
Fig. 30. Diagrammatic profile of an aquod (podzol).

2. Spodosols

These are high-latitude podzols or modified podzols with a distinctive ash-grey colour. They are strongly leached soils, the result not of heavy precipitation (here usually less than 500 mm per annum) but of the sudden release of snow-melt water in the spring. The sub-order *aquods* (*see* Fig. 30) refers to soils that are wet for long periods. Acidity in spodosols is also high. Organic substances formed by the decomposition of forest waste remove iron and aluminium oxides and leave behind a leached horizon, often composed of pure quartz sand, immediately beneath the acid humus layer of partly decomposed conifer litter of the A horizon. The oxides are washed down into the B horizon where they often form a reddish-brown "hard pan". Soils become waterlogged if there is a well-developed "pan" or where they occur in depressions.

There is a close association between the spodosols zone and the *tayga*.

> Its strength and magic lie not in the size of its giant trees nor in the depth of its deathly silence, but rather in the fact that perhaps it is the migrant birds alone of all living creatures that know its limits. . .   (Chekhov).

The *tayga* or boreal forest is predominantly coniferous and occupies 40 per cent (895 million hectares) of the USSR (*see* Fig. 31). Commercial forestry for soft wood and its products is the main economic activity within the *tayga*.

Fig. 31. Boreal forest (*tayga*) extends as a broad belt across the middle latitudes of the Soviet Union. The forest is composed of extensive stands of a few species and is underlain by ashen-coloured aquods (podzol).

Conifers need little of the calcium, magnesium, potassium and phosphorus that many other plants require. Spruce and Scotch pine are the dominant trees, especially in the western portion of the *tayga*, the latter on sandy soils. In the eastern part Siberian trees, especially Siberian larch, Siberian fir and Siberian pine, are mixed with spruce and Scotch pine. In some of the Russian Lowland (e.g. the Pripyat area), more particularly in the West Siberian Lowland where gradients are imperceptible, spring flooding gives rise to widespread inundations and there are vast expanses of marsh and bog with highly organic bog peat soils.

3. *Alfisols*
These have sub-surface horizons of clay accumulation and a medium to high base supply. They occur in middle latitudes and equate with

the grey-brown podzolic degraded chernozems of older soil classifi-
cations. Their organic status and structure is better than that of the
spodosols and they are not so acidic. Indeed, with adequate lime
and fertiliser they can support the continued production of a variety
of crops. Their grey-brown surface horizons are a reflection of the
slightly higher summer temperatures, increased evaporation and
weaker leaching arising from their somewhat more southerly location.
The sub-order designation *boralfs* (cool) applies to the bulk of the
alfisols in the Soviet Union. It is only along the western margins of
the country that moist temperate *udalfs* (similar to those in the
eastern part of England) make an appearance.

In Siberia, alfisols carry boreal forest, but in the European part
of the country where the natural vegetation was mixed coniferous
and deciduous forest of hornbean, oak, maple, birch and aspen
(278 million hectares or 12.5 per cent of the USSR) there has been
much clearing for cultivation with large areas given over now to
meadow and pasture for dairying and commercial agriculture.
Productivity of forage crops from the pastures and hayfields is high
by Soviet standards. Although the soil is productive and provides
good farm land it needs careful manuring to maintain fertility.

4. Mollisols

These include brown earths, chernozem, chestnut soils and associated types such as solenetzic soils and are distinguished by nearly
black organic-rich surface horizons and a high base supply. They
are formed under steppe vegetation in semi-arid and sub-humid climates and extend in a wide belt south of the alfisols. In its natural
state the steppe (168 million hectares or 7.6 per cent of the USSR;
348 million hectares or 15.7 per cent of the country if the wooded
steppe is included) consists of steppe turf grasses of which feather-
grass, needlegrass and fescue are the common species. Tall-growing
herbs also occur. The vegetation itself grows in separate tufts or
bunches, with bare ground between individual plants. Very little
of the original steppe now remains. The mollisols are highly fertile
and have long since been cleared for arable and mixed farming.
They are used intensively to support a variety of commercial crops.
Grains tend to dominate the croplands of the sub-type *borolls*
(where conditions are cool or cold); the sub-type *ustolls* (where
conditions are dry on more than 90 cumulative days each year)
carry mainly forage lands and are used for extensive grazing and
stock raising.

The dark organic-rich surface horizons which characterise borolls
(chernozems and black earths) occur in areas where decomposition
of organic matter is slowed down as a result of the frosts which
accompany the long and severe winters and also owing to the high

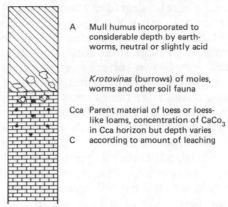

A   Mull humus incorporated to considerable depth by earth-worms, neutral or slightly acid

Krotovinas (burrows) of moles, worms and other soil fauna

Cca   Parent material of loess or loess-like loams, concentration of CaCo₃ in Cca horizon but depth varies
C   according to amount of leaching

(After Fig. 8.7 in *World Soils* By E.M. Bridges, Cambridge University Press, London, 2nd edn., 1978.)

Fig. 32. Diagrammatic profile of a boroll (chernozem). *Krotovinas* are the infilled holes of moles, worms and other soil fauna and are characteristic of borolls in the USSR. They appear whitish when formed in the humus horizon and are filled with secondary calcium from below, or are dark when in the carbonate horizon and filled with humic material from above.

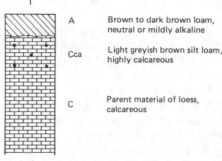

A   Brown to dark brown loam, neutral or mildly alkaline

Cca   Light greyish brown silt loam, highly calcareous

C   Parent material of loess, calcareous

(After Fig. 8.9 in *World Soils* by E.M. Bridges, Cambridge University Press, London, 2nd ed., 1978.)

Fig. 33. Diagrammatic profile of a ustoll (chestnut-brown soil).

rates of evaporation during the summer. There is no heavy leaching. Spring rain and snow-melt result in slight leaching from the A horizon, but the process is balanced by evaporation in the hot summers. The result is a zone of calcareous concretions one to one and a-half metres below the surface (*see* Fig. 32). The calcareous content promotes good soil structure and the humus assists in retaining moisture. These are excellent farming soils, but being friable are liable to wind erosion, and also to sheet wash, gullying and ravining during the heavy downpours accompanying and associated with the summer rains.

Ustolls equate with chestnut-brown earths (*see* Fig. 33). They have less humus than chernozem and have a brown rather than black upper A horizon. Calcareous material accumulates in the B horizon near the surface, giving the soil a friable structure. These soils carry a poor stunted grass cover. They are not infertile but are cultivated only under irrigation or dry farming methods.

5. Aridisols

These occupy the desert and semi-desert areas of Soviet Central Asia (345 million hectares or 15.6 per cent of the USSR). They extend from the Caspian Sea in the west to the mountain systems of Kopet-Dag-Pamir-Altay-Tyan-Shan in the south and east. These dry soils contain little organic matter or nitrogen (*see* Fig. 34). In many areas, salts accumulate on or near the soil surface to form crusts or hardpans. Since their nutrient content, excepting nitrogen, is often high, these soils can be highly productive with irrigation, but are vulnerable to salt accumulation.

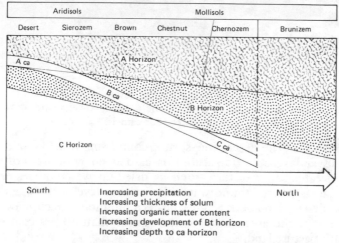

(Based on Fig. 11.9 in *Fundamentals of Soil Science* by H.D. Foth, Wiley, New York, 6th edn.)

Fig. 34. Generalised relationships between mollisols and aridisols, showing a gradual change in soil properties with increasing/decreasing precipitation.

A third of the desert area of the USSR is composed of shifting sands and clay depressions (e.g. Karakum and Kyzylkum) within which dunes (*barkhans*), varying in height up to more than 30 m, abound (*see* Fig. 252). Elsewhere there is a sparse and open vegetation reflecting the generally arid condition. Two types may be recognised, namely desert semi-shrub and desert tree-shrub. The desert semi-shrub, characterised by wormwood, saltwort and saltbush, is found in ragged clusters on clays, loams and stony desert

(Novosti)

Fig. 35. The bare patches and poor scant vegetation of the clay flats (*takyr*) of the desert give the landscape an unfriendly appearance. Camel thorn is an excellent feed for camels.

(*see* Fig. 35). The desert tree-shrub, comprising tree-like saltbushes (saksuls and xerophytic shrubs), is associated with areas of somewhat greater soil moisture, such as dried-up watercourses or light sandy areas where ground water lies at root level. The forage lands of the desert, semi-desert and southern mountains occupy 60 to 70 per cent of the area and constitute more than 60 per cent of the nation's pasture land.

6. Entisols

These are found in the arid area between the Kara-Bogaz-Gol and the Aral Sea, including the Ust-Yurt Plateau. They occur on freshly exposed rock and are low in organic matter; they have no clearly identified horizons. In the USSR they are agriculturally negative, but in other parts of the world (e.g. China) they are fertile and support dense populations.

PHYSICAL GEOGRAPHICAL REGIONS

A synthesis of the several aspects of the physical environment of the Soviet Union, including climate, soils and vegetation (Chs. II-IV),

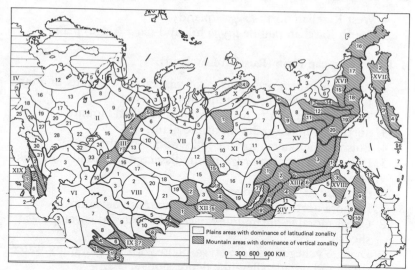

Fig. 36. Soviet Union: physical-geographical regions.

is presented in Fig. 36, based on Plates 248-9 of the *Physical-Geographical Atlas of the World*.

The regions are based on the "principal patterns of distribution and development of natural complexes, as determined by their latitudinal and elevational position on the continent, and within the system of atmospheric circulation, relief and geological structure, the effect of man's activities, and other causes".

On that basis the USSR has been divided into "natural countries" (I, II, etc.) and "provinces" (1, 2, etc.). By a natural country is meant part of a continent with a unity of geological-geomorphological structure and atmospheric circulation characteristics related to its geographical location. Major relief features and conditions of climate formation determine the composition, character and degree of distinctiveness of latitudinal natural zones in the plains, and of vertical zones in the mountains. A natural province is part of a country, and is distinguished mainly by the combination of bio-climatic characteristics and the character of the relief. Provinces are grouped in the plains according to zonal criteria, and in mountains according to the character of vertical zonality.

The regions are described as follows.

I. Fennoscandia:

    1. Murman dissected coastal tundra plateau;
    2. Kola north-*tayga* and mountain-tundra low mountains;
    3. White Sea hill-and-ridge north-*tayga* lake lowland;

4. West Karelian north-*tayga* upland;
5. South Karelian middle-*tayga* hill-and-*selga* (ridge) plain.

II. East European Plain (Russian Lowland):

1. Arctic platform archipelago of plateau-like islands of Franz Josef Land with ice sheet and Arctic desert.
2. Timan-Kanin tundra plain with low residual mountains;
3. north-east hilly tundra maritime plain;
4. Bolshezemelskaya moraine-hill wooded-tundra plain;
5. Dvina-Mezen north-*tayga* plain, dissected by broad valley-like depressions;
6. north-*tayga* Timan ridge;
7. Pechora north-*tayga* lowland with extensive swamps;
8. Onega moraine-hill middle-*tayga* plain with flat, swampy watersheds;
9. Dvina-Vychegda middle-*tayga* plain with flat, swampy watersheds and broad valley-like depressions;
10. middle-*tayga* Timan ridge;
11. Pechora middle-*tayga* upland plain;
12. Baltic moraine-hill lake plain with mixed forest;
13. Valday-Smolensk-Moscow upland with moraine hills and mixed forest;
14. Upper Volga plain with swampy lowlands in mixed-forest zone;
15. Vyatka-Kama south-*tayga* upland plain;
16. swampy outwash plain of the Polesye with pine-broad-leaved forest;
17. north of Middle Russian upland with broad-leafed and coniferous sub-*tayga* forest;
18. Volhynian-Podolian wooded-steppe upland with broad-leaved forest;
19. Dnieper low wooded-steppe plain;
20. middle Russian wooded-steppe upland dissected by gullying;
21. Oka-Don (Tambov) wooded-steppe alluvial plain;
22. Volga wooded-steppe upland, dissected by gullying;
23. Trans-Volga wooded-steppe, dissected by gullying;
24. Trans-Volga high wooded steppe, dissected by gullying;
25. Black Sea steppe low plain;
26. Dnieper steppe upland;
27. Donets ridge, rolling steppe plateau with islands of wooded steppe replacing eroded mountain massif;
28. Don-Volga steppe elevated dissected plain;
29. Yergeni dry-steppe upland;
30. Kuban steppe plain;
31. Stavropol steppe upland, plateau-like dome-shaped uplift, and northern foothills of Caucasus;

32. Trans-Volga steppe alluvial low plain;
33. Trans-Volga steppe *syrt* uplands.

III. Ural-Novaya Zemlya country:

1. middle-elevation mountains of Novaya Zemlya north island with extensive ice sheets and Arctic tundra;
2. Arctic-tundra low mountains and hilly plains of the south of Novaya Zemlya;
3. Pay-Khoy residual hilly tundra upland;
4. Polar Ural, middle-elevation mountains with alpine relief forms and denuded-summit tundra vegetation;
5. sub-polar Ural with alpine relief forms and north-*tayga* forest at its foot;
6. middle-elevation Northern Ural with middle-*tayga* forest at its foot;
7. low-mountain and hill-ridge south-*tayga* Middle Ural;
8. wooded-steppe South Ural with mountain-*tayga* slopes and alpine meadows on summits;
9. Trans-Ural steppe peneplaned upland;
10. Mugodzhar desert-steppe residual upland.

IV. Alpine-Carpathian country:

1. middle-elevation Carpathian with coniferous-broad-leaved forests on slopes and steppe summits;
2. Trans-Carpathian plain with broad-leaved forests.

V. Crimean-Caucasian country:

1. mountain Crimea with mountain forest on slopes and steppe summits;
2. mountain ranges of North Caucasus with steppe at foot; mixed forest on slopes, alpine meadows and glaciers;
3. Dagestan mountain desert;
4. west Caucasus province of humid sub-tropical forest;
5. east Trans-Caucasian province of sub-tropical dry forest and steppe;
6. Kura lowland with sub-tropical steppe and dry forest.

VI. Caspian-Turanian country:

1. Caspian semi-desert low plain;
2. Ural-Emba semi-desert upland;
3. Caspian desert lowland;
4. Trans-Caspian desert plateau;
5. Karakum sandy desert plain;
6. north Aral sand-and-clay semi-desert plain;

7. Kyzylkum sandy desert plain;
8. Kyzylkum residual desert plain;
9. desert plains of Betpak-Dala and Muyunkum;
10. Balkhash sandy desert plain.

VII. West Siberian country:

1. Yamal-Gydan flat tundra lake lowland;
2. Yamal-Taz rolling and hilly tundra lake plain;
3. Gydan-Yenisey hill-ridge tundra plain;
4. Ob-Taz rolling wooded-tundra plain;
5. Turukan lake-hill moraine wooded-tundra plain;
6. Ob-Lyapin dissected elevated plain with northern-*tayga* forests and swamp;
7. Kazym-Pur rolling swampy north-*tayga* lake plain;
8. Taz-Yenisey moraine-hill elevated north-*tayga* plain;
9. Konda-Sosva middle-*tayga* elevated plain;
10. Konda swampy middle-*tayga* lake plain;
11. Ob middle-*tayga* lowland;
12. Key-Yenisey middle-*tayga* elevated plain;
13. Tura swampy south-*tayga* plain;
14. Tobol-Vasyugan swampy south-*tayga* lake plain;
15. Ket-Chulym slightly swampy south-*tayga* elevated plain;
16. Kurgan wooded-steppe plain;
17. Ishim wooded-steppe lake plain;
18. Baraba ridge-and-vale wooded-steppe lake plain;
19. Ob ridge-and-vale wooded-steppe plain;
20. Irtysh elevated steppe plain with deep lake depressions;
21. Kulunda steppe plain with vales and basins.

VIII. Kazakh hill lands:

1. Turgay steppe tabular upland;
2. Kazakh hill-land steppe;
3. Turgay semi-desert low plain;
4. Dzhezkazgan semi-desert hill upland;
5. Kazakh hill-land semi-desert;
6. Zaisan semi-desert basin.

IX. Mountains of Central Asia:

1. high ranges of Tadzhikistan with vertical zonation from semi-desert to alpine;
2. desert highland of East Pamir;
3. south Tadzhikistan desert middle mountains;
4. south Tyan-Shan ranges with dominance of desert vegetation;
5. west Tyan-Shan ranges with dominance of mountain steppe and islands of forest on slopes;

6. Fergana desert-and-steppe basin;
7. high mountains of north Tyan-Shan with flat-topped *syrt* summits, forest belts on outer (northern) slopes and steppe on inner slopes;
8. Dzhungarian *syrt* highland with vertical zonation from desert to alpine meadows;
9. Tarbagatay middle mountains with adjoining desert piedmont.

X. Taymyr-Severnaya Zemlya country:

1. Severnaya Zemlya archipelago, low-mountain Arctic-desert plateau with ice sheets;
2. north Taymyr Arctic-tundra ridge plain;
3. Taymyr Arctic-tundra elevated plain;
4. low-mountain, flat-topped Arctic-tundra Byrranga range;
5. Pyasina-Khatanga lake-hill tundra lowland;
6. Anabar-Olenek tundra ridge plain;
7. Kheta lake-hill wooded-tundra plain.

XI. Middle Siberian plateau:

1. middle-elevation mountain-tundra Putorana trap plateau;
2. Vivi-Tutonchana open woodland tundra trap plateau with north-*tayga* forest in valleys;
3. north Anabar mountain-tundra plateau with open north-*tayga* woodland on slopes;
4. Anabar denuded summit, open woodland tableland;
5. Moiero-Kotui lake basin;
6. Anabar-Olenek residual plateau with open woodland;
7. Olenek limestone plateau with open woodland;
8. Olenek-Vilyuy north-*tayga* ridge plateau;
9. Yenisey north-*tayga* trap plateau with denuded summits;
10. middle Tunguska middle-*tayga* plateau;
11. upper Vilyuy low middle-*tayga* plateau;
12. upper Tunguska dissected plateau with middle-*tayga* forest;
13. Velmo-Kamo low plateau with middle-*tayga* larch and dark-coniferous mountain-*tayga* forest;
14. Lena-Tunguska heavily dissected plateau with larch-pine and dark-coniferous forest;
15. middle-elevation Yenisey ridge with dark-coniferous mountain-*tayga* forest;
16. middle Angara lightly dissected plateau with larch-pine and dark-coniferous forest;
17. upper Lena elevated plateau with south-*tayga* larch, larch-pine and dark-coniferous mountain-*tayga* forest;
18. Krasnoyarsk-Kansk rolling wooded-steppe plain;
19. Irkutsk-Balagansk rolling wooded-steppe plain.

XII. Altay-Sayan mountains:

1. Altay mountains with denuded summits, *tayga* and alpine meadow on slopes and steppe in depressions;
2. Kuznetsk-Salair middle mountains with steppe depressions and dark-coniferous mountain-*tayga* forest;
3. Minusinsk wooded-steppe basin;
4. Sayan denuded summit and *tayga* highland;
5. Tuva highland with denuded summits, dark-coniferous mountain-*tayga* and stone pine-and-larch forests on mountain ranges and steppe and semi-desert intermontane basins.

XIII. Baykal country:

1. Patom-North Baykal highland with mountain-larch forest on slopes and denuded summits;
2. Stanovoy highland with mountain-*tayga* and denuded summits;
3. Aldan tableland with denuded summits and mountain-larch forest;
4. Olekminsk highland with middle-*tayga* forest and open woodland below denuded summits;
5. Stanovoy middle-elevation mountain-*tayga* range with mountain-larch forest and mountain tundra;
6. Upper Zeya middle mountains with middle-*tayga* larch forest and *mari* (hillocky forest swamps);
7. Baykal highland with denuded summits and *tayga* vegetation, meadow-bog and steppe basins;
8. Vitim mountain-*tayga* tableland with meadow-bog basins;
9. Selenga middle mountains with south-*tayga* forest on slopes and steppe basins;
10. Henteyn-Chikoy highland with South Siberian mountain larch forest;
11. Chita wooded-steppe middle mountains.

XIV. Daurian country:

1. Daurian high steppe plain.

XV. Yakutian basin:

1. lower Lena north-*tayga* plain;
2. Lena-Vilyuy forest-meadow middle-*tayga* lake plain with sections of meadow steppe on permafrost;
3. middle Lena middle-*tayga* sloping plain;
4. Aldan-Amga gently rolling middle-*tayga* plain with occasional meadows.

XVI. North-east Siberia:

1. archipelago of low Arctic-desert New Siberian Islands;
2. low-mountain, Arctic-tundra Wrangel Island;
3. Yana-Kolyma maritime tundra lowland;
4. low-mountain tundra Chekanovskiy and Kharaulakh ranges;
5. Deputatskiy chain, a system of low mountain massifs with wooded tundra open woodland;
6. Alazeya rolling tableland with denuded summits and wooded tundra;
7. Indigirka-Kolyma lowland with open larch woodland;
8. Yana tundra and open woodland plateau;
9. Verkhoyansk mountain system with denuded summits and open woodland slopes;
10. lower Lena lowland with floodplain meadows and open larch woodland;
11. Yana-Oymyakon tundra and open woodland tableland;
12. Cherskiy high-mountain system with denuded summits and open larch woodland on slopes;
13. Momsk-Seimchan system of depressions separated by mountain ranges with open larch woodland;
14. Momsk high-mountain ranges with denuded summits;
15. Yukagir tundra-larch open woodland tableland;
16. Chukchi tundra highland;
17. Anadyr-Anyui mountain-tundra highland;
18. upper Kolyma tundra and open woodland highland with dwarf stone-pine growths;
19. Magadan tundra and north-*tayga* highland with dwarf stone-pine;
20. Suntar-Khayata denuded summit highland;
21. Okhotsk mountain and hill-and-plains coast with open larch woodland and sections of wooded tundra.

XVII. Kamchatka-Kuril country:

1. Anadyr-Penzhina tundra lowland with residual mountains;
2. Koryak tundra and denuded summit mountain group with dwarf alder and stone-pine;
3. Kamchatka tundra-and-forest middle-elevation inner range;
4. east Kamchatka volcanic province with mountain-tundra volcanic massifs and plains occupied by larch forest and Erman's birch;
5. west Kamchatka meadow and forest plain with sphagnum bogs and Erman's birch growths;
6. Kommandor and North Kuril volcanic islands with Erman's birch and sub-arctic grass vegetation;

  7. middle Kuril volcanic islands with dwarf stone-pine and heath and lichen-covered rock waste;

  8. south Kuril volcanic islands with vertical zonation from broad-leaved forest to lichen-covered summits.

XVIII. Amur-maritime country:

1. Dzhugdzhur maritime province with mountain-*tayga* larch and dark-coniferous forests and denuded summits;
2. low-mountain middle-*tayga* ranges of the lower Amur and Amgun Rivers;
3. Bureya-Khingan middle mountains with denuded summits, mountain-*tayga*, dark-coniferous and larch forests;
4. Tukuringra-Dzhagdy range with south-*tayga* larch forest and *mari* (hillocky forest swamps), mountain larch and dark-coniferous forests;
5. Amur-Zeya south-*tayga* plain with larch forest;
6. Amur plain with grassy coniferous-broad-leaved forest and wooded steppe;
7. lower Amur swampy meadow and forest plain;
8. Ussuri-Khanka plain with broad-leaved grassy forests and meadow steppe;
9. northern Sikhote-Alin with coniferous forest in lower zone;
10. southern Sikhote-Alin with coniferous-broad-leaved forest in lower zone;
11. north Sakhalin middle-*tayga* plain with light-coniferous forest;
12. middle-mountainous south Sakhalin with coniferous forest and open woodlands of Erman's birch.

XIX. West Asian highlands:

1. Armenian volcanic steppe highlands with mountain broad-leaved forests, alpine meadows, xerophile open woodlands and deserts in intermontane basins;
2. Talysh mountains with sub-tropical mountain-broad-leaved-forest;
3. Kopet-Dag mountain steppe and desert middle mountains;
4. Badkhyz-Karabil desert-steppe upland.

PART TWO: THE ECONOMIC FRAMEWORK

CHAPTER V

Agriculture, Fisheries and Forestry

AGRICULTURE

Agriculture employs approximately 23 per cent of the working population of the USSR and accounts for 17 per cent of the national income. Of the total land area of the USSR, barely 10 per cent (225.7 million hectares in 1976, 217.7 million hectares in 1977 and 227.0 million hectares in 1979) is cultivated. The remaining 90 per cent, at present of limited agricultural value, includes great areas of boreal forest, tundra, mountain and bog which are too cold for cultivation, and other large expanses, as in Trans-Caucasia and Soviet Central Asia, which are either mountainous or, at worst, sheer desert.

The cultivated one-tenth is broadly confined within a triangle, its apex near Novokuznetsk and its two sides bounded by lines drawn therefrom to Leningrad and Odessa. Within this triangle the USSR has certain geographical advantages for farming, as well as many off-setting shortcomings. The countryside presents level or gently undulating surfaces, admirably suited to mechanised farming, but a large part is subject to unreliable — and thus not always adequate — precipitation. The "dry" areas, and they include those astride the lower Volga and Southern Ural and those in Western Siberia and Kazakhstan, account for about 40 per cent of the area sown to grain. Evaporation in summer takes a further toll of a rainfall which fluctuates from year to year with inevitable effects on the harvest yield.

The north of the agricultural heartland is occupied by alfisols (podzol and degraded grassland soils). These soils extend as a wedge from European USSR eastwards to near Perm in the Urals, and beyond as a narrow belt as far as the Ob. Maritime (i.e. Atlantic) influences upon the climate in this area are evident in the slightly increased annual precipitation. This land was originally forested with a mixture of deciduous and coniferous trees, but early inhabitants were able to maintain themselves by agriculture in the clearings. With increased settlement clearings were extended by cutting and burning. The somewhat longer frost-free period in this zone, compared with the shorter one in the boreal forest (*tayga*) to the north, allowed deciduous trees to grow here. Their heavier leaf fall increased the supply of humus to the surface layer of the soil and the consequent richer undergrowth, consisting mainly of perennial grasses, encouraged the rearing of farm animals.

This mixed forest zone played an important part in the history of the country, for it was here that the early Slavs, fleeing from the Asiatic invaders of the steppes, found shelter (*see* Chapter IX). Under the influence of a settled agricultural life the Slavs and Finno-Ugrians were welded into groups which later coalesced to form the first Russian state.

Given adequate lime and fertiliser, alfisols will support the continued production of a variety of crops. All suitable land has long been cleared of trees and cultivated, and the hardier cereals are grown. Flax and hemp have long provided fibres for industrial use and potatoes are a widely-grown crop. Hay, alfalfa (lucerne) and other forage crops do well and support dairying and stock raising.

South of the alfisols come the highly fertile mollisols (brown forest, chernozem or chestnut soils). These tend to coincide with the so-called "tillable steppes". The higher humus content of the black upper layers of the mollisols (3-6 per cent), compared with that of the grey alfisols, accounts for the greater agricultural productivity achieved in these lands. The mollisols extend from the Ukraine into western Siberia and have produced grain for many centuries, seemingly without any great loss of fertility. The main handicaps to their utilisation are largely climatic. Recurrent droughts give rise to serious failures. In summer, the dry soils are particularly liable to wind erosion, while heavy rain showers give rise to gullying and the loss of precious topsoil. Large-scale mechanised agriculture tends to accentuate these difficulties. The diversification of crops, construction of tree belts for wind-breaks (*see* Fig. 37) and utilisation of the waters of the Volga, Don, Dnieper and Dniester for irrigation assist in counteracting the effects of these hazards, but the serious difficulties in agriculture persist.

Ustolls extend from the steppes of the Crimea across the Volga delta and through northern Kazakhstan to the extreme south of western Siberia. They are the result of extreme temperatures, low rainfall and high summer evaporation and show tendencies towards salinity. Ustolls are very fertile when supplied with enough water,

(*Novosti*)

Fig. 37. Shelter belts in the arid steppelands of the Volga region. Shelter belts in the drier agricultural zones of the USSR aid snow accumulation in winter (a valuable source of soil moisture), modify local microclimates, and act as year round moisture retainers and as windbreaks.

but their irrigation has to be carefully controlled. A rise in the water table is liable to produce alkalinity at or near the surface and leads to the formation of solonchak and solonets (*see* p. 47).

The agricultural heartland so defined has a cool continental semi-arid climate, not unlike that of the spring wheat region of the Prairie provinces of Canada or the Dakotas of the United States of America. In the north, mixed farming is the rule. Root crops, oats, rye and wheat are widely grown together with flax on the better clay soils and potatoes on the sandy soils. A great deal of woodland remains, but there are some good pasture lands. Market gardening (truck farming) and dairying, related to the market rather than to favourable conditions of climate, relief and soil, are found around most towns. Pigs and poultry are additional enterprises.

On the steppelands to the south in the zone of the mollisols, grain cultivation (particularly autumn-sown wheat) is the main agricultural enterprise. Sunflowers and other industrial crops, dairying, beef, poultry and sheep raising are important additional activities. On the north-western humid margins of the steppelands, as much as 60 per cent of the land is arable. The proportion of land under the plough is far less in the drier east and south. Crop yields in the south, where the unreliable character of the meagre precipitation tends to make the harvest somewhat precarious, are lower than they are farther north. For this reason, irrigation has been introduced in certain areas, particularly along the Dnieper, lower Don and lower Volga.

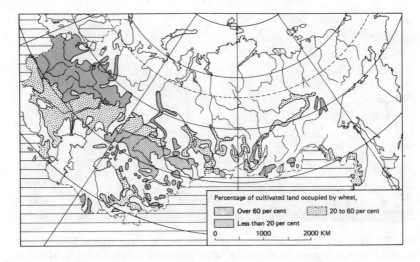

Fig. 38. Soviet Union: distribution of wheat-growing areas.

The agricultural heartland tapers off in Siberia, where the growing season is shorter, precipitation is unreliable (averaging only 250-400 mm) and climatic conditions generally are more extreme. In northern Kazakhstan, spring wheat constitutes the main crop, and dairying, raising of beef cattle and sheep are ancillary activities.

The areas devoted to individual crops and to livestock are shown in Figs. 38-51. Relative sowing areas in 1977 are given in Fig. 52.

Grains
Grains make up practically 60 per cent of the sown area of the Soviet Union and provide the basis of all agricultural production in the country. They satisfy the bread needs of the population, fodder for livestock and various raw materials for the food industry. Wheat is the main grain, providing almost 50 per cent of the country's total grain production of 189.2 million tonnes in 1980 (*see* Fig. 38). *Winter wheat,* sown in the autumn and protected from the winter cold by a layer of snow, dominates in the south-western part of European USSR — the Ukraine, North Caucasus and the Central Chernozem regions. It is grown with other grains, legumes and industrial crops alongside animal husbandry as part of an intensive system of agriculture and matures in four to four-and-a-half months. *Spring wheat* is grown further east, in Northern Kazakhstan, West Siberia and the Urals where climatic conditions are more severe and a protective snow cover for germinating seeds is not available. This category of wheat requires only three to four months to mature. It is grown extensively over vast areas under a system of virtual monoculture. Because of the low precipitation (400 mm in the north

to 200 mm in the south), the spring wheat belt suffers from a continuous threat of drought. Consequently, dry farming methods have to be employed whereby the land is allowed to lie fallow for two to three years between crops to help restore soil moisture humus. A total of 90.1 million tonnes of wheat was produced in the USSR in 1979 and 98.1 million tonnes in 1980.

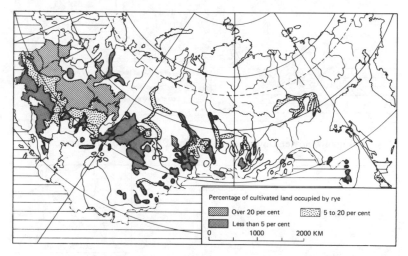

Fig. 39. Soviet Union: distribution of rye-growing areas.

Rye, a winter crop, is grown principally in the north-western part of European USSR in areas such as Belorussia and the Baltic Republics which are too damp for wheat (*see* Fig. 39). It is virtually absent east of the Urals. Rye provided the main breadstuff of the peasant in Czarist Russia but sowings have declined steadily during the Soviet period (8.1 million tonnes in 1979, and 10.2 million tonnes in 1980). *Buckwheat* and *millet* are minor grains in Soviet farming. Buckwheat, well adapted to cool moist conditions, is a traditional crop of the clearings in the mixed forest zone; millet is important in the drier areas of the Volga and Western Siberia. *Barley,* with about a quarter of the area sown to grains, is used chiefly as an animal feed grain with some for malting and brewing. It is grown mainly within the winter wheat belt.

The cultivation of *oats,* a food and forage crop, has suffered a similar fate to rye following a change in diets away from the traditional Russian gruels (of low nutritional value) and following the reduction in draught animals consequent upon the mechanisation of agriculture.

The opening up of new wheatlands in the previous virgin and unused lands of North Kazakhstan and Western Siberia facilitated

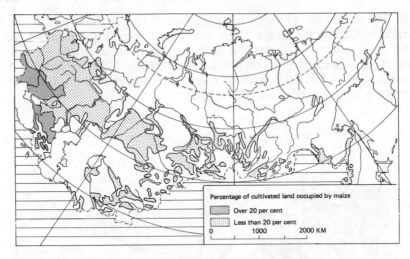

Fig. 40. Soviet Union: distribution of maize-growing areas.

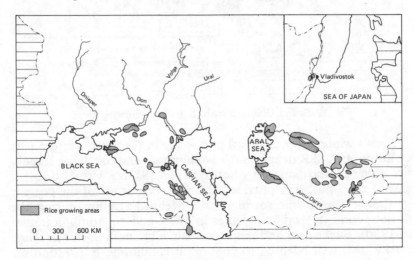

Fig. 41. Soviet Union: distribution of rice-growing areas.

the introduction of *maize* (corn) into the old wheat land of European USSR, but it is only in the south of the Ukraine, the Kuban valley of North Caucasus and Georgia that moisture and heat are sufficient to ripen the crop for grain (*see* Fig. 40). Elsewhere maize is cut for silage and as green fodder for cattle. Production in 1979 was 8.4 million tonnes and 9.7 million tonnes in 1980.

Rice is produced in irrigated areas in Soviet Central Asia, Kazakhstan, North Caucasus and the south of the Ukraine, and also the lowlands of the Soviet Far East between the upper Ussuri and Vladivostok where it is the main cereal (*see* Fig. 41). Grown on a comparatively small scale, its production, nevertheless, has increased phenomenally in recent years (2.4 million tonnes in 1979 and 2.8 million tonnes in 1980).

The size of the annual cereals crop in the Soviet Union provides the single most important consideration in an assessment of the Soviet agricultural performance. Production in recent years has been as follows.

Year	Million tonnes	
1972	168.2	
1973	222.5	
1974	195.6	
1975	140.1	
1971-75	181.6	(actual annual average)
1976	223.8	
1977	195.5	
1978	235.0	
1979	179.0	
1980	189.2	
1976-80	220.4	(planned annual average)
1976-80	205.0	(actual annual average)
1981	238	(planned)
1981	170	(Western estimate of actual)*
1982	240	(planned)
1982	150-175	(Western estimate of actual)*

*By September 1982 no total figures for the actual 1981 or 1982 harvests had been provided by the Soviet authorities. American agricultural experts put the USSR's probable grain import requirements over the year 1982-83 as nearly 50 million tonnes.

The disappointing harvests of recent years have seriously affected Soviet economic growth with cut backs in expenditure in several sectors of the economy and extensive grain imports (25-30 million tonnes annually) from the USA, Canada, Argentine, Australia, New Zealand and Western Europe. Unreliable weather, including early frosts, late snows, heavy rains, excessive heat and drought, have caused disastrous harvests in several parts of the country at various times, although bad planning and inefficiencies have been implicated. The consumption of bread and other cereals remains high in the Soviet Union but there is a rising demand for meat on the part of an increasingly affluent society (though consumption is still 40 per cent below the American level), with the consequent need for feed grains, especially maize, for its livestock.

Industrial crops
So-called industrial or technical crops play an important role in the national economy of the USSR by providing raw materials for the light and food industries and fodder for cattle. They include cotton, sugar-beets, sunflowers and flax. Potatoes too, while providing food

for human consumption as well as for pigs, are also used in making vodka and industrial alcohol. The most important role in the production of industrial crops is played by *cotton*, which provides the textile industry with valuable raw material. Conditions suitable for this heat-loving and drought-resistant crop are limited to Central Asia, southern areas of Kazakhstan, Azerbaijan SSR and Armenian SSR (*see* Fig. 42). However, the uncommonly dry climate of these areas and the extreme shortage of moisture accounts for the cultivation of cotton only on irrigated lands. The average annual output was 7.7 million tonnes during the 1971-75 period and 8.9 million tonnes during the 1976-80 period whilst the average annual output planned for the 1981-85 period is 9.2-9.3 million tonnes.

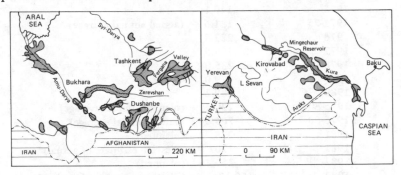

Fig. 42. Soviet Union: distribution of cotton-growing areas.

Uzbekistan (especially the Fergana Basin) is the most important region, producing about 65 per cent. Well over 50 per cent of the crop is now machine-harvested compared with 32 per cent in 1975. Soviet sources indicate that, while yields may be increased in the future, there is little scope for actually extending the area in which cotton can be sown short of the construction of extensive irrigation works. However, there are plans to bring 450,000-465,000 hectares of irrigated land under cultivation during the Eleventh Five-year Plan (1981-85).

Sugar-beet provides not only sugar and alcohol but also high-quality animal fodder. The USSR is easily the world's largest beet producer. Production is concentrated largely in the wooded steppe-lands of the Ukraine, Moldavia, North Caucasia and the Volga, where climatic and soil conditions are best, but relatively new areas have been opened up in Central Asia and Kazakhstan (*see* Fig. 43). Production averaged 88.7 million tonnes during the 1976-80 period, with 100-3 million tonnes the planned annual average for 1981-85. The aim was to achieve 95 per cent self-sufficiency in sugar-beet by 1980. Sugar-beet output has increased markedly (*see* Table 5), but large imports of cane sugar from Cuba (a member of Comecon) must involve the USSR in finding export markets.

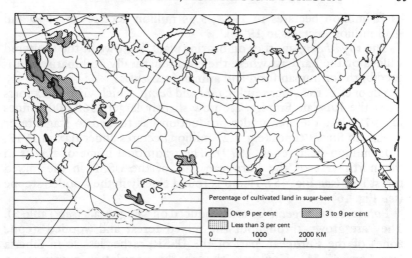

Fig. 43. Soviet Union: distribution of sugar-beet-growing areas.

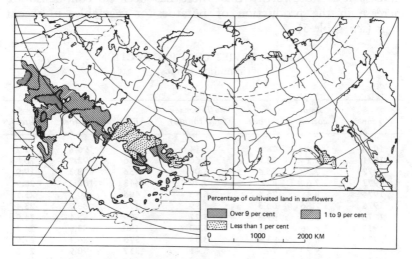

Fig. 44. Soviet Union: distribution of sunflower-growing areas.

Sunflowers, grown for fodder (leaves, oil-cake), yellow dye (flowers) and food (equal to olive or almond oil for culinary purposes) are traditional in the drier steppe country of the Ukraine, Moldavia, Northern Caucasus and Middle Volga-Urals region (*see* Fig. 44). The production of sunflowers (average annual output of 5.32 million tonnes of seed during the 1976-80 period and 6.8 million tonnes annually planned for the 1981-85 period, or about 85 per cent of the world's output) is being encouraged in the USSR, and in recent years the area under the crop has been much enlarged

(0.98 million hectares in 1913, 3.54 million hectares in 1940 and 4.33 million hectares in 1979).

The *soya bean,* another oil-bearing plant, is grown in the sheltered valleys of the Far East where the crop is naturally acclimatised. It is used both for human food and animal feedstuffs.

Supplies of the older staples, *flax* and *hemp,* which yielded exports from the Russian Empire, are now slightly larger (368,000 tonnes in 1979) but the area under production has tended to stagnate or decline in Soviet times (e.g. 1.25 million hectares under flax in 1913, 1.05 million hectares in 1979). The traditional home of flax is in the north-west of the European part of the USSR in the mixed forest belt (*see* Fig. 45). Hemp is found chiefly in the wooded steppe (*see* Fig. 46).

Potatoes and *vegetables* are produced on a large scale (*see* Table 5). They are grown throughout the mixed forest and wooded steppe zones of the European part of the USSR, rather less so in Siberia (*see* Figs. 47-51). However, though the population continues to increase it is noteworthy that there has been no commensurate increase in the production of potatoes or vegetables in recent years (*see* Table 5).

TABLE 5. SOVIET CROP PRODUCTION
(in million tonnes)

Year	Raw cotton	Sugar-beet	Sunflower seed (000 tonnes)	Flax	Potatoes	Vegetables
1970	6.9	78.9	6.14	456	96.8	21.2
1971	7.1	72.2	5.66	486	92.7	20.8
1972	7.3	76.4	5.05	456	78.3	19.9
1973	7.6	87.0	7.39	443	108.2	25.9
1974	8.4	76.4	6.76	406	80.7	23.1
1975	7.86	66.3	4.99	478	88.7	23.4
1976	8.28	99.8	5.27	509	85.1	24.9
1977	8.76	93.1	5.90	480	83.6	24.2
1978	8.5	93.5	5.33	376	86.1	27.9
1979	9.2	76.2	5.41	317	90.9	27.2
1980	9.96	79.6	4.65	291	66.9	25.9
1976-80 (av.)	8.9	88.4	5.32	394	82.5	26.0
1981	9.6	60.6	4.6	—	72.0	25.6
1982	9.3	71.0	5.3	—	78.0	29.0
1981-85 (plan.)	9.2-9.3	100-3	6.8	—	—	29.4

NOTE: Dashes indicate no information available.

Source: *Narodnoye Khozyaystvo SSSR*
(Central Statistical Board, Moscow) annual.

Forage crops

A reliable supply of fodder is basic to the livestock industry. There are vast areas of haylands in Western and Eastern Siberia, Kazakh-stan and Central Asia, Trans-Caucasia, the highlands of the North

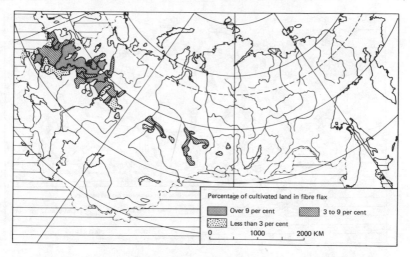

Fig. 45. Soviet Union: distribution of fibre flax-growing regions.

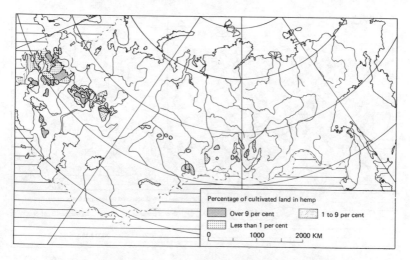

Fig. 46. Soviet Union: distribution of hemp-growing regions.

Caucasus and along the Volga, and extensive natural forage lands in the Belorussian SSR, the Ukrainian Polesye, the Baltic Republics, the north-west and the Urals. Despite the practice of ley farming and large increases in the area sown to maize for grain, silage and green fodder, the forage reserves do not, as yet, meet the requirements of the country's livestock industry (*see* p. 68). Urgent measures aimed at improving the forage reserves include not only the improvement of existing pastures by the inclusion of clover and

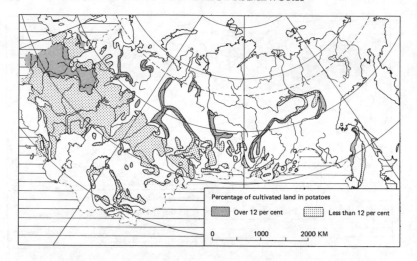

Fig. 47. Soviet Union: distribution of potato-growing regions.

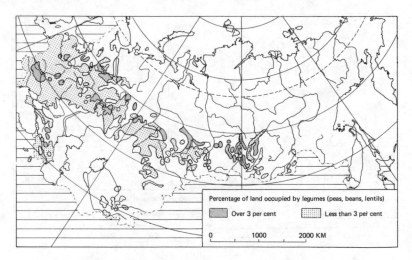

Fig. 48. Soviet Union: distribution of legume-growing regions.

alfalfa, but also more sowings of feed grains, legumes, sugar-beets and turnips.

Livestock

Collectivisation (*see* p. 77) had a shattering effect on the livestock industry of the USSR because the peasants, and more particularly the more successful ones (*kulaks*), were more than reluctant to hand over their stock to the communal ownership of the collective

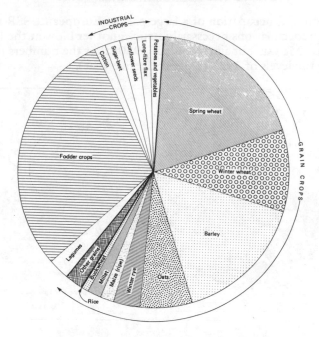

Fig. 49. Soviet Union: relative sowing areas, 1977.

farm (*kolkhoz*). The Government had to compromise by allowing the peasants to rear animals on their private plots (in early 1978, these plots accounted for one-fifth of the total animal population). As a result, before the Second World War, between two-thirds and three quarters of them remained in peasant ownership. The German

TABLE 6. NUMBERS OF LIVESTOCK IN THE USSR FOR SELECTED YEARS 1928-82
(in millions)

Year	Cattle (of which Cows)		Pigs	Sheep and goats
1928	66.8	33.2	27.7	114.6
1938	50.9	22.7	25.7	96.6
1961	81.9	36.3	66.4	144.1
1975	109.1	41.9	72.3	145.3
1978	112.7	42.6	70.5	146.6
1979	114.1	43.0	73.5	148.1
1980	115.1	43.3	73.9	149.4
1981	115.5	43.4	73.5	147.0
1982	115.9	43.7	73.3	148.5

Source: *Narodnoye Khozyaystvo SSSR*
(Central Statistical Board, Moscow) annual.

invasion and occupation of a large part of European USSR and war-time preoccupations necessarily struck another blow at the livestock industry. It was not until the late 1950s that the numbers had risen above the levels of 1928 (a pre-collective year).

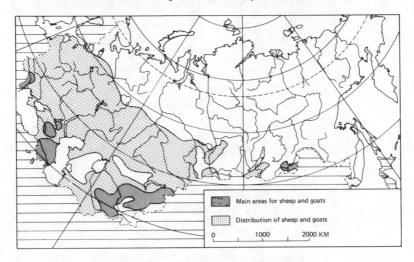

Fig. 50. Soviet Union: distribution of sheep and goats.

In addition to the availability of fodder, transport to consumers is a key factor in animal husbandry. Thus dairy herds for fresh milk and beef cattle for meat are concentrated near the urban centres. In more distant parts milk is converted into cheese, butter and sour cream, while more of the meat is canned or reduced to extracts, and hides and fats become important. *Sheep raising* is concentrated mainly in Kazakhstan and Central Asia where the karakul is an important traditional breed, and in Northern Caucasus and Trans-Caucasia where the merino is now common (*see* Fig. 50). *Pig farms* are found chiefly in areas which provide cheap grain and potatoes, and especially near large towns, particularly in the Ukraine and Northern Caucasus (*see* Fig. 51). *Reindeer,* used for draught purposes and pack animals and also for meat, milk and skins, are wide-spread in the tundra and *tayga* where there are about two-and-a-half million (*see* Fig. 52). *Camels* are bred for carrying goods in the desert and semi-desert areas of Soviet Middle Asia.

The production of major animal products in recent years is given in Table 7.

The agricultural sector of the Soviet economy still faces several underlying problems which have hindered growth for many years. In addition to the vagaries of the weather, these include: the poor quality of the rural labour force and generally low levels of education;

TABLE 7. SOVIET ANIMAL PRODUCTION

	Average annual output					
	1971-75	1976-80	1980 (actual)	1981 (actual)	1982 (actual)	1981-85 (planned)
Meat (slaughter weight) (million tonnes)	14.0	14.8	15.1	15.20	15.24	15.2
Milk (million tonnes)	87.4	92.6	90.9	88.9	90.1	88.5
Eggs (thousand million)	51.4	63.1	67.9	70.9	72.1	70.9
Wool (thousand tonnes)	442.1	460	443.0	460.0	450.0	454.0

Source: *Narodnoye Khozyaystvo SSSR*
(Central Statistical Board, Moscow) annual.

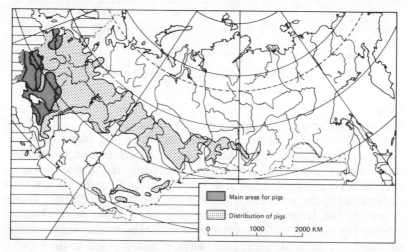

Fig. 51. Soviet Union: distribution of pigs.

shortage of fertilisers and capital equipment (notably tractors and lorries), and difficulties in obtaining spare parts for existing equipment; the drift of population, particularly young people, away from rural areas; and inefficient management and organisation. In recognition of these problems, the Soviet authorites have in recent years allocated large sums in investment to agriculture, putting special emphasis on all-round intensification of agricultural output; increasing the supply of capital equipment (tractors, combines, multi-row harvesters, grain storage buildings, etc.), chemical fertilisers and the provisions of irrigation and rural electric power supply facilities. For instance, under an agreement signed in January 1978 the Soviet Union is to invest some $2 billion (one thousand million) in Moroccan phosphate deposits and, in return, receive phosphate supplies for a period up to thirty years.

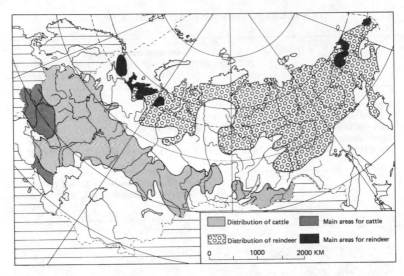

Fig. 52. Soviet Union: distribution of cattle and reindeer.

Furs
Hunting for fur-bearing animals in the tundra and *tayga* was an early attraction (p. 136) and "wild" furs continue to be a major resource. These include squirrel, mink, Arctic fox, sable, ermine, hare, silver fox and muskrat. There has been serious depletion of the more valuable species such as the ermine and silver fox, and fur-farms are now widespread in the northern regions of the country. The Soviet Union is one of the largest producers of furs, the output of mink alone amounting to ten million pelts a year. Sales at the annual international auctions at Leningrad average about four million pelts, half of them mink.

Conditions for agriculture
The agricultural heartland is bordered on the north and north-east by immense expanses which are forest-covered, underlain by permanently frozen ground, or are generally too cool for regular agriculture. The high latitudes virtually ensure a high proportion of boreal forest and tundra. In fact, 1,240 million hectares, or 56 per cent of the USSR, are so covered. Agricultural activities in the tundra regions are limited to reindeer herding and, in the occasional clearings in the *tayga*, to cattle raising and to the growing of potatoes, cabbages and some cereals. The middle Lena valley is a favoured area. Here, with alfisols, a short hot summer, and permafrost helping to conserve the limited rainfall, cattle are raised and some millets, oats and rye cultivated.

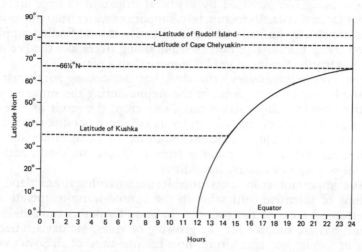

Fig. 53. Length of day and night at various latitudes on 21st June and 21st December.

Any northward expansion of the agricultural frontier has to meet very unfavourable conditions. Summers are short, cloudy and cool, although compensated somewhat by the unusually long days at this time of the year, which permit increased photosynthesis in crops and vegetation (*see* Fig. 53). The frost-free period is brief, little more than 160 days at Leningrad, 130 at Moscow and 95 days at Irkutsk (*see* Fig. 23), and precipitation decreases sharply eastwards, away from the Baltic (*see* Fig. 24). The spodosols of the northern latitudes are deficient in soluble plant foods, low in colloids, poor in structure and are acidic. They require heavy manuring and liming if they are to sustain agriculture, but even where this is possible yields are so low that the cost of the treatment seem unjustified. Only the surface layers of the permafrost thaw during the short summer and the frozen subsoil impedes drainage and cultivation. There are vast areas of badly drained land near Leningrad and Moscow and in Belorussia, and huge expanses of bog in the Western Siberian Plain.

The thermal regime of the lands to the south and east of the agricultural heartland of the USSR is favourable for agriculture, but here again expansion of agricultural land is restricted. Precipitation is slight and high rates of evaporation reduce its effectiveness. Because of the variability of the rainfall both in amount and in distribution, only occasional years have sufficient moisture for crops in such areas as the middle and lower Volga lands (Povolzhye) and complete crop failure is commonplace. In the Aral-Caspian Basin precipitation is totally inadequate for crops and there are 300 million hectares of desert and semi-arid steppe. Lack of precipitation is now being compensated by artificial irrigation in large areas of Soviet Central Asia. Unfortunately, supplies of water from the mountains are strictly limited and the imaginative idea of finding supplies by reversing the flow of northward-draining rivers like the Pechora and the Irtysh remains as yet little more than a plan.

The dreaded·*sukhovey*, the dry, hot desiccating south-east or southerly wind which blows in the steppe during the summer, can destroy within a single day a promising crop, the result of a year's adequate rainfall. Plants wilt under its influence because their roots are unable to supply sufficient mositure to compensate for the high transpiration rates resulting from the blasts of hot air and the accompanying low relative humidities.

The important crop areas outside the agricultural heartland are regions of intensive cultivation in the limited warm-temperate and sub-tropical areas of the country. In Trans-Carpathia and Moldavia, conditions are suitable for the growing of vines. Moldavia, once an area of subsistence agriculture, now has one-third of all Soviet vineyards. The southern coastlands of Crimea and the lower slopes of the Great Caucasus are suitable for apples, pears, plums, peaches, apricots, figs, grapes and tobacco.

The Kolkhida and Lenkoran Lowlands of Trans-Caucasia are the only areas of the Soviet Union which combine high temperatures and heavy rainfall. The main crops here are tea, citrus fruits, tung oil, tobacco, grapes, vegetables, cotton and maize.

There are limited areas of highly productive farmland within the desert and semi-deserts of Soviet Central Asia. These are the irrigated lands which lie in the piedmont zone where mountains and desert meet, within mountain valleys (e.g. Fergana Basin) or in long narrow tongues along the main river courses through the desert. Specialisation tends to be in high-grade cotton. Alfalfa (lucerne), grown in rotation with cotton, provides the basis for livestock raising. Mulberry trees, fruit trees, vines, rice, sugar-beet, hemp, tobacco and soft fruit are also grown. Crop specialisation in local areas is a common feature of irrigated lands. In so vast an estate, the Soviet Union necessarily has a wide range of relief, climate and soil and there are, in fact, only a few basic crops which it cannot produce — notably natural rubber, true jute, coffee and cocoa.

The basic agricultural regions of the USSR are shown in Fig. 54. The regions are based on particular crop and livestock combinations as follows.

1. Hunting and reindeer herding.
2. Reindeer herding and scattered agriculture.
3. Dairying of the northern regions.
4. Animal husbandry and arable agriculture of Yakutia.
5. Flax, potatoes and dairying.

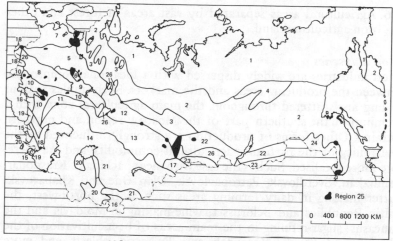

(After *Economic Geography of the USSR* by N.P. Nikitin, Moscow, 1966.)

Fig. 54. Soviet Union: agricultural regions. *See* text for explanation.

6. Dairying and potatoes.
7. Dairying and pigs (with fodder crops).
8. Sugar-beet, grains, dairying, beef and pigs.
9. Grains, potatoes, hemp, dairying, beef and pigs.
10. Grains, oil crops, dairying and beef.
11. Grains, dairying, beef and sheep.
12. Dairying, beef and grains.
13. Grains, dairying and beef.
14. Sheep raising of the desert and semi-desert pastures (and some cattle raising in the semi-deserts.
15. Mountain livestock of the Caucasus, with sheep, beef and dairying.
16. Mountain livestock of Central Asia, with sheep, beef and dairying.
17. Mountain livestock of the Altai, with sheep, beef and dairying.
18. Fruit, vines and tobacco.
19. Sub-tropical perennial crops.
20. Cotton.
21. Southern intensive crops and grains, with beef, dairying and sheep.
22. Grains and animal husbandry of southern Siberia and the Far East.
23. Animal husbandry of southern Siberia and the Far East.
24. Grains, rice, soya bean and animal husbandry of the Far East.
25. Suburban market gardening and dairying.

26. Agricultural areas separated by vast areas of forest and other non-agricultural land.

Food industries

Food industries are widely dispersed with a locational compromise between the producing areas and the markets. Such staples as flour milling are scattered throughout the main agricultural zone with a premium on the southern part of the Moscow region and northern Ukraine. Other forms of production are strongly influenced by the availability of the particular agricultural commodity and are therefore more localised. Such is the case with meat packing in Krasnodar, Leninakan, Sverdlovsk, Petropavlovsk, Ulan Ude and Khabarovsk; butter-making in dairy farming areas such as the north-west, the Baltic Republics and Belorussia; wine-making in Moldavia and the Caucasus; sugar-refining in the main areas of beet cultivation of the Ukraine and Kursk, Voronezh and Belgorod oblasts and more recently in Kazakhstan, Central Asia, Trans-Caucasia and Northern Caucasus.

ORGANISATION OF AGRICULTURE

An appreciation of the effects, direct and indirect, of politics, of the presence of the Communist Party, and of the ideas of communism, is essential to the proper understanding of the patterns of human activity in the USSR. Nowhere is this more evident than in agriculture, where the collectivisation of agriculture completely transformed the rural landscape.

Before the First World War, Russia was a classic example of a country with an overpopulated countryside. Agriculture supported over 85 per cent of the population, the bulk of whom were illiterate, poverty-stricken peasants. It was organised at a low level of efficiency, and what export there was (e.g. wheat through Odessa) was based on under consumption within the country itself rather than on an internal surplus. Some 42 per cent of the total agricultural land belonged either to the Tsar, to the Church or to the 30,000 or so country squires. Only 58 per cent belonged to the peasants. Of this amount, 23 per cent belonged to 3.4 million rich peasants (*kulaki*). The remainder belonged to 18.6 million poor (*biednyaki*) and medium-placed (*serednyaki*) peasants. There were about 11 million landless agricultural workers (*batraki*).

After seizing power in 1917, the Bolsheviks "socialised" all the land of the country and since 1929 agriculture has been organised on the basis of giant collective farms (*kolkhozy — kollektivnoe khozyaystvo*), and state farms (*sovkhozy — sovietskoe khozyaystvo*).

Individual peasant holdings no longer exist, except for some personal plots of between one-fifth and half a hectare attached to their dwellings for their own use.

The idea of collectivisation of agriculture, originally intended to take place on a voluntary basis, proved obnoxious to the peasants when, subsequently, it was introduced by Stalin. Its implementation was opposed in many ways, varying from refusal to join the *kolkhozy* to armed uprisings, some of which were widespread and prolonged. The Communists attributed the opposition to the *kulaks* and overcame it by a combination of administrative, military and economic measures (confiscation of property, banishment, the artificial famine of 1932-33, etc.). By 1934 some 71 per cent of all peasant holdings has been collectivised and by 1938 the figure had reached 93.5 per cent.

Through collectivisation agriculture was integrated into the rest of the socialised economy but its cost in terms of human suffering and material losses was extremely high. Millions of peasants died of starvation or were deported to forced labour camps.

The two forms of property, the collective farm (*kolkhoz*) and state farm (*sovkhoz*), are now firmly established and are used as instruments of Soviet economic and social policy. It is somewhat ironical that the essentially urban philosophy of Marx and Lenin, with its emphasis on all-out industrialisation, should have been first applied in a country so predominantly agricultural and rural as Russia.

The *kolkhoz* is a co-operative and collective undertaking set up by the peasants themselves. The chairman of the *kolkhoz* is theoretically elected by its members, but the local Communist organisation usually influences the election of the successful candidate. Except for the land, which is state-owned and loaned rent-free to the peasants for their perpetual use, the means of production on the *kolkhoz* and the outbuildings belong to its members rather than to society as a whole. Members have full charge of their property, which is disposed of by the highest managerial meeting. This meeting decides annually how much of the farm's output is to be sold to the State, how much is to be distributed among its members and how much is to be left for the productive and other needs of the collective farm itself. This latter share is known as the common or indivisible fund. Payment is based on the socialist principle: "From each according to his abilities, to each according to his work". The economy of the collective farm is based on the output of the communal land which is the main source of property for the members of the collective. Because of the joint ownership, each *kolkhoznik* receives a share of the total income, both in money and kind, in proportion to the amount and quality of work performed. The actual value of the share depends upon two factors: the total income of the collective farm, and the extent to which the individual farmer participates in the common work. The basic measure for remuneration is the so-called "work-day unit".

Although obliged to participate in common work, each *kolkhoznik* is entitled to a small personal plot of land, the size of which is determined by decision of the general membership meeting. The smallholdings or allotments (*podsobnoye khozyaystvo*) can be used to keep a cow (several in semi-nomadic areas), small animals and poultry and grow subsidiary crops to provide extras for the family, or else for personal recreation. Currently they provide an important source of milk, meat, fresh vegetables, fruit, eggs and potatoes and, with productivity close or equal to that of intensive farming in Western Europe are reported to account for maybe as much as 40 per cent of the gross agricultural output of the country. There were 27,100 *kolkhozy* in the Soviet Union in 1978 and their cultivated area was 96.7 million hectares. Some were essentially mixed farms, others specialised in particular crops, e.g. sugar-beet in the Ukraine, cotton in Uzbek. Every effort is made to avoid the dangers of monoculture.

Sovkhozy (state farms), now considered more important than *kolkhozy*, are organised on lines similar to those of manufacturing industry, and workers are paid in accordance with existing rules governing pay and skill as in other state enterprises. Such farms are not only productive units, but are used also for experimental work aimed at raising agricultural standards. Some specialise in plant breeding, others in livestock breeding. Many have been located in areas not previously cultivated, such as the virgin and long-fallow lands of Siberia and Kazakhstan (*see* p. 365). There were 20,066 *sovkhozy* in the Soviet Union in 1978 with a total cultivated area of 111.9 million hectares. The efficiency and productivity of the *sovkhozy* are greater than those of the *kolkhozy*.

Nearly all of the collectives and about half of the state farms are now combined into a new type of association which, it is thought, will result in the virtual disappearance of the division between existing collective and state farms. Possessing corporate status, the associations operate under a single management and often include related industrial activities, such as food processing, textiles and leather. The aim of the reorganisation is to achieve a better use of resources through the concentration and specialisation of agricultural enterprises. It is still a matter of debate as to whether or not the ideological system of agriculture practised in the USSR is the best for the country.

FISHERIES

The Soviet Union, despite very limited direct year-round access to the high seas, has become one of the world's chief sea-fishing nations since the Second World War. She shares in the rich grounds of the Pacific as well as of the Atlantic (*see* Table 8). Her fishing operations are highly organised and, except for a few local, coastal activities, are fully controlled by the central government through the Ministry of Fisheries. In this respect the USSR differs from the high-seas

TABLE 8. DISTRIBUTION OF SOVIET FISH CATCH
(in thousands of tonnes)

Fisheries	1960	1970	1975
Marine	2,736	6,704	9,109
North-east Atlantic	1,128	1,566	2,406
North-west Atlantic	285	812	1,167
West-central Atlantic	—	—	—
East-central Atlantic	44	613	1,167
South-east Atlantic	—	423	421
South-west Atlantic	—	421	9
Pacific Ocean	856	2,195	3,367
Indian Ocean	—	47	37
Inland	775	1,079	1,202
Inland seas:	562	746	719
Azov-Black	153	294	350
Caspian	367	438	357
Aral	42	14	12
Freshwater	214	333	484

Source: *Soviet Geography*, XIX (6), (1978).

NOTE: Dashes indicate that the Soviets did not fish these waters in these years. The marine catch includes that from seas other than those listed.

fishing fleets of other countries, which tend to be dominated by large capital companies.

The main species caught by the Soviet Union in the Atlantic are capelin, herring, cod, haddock, pollock and redfish. Sea mammals such as the harp seal are also taken but whaling is now on a small scale. Ice-free Murmansk (*see* Fig. 123) is the major Soviet fishing port, handling each year more than all British fishing ports put together. At one time it served as the base for the Atlantic fishery but is now more exclusively concerned with the Barents Sea fishery.

In the Pacific, the main species caught are ocean perch, pollock, sablefish, halibut, mackerel, hake, herring and flounder. In the Sea of Okhotsk, off the west coast of Kamchatka, there is an import king crab industry. The port of Petropavlovsk-Kamchatskiy plays a role in the Pacific similar to that of Murmansk, although the catch passing through the port is currently only about half of the latter.

Salmon originate in the spawning areas drained by streams and rivers along the Siberian coast, migrate to sea where they spend varying periods of time growing to maturity, then return to their parent nursery areas to spawn and die. The Soviet salmon fisheries appear to have been insignificant until the 1920s after which they followed a pattern similar to those of North America (a rapid rise during the early decades of the twentieth century, peaking in the 1930s, and a drastic decline in recent years). Soviet salmon production reached a peak in the 1940s. Like Canada and the USA, the USSR now limits her salmon fishing to the interception of returning mature salmon within her territorial waters. Since the 1950s, there has been considerable Soviet investment in fleets of modern fishing, processing and support vessels and reorganisation of shore-based processing centres to meet this transformation. In 1976, the USSR like other nations adopted a 200-mile (322 km) "economic zone" to protect its fish stocks. This has had an adverse affect on the fishing industry and caused a growing take from deep-sea fishing grounds. Consumption of fish (always an important feature of the Russian diet) is being stepped up to compensate for the difficulty of raising meat production.

The most important fish-processing and canning centres are Khabarovsk and Vladivostok in the Far East, Arkhangelsk and Murmansk in the Arctic, Zhdanov and Kerch on the Sea of Azov, Odessa on the Black Sea and Guryev and Astrakhan on the Caspian. Factory ships process fish offal on board to make fish-meal, fish protein solubles and liver oils.

FORESTRY

Timber is one of the great natural resources of the Soviet Union. *Lesa SSR* (Moscow, 1961) credits the USSR with 832 million hectares of timber-covered land. This is divided between 300 million hectares of inaccessible forest and 532 million hectares of accessible, economically exploitable forests (the distinction between total forest area and immediate exploitation forest which should be borne in mind).

Tseplyaev (1966) gave the forested area as 681 million hectares; Vasilev (1971), on the other hand, gave the area of forest as 916

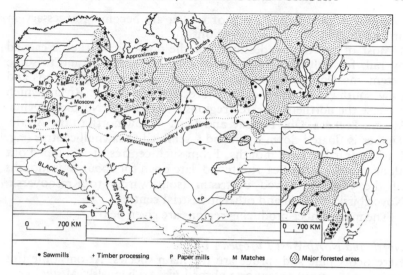

Fig. 55. Soviet Union: forestry, timber processing and products.

million hectares, 626 million hectares "with timber producing species" and 328 million hectares "where industrial extraction is being or can be undertaken" (i.e. exploitable). Conflicting information such as this is due largely to variations in assumptions and definitions. Some of the "forests", for instance, are not actually covered by trees. The Russians also include in their forest statistics areas which are in reserves, parks, etc., which would have rather limited potential for exploitation. The forested areas also contain non-timber species.

On the basis of area, the Soviet Union may be justified in claiming more than a quarter (27 per cent) of all the world's forests, rather than less than one-quarter (24 per cent) of the total timber reserves, and over half (60 per cent) of the world's softwood resource. The reserves of conifers represent the world's largest remaining source of softwoods. By area and volume (timber stand of 79 billion m^3) the exploitable forests of the USSR are comparable to the combined resources of the USA and Canada or of Brazil.

The forests are unevenly distributed (see Fig. 55). The European part of the country, with 80 per cent of the population, has less than a quarter of all the Soviet forests. In the Asiatic part the situation is reversed. Yet, even in the European USSR, the densely populated and industrially developed central and southern regions either lack forests completely or have a great deficiency of them. It is the northern and eastern parts which have the surplus. Increasingly longer and uneconomic hauls of timber are becoming necessary in order to supply the deficient regions.

Most of the timber destined for the domestic market is carried by rail, for only the Volga River and its tributaries, and to some extent the Dnieper River, which originate in wooded regions and flow southwards, offer cheap water transportation. Rivers which traverse the northern forested regions — the Onega, Northern Dvina, Mezen, Pechora, Ob, Yenisey and Lena — flow north to the Arctic. Timber is floated down them and assembled at sawmill centres (e.g. Igarka) near the river mouths. From such centres, it is shipped out along the Northern Sea Route (to date open for about four months of the year) or towed upstream (southwards) to Krasnoyarsk, Novosibirsk, Barnaul and other industrial centres.

The main timber-producing regions are given below.

North and North-West European USSR
Here Scots pine and spruce are the main species. At one time this region was geared to exports abroad via Arkhangelsk, Mezen, etc., but increasing amounts of timber are now despatched along the White Sea-Baltic Canal to sawmills and pulp and paper mills around the shores of Lake Ladoga in Karelia.

West European USSR
With broad-leaved and pine forests in the Baltic Republics, oak and pine in Belorussia, and pine, fir, beech and oak in the Carpathians, the region suffered from overcutting and devastation during the Civil War, in both World Wars and in the period since the last war, but is favourably located for transport facilities and markets.

Central Industrial Region
This region has coniferous and mixed forests. It occupies an intermediate position between the mainly timber-producing parts (upper and central Volga) and the mainly timber-consuming parts (the *oblasts* of Moscow, Kaluga, Orel and Tula). The region enjoys good rail and water transport facilities and has a third of the wood-processing plant of the USSR.

Urals
Here spruce and pine are the main species. Large quantities of timber are either floated down the Kama and other large tributaries or as deck cargo via the Volga system to south European USSR, or else transported westwards by rail.

West Siberia
This area has vast supplies of larch, fir and Siberian "cedar" (pine).

The latter is of high quality and particularly suitable for veneers, furniture, packing boxes, pencils, structural timber and other industrial uses.

Eastern Siberia and the Soviet Far East
These regions have larch, pine, spruce, fir and broad-leaved forests, as well as birch, maple, aspen, basswood, walnut, oak, elm and ash. At present only conifers are cut for timber. There are vast areas of mature and over-mature forest in Siberia and the Far East of which no more than 40 per cent can be regarded as exploitable. Harvesting of that which is exploitable presents serious problems. Much of the forest is on soils which are permanently frozen and the use of machines such as tractored vehicles during the summer thaw leads to serious long-term damage to both the soil and vegetation. The laying of adequate foundations for the construction of roads and buildings presents further formidable problems and there is the ever-present fire hazard. Vast tracts of forest will be opened up by the Baykal-Amur Mainline (BAM) railway (*see* p. 120).

Caucasus
In this region forests are restricted to the foothills and slopes of the Great Caucasus. Oak, beech and fir are the main species with admixtures of ash, maple, hornbeam and birch. The forests are highly productive, but logging is difficult.

Prolonged over-exploitation (especially of Scots pine and spruce forests in European USSR), destruction during the Civil and World Wars, and the need to bring in timber from ever-increasing distances have led to a progressive shift of sawmills, cellulose and paper plants and other wood-using industries from the southern, western and central regions of European USSR, to north-east European USSR, to the Urals and to Siberia. Something like three-quarters of the total annual cut is now concentrated in these regions.

Several integrated wood industry complexes have been constructed in Northern European USSR, Siberia and the Far East. The Bratsk combine in Siberia is the best-known example. These complexes obtain cheap power from massive hydro-electric stations in the area.

Not without good reason is wood called "the universal raw material". Besides fuel (nearly half of the timber cut in the Soviet Union is for fuel wood), it is used for wood pulp (producing cellulose, cellophane, rayon, artificial wools and many plastics), paper, card, fibre board, wood-chip and associated products, sawn planks, structural timber (joists, rafters), prefabricated houses, railway sleepers, telegraph poles, turpentine, resin and other wood chemicals, veneer, plywood, furniture, door panels, packing boxes and a host of other purposes (*see* Table 9). Trees also provide valuable shelter-belts, as in the Kamyshin-Volgograd (*see* Fig. 37) and the Belgorod-Don areas and along 1,200 km of railway in the Povolzhye.

TABLE 9. SOVIET WOOD PRODUCTION

Type of product	1975	1976	1977	1978	1979	1980 (planned)
Wood removals (million m³)	313	306	293	—	—	320
Cellulose (thousand tonnes)	6,840	7,200	7,448	7,581	7,047	9,165
Paper (thousand tonnes)	5,215	5,389	5,459	5,548	5,249	5,958
						5,300 * (actual)
Cardboard (thousand tonnes)	3,368	3,527	3,605	3,688	3,480	—
Chipboard (thousand m³)	3,368	3,527	3,605	—	—	6,593

*5,400 thousand tonnes in 1982

Source: *Narodnoye Khozyaystvo SSSR* (Central Statistical Board, Moscow) annual.

Past destruction and over-exploitation of forests is causing concern and there is currently in European USSR an accent on conservation, re-afforestation and utilising low-quality timber and wood waste. Growth in timber production is confined to Siberia where additional timber complexes are planned along the route of the Baykal-Amur Mainline (BAM) railway. It would seem that, despite the vast under-utilised forest resources, the Soviet Union is unable to satisfy her own timber needs. A surplus of forest products for export in either the short or the long term seems unlikely.

CHAPTER VI

Fuel, Power and Mineral Resources

It is in its mineral resources that the great natural endowments of the Soviet Union appear most conspicuous. Resources of coal, petroleum, natural gas and iron ore are large, and there are abundant reserves of most of the important non-ferrous minerals, with the possible exceptions of nickel, tin and wolfram.

COAL

The country's natural endowment is probably richest in respect of coal. The Soviet Union claims to have 58 per cent of the world's reserves (5,730 thousand million (billion) tonnes, of which 97 per cent are in Siberia and the Far East). The most productive coalfields are the Donets (Donbass), Kuznetsk (Kuzbass), Ekibastuz, Karaganda, Urals, Kansk-Achinsk and Pechora (*see* Table 10 and Appendix I).

TABLE 10. PRODUCTION IN THE MAIN SOVIET COALFIELDS
(million tonnes)

Coalfield	1965	1970	1975	1979	1980	1982	1985 (planned)
USSR total	578	624	701	719	716	718	770-800
Moscow Basin	41	36	34	27	–	–	–
Pechora Basin	17.6	21.5	24.2	28.9	–	–	–
Urals	55	47	36	34	(33)*	–	–
Kuznetsk Basin	97	110	139	(150)*	–	–	167
Kansk-Achinsk	14	19	28	33	–	–	–
Donets Basin	206	216	222	(208)*	(203)*	–	–
Karaganda	30	38.6	46.3	47	49	–	49
Ekibastuz Basin	14.3	22.8	45.8	59	67	–	–

*Figures in brackets are estimates.

Source: *Soviet Geography*, XIX (6), 1978.

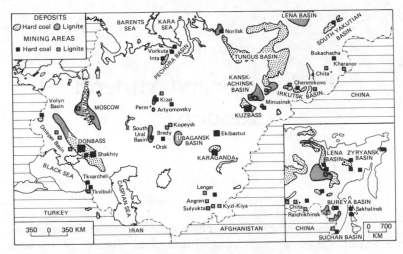

Fig. 56. Soviet Union: coalfields.

The earliest field to be developed was the Donbass in the steppes of eastern Ukraine and adjacent Rostov Oblast in the RSFSR (*see* Fig. 56). The northern limit of the coalfield is marked by the Northern Donets River, from which it derives its name, and through the centre of the field runs the Donets Ridge rising to 365 m. The exploited coalfield covers nearly 23,000 km^2, but proved deposits extend west along the middle Dnieper to Polesye. The "Greater Donbass" covers more than 60,000 km^2, but the western extension is exploited only locally and on a small scale.

The vast reserves of the Donbass include much coal of high quality. Of the proved reserves 32 per cent are anthracite or sub-anthracite, 21 per cent are coking coals, and 47 per cent bituminous or sub-bituminous. The coal is of Carboniferous age, preserved in a deep trench within the underlying crystalline foundation of the Russian Platform. The seams vary in thickness but rarely exceed 1½ m; the average is just under 1 m. Faulting is considerable along both the northern and south-western margins and mining costs generally are high. Production in 1980 was about 203 million tonnes, or approximately 31 per cent of the national total. This represents a decline from a high point of 224 million tonnes in 1976. Donbass coal is the basis for large-scale heavy industry in the Ukraine.

The second largest producer is the Kuznetsk Basin (Kuzbass) in Southern Siberia, 3,500 km east of the Donbass. The coal seams extend from near Anzhero-Sudzhensk to 65 km south of the town of Kuznetsk and westwards to the Ob River and underlie an area of about 12,000 km^2. The quality of the coal is high and there is a considerable proportion of good coking types. Seams vary in thickness from as little as 1 m to as much as 30 m; the commonest seam thickness is about 2 m. The Kuznetsk Basin has been distinguished by a high rate of growth, averaging about 5 per cent per annum. Production in 1979 was 150 million tonnes, or just over 20 per cent of the national output. Planned production for 1985 is 167 million tonnes. Long hauls are involved in transporting Kuzbass coal to consumers in the Urals and European USSR and also to Japan. Industrialisation within the Kuzbass itself began with the construction of a big metallurgical plant at Novokuznetsk (formerly Stalinsk) in 1932. Since then, ever-increasing amounts of coal are being used locally, and the metallurgical industry works on iron ores from deposits at Abakan brought in by the South-Siberian Railway.

The rapidly expanding Ekibastuz Basin in north-east Kazakhstan surpassed Karaganda in volume of production in 1977 and is now the third largest coal producer in the Soviet Union (though not in terms of coal quality). Production was 45.8 million tonnes in 1975 and 67 million in 1980. Planned production for 1985 is 85 million tonnes. The coals are non-coking and have a 40 per cent ash content. However, they are disposed in thick seams near the surface and can be won by open cast (strip) methods. The Bogatyr pit, responsible for much of the Ekibastuz output, is the largest strip mine in the USSR. Low mining costs make these lower-ranking coals competitive as a power source for thermal-electric generating stations in the Urals, adjacent parts of West Siberia and northern Kazakhstan. Projected pit-head, coal-fired thermal stations in the Ekibastuz Basin are to be linked ultimately with consumers in European USSR by extra-high voltage power transmission lines.

The Karaganda Basin, within the arid steppe of Kazakhstan, is now the fourth coal base in the USSR. Its deep-mined coals are high-grade and of coking quality but, because of their 20 per cent ash content, they have to be mixed with superior Kuzbass coals before use in the blast furnaces in the Ural and Central Asia regions. As in the Donbass, unfavourable geology in the Karaganda Basin creates high mining costs. Production was 49 million tonnes in 1980. Planned production for 1985 remains at the same figure, i.e. about 6.3 per cent of the total Soviet production.

In the north-east sector of European USSR, the Pechora Basin is important as the fifth producer of high-grade (coking) coals. Production commenced here in the 1930s, but it was not until the Second World War, after the construction of a railway link between Kotlas and Vorkuta in the 1940s, that it became significant. In 1965, production was 17.6 million tonnes; in 1979, 28.9 million tonnes, of which 18 millions were coking coal. Exploitation of this field, lying as it does within the Arctic Circle and subject to very harsh climatic conditions, requires the overcoming of many technical problems, but the high-grade coal seemingly makes the working of the field a justifiable and economic proposition. Most of the coal is exported to north-west European USSR (e.g. Cherepovets, Leningrad and Murmansk); the remainder is conveyed up the Ob and Irtysh Rivers to Siberia.

The Kansk-Achinsk Basin of southern Siberia is an important producer of lignite. As in Ekibastuz, large-scale deposits of brown çoal are being opened up by open-cast methods — a third of the Soviet coal output is won by these methods — to compensate for the gradual exhaustion of coal reserves in European USSR. Different from Ekibastuz the coals of Kansk-Achinsk cannot withstand long-distance transportation and must be burned in power stations near the mines. The world's largest thermal power station (6,400 MW) is being constructed to utilise the increased coal production which will result from the planned large-scale development of the Basin. Production was 14 million tonnes in 1965. By 1979 it had increased to 33 million tonnes with important prospects for further gains in output.

Production from the Ural fields, which lie on both the eastern and western slopes of the Ural Mountains, has declined markedly over recent years. The combined production of these fields was 33 million tonnes in 1980 (4.5 per cent of national output). The Kizel coals are the best but they are not of coking quality. The other deposits in the Ural fields are low-quality coals or lignite, those within Chelyabinsk Oblast being the most important. The coals are suitable for generating electricity but the lack of coal of coking quality has been a serious handicap for the metallurgical plants of the Ural Region. These rely heavily on Kuzbass coal, which has to be transported over 1,600 km, and on Karaganda coal, brought 1,000 km from Kazakhstan.

The lignite of the Moscow Basin in Tula Oblast has long provided fuel for electricity stations and for heating purposes in the Centre Industrial Region. It is not of coking quality and cannot be used in metallurgical industries. In spite of its low grade and high cost of mining, demand is such that the Moscow Basin ranks as sixth coal producer in the USSR. Production was 34 million tonnes in 1975 and 27 million tonnes in 1979. This reduction in planned production follows the increased availability of piped natural gas from western Siberia, the Volga-Urals area, the Ukraine and Azerbaydzhan. Natural gas, a cheaper fuel than coal, is being increasingly put to more use.

Apart from the hard coals of the Kuzbass and the brown coals of the Kansk-Achinsk Basin, there are many scattered coalfields in Siberia and the Far East. They include the Cheremkhovo-Irkutsk fields and the lignite deposits of the Minusinsk Basin. Some 60 per cent of the country's coal reserves lie within the Tunguska and the Lena Basins (Yakutia) of northern Siberia, a location so distant from the markets in southern Siberia or European USSR that transportation costs would seem to be prohibitive. Even so, work has began on the coking coal fields of South Yakutia for which Japan is supplying equipment in return for 5 million tonnes of coal a year. The first train-load of coal left the newly-opened Neryungri open cast mine in southern Yakutia in July 1981 on the BAM minor line (*see* p. 120) which connects the area with the main Baykal-Amur Mainline. This is a rare example of the Soviet Union using coal in foreign trade; exports are usually negligible, except for coking coal for the Comecon countries of East Europe. Mining at Norilsk is undertaken for local copper and nickel smelting. In the Buryat ASSR and in Chita Oblast deposits of brown coal are used to power local industry and for locomotives on parts of the Trans-Siberian Railway. Scattered coalfields in the Maritime Provinces and on Sakhalin Island contain good coals, but at present these are used only for local heating and power generation and for shipping.

Supplies of coal in Central Asia are limited and of poor quality. A number of small deposits occur in the Fergana Basin and the surrounding mountains. They are worked for local needs, but have to be supplemented by coal from the Kuzbass or Karaganda fields.

The mining of coal in the Soviet Union mounted rapidly after the Second World War. Production, 261.1 million tonnes in 1950, had increased to 509.6 million tonnes (95 per cent increase) by 1960. A slackening off during the next decade resulted in a production figure of 624.1 million tonnes by 1970 (i.e. 22 per cent increase). In view of a need to economise on scarcer oil resources a fuel policy has recently been introduced which places greater emphasis on the coal resources of the country (together with water and nuclear power) for power generation. In consequence there was a planned increase of 104 million tonnes (29 per cent) from 701 million tonnes in 1975 to 805 million tonnes in 1980. Actual production was 716 million tonnes in 1980 and 718 million tonnes in 1982 with 770-800 million tonnes planned for 1985. The bulk of the increased production is to come from Siberian, Kazakhstan and Far East mines, rather than from the Ukraine or European USSR.

Average pay rises of 27 per cent for Soviet coal miners were commenced in September 1981 to help boost output and keep skilled men in the mines.

PETROLEUM

At the turn of the century, the Baku field in Azerbaydzhan (Caucasus) was the largest single oil-producing area in the world and was the mainstay of the Russian oil industry up to the Second World War. Though oil was first obtained from the naphtha area to the north-west of Groznyy, the real start of the Russian petroleum industry came in 1873 with the sinking of wells to the north of Baku. There are many wells at Baku, but most are on the Apsheron Peninsula to the north or else in the waters of the Caspian. Other fields of moderate size occur at Groznyy and Maykop. Pipelines run from the fields of the Caucasus foothills to the Black Sea at Tuapse and Poti, and from Baku to Batumi (*see* Fig. 57). Other pipelines link the fields with the Caspian at Makhachkala, whence oil is transported by tanker to the Volga.

TABLE 11. GEOGRAPHICAL DISTRIBUTION
OF SOVIET OIL PRODUCTION*
(million tonnes)

Oilfields	1975	1980	1982	1985 (planned)
USSR total	491	603	613	620-645
West Siberia				
(Tyumen, Tomsk)	148	312		385-395
Volga				
(Tatar, Bashkir, Kuybyshev)	186	149		(100)
Urals				
(Perm, Orenburg, Udmurt)	40	42		(35-40)
North-west				
(Komi)	11	21		(26)
North Caucasus	24	19		(15)
Khazakhstan	23.9	18.4		23
Azerbaydzhan	17.2	14		−
Turkmenia	15.6	8		6
Ukraine	12.8	8		−
Georgia	0.26	3		−
Belorussia	8.0	3		−
Sakhalin	2.5	3		4-5

*Includes natural gas liquids (estimated 14 million tonnes in 1980).

Source: *Soviet Geography*, XXII (4), 1981.

In 1956 Caucasus production was surpassed by that of the so-called "Second Baku" fields. These lie between the middle Volga and the Ural Mountains and were first opened in 1929. There are five major groups of oilfields:

(a) the Perm Oblast, with Krasnokamsk as the largest centre;

(b) along the Volga near Kuybyshev, with Samarska Lika as its centre;

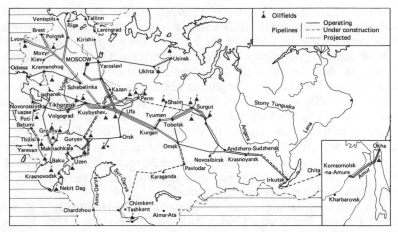

Source: *Soviet Geography*, XIX(8), 1978.
Fig. 57. Soviet Union: oilfields and oil pipeline network as of 1st January, 1978.

(c) the Tuymazy area (Bashkir ASSR), with its rich field at Shapovo and the town of Oktyabrskiy;

(d) Buguruslan in Orenburg Oblast;

(e) the Belaya Valley around Ishimbay and Sterlitamak (Bashkir ASSR).

Refining is carried out at a number of centres in each field, notably at Kuybyshev, Krasnokamsk, Ufa, Ishimbay, Perm and Syzran. Pipelines link the Volga-Ural oilfields with European USSR, and extend eastwards across Siberia to Irkutsk. The 5,330 km Comecon line, known as the "Druzhba" or "Friendship" pipeline, links Kuybyshev on the Volga with East European countries (Poland, East Germany, Czechoslovakia and Hungary), and there is an extension of this line to the Baltic port of Ventspils.

Since 1974 the traditional and conveniently located oilfields of Azerbaydzhan and the Volga-Urals region have been superceded by new fields in distant and difficult regions. They tap vast reserves in the roadless, swampy and inhospitable *tayga* of the middle Ob (Tyumen Oblast) in West Siberia (*see* Table 11). The West Siberian fields, which started commercial production in 1964, now compensate for the declining production elsewhere in the country, and account for about 52 per cent of USSR oil output. Virtually all the West Siberian output stems from Tyumen Oblast. It came at first from the development of the giant Samotlor field near Nizhnevartovsk (population: 76,000 in 1977), but more recently also from a number of medium-size fields north of Nizhnevartovsk (e.g. Pokachev field), and north and north-east of Surgut (e.g. Fedorovsk field and Kholmogory field). A 650 km railway linking Surgut with

Urengoy currently under construction will facilitate the exploitation of both the Siberian oil fields and the large natural gas fields which lie astride the Arctic Circle to the north of the oil-producing region. West Siberian oil moves to refining centres at Omsk and Angarsk in Siberia, Khabarovsk and Komsomolsk in the Far East, Pavlodar in north-east Kazakhstan, Fergana in centra Asia and to refineries in European USSR and western oil export terminals along pipelines through Omsk to Chelyabinsk and Kuybyshev and also eastwards to Angarsk, near Irkutsk. To handle the increasing flow of west Siberia an additional outlet, a 120 cm diameter trunk pipeline practically 3,400 km long, is under construction from Surgut to the Novopolotsk refinery in Belorussia. *En route* this pipeline will serve refineries in Perm, Kstovo (near Gorkiy) and Yaroslavl.

Minor oil-producing areas in western Ukraine (Brody), Komi ASSR (Usinsk and Vozey fields), Turkmen (Nebit-Dag), Uzbekistan (Fergana), Kazakhstan (Emba and Mangyshlak), Georgia and Sakhalin Island maintain small, though constant, percentages of the country's total oil production.

The tremendous increase in crude oil production is an outstanding feature of Soviet economic development in recent years. Production in 1950 was 37.9 million tonnes, 55 per cent coming from the Caucasus and 29 per cent from the Volga-Urals fields. By 1960, production was 148.0 million tonnes, only 20 per cent coming from the Caucasus fields and 70 per cent from the Volga-Urals fields. The continued eastward shift of the centre of gravity of production became further evident in 1970 when, with a total Soviet output of 353 million tonnes, the newly developed fields in West Siberia accounted for 9 per cent and those in the Volga-Urals region for 59 per cent. The West Siberian (Tyumen Oblast) fields supplied 40 per cent of the 1975 total (491 million tonnes) and nearly 50 per cent of the 1980 total (603 million tonnes) and are expected to provide about 52 per cent of the 1985 planned total of 620-645 million tonnes. The output of 613 million tonnes in 1982 made the USSR the world's major producer of oil (*see* Appendix I). Thanks also to the 1973 price explosion the country is now the world's largest oil exporter (worth $6 billion in 1977). Current estimates of Soviet oil proven reserves range from 30,000 million barrels to over 50,000 million barrels.

In 1979 the USSR earned 57 per cent of its total hard currency export receipts from oil alone and guaranteed delivery during 1981-85 of 80 million tonnes of oil to other members of Comecon.

USSR the world's major producer of oil (*see* Appendix I). Thanks also to the 1973 price explosion the country is now the world's largest oil exporter (worth S6 billion in 1977). Current estimates of Soviet oil proven reserves range from 30,000 barrels to over 50,000 million barrels.

NATURAL GAS

At first, natural gas in the Soviet Union was closely associated with oilfields. The associated *wet* gas was previously allowed to burn off, but, since about 1955, it has been collected and transmitted throughout much of the country by a network of pipelines. *Dry* gas is derived from gas fields. These are separate from oilfields but are sometimes located in the same general regions. At one time the main sources of this primary fuel were in the North Caucasus (Stavropol, Krasnodar), Trans-Caucasia (Baku), Ukraine (Dashava, Shebelinka), Povolzhye (Saratov), Urals (Orenburg Oblast) and Central Asia (Bukhara Oblast, Turkmenia, Fergana). The fields in Central Asia (especially Turkmenia) have witnessed a rapid growth of production but, since the early 1970s, these, like the others, have in their turn been eclipsed by spectacular gains in West Siberia (*see* Fig. 58). The giant Urengoy and Medvezhye gas fields in the harsh,

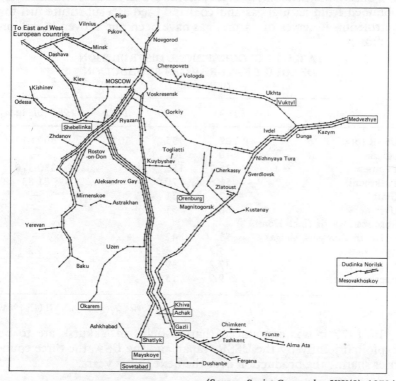

(Source: *Soviet Geography*, XIX(8), 1978.)

Fig. 58. Soviet Union: diagram of natural gasfields and gas pipelines. The major fields are boxed.

sub-arctic swampy environment of the northern part of Tyumen Oblast, accounting for 22 per cent of the Soviet output in 1975, have now overtaken Turkmenia and the Ukraine fields and account for 41 per cent of the national total (*see* Table 12). Total Soviet national gas production increased from 3.2 billion m³ in 1940 to 289 billion m³ in 1975 and 501 billion m³ in 1982. The planned output for 1985 is 600-640 billion m³ (*see* Appendix I). It is expected that, by the end of the century, gas will be the main source of energy in the Soviet Union and that exports of gas will be its main trade commodity. The country is already committed under long-term contracts to supply 40,000 million m³ of natural gas annually to Austria, West Germany, France and Italy, with deliveries planned to start late in 1984. The gas is to be transported along a new trunk pipeline which will link West Siberian fields with both East and West Europe. Gas is also an important feedstock for the petrochemical industry. The UK Company Davy Powergass has supplied the Soviet Union with two methanol plants (one to be sited at Tomsk). Methanol is an important industrial alcohol which can be obtained from natural gas and coal and used as a substitute fuel for petroleum. Reserves of natural gas have been put at over 25 million million m³.

TABLE 12. GEOGRAPHICAL DISTRIBUTION
OF SOVIET NATURAL GAS PRODUCTION
(billion m³)

Region	1975	1980	1982	1985 (planned)
USSR total	289	435	501	600-640
Siberia	40	161		–
Tyumen	35.7	156		330-370
Turkmenia	51.8	70.5		81-83
Urals	22	51		–
Ukraine	68.7	51		–
European Russia (incl. Komi, North Caucasus, Volga)	53	42		–
Kazakhstan	5.2	4.3		5.3
Uzbekistan	37.2	39		–
Azerbaydzhan	9.9	15		–

Source: *Soviet Geography*, XXII (4), 1981.

In 1977 it was announced that gasfields in Yakutsk are to be exploited jointly by the USSR, Japan and the USA, the three countries sharing the production over the next thirty years.

ELECTRICITY

Eighty per cent of the electricity generated in the USSR comes from thermal stations using coal, lignite, natural gas, oil, shale and peat (*see* Table 13). The potential for hydro-electricity, particularly in the Asiatic regions, is enormous but only 14 per cent at present comes from these sources. To conserve oil, gas and the better quality coals, it is expected that the future contribution of thermal sources will be nearer 66 per cent rather than the present 80 per cent; a decrease which will be partly compensated by a corresponding increase in nuclear power, mainly in the western regions of the USSR.

TABLE 13. SOVIET ELECTRIC POWER GENERATION
(billion kWh)

	1965	1970	1975	1977	1978	1980	1985 (planned)
USSR							
total	507	741	1,039	1,150	1,202	1,295 *	1,550-1,600
Thermal	424	613	892	969	(1,005)	(1,050)	1,100-1,140
Hydro	81.4	124	126	147	(154)	(180)	230-235
Nuclear	1.4	3.5	20.2	34	43	(65)	220-225

Source:*Soviet Geography*, XXII (4), 1981.
*1,325 billion kWh in 1981 and 1,366 billion kWh in 1982.

Large thermal generating stations (2.3 to 3.6 million kW) have been sited or are being built in the more populated areas such as the Centre, Donbass and the Urals where the power is required (e.g. Reft station, east of Sverdlovsk in the Urals, 2.3 million kW; Zaporozhye station at Energodar in the Ukraine, 3.6 million kW). New (4.0 to 4.8 million kW) thermal stations (e.g. at Perm and Ekibastuz) are planned for the 1980s. Hydro-electric stations are more restricted in their distribution than are thermal stations, and are found mainly in the eastern regions of Siberia and Central Asia. They suffer from the usual problems of remoteness from centres of population and the necessity to transfer surplus electricity to consumers in European USSR (*see* Fig. 59).

Great rivers such as the Dnieper (Kakhovka, Dneproges, Dneprodzerzhinsk, Kremenchug, Lomev and Kiev — total capacity 3.5 million kW) and the Volga (Gorodets, Cheboksary, Kuybyshev, Balakovo and Volgograd, each with a capacity of 2.5 million kW) in European USSR, and the Yenisey (Krasnoyarsk, Sayan-Shushenskaya), Angara (Irkutsk, Bratsk), Ob (Novosibirsk) and Irtysh (Bukhtarma) in Siberia have been harnessed for hydro-electric purposes. The buttress dam at Bratsk on the Angara has created one of the world's largest reservoirs with a capacity of 170,000 million m^3. This in turn provides energy for one of the world's larger hydro-electricity stations with a capacity in excess of over 4.5 million kW. A capacity

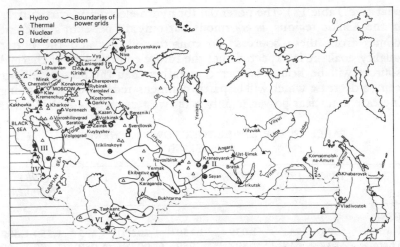

After Pokshishevsky, 1974.

Fig. 59. Soviet Union: electricity generating stations and power grid areas.

of 0.6 million kW is reported for the Irkutsk station and 3.8 million kW for the Ust-Ilimsk plant of the Ilim River, 6 million kW for that at Krasnoyarsk on the Yenisey and 6.4 million kW for the station at Sayan-Shushenskaya further upstream. The latter is the most power-ful in the world. Navigation, irrigation and recreational facilities are often important adjuncts of the electrical function.

Despite the fact that, in Siberia, the USSR possesses the world's largest resource of hydrocarbons and vast resources of hydropower, it is nevertheless forging ahead with its nuclear development pro-gramme. Eleven or more nuclear power stations are now in operation in the USSR, including reactors at Obinsk (Moscow), Beloyarsk (Urals), Shevchenko (north-east Caspian Coast), Novovoronezh, Kursk (Kurchatov), Smolensk (Desnogorsk), Kalinin, Chernobyl (Pripyat), Leningrad (Sosnovyy Bor), Rovno (Kuznetsovsk), and Polyarnyye Zori (Kola). Thirty more stations are under construction, including a giant installation at Ignalia in Lithuania which, it is claimed, will be when completed the most modern and biggest in the USSR.

Nuclear reactors and other equipment required for the various projects are being produced at "Atommash" (nuclear manufacturing complex) at Volgodonsk in the Rostov region. Nuclear generating capacity in the USSR was 900 MW in 1965, 11,500 MW in 1977 and 17,800 in 1980. Some 21,800 MW are planned for 1985.

In the generation of electricity in the USSR the share of nuclear power tripled from 2 per cent in 1975 to 6 per cent in 1980. In the

European part of the country the nuclear share rose from 3.1 per cent in 1975 to 10 per cent in 1980. Reports suggest that the Soviets are switching away from conventional nuclear plant to fast breeder reactors and that they plan to reach the peak of this technology by the end of the century when it will be superseded by thermonuclear synthesis.

TABLE 14. GEOGRAPHICAL DISTRIBUTION OF SOVIET ELECTRIC POWER OUTPUT
(billion kWh)

Region	1975	1979	1980*	1985 (planned)
USSR total	1,039	1,238	1,295	1,550-1,600
RSFSR	640	766	806	950-970
European Russia	339	–	–	–
Urals	112	–	–	–
Siberia	189	–	–	–
Ukraine	195	231	236	280-290
Moldavia	13.7	14.2	15.6	22
Belorussia	26.7	32.8	34.1	37
Baltic	28.6	34.8	35.4	–
Lithuania	9.0	11.4	11.7	27
Latvia	2.9	4.0	4.7	–
Estonia	16.7	19.4	18.9	–
Trans-Caucasia	35.5	41.1	43.3	–
Armenia	9.2	12.1	13.5	–
Azerbaydzhan	14.7	15.2	15.1	20
Georgia	11.6	13.8	14.7	17
Kazakhstan	52.5	59.7	61.6	90-95
Central Asia	47.2	58.4	63.2	–
Kirghizia	4.4	7.8	9.0	11.4
Tadzhikistan	4.7	10.6	13.6	16
Turkmenia	4.5	6.4	6.7	12.5
Uzbekistan	33.6	33.7	33.9	44-45

Source: *Soviet Geography*, XXII (4), 1981.

*1,366 billion kWh in 1982.

Regional power grids provide high voltage links between the power sources and the consuming areas, although the problem of power losses when electricity is transmitted over long distances continues to engage the attention of Soviet scientists. Soviet production of electricity was 507 billion kWh in 1965, and 1.039 billion kWh in 1975 (i.e. 100 per cent increase in a decade). In 1980 it was 1,295 billion kWh and the target for 1985 is 1,550-1,600 kWh (*see* Table 14).

FERROUS METALS

In addition to her seemingly adequate resources of mineral fuels, the Soviet Union appears to be as fortunately endowed with *iron ore*. Different from the fuels and energy situation in which the centre of gravity lies in the eastern regions, Soviet iron ore resources are concentrated mainly in the European sector. This in turn has tended to attract steel-making capacity to the west of the country. Some of the largest reserves of iron ore are in the Ukraine (Krivoy Rog), Crimea (Kerch), Central European USSR (Kursk Magnetic Anomaly), North-Western European USSR (Kola Peninsula), the Urals (Magnitogorsk, Tagil, Bakal), Kazahkstan (Rudnyy, Lisakovsk and Karazhal) with other important deposits in Siberia (*see* Fig. 60 and Table 15).

TABLE 15. GEOGRAPHICAL DISTRIBUTION
OF SOVIET IRON ORE PRODUCTION
(usable ore: million tonnes)

Region	1975	1979	1980	1985 (planned)
USSR	235	242	244.8*	—
RSFSR	89	89	92.4	—
European Russia	46	47	51	—
Kola district	10	10	11	—
Kursk district	36	37	40	—
Urals	26	25	24	—
Siberia	16	16	16	—
Kazakhstan	21.4	25.3	25.8	27
Ukraine	123.3	126.0	125.5	—
Azerbaydzhan	1.3	1.1	1.1	—

Source: *Soviet Geography*, XXII (4), 1981.

*244.0 million tonnes in 1982.

By far the largest proportion (about 72 per cent) of the total Soviet production of usable iron ore (235 million tonnes in 1975, 244.8 million tonnes in 1980) comes from deposits in European USSR. The Ukraine accounts for 51 per cent of the Soviet total, and of the remainder 10.5 per cent comes from Kazakhstan and just over 6 per cent from Siberia. Some of the best ores are at Krivoy Rog in the Ukraine. Part of the production here comes from open-cast sites, but the bulk is mined underground. Another Ukrainian iron-mining centre is Komsomolsk on the Dnieper east of Kremenchug. Crimea has low-grade reserves (28 to 40 per cent metallic content) on the Kerch Peninsula.

The so-called Kursk Magnetic Anomaly (KMA) is experiencing very rapid expansion and now accounts for 16 per cent of all Soviet

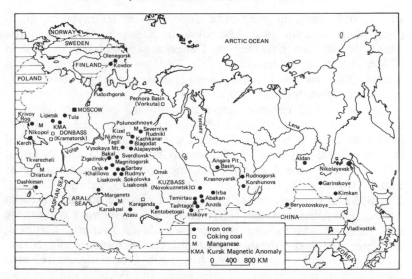

Fig. 60. Soviet Union: sources of iron ore, coking coal and manganese.

iron ore. Production from the two centres — Zheleznogorsk (Kursk Oblast) and Gubkin (Belgorod Oblast) — is on the increase since improved techniques have been introduced to exploit the deep seated, low-grade reserves and to upgrade them (benefication) for more efficient blast furnace use. Ore from the KMA is sent as far afield as the Urals (Novotroitsk, Chelyabinsk and Magnitogorsk) and the Cherepovets steel plant in northern European USSR, as well as to the Tula and Lipetsk iron and steel plants.

The iron ore mines at Olenogorsk and Kovdor in the Kola Peninsula are slowly expanding their production of local low-grade ores (31 to 32 per cent metallic content) to supply, mainly by rail, Cherepovets and iron and steel plants further east in the Urals, as well as to be exported through the port of Murmansk.

Production of iron ore from the Urals was between 25 and 27 million tonnes for many years, but latterly this has fallen to 24 million tonnes. At one time the high quality Magnitogorsk ore deposits in Chelyabinsk Oblast accounted for about half of the output. These are now practically exhausted and the balance has shifted to the Kachkanar deposit in Sverdlovsk Oblast. Even so, Urals ore production is insufficient to meet more than half of the needs of the Urals iron and steel industry. The balance is made up by shipments from Kazakhstan, the Kursk Magnetic Anomaly, the Kola Peninsula and Krivoy Rog.

Other ore deposits of significance are in Kazakhstan (Sokolovka and Sarbay low-grade magnetite deposits near Rudnyy, the high-phosphorus deposits near Lisakovsk in Kustanay Oblast and the Atasu deposit at Karazhal in Dzhezkazgan Oblast), in Siberia (Gornaya-Shoriya in the south of the Kuzbass and Zheleznogorsk in Irkutsk Oblast) and in Trans-Caucasia (Dashkesan magnetite deposits in Azerbaydzhan SSR (see Appendix I).

Manganese and *chrome,* important alloying metals in the steel industry, are abundantly available in the Soviet Union, the world's largest producer of both (see Appendix I). Manganese ores are mined mainly in two deposits — Chiatura (Georgia SSR) and Nikopol (Ukraine SSR) (see Fig. 60). Chrome ores are mined mainly at Sarany (Sverdlovsk Oblast) and Khromtau (Aktyubinsk Oblast). The USSR is the only major producer of chrome outside southern Africa and Albania. Other ferro-alloys which, besides manganese and chrome, add various properties such as strength, hardness, resilience and rust-resistance to steel are *nickel* and *cobalt.* Nickel ores come mainly from Norilsk (the main producing centre) near the mouth of the Yenisey, Monchegorsk and Pechenga in the Kola Peninsula, Orsk in the southern Urals, Tuva ASSR and Batamshinskiy in northern Kazakhstan. With an annual production of 150,000 tonnes (23 per cent of the world's output), the USSR is the world's major producer (see Appendix I). Verkhniy Ufaley in the eastern Urals is one source of cobalt but the bulk is produced by processing ores of various geological origins and composition in specialised smelters.

NON-FERROUS METALS

Deposits of ores of non-ferrous metals are plentiful in the USSR (see Fig. 61) but for strategic reasons details are not available (see Table 16).

Base metals
Kazakhstan (Kounradskiy, Dzhezkazgan) and the Urals (Krasnouralsk, Revda, Mednogorsk, Sibay, Uchaley, Kray) are the main producers of *copper,* but there are other deposits of significance in Armenia SSR (Kafan, Alaverdi, Kadzharan), Uzbek SSR (Almalyk), the Kola Peninsula (Monchegorsk, Pechenga) and northern Siberia (Norilsk). The output of 900,000 tonnes in 1970 had risen to 1,150,000 by 1979. The USSR is the world's second largest producer of copper (see Table 16).

Lead and zinc are in good supply in the Altay Mountains of east Kazakhstan (Leninogorsk and Zyryanovsk), central Kazakhstan (Kentau and Tekeli), in the northern Caucasus (Ordzhonikidze) and

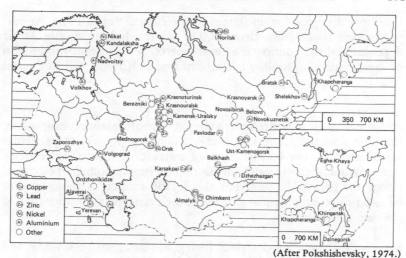

(After Pokshishevsky, 1974.)

Fig. 61. Soviet Union: main centres of non-ferrous metallurgy.

TABLE 16. PRODUCTION OF PRINCIPAL NON-FERROUS METALS
(thousand tonnes)

Metal	1975	1979	1980 (planned)
Copper	950	1,150	1,200
Nickel	155	150	185-200
Lead	480	590	530
Zinc	690	1,020	740
Platinum (in million ounces)	2.65	—	3.2
Chromium ore	2,000	—	2,200
Tin	30	—	30
Titanium	30	—	35
Primary aluminium	1,700	—	2,040-2,200
Manganese ore	8,000	—	—

Source: *Comecon to 1980*, D. Lascelles (1976).

in the Maritime Provinces of the Soviet Far East (Dalnegorsk, the former Tetyukhe). The most recent published data (1979) gave a figure of 590,000 tonnes for lead production and 1,020,000 tonnes for zinc, 73 per cent of the production coming from Kazakhstan (*see* Table 16 and Appendix I). *Cadmium* is recovered as a by-product of zinc-bearing ores at zinc smelters in Kazakhstan.

Tin is one of the few essential commodities in which the USSR is not self-sufficient. Mining takes place in remote areas of the Far East (Maritime Kray, Amur Basin and Chuckchi National Okrug).

Off-shore dredging for tin started in the Laptev Sea in 1974. Annual production is no more than 40,000 tonnes, half from the Arctic deposits, and the country is a net importer. A significant production of *mercury* and *antimony* is concentrated in Kirghiz SSR in Central Asia.

Light metals

Because of their high strength to weight ratio aluminium, magnesium, titanium and tantalum, the so-called light metals, are of particular significance in the construction of aircraft, spacecraft, electricity transmission lines, etc. Such metals require large amounts of electrical power for their reduction. For this reason reduction plants tend to be sited near large hydro- and thermo-electric plants rather than at the resource bases.

ALUMINIUM. There is a dearth of high grade bauxite in the USSR and recourse has to be made to low grade bauxite, to alumina-bearing materials and to imports (e.g. alumina from Hungary, bauxite from Greece). The aluminium industry is widely distributed through a variety of regional linkages, but a shift to low-cost hydro-electric power sources (power is the principal cost element in the aluminium industry) at Shelekhov (near Irkutsk), Krasnoyarsk, Bratsk, and Novokuznetsk has become evident in recent years. Production continues to increase at some of the longer-established sites in the Leningrad area (Volkov, Boksitogorsk), at Zaporozhye on the Dnieper, at Kamensk-Uralsky and Krasnoturinsk in the Urals and Yerevan and Sumgait in Trans-Caucasia. The plant at Volgograd relies on alumina imported from Hungary, that at Pavlodar (northern Kazakhstan) on Arkalyk (Turgay Oblast) ore and Krasnooktyabrskiy (Kustanay Oblast) bauxite, and Achinsk plant (in Siberia) on nephelite ore from the Belogorsk area 240 km to the south-west (*see* Appendix I). The USSR is the world's second largest producer of aluminium after the USA.

MAGNESIUM. This metal is extracted from magnesium-bearing minerals at refineries in Ust-Kemenogorsk in eastern Kazakhstan, Solikamsk and Berezniki in the Urals, and Zaporozhye on the Dnieper River. When alloyed with aluminium, magnesium produces light, very strong and stress resistant metals for use in air and spacecraft, rockets and ballistic missiles.

So little is known of the detail of the geology of vast areas of the country that there may well be large resources of minerals yet to be discovered. On present evidence it would seem that, in an emergency, there are very few naturally occurring minerals for which the Soviet Union would be dependent on outside sources.

CHAPTER VII

Major Branches of Industry

Manufacturing industry contributes about 53 per cent of the total national income of the USSR and employs about 38 per cent of the working population.

FERROUS METALLURGY

The fact that the bulk of the Soviet Union's iron ore resources are in the European sector has led to a concentration there of most of the country's iron- and steel-making capacity (*see* Fig. 62 and Table 17). The *Dnieper-Donets Basin* area of the Ukraine, with a sound raw materials base, is responsible for about 43 per cent of the production of pig iron and 36 per cent of the steel production. The main integrated iron and steel complexes are in Donetsk, Makeyevka, Yenakiyevo, Zhadanov, Kommunarsk (Voroshilovsk), Zaporozhe, Dneprodzerzhinsk, Dnepropetrovsk and Krivoy Rog. Water, required

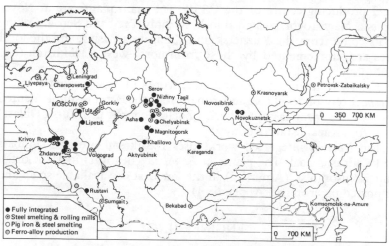

(After Pokshishevsky, 1974.)

Fig. 62. Soviet Union: ferrous metallurgical centres.

103

in large quantities for processing in ferrous metallurgy, is in short supply in the Ukraine (*see* Fig. 150). Further north there are lesser complexes at *Tula* and *Lipetsk* using Donbass coal and both Krivoy Rog and Kursk iron ore. The plant at *Cherepovets*, near the Rybinsk reservoir, uses coking coal from Vorkuta and iron ore from Olenogorsk, supplemented by some from Kursk. Together with the plant at Volgograd, which gets its pig iron from the Ukraine, the European USSR plant provide 54 per cent of the Soviet Union's total steel production.

TABLE 17. REGIONAL DISTRIBUTION OF SOVIET STEEL PRODUCTION
(million tonnes)

Region	1975	1980	1985 (planned)
USSR	141.3	147.9*	165-168
RSFSR	79.9	84.4	93-95
European Russia	23	27	33
Urals	42.6	43	44
Siberia	14	15	16
Ukraine	53.1	53.7	62-63
Kazakhstan	4.9	6	6-5
Others	3.4	4	4

Source: *Soviet Geography*, XXII (4), 1981.

*147.0 million tonnes in 1982.

Despite the deficiency of coking coal and depleting reserves of high-grade iron ore, the *Urals* represents the second main iron and steel producing centre of the USSR. The main plants are at Novotroitsk, Magnitogorsk Chelyabinsk, Nizhniy Tagil and Serov. Coking coals come from the Kuznetsk and Karaganda Basins, and the local ores are supplemented by those from north-west Kazakhstan (e.g. Rudnyy).

The two integrated iron and steel works in Novokuznetsk in the *Kuzbass* rely on local coal and iron ore, but the latter is supplemented by iron ore from eastern Siberia (Zheleznogorsk in Irkutsk Oblast) and from Kazakhstan (Rudnyy).

The *Rustavi* integrated works uses Dashkesan ore and Donbass and Caucasus coal. The plants at *Bekabad* (Begovat) in Uzbekistan and Komsomolsk (Amurstal) in the Far East use available scrap and imported pig iron (*see* Appendix I).

ENGINEERING

The products of the ferrous and non-ferrous metallurgical industries support a range of engineering activities. Engineering, in all its forms,

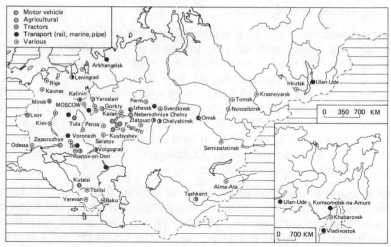

(After Pokshishevsky, 1974.)

Fig. 63. Soviet Union: engineering centres.

is currently the largest and most dynamic sector of Soviet industry. Two-fifths of the industrial workers are engaged in engineering which accounts for 34 per cent of Soviet industrial production. The engineering products, embodying skill, design and high value in relation to their bulk, can stand the cost of transport well and are, in consequence, widely dispersed. Even so, they tend to be concentrated in the larger and traditionally industrial districts in the European sector (*see* Fig. 63).

The engineering industry can be subdivided into a host of sub-sectors with an almost endless variety of products.

Heavy engineering
Heavy engineering is located in areas where the products are consumed and at the same time in proximity to raw material bases. This branch embraces the manufacture of equipment for coal and ore mining, oil drilling and metallurgical industries (e.g. heavy duty continuous steel casting equipment, rolling mills, pipe-making equipment). Because of the ready availability of steel, mining machinery, for example, is fabricated at such centres as Gorlovka, Kramatorsk and Voroshilovgrad (Lugansk) in the Donetz Basin, Kopeysk and Votinsk in the Urals and Prokopyevsk in the Kuznetsk Basin. Eastern Siberia makes special dredges and mining equipment for working gold and diamonds while oil drilling machinery is important in the Urals, the Volga area and Trans-Caucasia. Into the category of heavy engineering would come also equipment for the building, power, chemical and other industries.

Transport engineering

RAILWAY ENGINEERING. This widely dispersed activity involves the building of diesel and electric locomotives and rolling stock of various kinds. Diesel locomotives are built in Murom, Kolomna, Bryansk, Kuluga, Voroshilovgrad and Kharkov. Main line diesel locomotives equivalent to 3.8 million hp were being produced in 1980. The manufacture of electric locomotives takes place in Tbilisi and Novocherkassk. Main line electric locomotives equivalent to 3.4 million hp werc being produced in 1980. Rolling stock construction is widespread with Kremenchug, Kaliningrad, Moscow, Bryansk and Kolomna being important centres.

VEHICLE INDUSTRY. Previously the great bulk of the output of motor vehicles was in the form of buses and lorries. Within the last decade, however, motor cars have become an important part of the operation. Located mainly in the European part of the USSR the main centres are at Minsk (MAZ), Moscow (ZIL, AZLK), Yaroslavl (Ya MZ), Gorkiy (GAZ), Saransk, Miass, Engels, Ulyanovsk (UAZ), Lvov, Kremenchug (KrAZ), Togliatti (VAZ), and Naberezhnyye Chelny (KamAZ). Of the total of 2,199,000 vehicles produced in 1980, 1,327,000 were cars, 787,000 lorries and 85,000 buses. The production of cars increased four-fold during the 1970s, with VAZ plant at Togliatti producing 2,500 cars per day.

AEROSPACE INDUSTRIES. The aerospace industry is a creation of Soviet times. It plays an important part in transport and agriculture and is probably second in size only to that of the USA. Detailed inform-ation on the location of the engine, airframe and components industries is incomplete, but it is known that aircraft assembly takes place in Moscow, Kiev and Kazan and that aero engines are produced in Zaporozhe. The state airline, Aeroflot, uses several subsonic aircraft for civil flight, but has also developed the Tu-144 supersonic trans-port. Spacecraft of various kinds — information, surveillance, space laboratories, communications, weather watch, etc. — with which are associated such names as *Cosmos, Prognoz, Molniya, Soyuz* and *Salyut* testify to spectacular Soviet achievements in the sphere of space technology. The docking of manned craft with orbiting space stations and the launching of eight or more satellites by one rocket are but two recent achievements to indicate the high levels of tech-nology and human endeavour attained. The Baykonur "cosmodrome" and the city of Semipalatinsk in Kazakhstan are but two of the locations with which spaceflight and rocketry are associated.

SHIPBUILDING. Of the estimated thirty or so shipyards in the USSR (e.g. Leningrad, Tallin, Riga, Kaliningrad and Nikolayev), most of the capacity is earmarked for naval production. Traditionally the

Soviets import twice as much merchant shipping as they build themselves, mainly from Poland, the German Democratic Republic, Finland, Romania, Bulgaria and Yugoslavia. Even so, cargo ships, coasters, tankers and supertankers, container ships and bulk carriers are constructed in the USSR.

River vessels are built at centres on the Volga, Dnieper, Dvina, Irtysh, Ob, Yenisey, Upper Lena and Amur Rivers.

Electrical and power engineering
This branch of engineering depends a great deal on the inherent skill and "know-how" of the workforce, on complex design and advanced engineering techniques. As such, it is best suited to the older and larger industrial areas such as Leningrad or Kharkov which specialise in the production of turbines and generators, or Moscow which produces transformers, electric motors, lighting equipment and radio and television receivers. More recently, there has been some development of electrical and power engineering in other parts of the country such as Novosibirsk and Barnaul. Big capacity power units, hydraulic and automatic compressors for gas pipelines, equipment for thermal and nuclear power stations, gas turbine generators, boilers and diesel engines come into this category.

Agricultural engineering
Widely distributed, agricultural engineering (e.g. tractors and combines, potato harvesters, flax processing machinery) tends to reflect local needs. Plants are located both in the countryside and in engineering centres. Leningrad, Kharkov, Volgograd, Rostov-on-Don, Chelyabinsk, Perm, Kurgan, Vladimir, Minsk and Tselinograd are among the many established centres, though several additional works have been opened to ensure regional independence in respect of agricultural equipment.

Machine tools and instruments
This is one of the leading branches of engineering. It includes the production of metal-cutting lathes, forges, presses and casting machines. The largest machine-tool plants are in Moscow, Leningrad, Novosibirsk, Kharkov, Kiev, Kramatorsk, Minsk and Odessa.

CHEMICALS INDUSTRY

The chemical industry makes products used in practically every aspect of life. From such ordinary raw materials as coal, salt, limestone, sulphur and petroleum, the chemical industry turns out a prodigious number of compounds that are essential to the operations of every other industry (*see* Fig. 64). The tremendous upsurge in

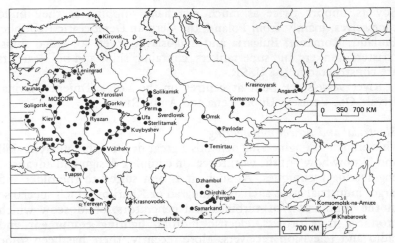

(After Pokshishevsky, 1974.)

Fig. 64. Soviet Union: centres of the chemical industry.

gas and petroleum refining during recent decades has stimulated the development of many petrochemical industries. At the same time, the need to raise the productivity of agriculture has also meant priority consideration for mineral fertilisers. The USSR is now the world's largest producer of fertilisers.

Mineral fertilisers

There are three main classes of mineral fertiliser — phosphatic, nitrogenous and potash. *Phosphatic fertilisers,* for which apatites and phosphorites are the main raw materials, are associated with plants at Voskresensk in Moscow Oblast (using apatite concentrate from the Kola Peninsula), Dzhambul and Chimkent in Kazakhstan, and Samarkand, Kokand and Chardzhou in Central Asia (the latter using Kara Tau phosphate rock). Most of the country's phosphate and superphosphate plants continue to rely on apatite from near Kirovsk in the Kola Peninsula. This of necessity involves costly transfer of bulky raw material over long distances. However, the share of apatite in the domestic fertiliser supply is now declining at the same time as that from phosphate rock is increasing.

The manufacture of sulphuric acid, basic in chemical production and closely linked with superphosphate production, relies on sulphur deposits (brimstone) in the Carpathian foothills of the Ukraine and in the Volga valley near Kuybyshev, on iron pyrites mined at several sites in the Urals and on "secondary" sources of sulphur (by-products, waste). Because of the dangers of transporting sulphuric acid in bulk the raw materials are moved to new superphosphate plants where the acid is both manufactured and used.

Nitrogenous fertilisers are produced in plant scattered throughout the agriculturally-productive parts of the country. The location of the individual plants is related to the availability of ammonia, the processing of which relies, in turn, on a source of hydrogen. Previously, hydrogen was obtained from coal-coke-chemical centres (e.g. sulphate of ammonia from coal by-products in the Donbass and Urals). Nowadays the raw material is natural gas, supplied by pipeline, and is available in many parts of the country.

Nitrogenous fertiliser works are now found in association with supplies from the Central Asian gasfield (e.g. Navoi, Chirchik), Volga-Urals oilfield gas (e.g. Togliatti, Salavat), the Shebelinka gasfield (e.g. Cherkassy, Gorlovka), the Dashava gasfield (e.g. Rovno, Grodno, Jonava) and the North Caucasus gasfield (e.g. Nevinnomyssk, Severodonetsk, Novomoskovsk, Kohtla-Järve).

Potash fertilisers are manufactured in association with a major deposit of potash in the Kama basin and in the Urals (Berezniki-Solikamsk), at Soligorsk in Belorussia and Kulush and Stebnik in Lvov Oblast.

The USSR is now the world's largest producer of fertilisers and should be well supplied with industrial fertilisers by the 1980s.

The Soviet Union is pushing forward relentlessly with expansion plans for the chemical industry which rely heavily on Western help. The investment programme under the tenth Five-year Plan was double that of the previous Five-year Plan, with top priority given to agricultural chemicals, plastics and man-made fibres.

Industrial alkalis

The production of soda ash and caustic soda, vital in the production of glass, soap, paper and pulp, detergents, textiles, etc., is dependent to a large extent on the availability of salt, limestone, coal or cheap electric power. Such resources are found in combination in the Donbass (Donetsk, Slavyansk) and in the Urals (Sterlitamak, Beresniki).

Artificial and synthetic fibres

These are man-made fibres, the artificial fibres derived from cotton and timber linters (cellulose fibres), the synthetic fibres produced by wholly chemical processes. The cellulose fibres (viscose rayon and acetate rayon) dominate, though the production of wholly synthetic fibres is increasing rapidly. Centres of the viscose rayon industry include Mogilev, Leningrad, Lesogorskiy, Svetlogorsk, Klin, Kalinin,

Shuya, Atamil, Namangan, Krasnoyarsk, Barnaul and Balakovo. Natural gas, now widely distributed through a network of pipelines, affords a cheap source of acetylene for acetate rayon. Acetate plants using this feedstock are sited at Engels, Kaunus, Kirovakan and Serpukhov.

The synthetic fibres include *kapron* (a polyamide fibre produced from cabrolactum, associated with ammonia synthesis), *lavsan* (polyester fibre) and *nitron* (acrylic fibre). Kapron is associated with both coal-based and natural-gas-based chemical complexes, and manufacturing plant are widely scattered in Lithuania (Daugavpils), the Ukraine (Zhitomir, Chernigov), Georgia (Rustavi, Volzhskiy) and elsewhere. Kapron and the other synthetic fibres are also produced in Klin, Kursk, Novomoskovsk, Barnaul, Ufa, Saratov, Yerevan, Kiev, Mogilev and Vilnius.

Chemical fibre production was 955,000 tonnes in 1975, and 1,100,000 tonnes in 1977. By 1980, according to the Tenth Five-year Plan, the USSR expected to produce 1,460,000 tonnes.

Synthetic resins and plastics

Based largely on gas, oil and petrochemicals, synthetic resins and plastics industries are widely dispersed. Urea resins, derived from ammonia, are associated with nitrogenous fertiliser plants. Vynyl resins include polyvynyl chloride (PVC) with the production of chlorine, plastics such as polypropylene and polyethylene with oil-refinery gases, etc. Intermediates such as propane, isobutane and isopentane produced in petrochemical plants are transported to plants which make the final plastic products. Production of polyethylene, PVC, polypropylene and polystyrene is to increase to meet the demands of engineering, building and packaging.

Synthetic rubber

Synthetic rubber now supplies upwards of two-thirds of the Soviet Union's rubber requirement. Industrial alcohol derived largely from potatoes was first used in the manufacture of butadien-sodium rubber (Buna). This was later replaced by ethyl alcohol, a by-product of oil refining. Methol is no longer used in the manufacture of synthetic rubber; it has been replaced by oil-refining gases and natural gas derivatives, while Buna rubber has been superseded by more advanced types. Synthetic rubber works, often associated with petrochemical complexes, are located in Vladimir, Kalinin, Klin, Voronezh, Yerevan, Sterlitamak, Kuybyshev, Gudermes (east of Groznyy), Shagal (Central Asia), etc.

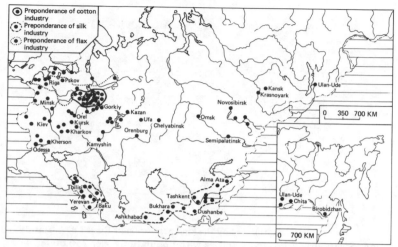

(After Pokshishevsky, 1974.)

Fig. 65. Soviet Union: centres of the textile industry.

TEXTILE INDUSTRY

The Industrial Centre, the Ukraine, the Baltic Republics and the Volga region supply the bulk of the cotton, woollen, linen and silk (mostly man-made) textiles of the USSR (*see* Fig. 65). Central Asia produces the bulk of the Soviet cotton crop (about 10 per cent of the world output), the remainder comes from Trans-Caucasia, yet practically 80 per cent of Soviet cotton cloth is produced in the European regions, two-thirds in the Moscow-Ivanovo area. Half-hearted attempts have been made to re-locate the industry away from Moscow, Ivanovo, Kalinin and Vladimir Oblasts by establishing new mills in the cotton-growing areas, in Tashkent, Fergana, Ashkhabad and Dushanbe in Central Asia and Leninakan, Kirovabad and Baku in Trans-Caucasia. Even so, the latter continue to produce little more than 10 per cent of the total cotton textiles.

The *woollen* industry, like cotton textiles, is also concentrated in the European part of the country to the extent that 90 per cent of the total output is produced there. The oldest centres of the industry are in the Baltic areas and the Industrial Centre, marking their earlier dependence on imported wool. Latterly, these areas have tended to concentrate on mixtures of wool and synthetic fibre. New woollen mills have been set up in Trans-Caucasia, Kazakhstan, Central Asia and elsewhere where domestic wool supplies are becoming increasingly available with the expansion in the numbers of sheep.

Linen is the only textile industry which is located within the

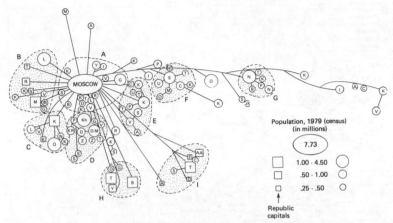

(Reproduced by the kind permission of Russell B. Adams, 1977.)

Fig. 66. Soviet urban hierarchy (cities with populations over 250,000 in 1976) showing the major linkages direct and presumed. The urban regions and their largest cities are:

A. The Centre — Moscow
B. West and Baltic — Leningrad
C. South-West — Kiev
D. Eastern and Southern Ukraine — Kharkov
E. Volga — Kuybyshev
F. Urals — Sverdlovsk
G. Western Siberia — Novosibirsk
H. Trans-Caucasia — Baku
I. Central Asia — Tashkent

growing area for flax and at the same time well-situated for its market. Mills are located in Vladimir, Kostroma, Bryansk, Yaroslavl and Ivanovo Oblasts, Belorussia, the North-West and Baltic Regions.

TERRITORIAL-PRODUCTION COMPLEXES

The major branches of manufacturing industry may be grouped to form industrial regions. The major urban zones of the Soviet Union and the linkages between them (*see* Fig. 66) serve also to show regions, centres and nodes where manufacturing is concentrated. However, such regions, centres and nodes take no account of other components of industrial production such as support industries, services and social infrastructure. In recognition of not only the dominant, but also the supporting, components of an industrial region, and in keeping with the planned nature of the economy of their country, Soviet economic geographers have introduced the concept of the "territorial-production complex" in preference to the more generally recognised "industrial region".

Territorial-production complexes evolved mainly in the new regions lying to the east of the Volga with simple economies; such complexes are more difficult to introduce into the older regions lying west of the Volga where economies are well developed. They

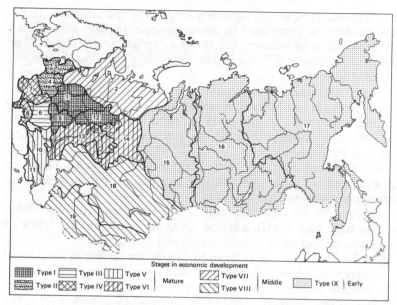

(Based on Moshkin, 1976.)

Fig. 67. Economic regions classified into territorial-production complexes.

relate to the spatial organisation of the Soviet economy and represent a complicated system of linkages encompassing all elements in the economy. The territorial-production complex is, in fact, a highly integrated regional economic organism. The framework of each is the industrial centre or node (usually a city) each with its own internal production, technological and economic linkages with other industrial centres. The transport system provides the necessary circulatory system for the over-all integration of the territorial-production complex.

On the basis of intensity of linkages within and between cities (i.e. an integration factor) and level of transport development (i.e. a transport factor), the official economic regions of the USSR (*see* Chapter XI) have been classified by Moshin (1976) into nine types of territorial-production complexes (*see* Fig. 67). These are described below.

(a) *The Centre, Volga-Vyatka and Central Chernozem Regions.* These regions are distinguished by high coefficients of integration and transportation as well as by high economic potential, a diversified and efficient production structure and a far-flung system of industrial nodes and centres.

(b) *The Baltic and Belorussian Regions.* These are distinguished by high coefficients of integration, comparable levels of economic development, production structure and farm specialisation (territorial-production complexes in which agriculture plays a significant role in addition to industry are termed "agricultural-industrial" or "industrial-agricultural" complexes, depending on which is the predominant sector).

(c) *The Donets-Dnieper Region* (one of the most highly urbanised regions in the Soviet Union), Kharkov and Zhdanov. The integrating industries here are iron and steel, machine building and chemicals. The system of linkages is extremely intricate and the rail transport system is highly developed.

(d) *The South-West and South Regions and Moldavia.* These are distinguished by their high levels of integration, industrial-agrarian economies and dense settlements.

(e) *The North Caucasus and Trans-Caucasian Regions.* Both regions have high coefficients of integration and similar levels of development, industrial specialisation and agriculture.

(f) *The Urals and Volga Regions.* These are similar in their levels of integration, economic potential and diversification of industry. The intense and intricate system of economic and technological linkages in the Urals are mainly in a north-south direction along the eastern and western foothills. Linkages between the nodes along the Volga reflect the same linear pattern.

Complexes (a) to (f) are classed as mature in terms of economic development.

(g) *North-west Region.* Similar to (a) in respect of economic potential, diversification and significance in the national division of labour but with a low integration coefficient (similar to that of Kazakhstan and Central Asia).

(h) *Kazakhstan and Central Asia Regions.* Both regions have low levels of integration and have poorly developed transport systems. Pavlodar-Ekibastuz and South Tadzhik complexes are designated under the Eleventh Five-year Plan (1981-85).

Complexes (g) and (h) are considered to be in the middle stage of economic development.

(i) *West Siberia, East Siberia and the Far East Regions.* Integration in these regions is at a very low level and the transport linkages are poorly developed. Territorial-production complexes here are in an early stage of economic development, but under the Five-year Plan 1981-85 new West Siberian, Sayan, Angara-Yenisey and South Yakutia complexes are to be developed.

CHAPTER VIII

Transport

For the economic development and integration of an area so vast as the Soviet Union, the importance of an adequate transport system is obvious. To satisfy such needs the Soviet government has developed a unified transport system in which the various media — railway, road, airway, sea and pipeline — are interrelated and integrated. Wasteful competition is thereby eliminated.

By far the largest proportion of freight (56 per cent by tonne kilometre (t km)) is moved by rail (in Britain, by contrast, 80 per cent of the freight is moved by road) (*see* Table 18). The railway is the basic and almost universal form of transport in the Soviet Union and is an all-purpose land carrier — it handles 40 per cent of the inter-city passenger traffic and almost two-thirds of the internal freight throughout the year in every direction. The vast and generally flat terrain of much of the country has greatly facilitated the laying of the permanent way. Water transport on river and lake is important for certain kinds of bulk cargo, but winter ice imposes an annual standstill. Little more than 4 per cent of the country's freight by tonne kilometre is moved on inland waterways. The rigours of the climate along the northern and eastern coasts reduce maritime transport (14.2 per cent by tonne kilometre) to two to three months a year. (In 1977 the first convoy used the Northern Sea Route in April, i.e. a month earlier than usual, and the route remained open until February 1978. By the end of the Tenth Five-year Plan (1980) year-round navigation was considered possible. This success has been due to the rapid expansion of the icebreaker fleet which now includes three nuclear-powered icebreakers (*see* Fig. 68).) Road transport, speedy and flexible for short hauls, is still relatively unimportant and accounts for rather less than 7 per cent of freight by tonne kilometre. Few motor roads exist, so that haulage concentrates mainly on the carriage of goods within towns and cities. Inter-city road freight transport is increasing, but certainly not to the same extent as, say, in Western Europe or the United States of America, where the excellence of the road

TABLE 18. FREIGHT TRAFFIC BY ALL TYPES OF GENERAL-PURPOSE TRANSPORT

Type of transport	1940 000,000 t km	%	1950 000,000 t km	%	1960 000,000 t km	%	1970 000,000 t km	%	1979 000,000 t km	%
Railway	420.7	85.0	602.3	84.4	1,504.3	79.8	2,494.7	65.3	3,349.3	56.0
Marine	24.9	5.0	39.7	5.6	131.5	7.0	656.1	17.1	851.1	14.2
Inland waterway	36.1	7.4	46.2	6.5	99.6	5.3	174.0	4.5	232.7	3.9
Pipeline	3.8	0.8	4.9	0.7	51.2	2.7	281.7	7.4	1,140.7	19.1
Motor vehicle	8.9	1.8	20.1	2.8	98.5	5.2	220.8	5.7	407.9	6.8
Aircraft	0.02	–	0.14	–	0.56	–	1.88	–	2.9	–
	494.4	100.0	713.3	100.0	1,885.7	100.0	3,829.2	100.0	5,984.6	100.0

Source: *Narodnoye Kbozyaystvo SSSR*, v. 1979, Moscow, 1980.

NOTE: Figures are rounded to significant places.

(Fotokhronika Tass)

Fig. 68. The nuclear-powered ice-breaker *Arktika* leading a convoy of ships through the Kara Sea. In a dramatic display of her power *Arktika* made a successful voyage to the North Pole in August 1977 — the first surface ship ever to do so. Year round navigation was planned for the Northern Sea Route by the end of the tenth Five-year Plan in 1980. This was considered possible by the rapid expansion of the ice-breaker fleet.

system and the flexibility of the lorry and truck have combined to make road transportation a serious rival of the railway for many long-distance hauls. However, the proportion of the road passenger traffic per passenger kilometre conveyed by motor bus has risen in recent years from 33 per cent in 1965 to 43 per cent in 1977, while that for the railway has declined from 55 per cent to 40 per cent in the same period. Pipelines for the transport of petroleum and natural gas (16-17 per cent per tonne kilometre) are becoming increasingly important as are transmission lines for electricity.

RAILWAYS

The railway system of the USSR is the backbone of the country's

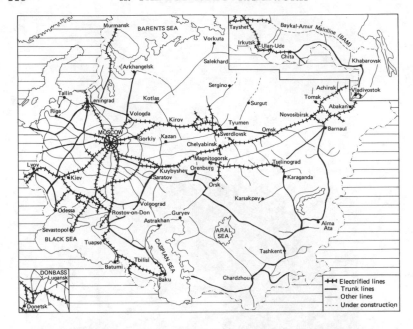

Fig. 69. Soviet Union: railways (including electrified sections).

unified transport system. It accounts for almost two-thirds of the
internal freight and about 40 per cent of the inter-city passenger
traffic. With 141,800 km of mainly broad-gauge (1½ m) lines in
1980, it is also the second largest national network in the world.
At the time of the Revolution in 1917, the route length was only
70,300 km. Most of the lines are in the European part of the
USSR (*see* Fig. 69). Eleven radiate from Moscow, the focus of the
system. East of the Volga there is no real network and many of the
railways are isolated single-track trunk lines with a small number of
feeders extending into Siberia, the Far East, Central Asia and Trans-
Caucasia, reaching out to productive agricultural areas and mining
areas and providing inter-regional links.

Trunk lines such as those which now link Moscow and Leningrad,
Moscow and Gorkiy, Leningrad and Warsaw, Moscow and Sevastopol, and Moscow and Rostov, were completed in the second half of
the nineteenth century. Local and shorter branch lines within the
Donbass and within the Ukraine generally were laid in the same
period. The main emphasis at that time was on lines to bring coal
and metals from the Donbass to the Moscow region, and grain to
the Baltic and Black Sea ports. Eastward in the Urals, the line
linking the metallurgical centres of Sverdlovsk and Perm was not

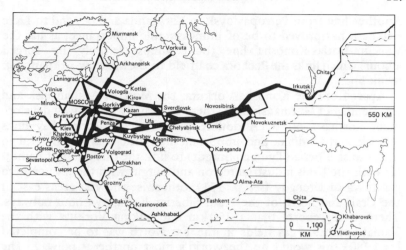

Fig. 70. Soviet Union: density of rail freight movements. The width of the lines corresponds to volume of goods traffic in main directions.

joined to the Russian network until 1896. The longitudinal Sverdlovsk-Orsk line, skirting the eastern Urals, was laid much later.

The *Trans-Caspian* (after 1889, the *Central Asian*) was the first railway to be built in what is now Asiatic USSR, running from Krasnovodsk to Samarkand (1888) and thence to Tashkent (1899). It was not linked with the main system until the *Trans-Aral* trunk line (the "cotton line") from Tashkent to Orenburg (formerly Chkalov) was completed in 1906. The *Trans-Siberian* is a true transcontinental line which links the European and Asiatic parts of the Soviet Union. It is the longest railway in the world (Moscow to Vladivostok: 9,297 km) and probably the most important. Not completed until 1916, when the Chita-Khabarovsk section was opened to traffic, it has been instrumental in opening up the vast resources of Siberia and in spreading Great Russian influences eastward. The 5,190 km section Moscow-Irkutsk is now electrified (*see* Fig. 69). The *South-Siberian* line runs from Magnitogorsk in the Urals to Prokopyevsk and Novokuznetsk in the Kuzbass via Tselinograd (formerly Akmolinsk) and Pavlodar, and helps to relieve the heavily worked section of the Trans-Siberian line between Chelyabinsk and Novosibirsk (*see* Fig. 70). This line has been further extended via Abakan to Tayshet on the Trans-Siberian Railway. The *Turk-Sib* line, completed in 1930, links Tashkent and Alma-Ata with Novosibirsk on the Trans-Siberian Railway. The lines from Leningrad to Murmansk and from Kazan to Sverdlovsk were among the first major railway constructions undertaken by the Soviets.

Another line from Petropavlovsk to Karaganda and beyond to Lake Balkhash has proved to be of immeasurable importance, as has the Vorkuta-Kotlas-Konosha line (built almost entirely by forced labour) which links the Pechora coalfield to the Moscow-Arkhangelsk trunk line.

Apart from the Konosha-Vorkuta, the Moscow-Arkhangelsk and the Leningrad-Murmansk lines, there is virtually no railway development north of 60° N. A double-tracked electrified railway links Norilsk and Dudinka and important new tracks are being laid in north-west Siberia (Tyumen-Surgut) to link the oil region of Samotlar with the Urals industrial region and Surgut with the far northern gas town of Urengoy (*see* p. 371), otherwise the vast areas east of the Urals and north of the Trans-Siberian line are without railways. There were reports that a 250 km line linking Vorkuta with the Yamal peninsula gas fields in the Far North was to be completed by 1980: this would be the world's most northerly railway. The long projected 3,200 km North-Siberian Railway, planned before the Second World War to pass around the north of Lake Baykal and to link Tayshet on the Trans-Siberian with Sovetskaya Gavan on the Pacific coast (Sea of Japan) is now half completed. It is being constructed with considerable investment of capital and man-power ("The Construction of the Century") under, first the Ninth, then the Tenth and now the Eleventh Five-year Plan (1981-5). The project, known as the Baykal-Amur Magistral (BAM), will take the strain off the existing Trans-Siberian line and open up vast untapped areas said to be rich in mineral and forest resources (*see* p. 412). A western section now extends from Tayshet through Bratsk and Ust Kut to Nizhneangarsk on the northern shore of Lake Baykal; in the east, Sovetskaya Gavan is linked with Komsomolsk and Khabarovsk. There is also a link with the Trans-Siberian Railway between the towns of Bam and Tynda (*see* p. 407).

While the general features of much of the country are an advantage in railway construction, many difficulties exist in railway working and maintenance. In areas of permafrost the instability of the ground, in association with the expansion of underground waters on freezing and solifluction in surface layers on thawing, causes damage to railway lines, cuttings, embankments, bridges and other structures. Concrete and gravel are used to consolidate surfaces. In the same areas water for locomotives — being in short supply — has often to be obtained from deep wells that penetrate the permafrost. Bridging some of the wide rivers also requires specialised engineering, as does the laying of track in the swampy areas of western Siberia or the mountainous areas of eastern Siberia and the Caucasus. Shelter belts consisting of one or more lines of trees or bushes are planted as protection against drifting snow (*see* Fig. 37). In parts of Central

Asia there is the hazard of drifting sand and, where railway lines are in danger of being buried by this, grasses and bushes are planted alongside the lines in belts several hundred yards wide.

Following thorough modernisation over the last quarter of a century, Soviet railways are now among the most modern in the world with most goods hauled by diesel or electric engines. Thirty-five per cent (1981) of the track is electrified (see Fig. 69) but the figure is higher for trunk lines where over 50 per cent of the freight is hauled by electric engines. Electrification of the Moscow-Brest line and of the Trans-Siberian Railway from Moscow to Chita gives the USSR the world's longest electrified line. This important freight route or "land bridge" provides a quicker and cheaper route between Western Europe and the Far East. It is taking an ever-increasing amount of container traffic and causing some alarm in Western shipping circles. Currently there is a marked imbalance in the "Trans-Siberian Landbridge" cargo, 72 per cent is westbound (mainly to Germany, the UK and Iran); 28 per cent is eastbound (to Japan).

INLAND WATERWAYS

Despite the fact that the Soviet Union has the world's greatest system of inland waterways, its use is severely restricted by several factors, mostly related to climatic conditions. The winter cold causes a freeze-up of most rivers for long periods each year. At Kiev on the Dnieper, at Rostov on the Don and at Astrakhan on the Volga, the freeze-up and consequent closure lasts for three months. Northwards and eastwards the freeze-up lasts longer: more than six months on the Pechora and over seven months in the lower reaches of the Yenisey and Lena in Siberia.

Another drawback to using the river systems is the south-north direction of flow of the majority of rivers which, in Siberia especially, does not accord with the longitudinal movement of people and freight. Furthermore, rivers flowing northwards discharge into a sea which is frozen for nine months, or longer, every year. Spring floods caused by melt-water and decreased volume in the dry months are additional disadvantages. On the other hand, because of the flatness of much of the countryside, gradients are slight, currents slow and rates of discharge relatively small. The flatness of the terrain has also fostered the cutting of canals to link important rivers, e.g. the Volga-Baltic, Moscow-Volga and Volga-Don Canals (see Fig. 209). The Volga-Baltic (the reconstructed and modernised eighteenth-century Mariinsk Canal system) links the Rybinsk Reservoir with Beloye Lake and Lake Onega, where connections are made via the Belomor (White Sea) Canal (built almost

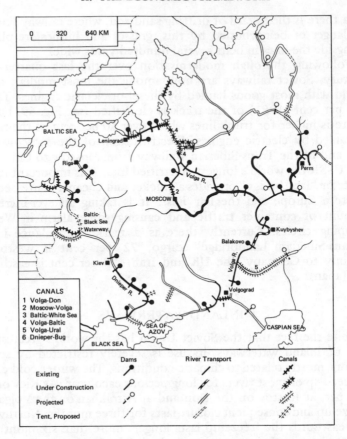

Fig. 71. Navigable waterways in European USSR.

entirely by forced labour in conditions of extreme hardship) west-wards to the Gulf of Finland and northwards to the White Sea. (The intention was to introduce year-round navigation on the Volga-Baltic Canal during the Tenth Five-year Plan (1976-80). The Volga-Don Canal (101 km), built largely by forced labour, was opened in 1952 joining the lower Volga with the Don and thence with the Sea of Azov. Moscow has since then been an inland "port of five seas" (*see* Fig. 71).

The Volga has been an artery of communication for centuries and is the key to the Soviet inland waterway system (*see* Fig. 72). Aided by a series of dams which impound the Volga waters for hundreds of kilometres upstream (the impounding and consequent slowing down of the flow of water reduces the ice-free period by ten days), navigation for steamers during the ice-free period is ensured upstream as far as Kalinin and downstream to Astrakhan.

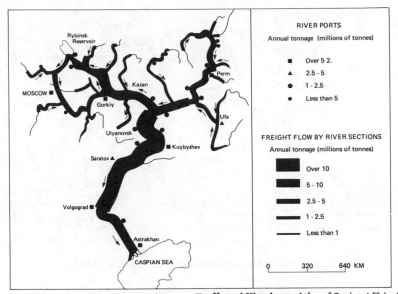

RIVER PORTS

Annual tonnage (millions of tonnes)

■   Over 5 2.

▲   2.5 - 5

●   1 - 2.5

•   Less than 5

FREIGHT FLOW BY RIVER SECTIONS

Annual tonnage (millions of tonnes)

Over 10

5 - 10

2.5 - 5

1 - 2.5

Less than 1

0   320   640   KM

(Source: Taaffe and Kingsbury, *Atlas of Soviet Affairs*.)

Fig. 72. Volga River system: ports and freight density.

The Dnieper is the second most important river for water transport. The barrage (Dneproges) at Zaporozhye impounds a reservoir some 90 km long which has drowned the cascade of rapids formerly interrupting navigation at this point. The Kakhovka Reservoir below the Zaporozhye Dam, completed in 1956, is even larger (200 km long) and facilitates navigation in the lower reaches of the river. Nevertheless, the final entry of the Dnieper into the Black Sea remains a long shallow estuary. The Northern Dvina is much used for the floating of timber.

The great Siberian rivers, Irtysh, Ob and Yenisey, would be navigable almost throughout their entire courses, but their development is restricted since the ice-free period is so short (*see* Fig. 73).

SEAS

Like many of the rivers, the surrounding seas are adversely affected by ice. Ports on the Sea of Okhotsk are closed for over six-and-a-half months. Further south, Nikolayevsk-na-Amure and Sovetskaya Gavan on the Pacific are closed for considerable periods, although Vladivostok, frozen over for three to four months, is kept open by ice-breakers. Nearby Nakhodka is also kept open for navigation the year round. Most Arctic Ocean ports are ice-bound for over eight months, some ice persisting throughout the year. Ports such as

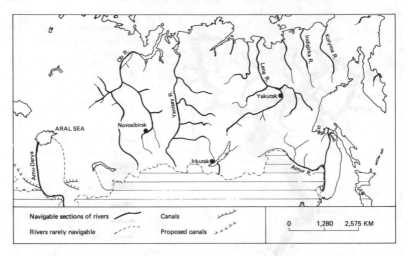

Fig. 73. Navigable sections of rivers in Asiatic USSR.

Arkhangelsk in the White Sea have ice for over five months (November to March) and are kept open only with difficulty. Murmansk on the Barents Sea benefits from the ameliorating influence of the North Atlantic Drift (*see* Fig. 123) and is open for navigation the year round. The Northern Sea Route between Murmansk and Vladivostok is kept open during the summer at great cost (*see* p. 7). Icebreakers are essential, and aircraft are used for ice observation (*see* Fig. 68). Ports along the route — Zelenyy Mys (Kolyma), Tiksi (Lena), Dikson (Yenisey), Salekhard (Ob), Naryan-Mar (Pechora) — are located near the river mouths for the transhipment of cargoes between ocean-goining vessels and river boats. From Moscow to Tiksi is 5,290 km via Arkhangelsk and the Northern Sea Route, 9,420 km by the most direct overland route via Irkutsk. The 11,000 km from Murmansk to Vladivostok is half the distance via either Suez or South Africa. In recent years the icebreaker fleet has managed to lengthen the navigation season; it now runs approximately from May to December (*see* Fig. 68). The maintenance of this route must be for prestige or strategic reasons, for it handles less than 10 per cent of the maritime traffic of the USSR.

The principal ports in the east Baltic and the Gulf of Finland are kept open by icebreaker, but others are closed for periods of up to four months. Ice also occurs along the north coasts of the Black Sea and the Sea of Azov, but the main ports can be kept open by icebreakers.

The Soviet merchant fleet is expanding fast and is now the sixth largest in the world. It handles about 45 per cent of the cargoes between the USSR and other countries and is endeavouring to acquire a larger share of international seaborne trade (*see* Table 19). Most sea transport is handled by the ports of the Black Sea and the Sea of Azov, especially by Novorossiysk which is the base for Soviet tankers, and by Odessa-Ilyichovsk. Terminals to handle container traffic from the "Trans-Siberian Landbridge" (*see* p. 121) have been contructed at Vostochny (Nakhodka) on the Pacific and at Ventspils, Riga, Tallin, Murmansk, Arkhangelsk and Ilyichovsk.

TABLE 19. SHIPPING ACTIVITIES OF
THE SOVIET MERCHANT MARINE

	1976	1977	1978 (planned)
		(millions of tonnes)	
Total shipments by Soviet merchant marine	214.5	219.3	226.9
Soviet foreign-trade cargoes	104.1	111.4	117.3
Shipments between foreign ports (cross trade)	14.2	13.8	13.2

Source: T. Cruzheno in *Soviet Weekly*, 10th Feb. 1979.

ROADS

Road haulage is responsible for about 7 per cent by tonne kilometre of freight in the USSR, but is expected to account for a growing share in the future. The adverse effects of snow, frost, drifting sand, earthquake and flood make road maintenance and expansion of the system both costly and difficult and, though the road network is now many times longer than before the Revolution, it still amounted to less than 1.5 million km in 1978. That same year the total length of "motor roads" (i.e. with a hard surface) was 741,600 km.

The main trunk roads, such as those radiating from Moscow to Leningrad, Minsk, Riga, Simferopol, Tbilisi, Orsk, Murmansk, Arkhangelsk and Ulan-Ude, are generally asphalt or grit-covered (concrete suffers adversely from frost). Apart from these there are few metalled roads away from the larger towns, and transport is often difficult in winter and early spring. There is still no east-west road across Siberia.

In the Great Caucasus, mountain roads such as the Georgian, Osetian and Sukhumi Military Highways are justly famous. In eastern Siberia, Yakutsk is connected by three roads to the coast at Magadan (Kolyma Highway), Okhotsk and Ayan; and to Never on the Trans-Siberian Railway (Aldan Highway). In the permafrost zones, current transport policy favours roads against railways since they are cheaper both to build and to maintain. The lofty mountainous country of Tadzhikistan in Central Asia is served by the Pamir Highway linking Dushanbe (formerly Stalinabad) and Kashgar in Sinkiang, while the traditional caravan route through the Dzhungarian Pass is now followed by a road from Alma-Ata to Urumchi. The capital of the Mongolian People's Republic, Ulan Bator, is linked to the Trans-Siberian Railway at three points, at Novosibirsk by the Chuya Highway, at Achinsk by the Usa Highway and at Ulan-Ude. The route Ulan-Ude to Ulan Bator is followed by both road and rail and is continued into China (Peking).

The main function of road transport in the USSR is to cater for local needs, primarily in retail trade, agriculture and construction, but also for deliveries to and from railway and river terminals. There is very little long-distance traffic (the average distance for a road cargo is 15 km) except where rail transport is not available. Two-fifths of all passenger movement is by bus, mainly over short distances within cities.

AIR

The main purpose of air transport in the USSR is the carriage of passengers and mail and the rapid delivery of high-value freight. Supplies for remote mining camps and Arctic stations are also carried by air. Regular services by the Soviet state domestic and foreign airline, *Aeroflot*, by far the largest airline in the world, serve the principal towns within the Union as well as ninety-five countries in Europe, America and Asia. Moscow, with four airports, is the centre from which the majority of the services radiate (*see* Figs. 74 and 75). Jet aircraft, mainly Ilyushin 62, Tupolev 134 and Tupolev 154, carry between 40 and 50 per cent of all passenger air traffic in the USSR (over 100 million a year). The supersonic passenger aircraft Tu-144 ("Concordski", the Soviet equivalent of the Anglo-French Concorde) began regular flights between Moscow and Alma-Ata in November 1977, and a service to Khabarovsk in the Far East was planned later. (The fleet of Tu-144s was withdrawn from service in the summer of 1978 following a crash: a new modified version flew to Khabarovsk in June 1979. However, the aircraft has been excluded from Soviet aviation planning until after 1985 and Western experts doubt that it will fly again.)

Auxiliary uses of aircraft, for which light piston-engined planes and helicopters are used (e.g. Yak-40, Antonov 20), include surveying, ice reconnaissance, pipeline monitoring, weather observation, spotting shoals of fish for trawlers, crop spraying, ambulance service and forest patrols. Such activities give Aeroflot the reputation of being the world's largest "bush airline".

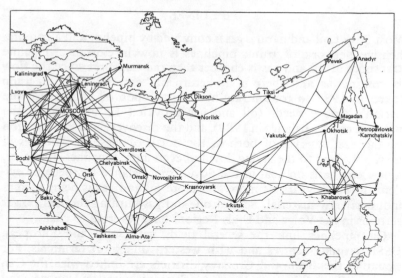

Fig. 74. Internal air routes (simplified) of major interregional significance operating in 1982. (Source: Aeroflot publications, *Atlas Razvitiye*. Reproduced
(simplified) with permission, from *Russian Transport: an Historical and Geographical Survey*, L. Symons and C. Whyte, Bell, London, 1975.)

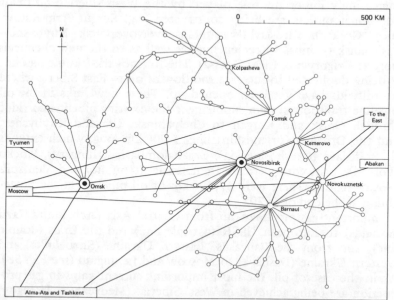

Fig. 75. The Aeroflot network in part of Western Siberia. The map gives an
indication of the hierarchy of services from transcontinental to local. (Source:
Aeroflot publications. Reproduced with permission, from *Russian Transport:
an Historical and Geographical Survey*, L. Symons and C. Whyte, Bell, London,
1975.)

PIPELINES

Most Soviet oil and natural gas is conveyed by pipeline and a comprehensive network of trunk pipelines is now in existence. Pipeline transport of oil and gas is cheaper than rail transport since the flow is continuous and there is no return of "empties". The decision taken in 1958 to concentrate henceforth upon oil and gas for the nation's energy needs (oil and gas provided 57 per cent of the national energy balance in 1980), and the discovery and exploitation of the vast reserves of both in the north of western Siberia will inevitably lead to the laying down of even more pipelines. However, a new emphasis on coal in the Soviet fuel balance has become evident in recent years, as more and more oil and gas is being used as industrial raw material. Several oil- and gas-burning thermal power stations in the Volga and Urals Regions have reverted to coal.

Oil pipelines link the several fields with local and European USSR refining centres and with western oil-export terminals. For example, the Baku and Groznyy districts are linked with the Caspian and Black Sea ports, the north Caucasus with the Donbass, and the Volga-Urals Region with the industrial and population centres in the western part of the Soviet Union and with the oil-export terminal at Ventspils (Latvia) on the Baltic Sea (see Fig. 57). With the increasingly important role played by the West Siberian oil fields additional outlets are being constructed, e.g. Surgut-Perm-Kstovo (near Gorkiy), Yaroslavl-Ryazan-Moscow-Novopoltsk; Kuybyshev-Lisichansk (Donbass)-Kremenchug, as well as to the new chemicals port at Grigoryevsk (near Odessa). The Krasnoyark-Irkutsk pipeline is being duplicated to increase the flow of oil to East Siberia where no oilfields have yet been opened up. These new links in the oil pipeline transport system supplement the existing pipeline corridor through Omsk and Kurgan to Chelyabinsk, Ufa and Kuybyshev, and the Druzhba (Friendship) line, 5,000 km long, which extends to Bratislava (Czechoslovakia), Szazhalombatta (Hungary), Plocko (Poland), Schwedt (German Democratic Republic) and Ventspils (Soviet Baltic). There were 67,400 km of oil pipeline in the Soviet Union at the end of 1979.

Important gas pipelines run from Central Asia (Achak and Gazli gasfields) to European USSR (a triple line) and the Urals (double line), and from the Caucasus, Eastern Ukraine (Shebelinka) and Western Ukraine (Dashava) to Moscow and Leningrad (see Fig. 58). As in the case of oil, the most important current gains in gas production are being achieved in West Siberia (Medvezhye, Urengoy, Vyganpur). Pipeline outlets from here are westward through Perm to European USSR and southwards to Chelyabinsk. Another important and recent development in the gas pipeline network has been the 2,670 km link between Orenburg and Uzhgorod on the Soviet-Czechoslovak border. Gas pipeline distances increased practically 12 per cent between 1975 and 1979, from 98,800 km to 124,000 km.

PART THREE: HUMAN RESOURCES

CHAPTER IX

The Peopling of the
Soviet Lands

The subject of history is the life of peoples
and of humanity. To catch and pin down in
words — that is, to describe directly the life,
not only of humanity, but even of a single
people, appears to be impossible.

War and Peace, L. Tolstoy.

To relate, even sketchily, the long history of Russia from Palaeo-lithic times to the present day would be a formidable task and one not really relevant to this study. Instead, a series of phases, considered to be significant for a proper understanding of the life and culture of the Soviet Union of today, has been selected.

KIEV RUS*: NINTH TO THIRTEENTH CENTURIES

Primitive Finno-Ugrian tribes, belonging to the Ural-Altaic group of people, migrated westward from Siberia and settled in the forests of northern European Russia towards the beginning of historical time. To the south, in the marsh and mixed forest lands between the Dnieper, Western Dvina and Dniester, lived eastern Slavonic tribes. Into the open steppe-lands of the south came wave after

*There is no universally agreed meaning and derivation of *Rus* from which it is thought the modern word "Russia" is derived. A consensus suggests that the word comes from the Finnish name for Sweden but that it referred only to the Swedes in Russia (never of the Swedes in Sweden). In course of time it came to include not only Swedes (Scandinavians) but also those who lived under their sovereignty, including subject Slavs. Later the term was used to denote the country, though it was not until the fifteenth or sixteenth century that the term "Russian State" was officially adopted. (*See: A History of the Vikings*, Gwyn Jones, OUP, 1978.)

wave of conquering nomadic peoples: Iranians, Cimmerians, Scythians, Sarmatians, Germanic Goths, Turko-Mongols and Turko-Avars. In the seventh century the Avars themselves were overrun by the Khazars, whose domination of the steppe lasted until the tenth century. The Khazars, a Turkic-speaking people of Asiatic origin, spread over the whole of the immense plains of southern Russia from the northern shores of the Black Sea and the Caspian Sea to the Ural Mountains, and to the Volga River beyond Kazan. The Crimea was also in their hands. Certain eastern Slavonic tribes that had settled in the middle Dnieper, chiefly around Kiev, came under Khazar subjection. Other Slavonic people who had settled farther north were much influenced by Swedes called either Varangians, Norsemen or Rus. The Varangians came to Russia from the Baltic, first as pirates and adventurers and later as traders. Following the waterways and making short portages along the Neva, Lake Ladoga, the Volkhov, Lake Ilmen, the Lovat, Western Dvina and Dnieper — "the Water Road from the Varangians to the Greeks" — and also other routes further east via the Volga — they made their way to Byzantium (Constantinople) where they had established trading links by the end of the eighth century.

By the closing decades of the ninth century, the Varangians (Rus) and subject Slavs had been organised into small principalities or city states at such places as Novgorod on the River Volkhov, and Smolensk on the Dnieper. The end of the century saw the Rus settled also in Kiev, an outpost on the forest-steppe fringe. Here, near the confluence of the Dnieper, Desna and Pripyat, and under Oleg who united the city with Novgorod, Kiev achieved primacy and became the main seat of the Rus power in Russia (*see* Fig. 76).

By the twelfth century, Kiev had become the cradle of Russia. Even Novgorod, a great trading centre and member of the Hanseatic League, was obliged to accept its leadership. A steady process of assimilation with the Slav population, through concubinage, intermarriage, a change of language and religion and the adoption of Slavonic customs, witnessed the progressive erosion of the Varangian-ness or Norseness of the Rus. Ultimately, a far greater part in the foundation and development of the Russian state was played by the east Slavs than by the Rus (although to the east Slavs must also be added Byzantine, Muslim and Turkic influences).

The Dnieper-Western Dvina axis and Dnieper-Volkhov axis drew together the Baltic and Black Sea, and thus northern and southern Europe. This axis was the backbone and economic *raison d'être* of Kiev Rus. Kiev Rus itself provided furs, wax, salt, hemp, honey, hides and slaves, but it was from the transit trade that she gained her real wealth and importance. Kiev, "the Mother of Russian cities"*,

*Kiev celebrated its 1,500th anniversary in 1982.

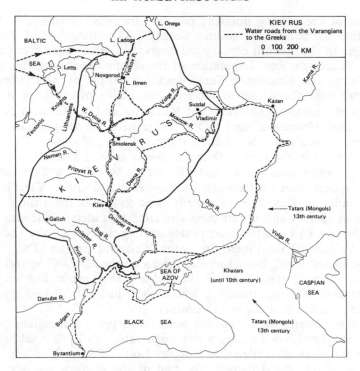

Fig. 76. Kiev Rus and the movements of the Rus.

and the Kievan State absorbed many elements of civilisation through contact with Byzantium, not the least of which were the Greek (Cyrillic) alphabet and Greek Orthodox Christianity.

Constant attacks by steppe nomads,* and internecine warfare of Russian princes during the twelfth century, brought about a decline in the power of Kiev Rus. Between 1237 and 1240, Kiev was overthrown and completely laid waste by Mongol and Tatar hordes (tribes) under Batu, Khan of the Golden Horde. For the next two centuries the Mongol peoples maintained complete supremacy over the steppelands.

MOSCOW RUS:
FIFTEENTH TO SEVENTEENTH CENTURIES

The frequent attacks of the steppe nomads and the general instability of Kiev before its fall in 1240 gave rise to Slav migration north-

*". . . a cloud of ruthless and idealess horsemen sweeping over the unimpeded plain – a blow, as it were, from the great Asiatic hammer striking freely through the vacant space" (H.J. Mackinder, 1904). The opera *Prince Igor* (Knaz Igor) by Alexander Borodin (1833-87) was set in this same period at a time when Kiev Rus was under Tatar pressure.

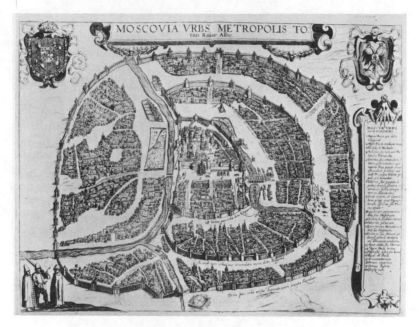

Fig. 77. Plan of Moscow, 1789.

eastwards. There, in the refuge of forest and marsh, Russian princely states began to emerge from the consolidation of several smaller states. The complete suppression of these individual principalities and the creation of the new Russian State, Muscovy, in the geographically important region between Oka and Volga was eventually attained by the ambitious and unscrupulous princes of Moscow. The Slav peoples from Kiev, speaking Great Russian, joined with the Finno-Ugrians and other Slavs who had earlier settled in the northern forest. Isolated villages dotted the forests and marshes, while the villagers practised subsistance agriculture, trapping and hunting. The environment in which these people lived was totally different from, and far less congenial than that of Kiev Rus. In the long hard winters of enforced hibernation, the peasants took to handicrafts. When the link with Byzantium was broken by the Mongol Tatars, Moscow became the new seat of the Metropolitan and the centre of the Russian Orthodox (Greek) Church (*see* Fig. 77).

The backbone of Moscow Rus was the Volga-Northern Dvina axis, and this remained for centuries "as closed and self-contained as the Arctic and Caspian Sea that link its ends". To the west, beyond the borders of the Russian homeland, the feudal monarchies

Fig. 78. Novgorod: eigthteenth-century view of this ancient Russian trading centre.

Fig. 79. Kazan: eighteenth-century view of the old Tatar centre at the great bend of the Volga.

of Lithuania and Poland disputed the Baltic lands with the Teutonic (German) Knights. Following their unsuccessful struggle with the Germans, the Lithuanians and Letts moved to absorb and rule over western Russia peoples. These Russians were later incorporated into the Polish Kingdom. They spoke different dialects, White Russian and Little Russian (Ukrainian). Mongol and Tatar hordes still occupied the steppelands to the south and south-east. The Russian homeland was thus hemmed in on the west, south and east; the only pioneer frontier was in the north-east.

Not until the reign of Ivan III (the Great), 1462-1505, did Muscovy finally emerge supreme over all the Russian States. By 1478, Novgorod (hitherto holding first place among the principalities, a rich and proud commercial city with territories stretching to the north, and possessed of an ancient system of republican liberties modelled on the Venetian type of municipal republic) was reduced to the rank of a provincial town (*see* Fig. 78).

In 1480, following a major stalemate on a battleground to the south of Moscow, the Tatar yoke was considered to be finally lifted. Even so, different groups of Tatars maintained independent states within Russia for a long time, particularly along the Volga and in the Crimea. Kazan on the Volga (*see* Fig. 79) was not captured until 1552 during the reign of Ivan IV ("the Terrible"), and Astrakhan not until 1556. The Crimea Khanate was not conquered by Russia until 1783. Thus, Muscovy was deprived of access to the Black Sea for some centuries to come.

The Russian (Slav) people became gradually separated into three large groups during the two-and-a-half centuries of Tatar rule: Great Russians, Ukrainians and Belorussians. The Great Russians, later to be the empire builders, had their original homeland in the mixed forest and woodland steppe. The Ukrainians (erroneously described as Little Russians, *Malorusy*) had theirs in the black earth steppe. The Belorussians (White Russians) inhabited the regions of the upper Western Dvina, upper Neman and upper Dnieper; they were the old Krivichi people, ethnologically a Lithuanian tribe who, after centuries of intermingling with neighbouring Slavs, adopted the Slavonic language and came to be considered a Slavonic people.

In the beginning of the sixteenth century, what is now the Ukraine became the goal of a considerable exodus both from Poland and from Russia. Serfs who desired escape from taxes and the tyranny of landlords, refugees from the law, daring and adventurous individuals, political rebels and similar elements, escaped eastwards and southwards to the great "No Man's Land" to become farmers or to join together in semi-nomadic fugitive and adventurer Cossack groups. These Cossacks (*kazaki,* not to be confused with the Kazakh, the people of Kazakhstan in Soviet Central Asia) were generally distributed over the southern plains, but tended to be concentrated around Kiev, the lower Don and near the present site of Zaporozhye on the Dnieper. It was this southward movement into the steppe, rather than the later eastwards movement into Siberia, which in Russian history is comparable with the westward migrations into the Great Plains of North America. The Cossacks were frontiersmen and freebooters who later became frontier guards. Polish kings used Cossacks to protect their State against incursions by the Tatars and the Turks; the Russian tsars (shortened from the Latin *Caesar*) en-

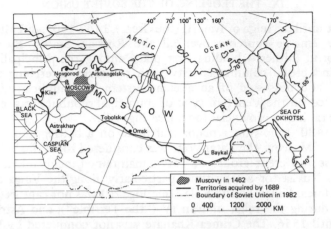

Fig. 80. Moscow Rus.

listed them as border defenders and later as advance troops for the extension of Russia beyond the Urals, the Caucasus and the Caspian Sea.

By the end of the fifteenth century, Muscovy was expanding eastward and northward (*see* Fig. 80). Adventurers, traders and hunters moved in boats along the rivers and made portages through the boreal forest (*tayga*) and along the White Sea shores in search of furs, walrus ivory, sealskins, blubber oil, tar, pitch and other forest products which were exported by Hansa merchants from Novgorod to Western Europe. This expansion reached the estuary of the River Ob by the sixteenth century. Here Russian and Tatar interests were brought into collision. An expedition organised by the fur-trading Strogonov family, and under the leadership of a Cossack officer named Yermak Timofeyevich, crossed the Urals and in 1582 conquered the small town of Sibir, a Tatar stronghold on the Irtysh near the present-day Tobolsk. Two years later, Yermak was drowned in the Irtysh during a Tatar counter-offensive. With his death, the Russians abandoned the country they called *Sibir* (Siberia). However, new bands of hunters and adventurers continued to move eastwards across the Urals through the sparsely populated Siberian *tayga* where they encountered only unorganised and ineffectual opposition from the primitive indigenous inhabitants. The movement eastwards continued roughly along the 55° N parallel, with much use being made of rivers when their direction coincided with that of the general advance. In this fashion the vast area now known as Siberia was conquered.

Illuminating descriptions of the extent of the territories of the Russians and of the Tatars in the sixteenth century, and of their religion, rites and way of life are given in Latin texts which accom-

Fig. 81. "Russia, Muscovy and Tartary": a sixteenth-century map taken from the *Theatrum orbis terrarum* of Abraham Ortelius (Antwerp, 1570). A translation of the Latin which accompanies this map is given on pp. 137-9.

pany the maps "Russia, Muscovy and Tartary" (*see* Fig. 81) and "Tartary, or the Empire of the Great Cham" (*see* Fig. 82). Translations of the texts which accompany the maps are also given below.

Russia (or the Empire of the Great Duke of Muscovy)
This map does not contain the whole of Russia, for Poland and Lithuania, which are also understood under the name of Russia, are missing. But it shows the whole of the empire of the Muscovite Duke which is bounded to the north by the Ice Sea and has for its neighbours the Tartars to the east, to the south the Turks and Poles and to the west inhabitants of Livonia and the King of Sweden. Sigismund Baro of Herberstein describes all these regions one by one, to whose writings we direct those who wish to read more of these matters. We have freely extracted from the same these few things concerning the religion, rites and way of life of the inhabitants.

As regards religion, they follow closely the rites of the Greeks. Their priests take wives. They worship images in the temples. When children are baptized, they are totally immersed in the water three times, the baptismal water being consecrated separately for each child. Although they have confession as part of the constitution, the common people look on it as necessary

Fig. 82. "Tartary, or the Empire of the Great Cham": a sixteenth-century map taken from the *Theatrum orbis terrarum* of Abraham Ortelius (Antwerp, 1570). A translation of the Latin text which accompanies this map is given on p. 139.

for princes and as appertaining to nobles. When the confession is finished, and penance according to the nature of the offence has been enjoined, they make the sign of the Cross on forehead and breast and cry with a loud voice: "O Jesus Christ, Son of God, have mercy on us". This is their communal prayer, for very few know the Lord's Prayer. They take Communion in both senses, mixing bread with wine, or the body with the blood. They give the Sacrament to boys of seven years saying that then is sin possible for man. The nobler men celebrate feast days by holding services, by eating, drinking and wearing fine clothes. The common people and slaves for the greater part work, however, saying that to feast and abstain from work is for masters. They do not believe in purgatory, but they have a service for the dead. Holy water is not sprinkled by any person other than by a priest only. They fast for seven weeks continually during Lent. They make marriage contracts and allow bigamy but scarcely consider it to be a lawful marriage. They allow divorce. Adultery is not so called unless a man takes another's wife.

The condition of women is most wretched, for they think none honourable unless she lives closed up at home and is so guarded that she can never go out. The people are cunning and deceitful and rejoice more in servitude than freedom. All confess themselves to be servants of the Prince. They rarely know peace for they are either engaged in war with the Lithuanians,

Livonians and Tartars, or if they are not waging war, they are in garrisons on the rivers Tanais (Don) and Occa to keep in check the ravages of the Tartars.

They wear rectangular tunics without pleats, whose sleeves fasten tightly somewhat like the Hungarians, and short leggings, usually red, which do not reach the knees. They have sandals strengthened with iron strips. They bind their thighs but not the stomach, so that as they become young men, the more prominent their stomach becomes, they loosen the belt.

They exercise justice actively against thieves but seldom punish theft and murder by execution. They have money of silver; not circular but rectangular and some sort of oval shape.

The region abounds in excellent and most precious skins which are exported thence throughout all Europe; almost the whole area is thickly wooded.

Tartary (or the Empire of the Great Cham)

Whoever wishes to describe the Tartars, must describe many nations which are far distant from one another. Tartary is usually called today that part of the earth from the Eastern Ocean or Mangicus, which is located between the Northern Ocean and Southern Sina [China], that part of India beyond the Ganges, Sacos, Oxus (now Abiamu); the Caspian Sea, the marsh of Meotis [the sea of Azov] and almost as far as Moscow to the west; because the Tartars occupied almost all these lands and lived in those places. So that it comprises thus the Asian Sarmatia of ancient writings, and both regions of Scythia, and Serica (which perhaps is Cathay today). The name of these was first heard in Europe in the year of grace 1212.

They are divided into "hordes", a word which means in their tongue "a gathering or multitude". But as they inhabit various widely separated provinces, so neither in morals nor kind of life do they all come together.

They are men of squat stature, with broad and heavy faces, slanted and deep-set eyes. They are rough only in respect of their beard, the rest is shaven. They have strong physiques and courageous spirits.

They feed on horse-meat readily and on other animals whatever way they are killed, except pork from which they abstain. They are most long suffering of hunger and lack of sleep; indeed if hunger and thirst assail them when riding, they will cut the veins of the horses they are riding on and assuage their need by drinking their blood.

And since they wander, having no fixed home, they are accustomed to direct their journeys by the sight of stars and chiefly by the Pole star which is in their tongue Selesnikol, that is the iron nail (according to Sigismund of Herberstein). They do not stay long in one place, considering it unpleasant and unlucky to remain for long in the same place. There is no system of justice among them. They are people most greedy of plunder and without doubt extremely poor, so that they are always striving after the goods of others. There is no use of gold and silver among them.

The Pacific coast, some 6,500 km or so from Moscow, was reached in 1647, sixty-five years after the conquest of *Sibir*. The area east and north of Lake Baykal, populated by Mongol Buryats, was subjugated during the period 1641-54. By the Treaty of Nerchinsk in

1689, China sanctioned the establishment of the Russians on the Pacific, at a time when they had still not reached the Black Sea (*see* Fig. 81).

However, the eastward course of Russia's empire still continued. In 1732, the Russians Gvozdov and Fedorov made the first European discovery of Alaska when they sailed across the Bering Strait. Bering rediscovered this part of the American mainland in 1741. A Russian-American Company was formed which was granted a monopoly over all commercial enterprises (e.g. hunting for sea otter for skins, furs, etc.) and also the governing of Russian America. With little economic gain accruing to Russia or the company shareholders, the colony was officially transferred from Russia to the USA in 1867 for the nominal sum of $7,200,000 (*see* Figs. 83 and 84). The only major addition of territory in east Asia after this date was the Amur basin and the coast to Vladivostok ("the Guardian of the East"), acquired from China in 1860.

Throughout the sixteenth and seventeenth centuries, the northern lands in Russia and Siberia flourished. Trade here was further stimulated by the discovery of the White Sea route to Muscovy by the Englishman, Richard Chancellor, in 1553. Three ships under the command of Sir Hugh Willoughby had set out from Gravesend, England, on 18 May, 1554, ". . . to seke the lands unknown". In August, they were separated by a storm and two of them wintered in Lapland, where Willoughby and his companions perished from exposure. However, the ship, *Edward Bonaventure*, commanded by Richard Chancellor, reached the mouth of the North Dvina River and Chancellor proceeded to Moscow where he was received by Tsar Ivan IV ("the Terrible") (1553-84). The Tsar expressed his willingness to receive English ships and, after negotiations, to allow free market and commercial privileges to English merchants. A charter was granted and the Muscovy Company formed in 1555. This northern outlet for Russia via Arkhangelsk outflanked the Baltic trade monopolists and enabled the English Tudor merchants seeking furs to satisfy the luxurious tastes of the court of Elizabeth I.

ST PETERSBURG RUSSIA: 1713-1918

Up to the end of the sixteenth century, the expansion of Muscovy eastwards into Asia was largely confined to the boreal forest. From the reign of Peter the Great (1689-1725), when Russia was proclaimed an Empire, the country assumed a wholly western orientation and became virtually part of Europe. For instance, Tsar Peter visited England in 1698; he lived at Deptford and studied shipbuilding techniques in the docks there. By 1721, Russia had emerged as one of the great powers of Europe. At the beginning of Peter's reign,

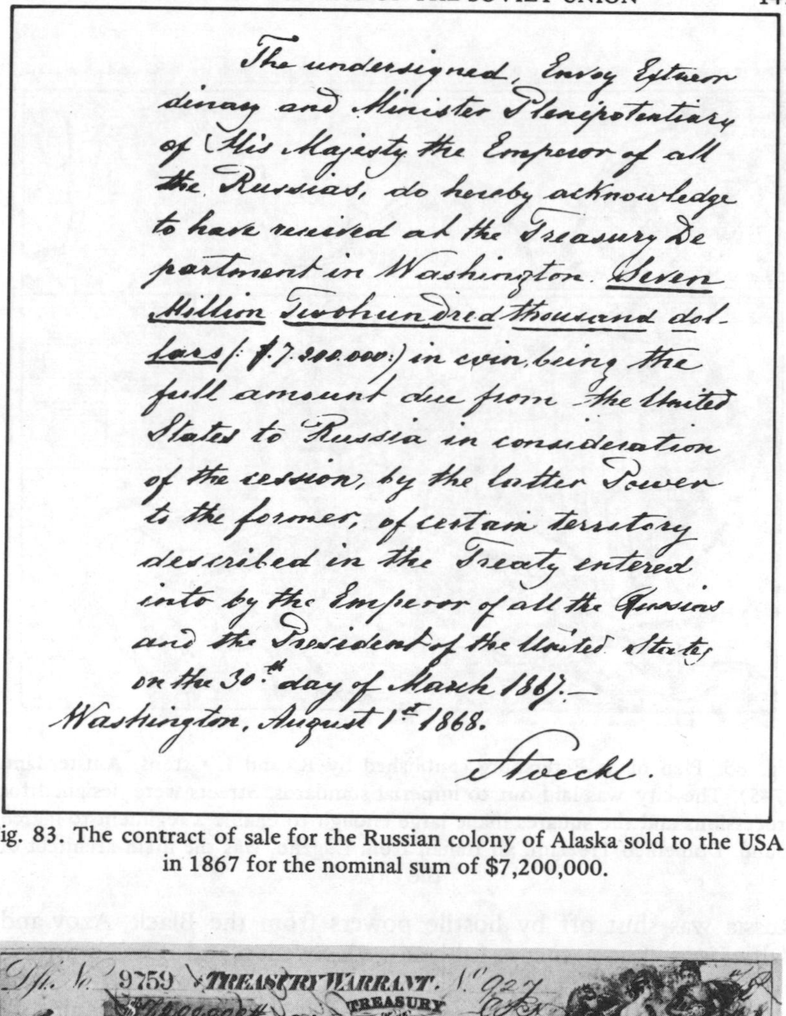

The undersigned, Envoy Extraordinary and Minister Plenipotentiary of His Majesty the Emperor of all the Russias, do hereby acknowledge to have received at the Treasury Department in Washington _Seven Million Twohundred thousand dollars ($.7.200.000.)_ in coin, being the full amount due from the United States to Russia in consideration of the cession, by the latter Power to the former, of certain territory described in the Treaty entered into by the Emperor of all the Russias and the President of the United States on the 30th day of March 1867. — Washington, August 1st 1868.

Stoeckl.

Fig. 83. The contract of sale for the Russian colony of Alaska sold to the USA in 1867 for the nominal sum of $7,200,000.

Fig. 84. Facsimile of the cheque paid for the colony of Alaska in 1867.

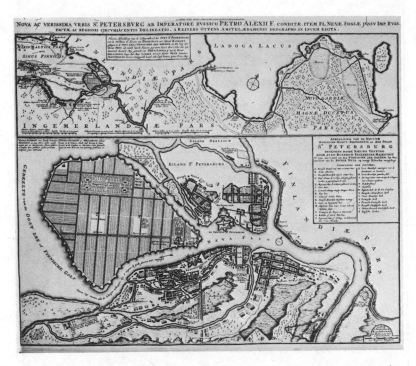

Fig. 85. Plan of St Petersburg (published by R. and I. Ottens, Amsterdam, 1745). The city was laid out to imperial standards. Streets were designed for processions and the squares made large enough to enable a regiment to march round. Domenico Trezzini, an Italian from Lugano, was the main architect of the city.

Russia was shut off by hostile powers from the Black, Azov and Baltic Seas, but a successful war with Sweden and the acquisition of the Swedish territories of Ingria, Karelia, Estonia and Livonia established a Russian hold on the Baltic. In 1702, the building of St Petersburg on the Baltic — Russia's first "window to Europe" — was begun (see Fig. 85). The Government was moved there from Moscow in 1713 and it remained in St Petersburg until 1918. (The name St Petersburg was changed to Petrograd in 1914, and to Leningrad in 1924.)

Under Peter's successors, Russian settlement in the southern steppe was intensified. It followed in the wake of marauding Cossacks and involved for the settlers a complete change of physical environment — from forested homeland to wooded and open steppe. It was not until early in the nineteenth century that the settlers changed from stock raising to large-scale wheat farming. Russian settlement in the southern steppe was reinforced by Germans and

Greeks, who gave to the region a decidedly multi-racial polyglot character.

The entire north shore of the Black Sea was eventually secured from the Turks, Prussians and Austrians by the Russo-Turkish War of 1774, after which what is now part of the Ukraine became New Russia (*Novorossiysk*). Bessarabia was acquired from the Turks in 1812. In the north-west the expansion was completed by the acquisition of Finland from Sweden in 1809. The boundaries of the Russian Empire now extended from their most western possession in Poland (all of which, including Warsaw, came under the Russian throne in 1795) to the Pacific.

The expansion into the Caucasian region began with the capture of Astrakhan in 1556, when the southern part of the country was reopened after 300 years. Cossacks pushed into the Kuban and established fortifications there, but it was not until the reign of Peter the Great that a concerted attack was made to the south. The Caspian shores as far as Baku were occupied in 1722-23, but the gain was shortlived for the frontier was later pushed back to the River Terek. A further advance during the latter part of the reign of Catherine II (1762-96)* reached the northern foothills, but it was not until the first year of the reign of Alexander I (1801-25) that the Russians were able to cross the Caucasus to gain Tbilisi (Tiflis) and eastern Georgia from the Persians. The conquest of the Caucasus was not finally completed until 1859 after the Turkish territory north of Batumi had been gained and the resistance of mountain guerillas broken. It brought under Russian control many peoples of ancient civilisation — Georgians, Armenians, Azerbaydzhans — each distinct in language, religion and cultural traditions. At the same time it brought Russia into contact with British influence in Persia.

Expansion into Central Asia had as its primary purpose the subjugation of the nomadic tribes that periodically foraged northwards into south-western Siberia and the south-eastern part of European Russia to harass the Russian settlers. Cossack military pioneers from Orenburg and the southern fringe of the Urals moved into the northern margins first, and later moved south of the Karakum and Kyzylkum to overthrow the Mahommedan centres of Tashkent (1865), Bukhara (1868), Samarkand (1868), Khiva (1873) and Kokand (1876). Any plans that Russia might have had for further expansion southwards had to take into account British interests in Afghanistan. In 1907, with her prestige at a low level following her defeat in the Russo-Japanese War (1904-5), Russia recognised these

*During the reign of Catherine II several English and Scottish officers were employed in the Russian Navy. Outstanding among these was Samuel Greig from Inverkeithing, Fife, who rose to the rank of Commander-in-Chief of the Russian Fleet.

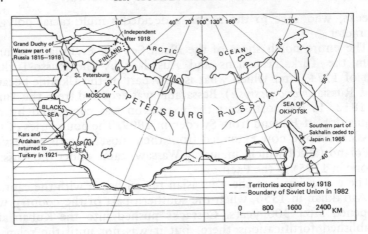

Fig. 86. St Petersburg Russia.

interests and has remained since within the present boundary (*see* Fig. 88). (China, however, continues to make occasional references to Soviet inroads into Sinkiang.)

SOVIET RUSSIA: 1918 TO THE PRESENT

Russia entered the First World War (1914-18) on the side of Britain and France against the Central Powers (Germany, Austro-Hungary and Turkey). She was unprepared, grossly mismanaged and lacking in good leadership. Furthermore, she was isolated from her allies except via the northern ports of Murmansk and Arkhangelsk (Archangel). Dissatisfaction among the Russian people was widespread and disorders commonplace. A revolution in March 1917 (known historically as "the February Revolution" since the Tsarist calendar was thirteen days behind the Gregorian calendar) brought about the overthrow of Russian tsardom and the setting up of a provisional government composed of liberal-minded members of the middle class (*Mensheviks*). A second revolution in October 1917 ("the October Revolution") brought the Communists (*Bolsheviks*) to power, and the capital was moved back from Petrograd to Moscow. The day after assuming power, the new Soviet Russian government proposed opening negotiations with Germany for a "just and democratic peace, without annexations or indemnities". It was not until March 1918, however, that the final peace treaty was signed with Germany at Brest-Litovsk. The price of surrender was high. Russia was obliged to renounce control over Estonia, Latvia, Lithuania, Poland and a major part of Belorussia. She was also obliged to cede to Turkey the districts of Kars, Ardahan and Batumi. The independence of Finland and of the Ukraine was recognised (*see* Fig. 87).

Fig. 87. Changes in the Russian frontier since 1914.

In consequence Russia lost about 1 million km² and some 46 million people.

Russia's allies, alarmed at her seeming defection and the unleashing of revolutionary forces, attempted to rally anti-revolutionary ("White Russian" as opposed to "Red Russian") opposition by landing troops and supplies at Vladivostok, Arkhangelsk and also in Persia. Their intervention won little support and failed in its attempt to stamp out Bolshevism. The three years of civil war that followed brought widespread destruction and untold misery for the Russian people.

By the end of 1922, a new Russia emerged as the Union of Soviet Socialist Republics (USSR) with control over the bulk of the territories of the former Imperial Russia. Each of the Soviet Socialist Republics which make up the USSR is constitutionally of equal status, with "the right freely to secede from the USSR" (Article 72 of the Soviet constitution), although the Russian Soviet Federated Socialist Republic (RSFSR), which extends from the Baltic to the Pacific, is by far the largest in area and population. The RSFSR, together with the Ukrainian and Belorussian Soviet Socialist Republics, were the founder members of the federated USSR. It was some years before the borderlands were organised into various Soviet Socialist Republics on the basis of national cultures and admitted as full members of the USSR. Turkmen and Uzbek were admitted in

Fig. 88. Soviet Union: administrative divisions.

TABLE 20. USSR: CONSTITUENT REPUBLICS,
THEIR CAPITALS, AREAS AND POPULATIONS

Republic	Capital	Area (km^2)	Population (thousands) (Census 1979)
RSFSR	Moscow	17,075,400	137,552
Ukrainian	Kiev	603,700	49,757
Uzbek	Tashkent	447,400	15,391
Kazakh	Alma-Ata	2,717,300	14,685
Belorussian	Minsk	207,600	9,559
Azerbaydzhan	Baku	86,600	6,028
Georgian	Tbilisi	69,700	5,016
Moldavian	Kishinev	33,700	3,948
Tadzhik	Dushanbe	143,100	3,801
Kirghiz	Frunze	198,500	3,529
Lithuanian	Vilnius	65,200	3,399
Armenian	Yerevan	29,800	3,031
Turkmen	Ashkhabad	488,100	2,759
Latvian	Riga	63,700	2,521
Estonian	Tallinn	45,100	1,466
USSR	Moscow	22,402,200*	262,442

*Total area of USSR includes White Sea and Sea of Azov.

Fig. 89. Territorial readjustments in western Europe after the Second World War.

1925, Tadzhik in 1929, Kirgiz, Kazakh, Georgia, Azerbaydzhan and Armenia in 1936 (*see* Fig. 88).

Within each of the republics (*see* Table 20) there are administrative units of lower status enjoying varying degrees of self-government, namely *Oblasts* (provinces), *Krays* (territories), *Autonomous Soviet Socialist Republics* (ASSR), *Autonomous Oblasts* (AO) and *Autonomous Okrugs* (districts).

All the territories lost by Russia as a result of the First World War, except for Finland and part of Poland, were regained by the USSR at the end of the Second World War (*see* Fig. 89). Other territories which had never been part of Russia were also acquired, e.g. the Trans-Carpathian Ukraine (formerly the Ruthenian area of Czechoslovakia) and Kaliningrad Oblast (formerly the northern half of Germany's East Prussia) (*see* Table 21). Pieces of territory near Leningrad and in the far north were taken over from Finland. The Baltic States of Estonia, Latvia and Lithuania were reincorporated into the Soviet Union during the early part of the war. Bukovina and Bessarabia were taken from Romania and made into an enlarged Moldavian SSR, with a portion added to western Ukraine. Eastern Poland became part of either the Ukraine or Belorussia. In the Far East, southern Sakhalin and the Kuril Islands were regained from Japan.

TABLE 21. SOVIET LAND ANNEXATIONS SINCE 1939

Area	Former owner	Present Soviet status
Pechenga District	Finland	Murmansk Oblast (RSFSR)
Karelia (Salla)	Finland	Karelian ASSR (RSFSR)
Vyborg District	Finland	Leningrad Oblast
Northern East Prussia and Memelland	Germany	Kaliningrad Oblast (RSFSR) and Klaipeda Oblast (Lithuanian SSR)
Estonia	Independent	Union Republic
Latvia	Independent	Union Republic
Lithuania	Independent	Union Republic
Eastern Estonia and Latvia	Estonia and Latvia	Pskov Oblast (RSFSR)
Eastern Poland (Western Belorussia)	Poland	Four oblasts in Belorussian SSR and Vilna Oblast (Lithuanian SSR)
Transcarpathia (Ruthenia)	Czechoslovakia	Transcarpathian Oblast (Ukraine SSR)
Western Ukraine	Poland	Six oblasts in Ukrainian SSR
Northern Bukovina	Romania	Chernovtsky Oblast (Ukrainian SSR)
Central Bessarabia	Romania	Moldavian SSR
Southern Bessarabia	Romania	Izmail Oblast (Ukrainian SSR)
Tannu Tuva	Independent	Tuva ASSR (RSFSR)
Southern Sakhalin	Japan	Sakhalin Oblast (RSFSR)
Kuril Islands	Japan	Sakhalin Oblast (RSFSR)

RUSSIAN SOCIETY

Early Russians lived in small communities (clans), and society was organised on a tribal basis, practising a primitive form of communism. Property ownership as it is generally understood was non-existent. With the growth of Russia as a nation state under a bureaucratic and autocratic government, the peasants found themselves increasingly tied to the estates of the tsars and nobles under conditions which were far from idyllic. Peasants were not permitted to leave the estates of their landlords, nor to move to those of other landlords. Legal serfdom prevailed. Those serfs who escaped the authority of the landowners, the Church or the State and lived as freebooters in the southern steppelands were known as Cossacks (*see* p. 135).

It was not until 1861, during the reign of Alexander II, that the serfs were finally emancipated and their position eased. Liberated peasants were organised in village communities governed by elected elders. These were the village communes or *mir*. The peasants in the villages cultivated their lands on a co-operative and communistic basis, all fields being held in common. Land, and fishing and grazing rights, were continually re-allocated according to the strength and needs of different families. Individual peasants thus lacked permanence or continuity of ownership of land that belonged to the village community. In 1913, of the 368 million hectares classed as agricultural land, 154 million hectares were grouped in large estates belonging to the royal family, the nobles and the Church. The remaining 214 million hectares were divided up into over 20 million peasant holdings averaging a little over 10 hectares apiece. Among the peasant holdings were to be found those of a class of more substantial and wealthier peasants known as *kulaki*. These *kulaki* had taken advantage of new legislation introduced after the first Russian Revolution of 1905 which allowed peasants to leave the village community and consolidate their strips into independent farms. They developed their holdings as capitalist farms and employed their poorer neighbours for hire under conditions no less burdensome than those on the estates of the landowners.

The Revolution of 1917 which installed the Bolshevik government proceeded to set up the world's first socialist country of factory workers and agricultural peasants, based on Marxist-Leninist ideology. All land was declared national property and the big private estates of the tsars, the Church and the nobles were expropriated. Some expropriated land was allocated to peasants, later to demobilised soldiers and to settlers from the towns. On the industrial and commercial side, all the large industrial enterprises such as banks, means of transport and foreign trade, were nationalised. Unfortunately, there were too few people with the necessary technical and managerial skill to take over efficiently, and a period of painful adjustment to the new order followed. The country was beset by internal counter-revolution and the bitterest of civil wars, food requisitioning, food shortage, social tensions and a multitude of problems — all attended by immeasurable human suffering. It was not until 1928, after a compromise was reached under the New Economic Policy (1921-28) between the nationalised and private economy that production in most branches of the economy was back to, or a little above, the 1913 (pre-Revolution) level.

Economic life in the USSR since 1928 has been determined by a series of Five-year Plans which involve advance planning in all branches of the economic and cultural life of the country. As a result a centrally-controlled and intricately integrated national economic complex has emerged in the USSR (*see* Chapter XIX).

CHAPTER X

Population and Settlement

POPULATION

Over 268.8 million people (1st January 1982, USSR Central Statistical Board) inhabit the 22.4 million km^2 of Soviet territory. The population is the third largest of any world state, after China and India. Nevertheless, the total (6 per cent of the world's population) is small in relation to the vast area over which it is spread. Vast areas are unoccupied, and the over-all density is no more than eleven persons per km^2. This compares with an over-all density of approximately 433 persons per square kilometre in Bangladesh, 384 in Taiwan, 229 in the United Kingdom, 182 in India, 87 in China and 23 in the United States.

Despite the high degree of national autonomy within the country the Soviet Union is ruled by the Great Russians who make up just over half (52.3 per cent) of the total population. Together with the Ukrainians (16 per cent), Belorussians (3.6 per cent) and small numbers of Czechs, Slovaks, Poles, Bulgarians and Romanians,* they account for 72.8 per cent of the total population (*see* Table 22). This represents a decline from 77.1 per cent in 1959 and 74.6 per cent in 1970. They are of Slav origin and are traditionally Orthodox in religion. They form a homogeneous body in much of the Russian Lowland and Siberia and predominate in most cities and the newer farming areas of Soviet Central Asia and Kazakhstan. Their presence is also particularly striking in Estonia and Latvia.

After the Slavs, the Turkic peoples are the most numerous and important. The Turkic group (Uzbeks, Turkmen, Kirgiz, Kazakhs, Tatars, etc.) is most continuous in the Central Asian Republics and forms about 15.2 per cent of the total (11.1 per cent in 1959 and 13.4 per cent in 1970). In so far as there are any cultural links, other than those of history and language, which bind the Turkic people, they are those of Islam. Except for the Yakuts in the Lena Valley,

*The forebears of the Czechs, Slovaks, Poles, Bulgarians and Romanians in the USSR settled in Russia at different periods. They have no ethnic territories and live among other nationalities.

TABLE 22. MOST NUMEROUS NATIONALITIES IN THE USSR
(in millions)

Nationality	Number	Nationality	Number
Russians	137.4	Takzhiks	2.8
Ukrainians	42.3	Turkmenians	2.0
Uzbeks	12.4	Germans	1.9
Belorussians	9.4	Jews*	1.8
Kazakhs	6.5	Chuvashes	1.7
Tatars	6.3	Kirghiz	1.7
Azerbaydzhanians	5.4	Latvians	1.3
Armenians	4.1	Bashkirs	1.3
Georgians	3.6	Mordovians	1.2
Moldavians	2.9	Poles	1.1
Lithuanians	2.8	Estonians	1.0

Source: *Soviet Census* 1979.

*In the USSR Jews are classed as a national group; there is not necessarily a religious connotation associated with persons listed as Jews in the Soviet census of population. A high rate of assimilation, compounded by emigration, would account for the 16 per cent decline in the number of Jews in the 1970-79 period.

a north-eastern spread of the Turkic element now intermingled considerably with people of Slavonic blood, the Turkic peoples are all Moslem.

The so-called Caucasians comprise about 3 per cent of the total population. They include the Japhetic peoples of Georgia and Armenia, and other groups living in the mountain valleys.

The Finno-Ugrian groups of northern USSR have been increasingly pushed outward by Slav settlement. Finns are to be found mainly in the north and west and also in a belt of Finnish settlement in Asiatic Russia. Their territories lie north of the main Slavonic belt and extend to the River Yenisey, but there has been much intermingling with the incoming Slav population. Apart from the Finns of Karelia and the Estonians along the Baltic, the Finno-Ugrian nationalities number no more than 2 per cent of the total.

About 1.9 million Germans, 1.8 million Jews and 1.1 million Poles are scattered throughout various parts of the Soviet Union. The 2.8 million Lithuanians and 1.3 million Latvians belong to the so-called Slavonic-Baltic group of peoples. They are closely related to the Slavs, but display some features of other Baltic peoples. Traditionally, the Germans, Latvians, Estonians and Finns are Lutheran in religion, while the Lithuanians and Poles are Roman Catholic.

In the south-western part of the country, the Moldavians are of Romanian stock. The Tadzhiks of Central Asia are related to the Iranians (Persians). Some Mongol and Palaeo-Asiatic groups exist in

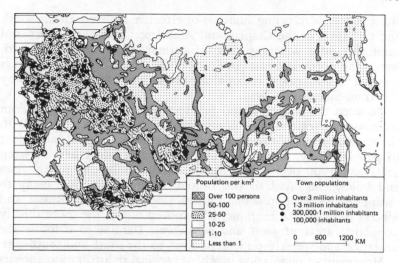

Fig. 90. Soviet Union: density of population and town populations of over 100,000.

Siberia and in the Soviet Far East; the Buryats form the largest Mongol group.

The Slav peoples occupy the economic core of the country; other groups are distributed largely peripherally. A growing proportion of Russians and Ukrainians are finding their way to those parts of the Caucasus, Central Asia and south Siberia, where economic development is taking place, although the ethnic results of the 1979 Soviet census seem to suggest a decline in the intensity of this outmigration. Indeed, evidence points to outmigration from Trans-Caucasia, Kazakhstan and Kirghizia.

The bulk of the population of the Soviet Union is contained in an area bounded by Leningrad-Sverdlovsk-Magnitogorsk-Rostov-Baku-Batumi and Odessa (see Fig. 90). Two-thirds of the population live south of latitude 60° N and west of the River Volga. Within this region there is considerable variation of density, ranging from moderate settlement (10-25 persons per km²) to closer settlement (40-50 persons per km²). In the wooded steppe country of the Ukraine, the countryside is closely settled and population densities are in excess of 50 persons per km². This is an area that has many towns.

Outside the main area of population and amid the empty vastness of Siberia there are outliers of moderate settlement (in the Kuzbass, around Omsk and around Irkutsk, etc.), and in the irrigated areas of Central Asia.

The distribution of the population reflects the distribution of extractive and manufacturing industry and of cultivated land. The latter reflects decreasing amounts of effective moisture to the south and east towards the Caspian and Aral desert areas, and short cool summers and a widening zone of permanently frozen subsoil towards the north and east. In Siberia, the zone of habitable land is reduced to a narrow corridor along the southern fringe traversed by the Trans-Siberian Railway.

Between the sixteenth and nineteenth centuries, when serfdom prevailed, movement and colonisation were severely restricted. With the emancipation of the serfs in 1861 there was a great movement of people, many, indeed, leaving the country altogether. Between 1891 and 1900 over half a million Russian subjects (mainly Jews and Poles) emigrated to the United States of America, many to escape political oppression. Others migrated within Russia and Siberia — those, for example, who moved out of the more thickly populated areas of west and south-west Ukraine to colonise the unsettled and sparsely populated areas to the south and south-east.

Movement of population involving regional redistribution appears to have been a continuous process both from area to area and from countryside to town. Movement has been directed to the Urals, Siberia, the Far Eastern territories and Central Asia. Much of it was officially encouraged; no small amount was made under compulsion. Under the tsars, a policy of exile was used as a means of colonising the empty spaces of Siberia. Political convicts and ordinary criminals were sent to Siberia in much the same way as Britain sent convicts to her colonies during the eighteenth and nineteenth centuries. Peasants (*kulaki*) who resisted collectivisation in the early 1930s were deported to Siberia, as were the intelligentsia from Polish, Estonian, Latvian, Lithuanian, Ukrainian and Romanian territories annexed by the Soviet Union during and after the Second World War. Mass deportations were not uncommon and forced labour was employed in road making, timber felling, peat cutting, building, mining, etc. Large camps for housing these workers (estimated at between four and six million) existed in desert areas in Kazakhstan and in the extreme north (e.g. Vorkuta) where climatic conditions are considered to be too difficult to attract normal voluntary labour (*see* Fig. 91). Up to about 1951, the Soviet administration also sent political prisoners and criminals to Siberia.

Planned settlement associated with industrial and agricultural developments has led to considerable movement of Russians and Ukrainians into Soviet Asia. In the case of the Virgin and Long Idle Lands Project (*see* p. 365) which was started in earnest in 1954, there was voluntary recruitment of new settlers. Grants were offered to cover the cost of removal, journeys were assisted and wage and other incentives were provided to attract manpower to the new territories. Members of the Communist Party were sometimes

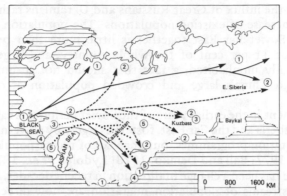

(Source: Taffe and Kingsbury, *Atlas of Soviet Affairs.*)

Fig. 91. Soviet Union: deportation during and after the Second World War. Arrows indicate origins and reported areas of exile of the following nationalities:

1. Crimean Tatars 3. Kalmyk 5. Checken-Ingush
2. Volga Germans 4. Karachai-Balkas

obliged to take up residence in new surroundings as a political duty.

The German occupation of much of the European part of the USSR during the Second World War and the consequent evacuation of industrial enterprises to the east; the acceleration of industrialisation in the USSR as a whole; the need to increase the exploitation of the enormous coal, oil and gas reserves, water power, ore deposits and timber resources of Siberia when those of the west could no longer meet industrial demands; the cultivation of the virgin lands and strategic considerations − all have contributed to an easterly displacement of the population of the Soviet Union (*see* Table 23).

TABLE 23.
POPULATION OF THE USSR, SIBERIA AND THE FAR EAST
IN SELECTED YEARS
(in millions)

Area	Year				Percentage increase (1939-79)
	1939	1959	1970	1979	
USSR	170.5	208.8	241.7	262.4	52.5
Siberia and the Far East	16.6	21.7	25.2	27.9	76.5
West Siberia	8.9	11.2	12.0	12.9	50.5
East Siberia	5.3	6.7	7.4	8.1	64.1
Far East	2.3	3.6	5.7	6.8	208.6

Source: *Soviet Census* 1979.

Much of the increase in Siberia and the Far East has been due rather to the influx of Great Russians and Ukrainians rather than to natural increase of existing populations. The population of Siberia and the Soviet Far East together is little more than twenty-nine millions or 11 per cent of the whole country, and large areas are still virtually uninhabited, a fact that should not go unnoticed in relation to China's large and crowded population of over 1,000 million.

Movement in the earlier years of the Soviet period was eastwards to eastern Siberia and the Far East, fostered largely by Government sponsored migration programmes, but analyses of recent population data (Shabad, 1977; Ball and Demko, 1978; Lydolph et al., 1978) suggest that there has been a change of direction in recent decades. Seemingly the mainstreams of population migration are now directed southwards to the Donbass-Dnieper Region, the Black Sea coastlands, the Crimea, North Caucasus and Central Asia. The Urals and western Siberia have experienced outmigration over the last twenty years (though doubtless the recent oil and gas developments in the Tyumen Oblast of West Siberia will stimulate movement into the region) and the settling of the Virgin Lands in Kazakhstan has been completed (indeed there is now an outflow to European Russia). The Central Asians have always displayed a marked reluctance to move to other parts of the Soviet Union.

Internal migration is doubtless important in building up populations, but of equal if not greater importance is natural increase. Natural population increase, related to birth and death rates, varies with the different ethnic groups and regions and between city (urban) and country (rural) regions. The Central Asians and Trans-Caucasians, for example, have higher birth rates and rates of national increase than have the Slavic and Baltic groups. The Tadzhiks and Latvians may be cited as representing extreme cases. In 1976 the birth rate in Tadzhik SSR was 38.2 per thousand, the death rate 8.5 per thousand and the natural increase rate 29.7 per thousand. In contrast the Latvian SSR had a birth rate of 13.8 per thousand, a death rate of 12.1 per thousand and a natural increase rate of 1.7 per thousand. The natural increase of the Tadzhik SSR was thus more than seventeen times that of the Latvian Republic. Regional fertility levels would appear to represent the main factor underlying regional variations in the role of population growth.

The high natural increase rates among the non-Slav groups in the four Central Asian SSRs are noteworthy, the more so when fertility levels among the Russians, Ukrainians and Baltic groups are falling to levels similar to those of Western Europe. According to present trends it seems likely that the Slav component of the total Soviet population will fall to below 50 per cent within the next decade. Migration and mobility of people within the USSR leads to ethnographic mixing. The future existence of the Slav and non-Slav groups as distinctive nationalities or cultural entities must inevitably be limited.

Because of several boundary changes early population statistics for Russia and the Soviet Union are not strictly comparable, but the following figures (related to the contemporary boundaries for the years shown) provide an indication of population growth.

Year	Population (millions)	
1724	20.0 (Russian Empire)	
1897	126.9 (Russian Empire)	
1913	159.2 (present frontiers)	
1939	170.6 (census)	Estimated losses of population in the Second World War, 20-22
1959	208.8 (census)	million of which total 7 million were military losses.
1970	241.7 (census)	
1975	253.3 (estimate)	
1978	260.0 (estimate)	
1979	262.4 (census)	
1981	266.6 (estimate)	
1982	268.8 (estimate)	

Fatalities and the consequent deficit of live births arising from the First World War, revolution, counter-revolution and civil war at the beginning of the Bolshevik regime gave rise to a severe reduction of numbers of the population centring on what was, at the time of the 1970 census, a 51-year age group (see Fig. 92). A similar constriction in the sex-age pyramid is evident at about the 36-year age group. This was due to the enforced collectivisation of agriculture in the early 1930s and the accompanying famines and death. Excessive losses during the Second World War, variously estimated at between twenty and twenty-two millions, gave a further constriction to the age structure of the Soviet population centring on age group 26-years. (The three constrictions in the sex-age pyramid (see Fig. 92(a)) would in 1982 be in age groups 63, 48 and 38 years.*) Such tumultuous events and their inevitable grave consequences have had effects on birth rates and the over-all excess of women in the population. In 1979 there were 140 million women and 122.4 million men in the USSR (52.8:46.0). A notable feature of the workforce is that 51 per cent or more is female. Nearly all able-bodied women are employed. About 70 per cent of the doctors and teachers for instance are women. Women are also employed in lumbering, construction, agriculture, mining and public services

---

*Age-sex data at the time of the 1979 census had, by September 1982, still to be published by the Soviet authorities. The most up-to-date information available is for 1974 (see Fig. 92(b)).

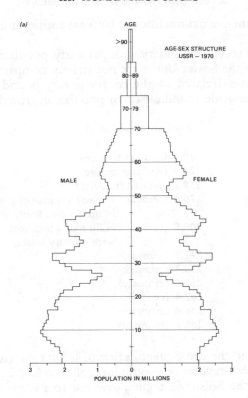

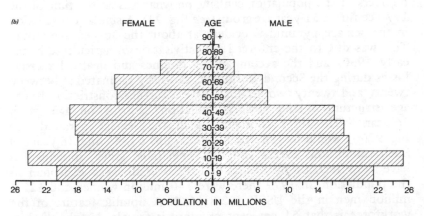

Fig. 92. Age-sex structure of the Soviet population *(a)* for 15th January, 1970 (based on data from Baldwin, G., "Estimates and projections of the population of the USSR by age and sex: 1950 to 2000", *International Population Reports*, series P-91,*(23)*, 1973, and *Itogi vsesoyuznoy pererpisi naseleniya 1970 goda*, II, pp. 12-13, quoted by Lydoph *et al.*, 1978); *(b)* for 1st January 1974 (source: *Naradnoye Kbozyaystvo SSSR*, v. 1973, Moscow, 1974).

generally, often in work more usually associated in the West with male workers.

The countrywide birth rate in the USSR declined from the 1940s until 1969 (see Table 24) when it reached 17.4 births per 1,000 of the population. From that date it rose slowly to reach 18.4 per thousand in 1976, declined to 18.2 per thousand in 1979 but since then has risen to 18.7 per thousand in 1981. The younger age groups are now having more children than formerly, although this development is not countrywide. Generally speaking, couples in European Russia and the Baltic republics do not marry until their late twenties and limit their families to one child; many have no children. This limitation in the size of families is considered to be a consequence of rising standards of living associated with increasing urbanisation and industrialisation. It is also due partly to the chronic housing shortage in the country. On the other hand, in the Central Asian Republics and in parts of the Caucasus early marriages are commonplace and families in excess of four children are typical.*

TABLE 24. USSR: VITAL STATISTICS 1940-82
(per 1,000 of the population)

Year	Births	Deaths	Natural increase
1940	31.2	18.0	13.2
1950	26.7	9.7	17.0
1960	24.9	7.1	17.8
1970	17.4	8.2	9.2
1971	17.8	8.2	9.6
1972	17.8	8.5	9.3
1973	17.6	8.7	8.9
1974	18.0	8.7	9.3
1975	18.1	9.3	8.8
1976	18.4	9.5	8.9
1977	18.2	9.7	8.5
1978	18.2	9.7	8.5
1979	18.2	10.1	8.1
1980	18.3	10.3	8.0
1982	18.7	10.3	8.4

The all-Union death rate has been exceptionally low. This is not

*Previously State subsidies to families in the USSR began only with the birth of the fourth child and did not affect most families outside Central Asia and parts of the Caucasus (see P. Lydolph et al., "Recent population trends in the USSR", Soviet Geography XIX (8), (1978), pp. 505-39, on which this section is based). Recently, however, measures have been introduced which encourage the first and second child rather than subsequent offspring. They range from higher family allowances and lump-sum payments for the first and second child, the guarantee of a minimum of one room for a young couple with a baby, a year's paid leave for mothers after the birth of a child and a further year's unpaid leave, and the provision for more part-time work for women (The Times, 12th June, 1981).

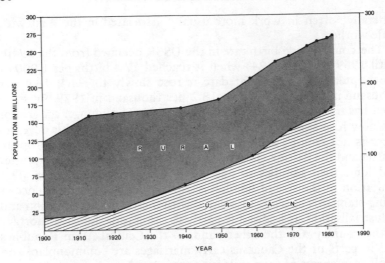

Fig. 93. Soviet Union: population growth 1900-1982.

so much a reflection of the health status or longevity of the population but rather of the fact that those who, under normal circumstances would now be reaching the end of their expectation of life, have already died as a result of one or other of the several calamities that have beset their generation during the last sixty-six years. The death rate reached a minimum of 6.9 per thousand in 1964 but since then has been rising due to an ageing population and now stands at just over 10 per thousand. A rise in infant mortality rate (i.e. deaths under one year) in the USSR over the past 10 years (24 per 1,000 in 1960, 30 per 1,000 in 1981) has so far gone unexplained.

The average life span in the USSR, 32 years in 1897-98 and 44 years in the period 1926-29, had lengthened to 67 years by 1955-56. In 1975, expectation of life at birth was 64 years for men and 74 years for women. The ten year spread in life expectancy between men and women in the Soviet Union is exceptional and appears to be greater than for any other country in the world. Vital statistics for the human resources of the USSR as a whole are not particularly meaningful in view of the heterogeneity of the Soviet population. The statistics mask wide variations in birth rates, death rates and natural increase rates among the several ethnic groups which in turn result in marked differences in population growth in the different parts of the country. However, in so far as planned economic growth requires a continuing supply of labour there is obvious concern on the part of the Soviet leaders for the continued growth of the Soviet population. During the intercensal period 1959-70 there was a more rapid growth of population (15.8 per cent) than was experienced during the preceding intercensal period 1939-59 (9.4 per cent) but between 1970 and 1979 the increase was only 8.6 per cent. The growth rate is obviously slowing down. Between 1960 and 1965 the total rose by 17 million, between 1965 and 1970 by 12.4 million, and between 1970 and 1979 by 20.7 million (8.6 per cent) (*see* Fig. 93). Feshback and Rapawy (1976) predicted the natural increase to be 9.9 per thousand in 1980, 7.5 per thousand in 1990 and 5.8 per thousand by the year 2000 (ranging from 29.1 in Central Asia to 14.2 per thousand in Trans-Caucasia, 1.7 per thousand in the Baltic Republics and only 0.1 per thousand in the RSFSR). It seems likely that as a result of current migration trends and regional discrepancies in the rate of natural increase the USSR will continue to experience severe regional imbalances between labour supply and labour needs in the foreseeable future.

SETTLEMENT

Rural
The varied conditions for the practice of many forms of agriculture in the Soviet Union give rise to widely contrasting variations in rural population density, settlement distribution and form. The administrative-territorial unit into which the rural area of each republic, *oblast,* or province is divided is the *rayon,* and the *rayon* centre is the basic unit in the network of rural settlements. These are called *derevnyas* and *syelos* in the Ukraine, Belorussia or European USSR and *stanitsas* in the historic Cossack resettlement areas. The Caucasian mountain settlements are *auls* and those in Central Asia *kishlaks.* In regions newly populated with peasant settlers the rural settlements are called *posyeloks.* There are also many new *kolkhoz* and *sovkhoz* settlements.

There were 3,176 *rayons* and 469,000 rural settlements in the Soviet Union in 1980, but with the perpetual drift of rural dwellers to the towns a pattern of rural population change is created which is likely to continue and might even intensify. Whereas in 1940, for instance, there were 131 million classed as rural dwellers (67 per cent), in 1970 there were only 105.7 million (44 per cent) and by 1979 the figure had dropped to 98.8 million (38 per cent). Not all of those classed as rural were engaged in agricultural or forestry pursuits: many were involved in work quite unconnected with farming. Some were employed in transport and industry within the *rayon,* others served as tradesmen, doctors, teachers, etc., or else worked in neighbouring towns.

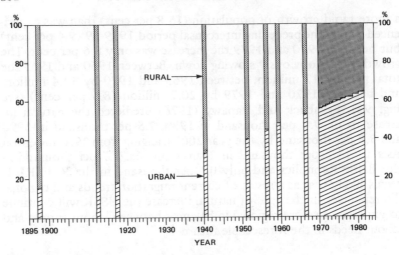

Fig. 94. Soviet Union: percentages of urban/rural population in the total population 1877-1982.

The current trend is for inhabitants of the smaller, more remote villages, lacking in facilities and amenities, to move to towns or nearer to the towns, thereby increasing the population density and size of settlements in the suburban zones or else move to larger and better equipped *posyeloks*. Thus, although the over-all number of rural settlements is decreasing noticeably with the fall in rural population, the number of larger *posyeloks* with more than 1,000 inhabitants is increasing (from 20,200 to 23,500 during the intercensal period 1959-70).

Urban
In less than sixty years, the Soviet Union has experienced perhaps the most rapid rate of urbanisation of any developed country within a comparable time span. From both internal migration and natural increase the urban population has risen from 18 per cent to 64 per cent of the national total in the Soviet era (*see* Fig. 94 and Table 25). Six persons in every ten now live in a town. In the United States (73 per cent) dwell in towns. (Despite the smaller rural population in the USA its productivity is four to five times greater than that in the USSR.) The greater part of the increase in urban dwellers in the USSR is currently accounted for by natural population growth in the towns themselves. Previously it was the result of movement from the countryside to the towns where increasing and intensive industrialisation provided a powerful magnet for peasants whose

TABLE 25. USSR: URBAN AND RURAL POPULATIONS 1917-82

Year	Population in millions			Percentage of total	
	Urban	Rural	Total	Urban	Rural
1917	29.1	133.9	163.0	18	82
1926	26.3	120.7	147.0	18	82
1939 (pre-war boundaries)	56.1	114.5	170.6	33	67
1939 (post-war boundaries)	60.4	130.3	190.7	32	68
1959 (census, January 15)	100.0	108.8	208.8	48	52
1963 (January 1)	115.1	108.0	223.1	52	48
1965 (January 1)	121.5	107.5	229.0	53	47
1970 (census, January 15)	136.0	105.7	241.7	56	44
1975 (January 1)	153.1	100.2	253.3	60	40
1978 (January 1)	162.5	97.5	260.0	62	38
1979 (January 17)	163.6	98.8	262.4	62	38
1980	166.2	98.3	264.5	63	37
1981	168.9	97.7	266.6	63	37
1982	171.6	97.2	268.8	64	36

Sources: *Statistical Yearbooks of the Central Statistical
Administration (Narodnoye Khozyaystvo
SSSR)*, Moscow, 1964, 1965 and 1982; *UN Demo-
graphic Yearbooks*; *Soviet News.*

labour had become redundant through the mechanisation of agriculture. Even so, within the towns themselves, the natural increase
continues to be greatest among the migrants from rural areas.

Moscow (8,011,000), Leningrad (4,588,000) and Kiev (2,144,000),
the three largest cities, together account for 8.4 per cent of the
total urban population; the 47 towns with populations over half a
million represent 30 per cent. The increase of and concentration of
population in the larger cities and towns is a characteristic of the
urbanisation process in the USSR as are the growing agglomerations
around nucleus towns (*see* Table 26).

TABLE 26. NUMBER OF CITIES IN VARIOUS POPULATION CLASSES

Population	Number of cities			
	1939	1959	1970	1979
Over 100,000	9	148	221	272
Over 500,000	6	24	31	45
Over 1,000,000	2	3	10	18
Over 2,000,000	2	2	2	3

During the period 1939-59 there was a remarkable increase of
population in towns in a zone extending from the middle Volga

into Siberia as far east as Krasnoyarsk. In this zone, which includes the Volga-Urals oilfields, almost all towns increased their populations by 50 per cent or more, but there were several centres, including a number of the larger ones, which doubled their populations. The latest available population figures (1 January 1979) for the same towns show continued increases (*see* Table 27).

TABLE 27. POPULATION CHANGES OF CITIES IN THE ZONE
MIDDLE VOLGA TO CENTRAL SOUTH SIBERIA 1939-79
(in thousands)

	1939	1959	1970	1979
Kuybyshev	390	806	1,045	1,216
Kazan	398	647	869	993
Saratov	372	581	757	856
Perm	306	629	850	999
Ufa	258	547	771	969
Sverdlovsk	423	779	1,025	1,211
Chelyabinsk	273	689	1,019	1,031
Omsk	289	581	821	1,014
Novosibirsk	404	886	1,161	1,312
Novokuznetsk	166	377	499	541
Barnaul	148	305	439	503
Karaganda	156	397	523	572
Krasnoyarsk	190	412	648	796

Outside this zone of urban development were other isolated centres with high growth rates. These included capitals of SSRs such as Minsk, Kishinev, Dushanbe, Frunze and Alma-Ata, together with Komsomolsk and Khabarovsk in the Far East.

More recent trends reveal high urban growth rates in certain of the larger cities such as Minsk (the fastest growing "millionaire" city in the USSR for most of the post-Second World War period), Kiev, Yerevan, Omsk and Tashkent and also in some of the intermediate sized cities. The latter are those in which industrial development has been rapid, in towns where industry has been stimulated by hydroelectric projects, in new chemical centres, or new metallurgical centres and include (with percentage increase between 1970 and 1979 shown in brackets) Togliatti (100), Bratsk (38), Temirtau (28), Sumgait (53), Cherepovets (41), and Cheboksary (43).

Table 28 and Fig. 95 provide an indication of the dynamics of the population in the largest cities during the period 1970-79.

Since the 1930s city growth in the USSR has been planned to take into account the exploitation of physical resources in underdeveloped and backward areas of the country and the principle of balanced growth and self-sufficiency in large regions. The rapid

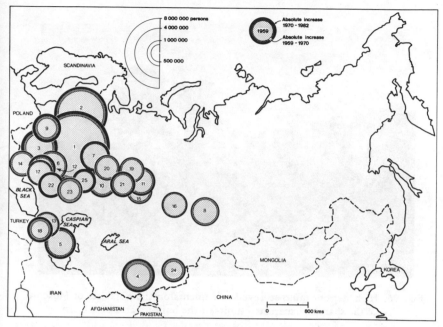

Fig. 95. Soviet Union: population changes in the largest cities 1970-79.

1. Moscow	7. Gorkiy	13. Tbilisi	19. Yerevan
2. Leningrad	8. Novosibirsk	14. Odessa	20. Kazan
3. Kiev	9. Minsk	15. Omsk	21. Ufa
4. Tashkent	10. Kuybyshev	16. Chelyabinsk	22. Volgograd
5. Baku	11. Sverdlovsk	17. Donetsk	23. Rostov-on-Don
6. Kharkov	12. Dnepropetrovsk	18. Perm	24. Alma-Ata
	25. Saratov		

growth of cities in Siberia and Central Asia reflected economic growth there, but Adams (1977) suggests that in the absence of a sufficient infrastructure, growth in most Siberian cities is slowing down and that the same will happen in the future with the Central Asian and Caucasus cities through falling birth rates. He further suggests that, with the gradual shift towards consumer needs, to more motor cars, quality housing and modern services, coupled with residential and occupation choice, there will be a reversal of the declining growth rates in the mature cities of European USSR.

The form of the old Russian town (*gorod*) reflected something of the long struggle against invaders. It was concentric, with streets radiating from the centre, the Kreml (*Kremlin* or fort), which was built originally of timber but later of stone. Another typical feature of Russian towns was the collection of low, wooden houses on the

Fig. 96. High density multi-storeyed apartments on the outskirts of Moscow.
Note the sharply demarcated limits of the built-up area of the city.

outskirts, of the same type as the peasant *izba* or hut. The smaller
towns were distinguished by a single, broad main street, which in
spring and autumn was a sea of mud (*rasputitsa*). A few of the cities
in the west, notably Kiev, obtained the Magdeburg rights (a civic
constitution) under Polish rule, and in some towns traces of Western
influence still remain. The influence of Byzantium was, however,
far stronger throughout European Russia and evidence of this may
be found in all the older towns. Painted minarets, domed mosques
and tombs in Samarkand and Bukhara show the influence of Allah
and his prophet Mahomet in Central Asia (*see* Fig. 275 and 276). In
Trans-Caucasia, monasteries and churches with spires and bells, and
cathedrals at Mtskheta and Echmiadzin bear witness to Christianity.
For all these subtle regional influences, every Soviet town and city
from the Baltic to the Pacific and from Central Asia to the suburbs
of Leningrad now bears the stamp of uniformity of pattern in the
shape of stiff, regimented high-capacity blocks of flats (*see* Fig. 96).
The only relief is provided by some public buildings, which have
been built with an abundance of Greek columns, gables and apexes,
according to the Soviet idea of classical design.

The morphology of the contemporary Soviet city differs markedly
from that of the western city. French (1979) cites differences
related to population densities, spatial differentiation of functions
and social groups, employment structure and public transport. He
notes that the Soviet city characteristically has high densities of

TABLE 28.
USSR: POPULATION CHANGES IN THE LARGEST CITIES 1970-79
(in thousands)

City	1970 (census)	1979 (census)	% increase
Moscow	6,942	8,011	13
Leningrad	3,987	4,588	15
Kiev	1,632	2,144	31
Tashkent	1,385	1,779	28
Baku	1,266	1,550	22
Kharkov	1,223	1,444	18
Gorkiy	1,170	1,344	15
Novosibirsk	1,161	1,312	13
Minsk	917	1,276	39
Kuybyshev	1,045	1,216	16
Sverdlovsk	1,025	1,211	18
Dnepropetrovsk	904	1,066	18
Tbilisi	889	1,066	20
Odessa	892	1,046	17
Chelyabinsk	875	1,031	18
Omsk	821	1,014	23
Donetsk	879	1,021	16
Yerevan	767	1,019	33
Perm	850	999	17
Kazan	869	993	14
Ufa	771	969	26
Rostov-on-Don	789	934	18
Volgograd	818	929	14
Alma-Ata	730	914	24
Saratov	757	856	13

population which extend to the outskirts. This relates to the huge increase in urban population in the country which has not been matched by a comparable growth in the housing stock. The limits of the built-up area of the city tend to be sharply demarcated, high-density multi-storeyed apartments extending to the periphery (*see* Fig. 96). The gradient of decreasing density towards the outer suburbs characteristic of the Western city does not exist.

Functional mingling, with all parts of the city containing residential, industrial and services functions, differentiates the Soviet city from the Western city which has its clearly distinguished business district (CBD), shopping precinct, industrial sector, zone of blight, etc. The mingling in the Soviet city reflects planning decisions, a great housing shortage and lack of a price mechanism of land values which in the West differentiates users by their ability to pay.

Spatial segregation by social or income groups is absent in the class-less Soviet society; what segregation there is is more by building than by street or area. The employment structure is characterised by a much higher proportion of the working population engaged in industry and a lower proportion in the services. Private car owner-ship is still minimal and there is heavy reliance on public transport for movement within cities.

Marxist-Leninist theory regards the town as the perfect milieu for the evolution of a Communist society and "the victory of the pro-letariat". It has always been looked upon as the force from which Marxism-Leninism is disseminated to the countryside which was for so long resistant to Communist views. Each territorial-administrative unit (oblast, kray, rayon, etc.) is viewed as a hinterland of its major "proletarian" centre. Such a view pervades the whole spectrum of Soviet regional planning and explains why, in the USSR, urban status is conceived in economic terms rather than on the basis of function, morphology or demography (see Fig. 66).

CHAPTER XI

Regional Divisions of the Soviet Union

I love my country, but with a strange love,
My reason will not conquer it!
But I love — I know not why —
The cold silence of its steppes,
The swaying of its boundless forests,
Its rivers which, in flood, are like the seas.

M. Yu. Lermontov, in *My Country*.

NATURAL, POLITICAL AND ECONOMIC DIVISIONS

Contrasts within the Soviet Union are legion. There are mountains and plains, tundras and forests, swamps and deserts, steppes and oases. One finds extremes such as Mount Communism in Tadzhikistan, 7,495 m high, and the Caspian Sea with its shores 26-28 m below sea-level, the cool, humid climate of the low rolling country around Moscow, the sub-tropical environment of Baku, the true desert of Turkmenistan, the monsoon-like conditions of the territories in the Far East, the extreme cold of north-east Siberia, and the "cold pole" near Verkhoyansk and Oymyakon. Tropical rain forest is the only major vegetation zone not found within the boundaries of the Soviet Union.

Russian geographers, following Berg (1950), distinguish ten main natural regions: tundra, *tayga,* mixed forest, forest-steppe, steppe, semi-desert, desert, sub-tropical areas, mountainous areas and broad-leaved forest. Others provide more elaborate physical-geographical regions (*see* Fig. 36). Such divisions are sometimes used for regional description within the framework of each of the main, traditional

169

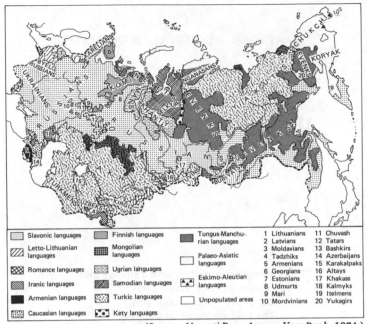

Slavonic languages	Finnish languages	Tungus-Manchu- rian languages
Letto-Lithuanian languages	Mongolian languages	
Romance languages	Ugrian languages	Palaeo-Asiatic languages
Iranic languages	Samodian languages	Eskimo-Aleutian languages
Armenian languages	Turkic languages	
Caucasian languages	Kety languages	Unpopulated areas

1 Lithuanians
2 Latvians
3 Moldavians
4 Tadzhiks
5 Armenians
6 Georgians
7 Estonians
8 Udmurts
9 Mari
10 Mordvinians
11 Chuvash
12 Tatars
13 Bashkirs
14 Azerbaijans
15 Karakalpaks
16 Altays
17 Khakass
18 Kalmyks
19 Itelmens
20 Yukagirs

(Source: *Novosti Press Agency Year Book*, 1974.)

Fig. 97. Soviet Union: peoples and languages.

divisions of the former Russian Empire, namely Russia, Siberia, Far East, Central Asia and Caucasia. Since these traditional divisions are obsolete and contrary to the spirit of Soviet policy, it would be illogical to perpetuate them.

The component states of the Soviet federation are based on the Marxist national territory principle. Such political recognition of nationality groups tends to stabilise internal boundaries while economic determination of the boundaries in such a rapidly developing country calls for almost constant change. Even so, the political divisions in the European part of the USSR appear much the same today as they did when they were first formed by the government of Catherine the Great in the latter part of the eighteenth century.

The present fifteen Soviet Socialist Republics ("Union Republics") based largely on the ethnic distributions of half a century ago (*see* Fig. 97 and Table 20), may be classified into three groups, representing three significant elements in Russian history.

(*a*) The Russian Soviet Federated Socialist Republic (RSFSR), with about three-quarters of the territory of the country and over 137.5 million people, equates broadly with the Muscovy core of the Russian state and the Muscovite Empire.

(*b*) The Soviet Socialist Republics of Georgia, Azerbaydzhan,

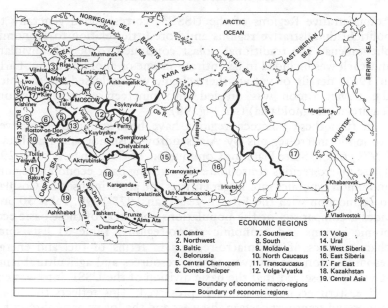

Fig. 98. Soviet Union: economic regions and economic macro-regions.

Armenia (Trans-Caucasia), Turkmenistan, Uzbekistan, Tadzhikstan, Kirgizia and Kazakhstan (Middle Asia) constitute a southern group which represents the southern expansion of Russia into the steppe and desert lands. This movement began in the seventeenth century with the conquest of nomadic peoples and involved the Russians in a new way of life.

(c) The Ukraine and Belorussian Soviet Socialist Republics, the Republics of the Baltic (Estonia, Lithuania and Latvia) and Moldavia constitute a western group along the European frontier. This group represents the westward orientation of Russia which began with Peter the Great and which continued after the Second World War with the advance of the frontier westward from Leningrad and into Finland, the material westward shift of the country of Poland to the Oder-Neisse line, and the recovery of the Baltic States and East Prussia early in that War.

Cutting across the major politico-administrative divisions (SSRs) are the systems of economic planning regions which involve the grouping of lower order administrative regions, i.e. *oblasts, krays,* etc. Between the 1920s and 1957, economic planning and production were based on fifteen economic regions. In June 1957, 105 new economic regions were created as "the further perfection of the organisation of administration in industry and building" (*Pravda,* April-June 1957). The new units, called "Economic

Administrative Regions of the USSR", corresponded generally to politico-administrative regions and bore little relation to economic phenomena. The traditional oblast continued to be held inviolate and each was included in its entirety in one or another region. Early in 1961, details of yet another scheme were released under which the Soviet Union was divided into nineteen economic regions (eighteen plus Moldavia) (*see* Fig. 98).

In turn these nineteen regions have been grouped into seven economic macro-regions by Aleksandrov, Kistanov and Ephshteyn (1974) of the State Planning Commission, of Gosplan (*see* Table 29). These macro-regions consolidate the existing basic economic regions and union republics into larger entities and are being used by Gosplan in connection with the Fifteen-year plan 1975-1990. Table 30 provides a comparison of the populations and areas of these basic economic regions and economic macro-regions; Table 31 lists some characteristics of the macro-regions in terms of fuel and energy resources, iron ore reserves, timber resources and agricultural land. It will be observed that the basic division of the USSR into western and eastern economic zones is preserved. This reflects the lower labour and transport costs in the west and the lower natural-resource costs in the east.

TABLE 29. MACRO-REGIONS AND CONSTITUENT ECONOMIC REGIONS

Economic macro-regions	*Basic economic regions*	
	In RSFSR	*In other republics*
1. North Central European USSR	North-West, Central (also Kaliningrad Oblast)	Baltic (Estonia, Latvia, Lithuania), Belorussia
2. South European USSR	Central Chernozem, North Caucasus	South-West, Donets-Dnieper, South (all in the Ukraine); Moldavia; Trans-Caucasia (Georgia, Azerbaydzhan, Armenia)
3. Volga-Urals	Volga-Vyatka, Volga, Urals	
4. Siberia	West Siberia, East Siberia	
5. Far East	Far East	
6. Kazakhstan		Kazakhstan
7. Central Asia		Central Asia (Uzbek, Tadzhik, Kirghiz and Turkmen SSRs)

After Aleksandrov *et al.*, 1974.

TABLE 30. COMPARATIVE POPULATIONS (1979) AND AREAS OF THE SOVIET ECONOMIC REGIONS

Region	Pop. * (000, 1979)	% total pop.	Area† (000 km²)	% total area	Persons (per km²)	Rank Pop.	Rank Density	Rank Area
North and Central European Russia		22.3		11.40				
Centre	28,947	10.9	485.2	2.17	58	1	6	9
North-West	13,275	4.7	1,662.8	7.42	7	11	15	5
Baltic	8,192	3.1	189.1	0.84	43	15	10	15
Belorussia	9,559	3.6	207.6	0.93	45	12	8	14
South European Russia		34.7		6.16				
Central Chernozem	7,797	2.9	167.7	0.75	46	16	7	17
Donets-Dnieper	21,045	8.0	220.5	0.98	94	4	2	13
South-West	21,578	8.2	269.0	1.32	72	3	4	11
South	7,134	2.7	110.7	0.49	63	18	5	18
Moldavia	3,948	1.5	33.7	0.15	116	19	1	19
North Caucasus	15,487	6.1	354.7	1.63	44	6	9	10
Trans-Caucasia	14,075	5.3	186.1	0.83	74	9	3	16
Volga-Urals		16.6		7.28				
Volga-Vyatka	8,343	3.2	263.2	1.18	31	14	11	12
Volga	19,393	7.4	680.0	3.04	28	5	12	8
Urals	15,568	6.0	680.4	3.04	23	7	13	7
Siberia		8.0		29.22				
West Siberia	12,959	5.2	2,427.2	10.81	5	10	16	4
East Siberia	8,158	3.4	4,122.8	18.41	2	13	18	2
Far East	6,819	2.7	6,215.9	27.75	1	17	19	1
Kazakhstan	14,685	5.6	2,717.3	12.13	5	8	16	3
Central Asia	25,480	9.5	1,279.3	5.71	19	2	14	6

*Total population of the USSR:

   1970 (census): 241.7 million (111.4 million males; 130.3 million females)
   1979 (census): 262.4 million (122.3 million males; 140.1 million females)
   1981 (July 1, estimate by Central Statistical Board): 267.7 million.
   1982 (January, estimate by Central Statistical Board): 268.8 million.

†Total area of the USSR: 22.4 million km²

TABLE 31. SOME CHARACTERISTICS OF THE
CONSOLIDATED ECONOMIC REGIONS OF THE USSR
(percentage of USSR 1979)

Parameters	1 North- Central European	2 South European	3 Volga -Urals	4 Siberia	5 Far East	6 Kazakh SSR	7 Central Asia
Potential fuel and energy resources	4.5	3.9	1.6	56.3	30.6	1.9	1.2
Predicted iron ore reserves	1.0	30.7	10.5	45.5	5.0	7.2	0.1
Timber resources	13.5	2.2	7.0	48.4	28.5	0.4	0.0
Agricultural land	8.2	17.4	15.7	10.8	1.2	33.9	12.8

After Aleksandrov, Kistanov and Ephshteyn, 1974.

To understand the complexities of the geography of the Soviet Union it is necessary to consider it in regions; yet ideas of man-land relationships or syntheses of the physical, historical and social geography of areas normally adopted by Western geographers for purposes of regionalisation are not readily applicable since the pattern of human geography in the USSR is, to a high degree, a reflection of the prevailing planned economic activity. In this book, therefore, the official economic regions and macro-regions have been adopted as the framework for regional description and analysis (see Fig. 98 and Table 28).

These economic regions have remained fairly consistent during the last two decades and continue to be used by the Soviets for statistical reporting and for purposes of planning as, for example, during the Eleventh Five-year Plan, 1981-85. Soviet geographers believe, on grounds of Marxist and Leninist dialectical materialism, that such regions really exist because their functional characteristics are created and fashioned by State planning decisions. For them the economic planning region is the unit of regional description.

Every aspect of the communal economy of the USSR is centrally planned according to economic laws. Decisions involve the selection and ranking of priorities for the use of resources of materials, people, finance and time. The activities of every industrial establishment and every economic enterprise (all owned and operated by the State) are planned such that at each stage the goods and services required to meet the needs of the national economy and the people are provided. Planners of the State Planning Committee of the USSR (Gosplan) determine policies and fix targets for various economic development plans for the country as a whole and for each of the economic regions. The plans are either long term, covering fifteen to twenty years, or Five-year Plans, which help fulfil the longer term plan, or annual plans, which represent the breakdown of the Five-year Plan. The plans represent a synthesis of centralised guidance and control and have the force of law. They are a comitment to specific goals backed by an appropriate allocation of resources and are binding on all concerned. Enterprises and individuals must strictly abide by the planned assignments fixed by the State. Matching of performance against the plan is an ongoing exercise and the results are published each year as a "Plan Fulfilment Report". Whether deviations of performance or achievement from the plan represent poor economic performance or bad planning is open to debate.

CHAPTER XII

North-Central European
Macro-Region

This macro-region consolidates the Centre and North-West basic economic regions of the RSFSR (including Kaliningrad Oblast), together with the Baltic (Estonia, Latvia and Lithuania) and Belorussia Economic Regions. It contains 11.4 per cent of the total area of the USSR, just over a fifth of its population and more than a quarter of its urban population. Aleksandrov *et al.* (1974) estimate that it contains 4.5 per cent of the country's fuel potential and energy reserves, 13.5 per cent of the timber resources and just over 8 per cent of the agricultural land (*see* Table 29). The macro-region has a high level of economic development and, whilst having noticeable internal contrasts, nevertheless preserves certain commonality among the principal production centres of the major economic regions — Moscow, Leningrad and the Baltic and Belorussian industrial regions — where the stress is markedly on manufacturing (iron and steel, chemicals, light industry and machine-building).

1. CENTRE ECONOMIC REGION

This economic region (*see* Fig. 99), transitional with respect to climate, soils, drainage, vegetation and agriculture is nevertheless distinguished by its high level of economic development. It is powerful in industrial production and employment, especially in lighter branches and government services with 40 per cent of the national total. Its core is the metropolis — Moscow — the political, administrative, economic and cultural centre of the Soviet Union, but with major linkages with twelve other cities with populations of more than 250,000, themselves industrial centres and nodes which form several concentric radial systems around Moscow (*see* Fig. 100 and Tables 32 and 33).

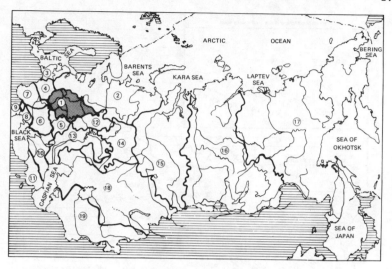

Fig. 99. Soviet Union: location of Centre Economic Region.

TABLE 32. CENTRE ECONOMIC REGION:
ADMINISTRATIVE UNITS, THEIR POPULATION AND DENSITY

Area: 485,200 km²
Population (1979): 28,947,000

Administrative unit	Area (000 km²)	Population (000, 1979)	Density (persons per km²)	Percentage urban
Kalinin Oblast	84	1,649	20	67
Smolensk Oblast	50	1,121	22	60
Kaluga Oblast	30	1,007	33	62
Bryansk Oblast	35	1,507	43	59
Tula Oblast	26	1,907	74	78
Moscow City	47	8,011	298	100
Moscow Oblast		6,360	306	75
Yaroslavl Oblast	36	1,425	40	78
Vladimir Oblast	29	1,581	55	75
Ryazan Oblast	40	1,362	34	58
Ivanovo Oblast	24	1,321	55	80
Kostroma Oblast	60	804	13	64
Orel Oblast	25	892	36	55

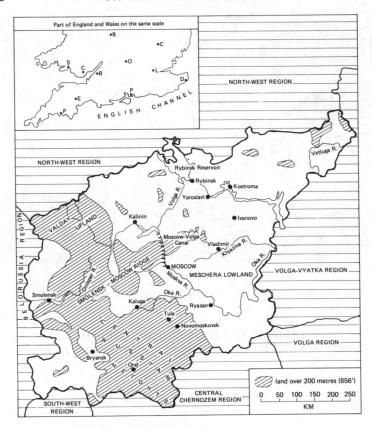

Fig. 100. Centre Economic Region.

PHYSICAL ASPECTS

Relief

Although the region occupies part of the Russian Lowland (the so-called Great Russian or East European Plain), relief tends to be varied, with general elevations between 100 and 200 m, and occasional parts over 300 m; the term "plain" is therefore somewhat inappropriate. Rather the region is one of monotonously rolling lowland (*see* Fig. 100). It rests on a relatively stable geological foundation of Pre-Cambrian crystalline rocks — the Russian Platform (*see* p. 12).

The region bears the evidence of Quaternary glaciation in fluvio-glacial drifts, drumlins and erratic boulders. Morainic hills, such as the Smolensk-Moscow Ridge, are interspersed with depressions occupied by lakes. Peat bogs and marshes are commonplace and the

TABLE 33. CENTRE ECONOMIC REGION:
TOWNS WITH OVER 150,000 INHABITANTS IN 1979

Town		Population in thousands 1970 (census)	1979 (census)	Percentage increase 1970-79
Moscow	proper	6,942	7,831	13
	with suburbs	7,061	8,011	13
Yaroslavl		517	597	15
Tula		462	514	11
Ivanovo		419	465	11
Ryazan		351	453	29
Kalinin		345	412	19
Bryansk		318	394	24
Orel		232	305	31
Vladimir		234	296	26
Smolensk		211	276	31
Kaluga		211	265	26
Kostroma		223	255	14
Rybinsk		218	239	9
Podolsk		169	202	20
Lyubertsy		139	160	15

sources and upper reaches of streams tend to be diffuse. The line of terminal moraines extending from Lithuania and Belorussian (Belorusskaya Gryada) and terminating in the Valday Hills (maximum height 310 m) in the north-west of the region constitutes the main water divide between drainage to north and south.

The more southerly parts of the region contain immense stretches of sand, which are succeeded southwards by loess and weathered mollisols (chernozem). The latter are better drained and drier than the soils to the north. Streams tend to have clearly marked sources, while their courses are usually distinguished by pronounced and high right banks and low left banks which are liable to flooding during spring high water.

Drainage
Practically the whole of the Centre Region is drained by the River Volga and its tributaries. This river rises amid swamps and marshes in the Valday Hills near Lake Seliger and flows eastwards in a circuitous and gently graded course, eventually to leave the region north-west of Gorkiy. The south and west are drained by the Oka River and its Klyazma and Moskva tributaries, the north-east by the Vetluga and Vyatka, and the west by the Rivers Dnieper and Desna. The economic usefulness of these rivers is seriously curtailed because they are frozen over for about six months each winter.

Despite this, the Volga, the largest river in Europe, is the most important waterway system of the USSR. It receives most of its water from melting snows in spring, when sizeable floods are likely, though, since the 1930s, these spring floods have been controlled by reservoirs. By such control, surplus water held back in the spring is used to maintain the level of the river during summer and autumn, at which periods shoals and shallows formerly interfered with river navigation.

A dam near Ivankovo has impounded the Volga Reservoir which raises the level on the upstream side to beyond Kalinin. Downstream from Ivankovo come first the Uglich Reservoir, then the Rybinsk Reservoir formed by two dams, one on the Volga and the other on its tributary, the Sheksna. These reservoirs provide water for the Moscow Canal and Moscow River, giving Moscow a deepwater route for navigation to the Volga River. A dam at Gorodets, 56 km upstream from Gorkiy, forms the Gorkiy Sea. On the middle Volga, beyond the limits of the Centre Region, other multipurpose reservoirs have been constructed, e.g. at Kuybyshev and farther downstream near Volgograd (*see* p. 331).

At Volgograd, the Volga-Don Canal provides an outlet from the Volga to the Sea of Azov and Black Sea, and thence to open sea (*see* Fig. 210). As a result of these constructions and of older canal systems and lakes, Moscow is provided with links to the Baltic, White, Caspian, Azov and Black Seas, and has come to be called the "Port of the Five Seas" (*see* Fig. 71).

Climate
The climate of the Centre Region is of the cold continental type with humid winters. Compared with the climate of Britain, winters generally are colder and summers only slightly warmer; rainfall aggregates are less and the annual distribution is different (*see* Fig. 101).

In summer, there are usually no more than five months with mean temperatures over 10 °C. In winter, three to five months have mean temperatures below freezing level (0 °C). Spring and autumn are brief. In the west, the temperature range is about 10 °C, but it increases in the east to 21 °C. Precipitation is everywhere slight, the humid western parts receiving no more than about 700 mm, the drier south-eastern margins less than 400 mm. Maximum precipitation occurs during summer at a time when rainfall effectiveness is appreciably reduced through evaporation. Much of the winter precipitation comes in the form of snow, which lies for four and a half to five months at depths of 30-40 cm. Atlantic influences penetrate into western parts of the region and winters here tend to be overcast

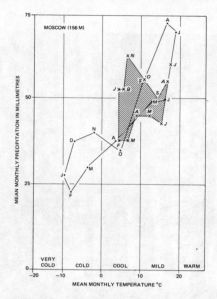

Fig. 101. Hythergraph for Moscow.

NOTE: The shaded hythergraph with X symbols in this and all other hythergraphy following is for Kew, London, England, and is added for comparative purposes.

and raw. In the east, however, away from the maritime influences and nearer the Siberian anticyclone, winters tend to be crisp and bright and the cold is intensified. The climate in the east of the region is not unlike that of the south of Canada east of the Rockies.

Natural vegetation and soils
The transitional nature of the region is further reflected in the natural vegetation and soils. Both occur in roughly parallel zones aligned west-east. In the north, the region is still essentially forested, with conifers (*tayga*) predominating. Between the Volga and the Oka, the conifers have admixtures of birch, oak, maple and ash (*see* Fig. 102). Spodosols, overlain by glacial deposits in the north and by immense stretches of sand in the south, underlie both the coniferous and the mixed forest zones. South of the Oka River there is a zone of predominantly broad-leaved forest, containing limes and poplars. This thins out to woodland steppe farther south. This zone of broad-leaved forest coincides roughly with mollisols (brown forest soils) which grade from borolls to ustolls farther south (*see* p. 45).

Fig. 102. Woodlands of graceful silver birch trees are characteristic of the country-side near Moscow. Birch is a deciduous tree of the *tayga*, in which other species are mostly conifers.

THE ECONOMY

Agriculture and forestry

The Centre Region has never been a leading agricultural area. The short, cool, growing season, the low annual rainfall (the effective-ness of which diminishes towards the south-east), and the generally infertile soils combine to produce an unfavourable physical environ-ment. Diversified mixed farming embracing such crops as rye, oats, wheat, potatoes, flax and cabbages is customary (*see* Fig. 103). Sheep, pigs and cattle are frequently kept. Farm output over-all is inadequate in grains and meat. Near the towns there is considerable market gardening and dairying. Where forest persists north of the Volga River, rather less than a quarter of the area is sown to crops. Paper, pulp and other forest industries are common. South of the Oka River the range of crops widens to include maize, sugar-beet, hemp, tobacco and deciduous fruits (*see* Fig. 104).

(Novosti)

Fig. 103. Cut flax drying in the open air near Uglich in Yaroslavl district. The USSR accounts for two-thirds of the world's flax crop.

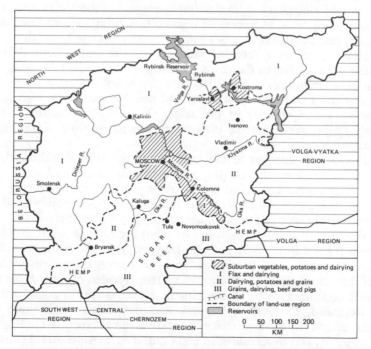

Fig. 104. Centre Economic Region: agricultural land-use regions.

Manufacturing

Manufacturing industry in the region is the result more of tradition and geographical inertia than of favourable location in relation to supplies of energy and raw materials. The courts of the tsars and the presence of the nobility in Moscow encouraged early artisan industries which relied on raw materials brought in from other regions. Today, the market afforded by the largest concentration of people in the USSR, the presence of a large and skilled labour force, an industrial tradition and government planning combine to maintain a modern industrial complex which, like the earlier industries, continues to look far afield for its raw materials and sources of power.

Lignite in the Moscow coal basin, peat (the Soviet Union has about 60 per cent of the world's peat resources), some iron ore near Tula, and scattered deposits of phosphate, and such agricultural products as flax, hemp and potatoes are the only raw materials available within the Centre Region for manufacturing industry (*see* Figs. 105 and 106). The lignite and peat are still used to generate electricity, but neither the electricity, iron ore or other resources are sufficient to meet local demand. Coal, iron ore, pig iron, steel, petroleum and a wide range of minerals, metals and raw materials have to be imported from other parts of the country. A substantial amount of electricity, generated at barrages on the Volga and elsewhere, is imported by means of high voltage transmissions lines, and natural gas, a basic fuel for both industry and electricity production, is piped from West Siberia (Medvezhye, Urengoy), Central Asia (Gazli, Achak), North Caucasus (Stavropol, Krasnodar), Volga-Urals (Saratov, Orenburg) and the Ukraine (Shebelinka, Dashava). Preference is given to gas over oil, coal and peat because of its high combustibility and absence of pollution. Oil is piped from the Volga-Urals fields, West Siberia (Samotlor, Pokachev), and Kazakhstan (Mangyshlak).

The long-established textile industry of the region, still the third major industry of the Centre, was originally based on local wool, flax and hemp. The wool was a by-product of sheep rearing for meat production, while flax and hemp were fibre crops suited to the relatively wet and cool climate and poor podzolic soils (alfisols) of the area. Additional supplies of wool are now brought into the region from Central Asia and the Ukraine, flax and hemp from the Baltic Republics and Belorussia, and raw cotton from Central Asia (90 per cent) and Trans-Caucasia. The woollen industry of the USSR continues to be located in the Moscow area at such centres as Kuntsevo, Pavlovskiy, Zagorsk and Posad, although there are some mills in the Ukraine (Kiev, Kharkov), in the North-West Region (Leningrad) and in Kazakhstan and Central Asia (Alma-Ata, Frunze). Cotton mills in the oblasts of Ivanovo (Ivanovo, Shuya, Kineshma),

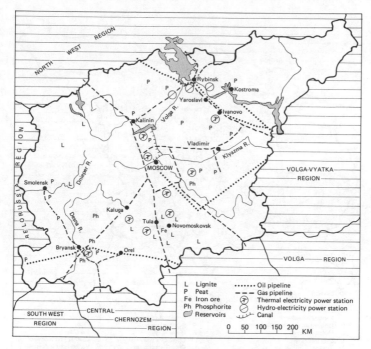

Fig. 105. Centre Economic Region: mineral and power resources.

Vladimir (Vladimir, Kovrov), Moscow (Moscow, Orekhovo-Zuyevo, Noginsk) and Yaroslavl are responsible for 75 per cent or more of the cotton textiles of the USSR. This is the largest cotton-textile producing region in the world. The Centre produces about 60 per cent of the country's linen goods; Kostroma and Yaroslavl are the main centres. Man-made and synthetic fibres are becoming increasingly important.

The iron, steel and metal-working industries at Tula and Lipetsk utilise local ores and ores from the Kursk Magnetic Anomaly in the Central Chernozem Region (*see* p. 245) for foundry work and for making cast steel. Elsewhere in the region the metallurgical industry, which first worked up iron ore found in the marshes between Kaluga and Gorkiy, relies on steel brought in from Krivoy Rog in the Ukraine and from the Urals, iron ores from Kursk and also on converted scrap metal. Around Moscow and elsewhere, there are steel converters and rolling mills which serve engineering works. These in their turn produce general machinery for other industries, motor vehicles, railway equipment, aircraft, machine tools, precision instruments and ball bearings.

Engineering in all its several forms (electrical, transport, etc.)

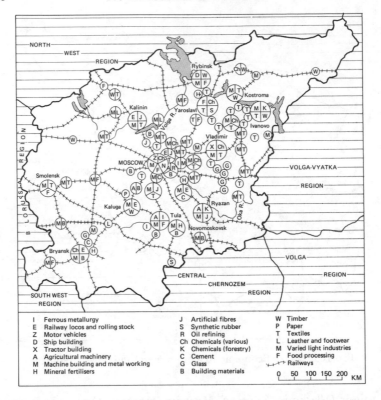

Fig. 106. Centre Economic Region: railways and industrial structure of towns.
NOTE: In this and in all other similar illustrations the town circles are relative only and are not in strict proportion to their populations.

occupies the leading place in the industrial make-up of the Centre. Hardly a town is not engaged in engineering of some kind or another, with specialisation and integration a characteristic feature: motor vehicles and railway equipment in Moscow; textile machinery at Ivanovo; railway waggons and locomotives in Bryansk; road building in Orel; electrical engineering in Kalinin; shipbuilding at Rybinsk, etc. (*see* Fig. 106).

The rapidly expanding chemical industry of the Soviet Union is well represented in the Centre Region. In fact, it is moving into second place after engineering both as regards the value of its output and its significance in the national economy. Moscow has a wide range of light chemical and pharmaceutical plants: Yaroslavl, Tambov, Voronezh and Yefremov produce synthetic rubber (based originally on industrial alcohol from potatoes, but now on petroleum (hydrocarbon) sources); Voskresensk and Novomoskovsk, sulphuric acid; Shchelkovo, Orekhovo-Zuyevo and Klin, synthetic fibres (19 per cent of all Soviet man-made fibres are produced in the Centre Region); and Lyubertsy, Klin and Vladimir, plastics. Synthetic substances and plastics are gradually pushing the old branches of the chemical industry (superphosphates, dyes, varnishes) into the background.

Woodworking and paper industries are also important, as are the service and food-processing industries serving the large urban markets. There is hardly a town in the Centre Region which does not engage in manufacturing of some kind. This is not to say that the industrial landscape is in any way as close-textured as that found in parts of England. The distance from Manchester to Bolton or from Birmingham to Wolverhampton in England is a mere 20 km; but the distance separating Moscow and Kalinin or Moscow and Vladimir is of the order of 160-180 km (which compares with London to Bristol or London to Birmingham). Rather is the Centre Region a series of industrial centres and nodes, e.g. Moscow and its satellite towns Ivanovo-Kineshma-Kostroma, Tula-Novomoskovsk, etc., separated by extensive rural areas. The integration of the industrial centres and the density of the transport net decrease with distance from Moscow.

POPULATION AND CITIES

It was in the area that has since become the Centre Region of the USSR, mainly between the Volga and the Oka Rivers, that the rebirth of Rus (Muscovy) took place after the Mongol invasions. Slavic people entered the area in spite of its originally wooded nature and unproductive soil. Today over 28 million people, mainly Great Russians, live in the region and in all twelve oblasts the urban population exceeds 50 per cent. The wealth of the region lies not in its farms, but in its cities, and of these Moscow is by far the largest and most important.

Moscow (population: 7,831,000; with suburbs: 8,011,000)
Kiev Rus near the transition zone of forest and steppe, and long exposed to the inroads of Mongol Tatars from the east, finally fell to Batu, the nephew of Genghis Khan, in the thirteenth century. The unity of Kiev Rus collapsed and the embryo state moved far to the north to the safety of the forest and marsh. Here the centres of influence were Novgorod and Moscow. Novgorod was a trading post, controlling routes to the Baltic and White Seas, and a member of the Hanseatic League; Moscow a frontier post, situated well to the east, became the rallying point where forces for the final breaking and pushing back of the Tatars were mustered, while Novgorod's fortunes gradually waned with the decline of the Hanseatic League.

In 1156, Yuri Dolgoruki, Prince of Suzdal, built a wooden *kremlin* (fort or citadel) at Moscow on the site of an earlier settlement, and around this, near an easy crossing of the Moskva River, the township grew. The site was on the outer convex bank of a north-swinging meander of the Moskva River, and between two small streams — the Neglinka and the Yauza — which joined the main river at this point (*see* Fig. 77). The water barriers were ineffectual defence lines, as was the surrounding flat and dismal countryside. Rather the site was a refuge in the backwoods between the Oka and upper Volga, well away from the Tatars. Even so, it held a commanding position in a central part of the Russian lowland near the hub of the great river systems of European Russia. By means of short portages, Moscow had links with the Dvina, Dnieper, Volkhov and Narva Rivers, in addition to its direct connection via the Rivers Oka and Volga to distant ports on the Caspian Sea and beyond.

Twice during the thirteenth century and once in the fourteenth century Moscow was burned and plundered by the Tatars, but by the second half of the fifteenth century, having annexed the majority of the surrounding principalities, the Grand Duchy of Moscow became the focus for the unification of a Russian state. Ivan III made Moscow the capital and himself "Tsar of all the Russias".

In the sixteenth century, the growth of Moscow was interrupted by fires and further Tatar invasion, but the presence there of state administration represented by the tsar's court, the boyars' *duma* (council of the upper stratum of society and state administration), the assembly of the *zemstvo* (an advisory organ drawn from elected representatives), the residence of the Russian Metropolitan (the "third Rome" after the fall of Constantinople in 1453), and the concentration of businesses and workshops, assured the city of a premier position in the life of the Russian realm. Moscow proved to be the cradle of the Russian people and the springboard for the conquest of enormous territories. Its political functions were eclipsed for some 200 years when, in 1712, the capital was transferred to St Petersburg, but it continued to play a leading role in the cultural and artistic life of the country and has remained its major commercial and industrial city. The government returned to Moscow after the Revolution of 1917. Today, besides being a symbol of the nation's past, Moscow is the largest city of the Soviet Union and plays the leading role in the political, administrative, economic, artistic, literary and intellectual life of the country.

With Moscow's increasing importance, the area occupied by the city has grown and its appearance changed. It now covers nearly 330 km². In the absence of pronounced physical obstacles the city retains its original radial-ring plan of streets (*see* Fig. 107) and presents a striking summary of the life of old and modern Russia. There

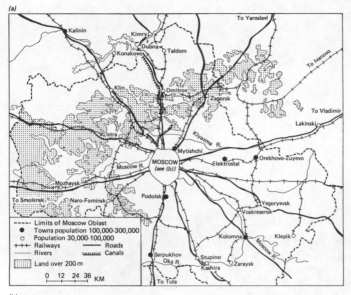

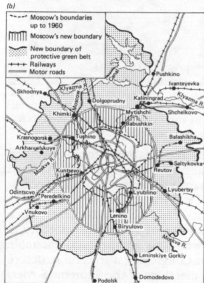

(After Pokshishevsky, 1974.)
Fig. 107. Position of Moscow
(a) Oblast; (b) city.

still remain in the suburbs some wooden houses reminiscent of the peasant *izba* of the villages, standing alongside large 15-20 storey blocks of flats built since the Second World War (including the Olympic Village, built for the 1980 Games which were held in Moscow), and, nearer the centre, town residences with pillared porticos which belonged to the former aristocracy. There are

(*Fotokbronika Tass*)

Fig. 108. Moscow Kremlin (citadel) with its three cathedrals — the erstwhile residence of the tsars and now the seat of the Supreme Soviet of the USSR — with the Palace of Congress, Armoury and many other buildings.

factories producing motor vehicles and machine tools, medieval Orthodox churches with the oriental splendour of gilded and painted domes, and sports stadia; there are narrow irregular lanes and recently widened sixteen-lane thoroughfares; and there is the Kremlin.

The Kremlin contains within its red-brick battlements three cathedrals, the tsar's palace and palaces of the former nobility, a museum and an imposing clocktower. This architectural ensemble was joined in 1961 by the Palace of Congresses, a graceful structure of glass and steel, in which are held meetings of the Supreme Soviet. In front of the Kremlin lies the vast space of Red Square, witness of many major events in Russian history. Across the Square to the east is the city's largest store (GUM or State Department Store) and towards the river to the south from Red Square stand conspicuously the brightly painted baroque onion-domed spires of St Basil's

Cathedral and the 3,000 bedroomed Hotel Rossiya.

To provide Moscow with a navigable waterway the 5½ m deep Moscow Canal was completed in 1937. It joins the Moscow River in Moscow with the River Volga, 130 km to the north, through a system of eight locks. A dam constructed with a hydro-electric power plant of 30,000 kW capacity on the Volga near Ivankovo (in the neighbourhood of Dubna) raises the water level on the river upstream as far as 70 km above the city of Kalinin to form the Volga Reservoir. One-third of the water collected in the reservoir is used to feed the Moscow Canal, the remainder to feed the Uglich Reservoir a little way downstream. As has been noted, Moscow, 650 km from the nearest sea, is yet accessible to five seas. Self-propelled barges, with a total load capacity of about 22,000 tonnes, reach the city during the seven-month ice-free period. River traffic, however, is slow and is economical only for the transport of such bulky low-cost goods as lumber, coal, building materials, petroleum products and grain.

In the mid-nineteenth century, Moscow became the focus of the railways of European Russia. Eleven trunk railways now connect the city with all parts of the USSR (see Fig. 107). The terminal stations are linked by an outer ring railway and an inner underground railway (the Metro). Each of the seventy earlier stations of the Moscow Metro Railway has a distinctive architectural style of its own, the more recent ones have a functional design. The Metro provides for one third of all Moscow's transport.

Moscow is not yet plagued by the congestion of motor traffic that characterises London, Paris, Rome or New York, although the public omnibus, trolley bus, and underground transport facilities are well used by commuters. Nevertheless, the development of motor transport aggravated the problem presented by narrow streets. This has been overcome by the straightening and widening of main thoroughfares, such as Gorkiy Street and Sadovaya Ulitsa, to as much as 30 m wide. In this process whole buildings were moved bodily, either backwards or about face.

The raising of the level of the Moscow River after the completion of the Moscow-Volga Canal necessitated the construction of eleven new bridges and the lining of the river with grand embankments. These now provide some of the chief thoroughfares of the city.

The use of aircraft introduced another element into the geography of Moscow's transport. The original civil airport at Vnukovo, 27 km south-west of the city centre, soon proved to be totally inadequate and another, international airport, Sheremetyevo, capable of handling 1,500 passengers an hour, was laid out in the north at the same distance from the city. A third airport, one of the world's biggest, at Domodedovo, 25 km to the south-east, has been in operation since March 1964 and there is a fourth airport called Bykovo. There are plans for a fifth airport to be built in the 1980s at a site 60 km north-west of the city, designed mainly to handle jumbo jets.

Despite the distances involved, the ease of rail transport over the generally flat expanses of the Union, the availability of natural gas and petroleum supplies via long distance trunk pipelines and hydro- and thermal electricity via high voltage transmission lines has encouraged the setting up of a wide range of industries in Moscow, which is now the country's largest industrial producing centre. Heavy industries take pride of place. Metallurgy, engineering and the textile industries together account for approximately 45 per cent of the gross production in these categories. Consumer goods industries are becoming increasingly important. Enterprises such as the *Likhachev* Car Plant, *Sergei Ordzhonikidze* plant (lathes), the Red Proletariat plant, Frezer and Kalibr (instrument-making) plant, the Hammer and Sickle (*Serp i Molot*) plant (high grade steel and rolled steel), *Stankolit* plant (machine parts) and the "Dynamo" plant (electric motors), *Elektrozavod* (transformers) and *Elektro-pribor* (electric measuring instruments) produce a wide range of industrial products and supply electrical fitments, machine tools and precision instruments. The *Pervyi Gosudarstvennyi Podship-nikovyi Zavod* is one of the largest ball-bearing factories in the world. There are also enterprises producing pharmaceutical and heavy chemicals, synthetic rubber, plastics, footwear, silk, wool, synthetic fibres and other products, which take advantage of the presence of abundant skilled labour and a large market of over 8 million people in the capital and its immediate environs and practically 29 million in the Centre Region as a whole. The Moscow area alone is responsible for approximately 16 per cent of the total industrial output of the USSR.

Yaroslavl (population: 597,000)
On the right bank of the Volga at its confluence with the Kotorosl River, Yaroslavl lies some 260 km north-north-east of Moscow. Founded in 1024, it was an important town in the Rostov-Suzdal Principality, but was annexed by Moscow early in the fifteenth century. During the next two centuries, it was a sizeable trading post on the White Sea-Volga-Near East route, but with the establishment and rapid rise of St Petersburg on the Baltic in the eighteenth century its industries and trade suffered a temporary decline. Today, Yaroslavl is a major industrial and oil refining centre and river port where the main railway line north from Moscow to Arkhangelsk crosses the Volga River. Among its manufactures are motor-vehicle

tyres made from petroleum-based synthetic rubber, petro-chemicals, textiles, motor vehicles, locomotives, ships, electrical engineering and instrument making.

Tula (population: 514,000)

The most important of the industrial centres of the Centre Region south of Moscow, Tula is situated on the Upa, tributary of the Oka River, 180 km south of the capital near the junction of the mixed forest zone and the steppe. Founded as a frontier fortress against the Tatars, it later grew as a metal-working centre specialising in armaments and samovars. Nowadays the emphasis is on arms, machine tools, sewing machines, agricultural and general machinery, electrical engineering, tanning, flour milling and sugar refining. In recent years, ores from the Kursk Magnetic Anomoly and natural gas from the Caucasus and West Siberia have considerably strengthened the resource base of Tula's integrated iron and steel plant. *Yasnaya Polyana,* the memorial estate of the Russian writer Leo Tolstoi, is near Tula.

Ivanovo (population: 465,000)

After Moscow, Ivanovo is the largest centre of the cotton textile industry in the Soviet Union. It is responsible for 20 per cent of the total output of textiles in the USSR. Its first mill, built in 1751, used imported cotton, but is now supplied from Central Asia. Other industries of the "Manchester of the Soviet Union" include man-made fibres, textile machinery and chemicals. Situated about 300 km north-east of Moscow, Ivanovo was a centre of strikes and revolutionary movements from the end of the nineteenth century and in the early twentieth century it was an important stronghold of the Bolsheviks.

Ryazan (population: 453,000)

On the right bank of the Oka River, 190 km south-east of Moscow, Ryazan has experienced a remarkable increase of population in recent years (29 per cent between 1970 and 1979). It is a flourishing industrial town within a generally agricultural area. It has a major petrochemical complex associated with a local oil refinery and factories for agricultural machinery, flour milling, fruit canning, distilling, railway equipment and construction, wood-working, shoe-making, clothing and electric light bulbs. The main railway from Moscow to Kuybyshev passes through the city.

Kalinin (population: 412,000)

Formerly Tver, Kalinin is situated on the main Moscow-Leningrad Railway at its crossing of the navigable Volga (*see* Fig. 107). In the thirteenth century it became capital of the important and independent principality of Tver and for a time rivalled Moscow, but fell to that principality in the fifteenth century. Its chief industries include textiles (cotton and flax), chemical fibres, engineering (railway rolling stock, textile machinery, excavators), timber-based industries, radios and electrical equipment.

Bryansk (population: 394,000)

At the head of navigation of the Desna River, 340 km south-west of Moscow, Bryansk is, with nearby *Bezhitsa,* an important industrial centre. It has the largest railway engineering works in the Soviet Union (conveniently sited at the junction of several routes), iron and steel works (in the northern suburb of Maltevsk), sawmills, flour mills, distilleries and cement works.

Orel (population: 305,000)

A market town near the transition between the wooded steppe and the steppe where the main Moscow-Kharkov railway crosses the Oka River, Orel is in a good agricultural area and markets grain and livestock. It manufactures farm machinery and textile machinery.

Vladimir (population: 296,000)

Founded in 1150 Vladimir is among the oldest of Russian towns, and was capital of the Grand Principality of Vladimir until it fell to Muscovy in the fourteenth century. It lies 184 km east of Moscow on the main Moscow-Gorkiy railway, but was comparatively insignificant until the 1930s, when textile, chemical, machine-tool, precision instruments and farm engineering industries were established to make it a thriving industrial city. Its population increased by 26 per cent in the period 1970-79.

Smolensk (population: 276,000)

Another very old Russian city dating from the ninth century, Smolensk is favourably located on the Dnieper River on the so-called "Water Road from the Varangians to the Greeks", and became an important trade and distribution centre. In modern times it manufactures linen (it has one of the largest linen mills in the Soviet Union), textile machinery, electrical goods and clothing. Other activities include flour milling, distilling, brewing and wood-working. In 1812, Smolensk (often referred to as the "western key to Russia" or "foremost guardian of Moscow") lay on the route of Napoleon's armies advancing on Moscow, and again in 1941, before the eastward advance of Hitler's armies; it was razed to the ground on both occasions. Its population increased by 31 per cent between 1970 and 1979.

Kaluga (population: 265,000)
Kaluga is a machine-building centre and railway junction on the Oka River, 145 km south-west of Moscow. Railway rolling stock (diesel locomotives), electrical, telephone and telegraph equipment, matches, glass and leather are among its varied products.

Kostroma (population: 255,000)
Situated on the left bank of the River Volga, 320 km north-east of Moscow, Kostroma is an old wood-working and linen centre with, in addition, footwear, engineering (mechanical excavators), flour, flax-seed oil and shipbuilding industries.

Rybinsk (population: 239,000)
A port on the River Volga at the southern terminal of the Volga-Baltic waterway (Mariinskiy Canal System), Rybinsk lies at the south-east end of the Rybinsk Reservoir and functions as a trading and transhipment centre for timber, oils, grains, building materials and fish. Local industries include sawn timber, matches, linen, aircraft engines, ships and agricultural machinery. The local hydro-electric station and piped natural gas are important elements in the energy supply of the city.

Podolsk (population 202,000)
Situated 25 km south of Moscow, Podolsk is a rapidly expanding industrial town with heavy engineering enterprises, electrical engineering works, a tin smelter and a reduction plant for magnesium and titanium.

Lyubertsy (population: 160,000)
Lyubertsy specialises in the manufacture of farm machinery and the weaving of worsteds and fine woollens.

2. NORTH-WEST ECONOMIC REGION

Leningrad is the supra-dominant centre of this vast peripheral region (*see* Fig. 109), although economic and population growth rates are now higher in certain other places in the region such as Arkhangelsk, Cherepovets and Murmansk. The North-West Region extends 2,300 km from Pskov Oblast in the south-west to Nenets AO in the north-east and it is 1,150 km from Murmansk in the north to Cherepovets in the south (*see* Fig. 110). It is as large as Spain, Portugal, Italy and the Benelux countries combined. On this account alone it is to be expected that it contains many obvious internal physical and economic contrasts, e.g. Leningrad Oblast (manufacturing) and Komi

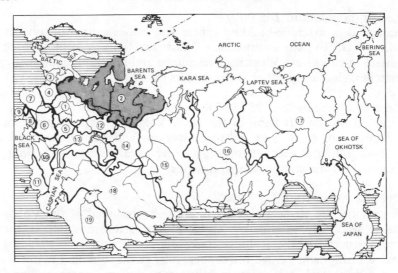

Fig. 109. Soviet Union: location of North-West Economic Region.

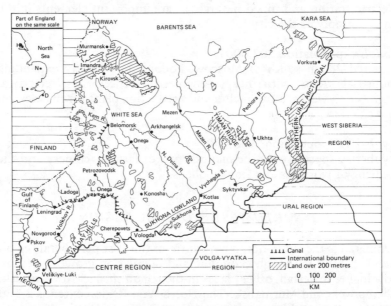

Fig. 110. North-West Economic Region.

ASSR (extractive industry), but commonality of the Leningrad area with its wide range of industries of all-Union and international importance and the industrial districts of the Centre Region (*see* pp. 184-7) provides justification for its inclusion in the North

Central European Russia Macro-Region. The common manufacturing specialisations of the Moscow, Leningrad, Baltic and Belorussian industrial districts make up the core of the macro-region.

The North-West as a whole is not as well integrated as the Centre in terms of economic linkages. In the sparsely populated Arkhangelsk Oblast and Komi ASSR, industrial centres and nodes are isolated in the *tayga;* the Leningrad Oblast, by contrast, has a diversified industrial complex concentrated in the Leningrad node (*see* Tables 34 and 35). This node plays a key role in shaping the territorial-production unity of the north-west, with a system of linkages fanning out from Leningrad to all other industrial centres of the region and reverse linkages extending back to Leningrad. The Cherepovets area, with its iron and steel plant also provides a substantial integrating role.

TABLE 34. NORTH-WEST ECONOMIC REGION:
ADMINISTRATIVE UNITS, THEIR POPULATION AND DENSITY

Area: 1,662,800 km²
Population (1979):   13,275,000

Administrative unit	Area (000 km²)	Population (000, 1979)	Density (persons per km²)	Percentage urban
Arkhangelsk Oblast	587	1,467	3	72
(incl. Nenets AO)	177	47	0.3	60
Komi ASSR	415	1,118	3	71
Karelian ASSR	172	736	4	78
Vologda Oblast	146	1,310	9	59
Murmansk Oblast	145	965	7	89
Leningrad City ⎫	86	4,588 ⎫	71	100
Leningrad Oblast ⎭		1,519 ⎭		64
Pskov Oblast	55	850	15	55
Novgorod Oblast	55	722	13	65

PHYSICAL ASPECTS

Structure, relief and drainage
The physical landscape is everywhere dominated by the effects of the Pleistocene glaciations. North of a line from Leningrad to Lake Ladoga to Lake Onega, Pre-Cambrian granites, peneplaned schists and gneisses belonging to the structural core of the country (the Fenno-Scandian Shield) were subjected to a succession of glacial advances and retreats. Bare rock surfaces, ice-scoured basins, whale-backed drumlins and sinuous eskers bear witness to glacial action. Everywhere there are lakes, big and small, named and unnamed, and

TABLE 35. NORTH-WEST ECONOMIC REGION:
TOWNS WITH OVER 150,000 INHABITANTS IN 1979

| Town | | Population in thousands | | Percentage increase |
		1970 (census)	1979 (census)	1970-79
Leningrad	proper	3,550	4,073	15
	with suburbs	3,987	4,588	15
Arkhangelsk		343	385	12
Murmansk		309	381	23
Cherepovets		189	266	41
Vologda		178	237	33
Petrozavodsk		192	234	22
Novgorod		128	186	45
Pskov		127	176	39
Syktyvkar		125	171	37

a labyrinth of rivers and waterways (see Fig. 110). The plateau-like Khibiny Mountains, 600-1,200 m high in the Kola Peninsual are an exception in a monotonously rolling landscape of lakes and swamps where heights above 450 m are rarely attained.

Where the southern edge of the Archaean Fenno-Scandian Shield abuts upon limestones and clays of Cambrian and Silurian age, a zone of differential erosion is marked by a prominent escarpment which runs south of Leningrad and westwards to near the Estonian coast where it is known as the "Glint". The broad depression at the base of the escarpment is occupied by lakes, of which the largest are Ladoga and Onega, covering 17,700 and 9,600 km² respectively.

To the south the countryside is one of low plateaux and marshy lowlands (Volkhov-Lovat), strewn with such glacial depositional forms as moraines and eskers and with sandy deposits and irregular heaps of detritus. The Valday Hills in the extreme south-east of the region constitute a prominent morainic ridge rising to over 200 m.

Drainage systems have been disturbed by glaciation and seem to have little obvious pattern. Rivers are immature and there are frequent rapids and waterfalls which afford potential for hydro-electricity production. The Gulf of Finland is linked with the Volga system via a series of canals and rivers. The waterway follows the River Neva from Leningrad, then skirts the southern shores of Lake Ladoga to the River Svir, thence via Lake Onega, the Vytegra and Kovsha Rivers to the River Sheksna which joins the Volga at Rybinsk Reservoir. The number of locks on this, the old Mariinsk Canal System, has been reduced from thirty-eight to seven, and the whole waterway completely renovated and renamed the Volga-

Baltic Canal, capable of handling ships with loads up to 2,700 tonnes. Another waterway link via the Sheksna River, Lake Kubenskoye and the Sukhona joins the Northern Dvina River. Ocean-going vessels can travel from the Gulf of Finland to the White Sea along the White Sea-Baltic Canal, but the route is reported to be little used. (Naval vessels as large as cruisers, however, are said to make use of this route between the Baltic and the White Sea (*see* p. 121.) The Volkhov River, flowing to Lake Ilmen and thence to Lake Ladoga once formed part of the historical "White Road" or "Water Road from the Varangians to the Greeks" (*see* p. 131) from the Baltic and Gulf of Finland to the Black Sea and Byzantium. The hydro-electricity generating station on this river is the largest of six supplying power to Leningrad.

Eastwards to the Urals is the Russian Lowland or East European Plain. It is a region of low and monotonous relief that owes its character in large measure to a very thick mantle of Quaternary glacial deposits rather than to any pre-Pleistocene processes. Except in the worn-down Palaeozoic Timan Ridge, stretching from Chesh-skaya Bay to the source of the Vychegda River, and in the Ural-Pay-Khoy Range in the extreme east, the countryside is mainly below 200 m. Broad valley-like depressions and minor relief features (moraines, eskers or fluvio-glacial material) are largely concealed by the ubiquitous boreal forest (*tayga*). The two headwaters of the Northern Dvina, the Vychegda and Sukhona Rivers, occupy an ancient valley formed by the damming of northbound drainage by the edge of the Pleistocene ice sheet. A long low ridge — which appears to be a terminal moraine — running along the southern boundary of the region, is the main water parting between rivers draining northwards to the Arctic and those draining southwards to the Caspian.

Drainage here is largely northwards to the Arctic, by the Northern Dvina and Mezen systems in the western section and the Pechora system in the eastern part. As few railways have been built, the rivers and their tributaries provide the chief means of communication. Unfortunately, their usefulness is curtailed by the long period during which they are frozen, six months each year in the south-west and over eight months in the north-east. Since the ice-free period is longer in the upper, more southerly courses of the rivers, interior navigation commences long before the river mouths are open for navigation.

Climate, soils and natural vegetation
In the western portion of the region, and different from most other parts of the Soviet Union, the climate is characterised by a relatively high frequency of maritime temperate air. It is also very strongly

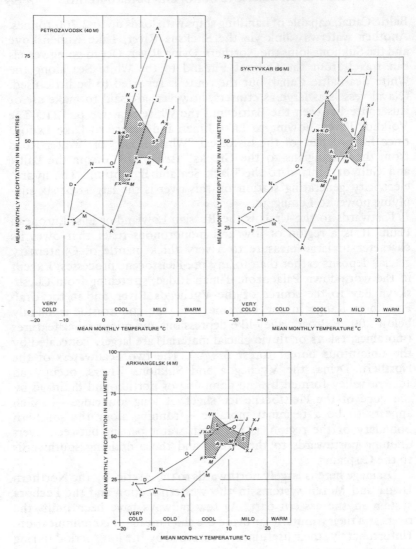

Fig. 111. Hythergraphs for Petrozavodsk, Syktyvkar and Arkhangelsk (Kew, London, shaded).

influenced by Arctic air masses which frequently enter the region. For its latitude, this is the most temperate part of the country, experiencing the least extremes. Even so, winters are long, cold and raw. Temperatures in winter average −7.5 °C near the head of the Gulf of Finland (Leningrad), −8 °C along the north coast of the Kola Peninsula (Murmansk) due to the ameliorating influence of the North Atlantic Drift and −11 °C near Cherepovets (*see* Fig. 111).

Skies are frequently overcast and there is much mist and fog. Occasional invasions of milder, moister air from the Atlantic cause temporary thaws (*ottepeli*). Summer days here are long and cool, with mean temperatures during the period April-October ranging from 4 °C to 10 °C, but in July average mean temperatures range from 15.6 °C in the south to 10 °C in the north. Precipitation aggregates range from about 635 mm on the Baltic Coast to less than 400 mm along the White Sea; maxima occur during the period July-September. Winter snow lies for about four months in the southwest and more than six months in the north, although depths rarely exceed 50 cm.

> On clear frosty nights is seen (from the Khibin
> mountains) a bright and beautiful aurora borealis.
> The whole sky blazes with multicoloured ribbons
> and shafts of light which continually change form
> and irridesce with endless hues.

> G.D. Rickhter, 1946.

The east and north-east of the region differs from the western portion primarily in its increased degree of continentality. Maritime temperate air masses occur only half as frequently as they do further west and maritime Arctic air masses are less common. Winters are prolonged and severe and accompanied by a heavy snowfall. January mean temperatures fall to −18° to −22 °C. Summers are short and cool, last no more than three to four months, and are broken by recurrent indraughts of polar continental air and associated cold spells. Summer warmth falls off latitudinally (July mean temperatures range from 18 °C in the south to 7° to 10 °C in the north). Spring has a sudden onset, and like autumn is a fleeting season (*see* Fig. 111). The northern part of the region tends to be generally cloudy, especially in the summer; it is prone to autumnal and winter gales and these give rise to snow blizzards. Except in the Urals, where annual aggregates of over 800 mm are received, precipitation is slight and rarely more than 400-500 mm. Though maxima occur in the period July-August in association with thunderstorms, winter precipitation gives rise to appreciable snow cover (depths 60-80 cm in the east and centre of the region) which lasts five and a half months in the south and over eight months in the north. Snow melt in the spring takes place over a period of four to five weeks, although individual days of maximum melting can produce as much as a 5 mm layer of water, conditions that are conducive to flooding. Floods, low rates of evaporation and, in the north, permafrost (there is a layer of frozen subsoil 1 to 2 m below the surface in the delta of the Pechora) together give rise to waterlogging and vast expanses of swamp and bog.

(Novosti)

Fig. 112. Malozemelskaya Tundra on the mainland Arctic coast south of Novaya Zemlya was part of the source area of the Oka glaciation.

The whole of the northern part of the region, including the Kanin Peninsula and most of the Kola Peninsula, lies within the tundra, e.g. Malozemelsk Tundra (*see* Fig. 112), Bolshezemelsk Tundra. This treeless expanse supports a dense growth of mosses, lichens, a few dwarf herbs and stunted shrubs. In some sheltered spots there are small copses of Arctic birch and similar dwarf species. The whole of the tundra is underlain by infertile aquepts (inceptisols) and perenially frozen ground. Southwards the tundra merges into a vast, dense *tayga* (boreal forest) of predominantly spruce, pine and birch in the west, fir, cedar and larch in the east, extending from the western border of Karelia to the Urals in eastern Komi ASSR. The forest is interspersed by immense tracts of marsh and bog and underlain by infertile and waterlogged aquods (spodosols), frequently in permafrost conditions. South-west of an approximate line from the southern shore of the Gulf of Finland to Vologda, there is a transition to mixed forests of broadleaf deciduous hardwoods and coniferous evergreen softwoods. These have been cut over many years and where the land is reasonably drained agriculture is practised. But soils are poor, well-leached and infertile and require heavy fertilising to keep them productive.

THE ECONOMY

Agriculture
Agriculture reaches its economic northern limits within the North-

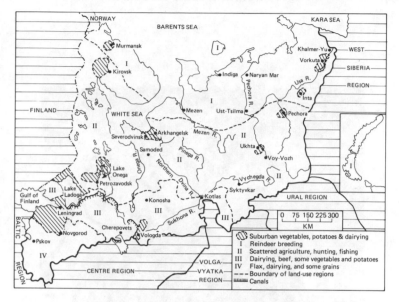

Fig. 113. North-West Economic Region: agricultural land-use regions.

West region. It is restricted by the harsh physical environment (the growing season for crops is short and cool, nowhere are there more than three months with temperatures above 10 °C) and the widespread forest cover. Modest amounts of small grains — primarily rye, oats and barley — flax, potatoes and cabbages are grown on small patches of cleared ground, usually along the southern margins of the *tayga* in the south-western oblasts of Pskov, Novgorod and Vologda (*see* Fig. 113). What agriculture there is is based heavily on animal husbandry, mainly dairying and pig raising. The livestock spend the greater part of the year indoors, though some use is made of riverside meadows in the summer. Fishing is also carried on and there are reindeer, both wild and domestic (wild reindeer are the caribou of North America) in the tundra and boreal forest (*see* Fig. 114).

Fishing

In the Barents and White Seas a continuation of the warm North Atlantic Drift meets the cold waters of the Arctic, and there is a supply of plankton (minute algae, protozoa, rotifers, crustacea, molluscs, etc.) which provide food for fish. Murmansk Oblast and Karelia are important for their fishing industry which is of national rather than local significance. Cod, herring, capelin and sea perch are caught and landed at the ice-free ports of Murmansk and Port Vladimir. Here fish is canned and processed, and there are ancillary

Fig. 114. Reindeer herding in the Murmansk Region. Reindeer, used for draught
purposes and pack animals as well as meat, milk and skins, are raised extensively
in the tundra and *tayga* of the USSR where they number about 2½ million.

activities of glue-making, cod-liver oil extraction and the making of
fish meal. Kandalaksha, Kem, Belomorsk and Arkhangelsk are
important fishing centres on the White Sea.

Forestry
Forest is the principal natural resource of the region which ranks
first in Soviet timber production. Karelia and Leningrad Oblast are
part of the traditional home of the Russian timber industry, but
the main harvested areas now are to the east of the White Sea in
Arkhangelsk Oblast (Northern Dvina Basin) and in Komi ASSR
(Pechora Basin). The more accessible Karelian forests have been cut
over more than those further east and the lower quality timber left
there is utilised primarily for the extraction of cellulose fibre used
in paper production. The North-West Economic Region now provides about a third of the country's paper and paperboard. The
better quality timber further east is cut during the winter from
stands along the Northern Dvina, Mezen and Pechora Rivers and

their tributaries and floated downstream on the spring thaw to collecting points and saw mills at Arkhangelsk, Kotlas, Mezen and Naryan-Mar. Here it is sawn into planks, pit props, railway sleepers and telegraph poles, pulped for paper-making and used for wood chemicals and turpentine.

Sawmills abound and pulp, paper, plywood, furniture, prefabricated houses, cellulose, matches, plywood and laminates are produced at centres along the Murmansk-Leningrad railway (e.g. Petrozavodsk, Segezha), around Lake Onega (e.g. Kondopoga), and Lake Ladoga (e.g. Petrokrepost, Lakhdenpokhya, Olonets), at Leningrad and Murmansk, along the Vologda-Arkhangelsk railway (e.g. Plesetsk, Konosha), the Pechora railway from Konosha to Novyy Port via Vorkuta (e.g. Kotlas) and along a branch line southeast up the Pechora railway (e.g. Syktyvkar).

Overseas timber markets are served by Arkhangelsk (the largest sawmilling centre of the Soviet Union), Severodvinsk, Murmansk, Leningrad, Belomorsk, Onega, Mezen and some lesser ports; domestic markets within the Soviet Union are served by timber-sawing and wood-working centres such as Vologda, Kotlas, Syktyvkar and Konosha by means of inland railway links.

Mineral extraction

Ever-increasing attention is being directed to the exploitation of the mineral wealth of the North-West Economic Region so much so that mining is now one of. its keynotes. In the Khibiny Mountains of the Kola Peninsula are to be found the largest reserves of apatite (phosphate rock) in the world (*see* Fig. 115). These, in turn, form the raw material base of a phosphatic fertiliser industry in the Kirovsk-Apatity district, in Leningrad, 800 km to the south, and in other superphosphate plants in the European part of the country. Much apatite is shipped 60 km northwards for export through Murmansk, the remainder being railed southwards. Kola apatite supplements local phosphate rock used in the ammonia phosphate industry at Kingissepp in Leningrad Oblast. Associated with apatite waste are nephelite ores, a source of alumina, potash and soda, which are used in chemical enterprises in Kirovsk, Kandalaksha and Volkhov. The Kola Peninsula is also one of the nation's producers of nickel, copper and cobalt ores (Nikel, Zapolyarnyy and Monchegorsk). Different from apatite and nephelite which, as raw materials, are mainly processed elsewhere, the integrated stages of mining and processing to the finished metals of nickel, copper and cobalt ores are completed within the area.

Bauxite, exploited first at Boksitogorsk, 200 km south-west of Leningrad, was the raw material base for alumina plants in Volkhov (where hydro-electric power was available) and Boksitogorsk, opened

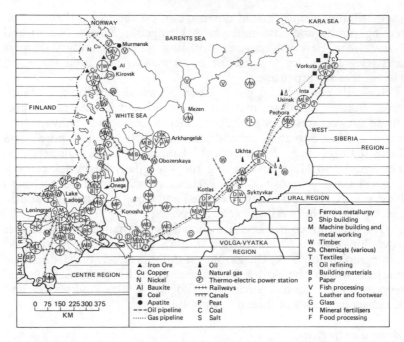

Fig. 115. North-West Economic Region: mineral resources, railways and industrial structure of towns.

within six years of each other, in 1932 and 1938 respectively. The former and another more recent alumina plant, constructed at Pikalevo in 1959, now use nephelite, while the Boksitogorsk plant relies on a major bauxite source in the northern Onega River valley near Plesetsk in Arkhangelsk Oblast. Alumina from these plants is reduced to aluminium at Nadvoitsy in Karelia, and Kandalaksha (where locally generated hydro-electric power is available), and also at Volkhov. While still important in the Soviet aluminium industry, the North-West Economic Region has been superceded in recent years by Siberia which, relying on alumina from the Urals and Kazakhstan, is able to capitalise on cheap hydro-electricity generated at major sites at Shelekhov, Krasnoyarsk and Bratsk.

Scattered deposits of low-grade iron ore (30-35 per cent iron content) occur in Karelia (Mezhozyorskoye, Pudozhgorsk, Kostamukshshkoye) and in the Kola Peninsula (Olenegorsk-Kirovogorsk, Kovdor). After enrichment (concentration), they are either railed over 1,300 km southwards to the Cherepovets iron and steel complex in Vologda Oblast or else exported through Murmansk. Kola and Karelia iron-ore producing areas supply the current ore requirements of Cherepovets which, in turn, provides practically all of the steel needs of the North-West Economic Region.

Fuels

The energy resources of the region include peat, lignite, coal, oil, natural gas and hydro-electricity. Coal was discovered along the western flank of the Ural Mountains and within the upper Pechora Basin (Komi ASSR) during the 1930s, but full-scale development did not commence until 1942, after a railway line had been laid by prisoners of war and political prisoners between Kotlas and Vorkuta (*see* Fig. 115), at a time during the Second World War when the Donets coalfield of the Ukraine had been overrun by the Germans. The coals are bituminous and some are of coking quality. Production in 1979 was 28.9 million tonnes or about 4 per cent of the all-Union total. Reserves are considered to be greater than those of the Donbass and their quality is as high. However, the fact that they lie deep beneath lacustrine and marine sediments in a sub-Arctic region of extremely rigorous climate and permafrost presents serious technical difficulties for their exploitation. The main mining centre is Vorkuta; Inta, Yunyaga, Gornyatskiy and Khalmer-Yu are subsidiary centres. Some of the coal is sent to Labytnangi for Arctic shipping, or by rail to cities in north European USSR and to the Cherepovets iron and steel plant 1,600 km away on the north shore of Rybinsk Reservoir.

Oil-bearing strata are being tapped near Ukhta, Usinsk and Voy-Vozh in Komi ASSR (*see* Fig. 115). Some of the oil is refined at Ukhta, though the bulk is conveyed by pipeline to refineries at Yaroslavl and Kirishi, 100 km south-east of Leningrad. Natural gas, not associated with petroluem, occurs near Voy-Vozh and Dzhebol. This is transported westwards to consuming areas along the major transmission corridors constructed to convey natural gas from the Medvezhye field in West Siberia to European USSR, thence, via Minsk, to the Czechoslovak border.

Peat and lignite, once important in local thermo-electric generating stations (e.g. Kirovsk power station serving Leningrad), have been superceded by coal, oil and natural gas from Vorkuta, Ukhta and Voy-Vozh respectively and by supplies brought in by rail or pipeline from further afield. Shale-oil gas from Slantsy (Leningrad Oblast) and Kohtla-Järve (Estonia SSR) is used in the Red October and Dubrovsk generating stations in Leningrad. Hydro-electricity is generated on the Volkhov, Svir, Narva and Vuoksa Rivers in the Karelian ASSR, and on several rivers south and west of Murmansk (which is not in the permafrost zone). On the Tuloma River, for example, there is a joint Finnish-Soviet project feeding power to Murmansk and another joint Norwegian-Finnish-Soviet scheme on the relatively small Pasvik River. The rivers employed are generally small and their hydro-electric potential a mere fraction of that of major Siberian rivers such as the Yenisey or Angara. The Kola

Peninsula has the most northerly electric grid transmission system in the world. It supplies Leningrad, where it supplements locally generated thermal electricity based on Vorkuta and Donbass coals. The presence of hydro-electricity generating stations in places gives rise to small industrial nuclei. Kandalaksha and Nivskiy in the Kola Peninsula have aluminium smelters using hydro-electricity generated on the Neva River. The Volkhov station provides power for aluminium smelters utilising bauxite mined at Boksitogorsk, 100 km to the south-east, and nephelite mined in the Kola Peninsula, 1,600 km to the north. The use of nuclear power in the Soviet Union to generate electricity is being rapidly expanded. It now accounts for 6 per cent of all the electricity generated. There are three stations in the North-West Region, one at Sosnovyy Bor, 80 km west of Leningrad (the world's largest), the other two in Murmansk Oblast (an area lacking in both fossil fuels and large rivers) referred to as the Kola and Polyarnyye Zori stations respectively.

Transport

The supply of energy for driving machinery and the movement of raw materials from source to processing and manufacturing centres and thence to consuming centres or export points presupposes an adequate transportation system. In this respect and considering its high latitude the North-West Region is reasonably well endowed. Leningrad is the chief nodal point with seven major railway lines focussing on it (*see* Fig. 115).

The 650 km line to Moscow, the first important railway to be built in Russia and one of the straightest in the world, was completed in 1842. It is electrified throughout and the Leningrad-Moscow journey can be completed in as little as five and a half hours, though six to eight hours is the more common time. The 1,500 km long Leningrad-Murmansk (Kirov) line, the first major piece of railway construction under the Soviets, not only aids the exploitation of Kola-Karelia but also enables Murmansk to function as the outport for Leningrad during the winter.

The Kirov line and the Moscow-Vologda-Arkhangelsk (Northern) line, completed in 1897, were linked by another between Belomorsk and Obozerskaya. This was built during the Second World War to provide a detour route between Murmansk and Moscow avoiding the German-occupied Leningrad region. Another railway construction arising from the special needs of the wartime economy at a time when the Germans had overrun the Donbass and were beseiging Leningrad was the line built north-eastwards from the Northern line through Kotlas to Vorkuta (Pechora line) to bring coal to the industrial areas of the Centre Economic Region. The branch of the Pechora line at Mikun northwards through Koslan to Yertom, and the railway from Arkhangelsk south-east to Karpogory, facilitate the exploitation and expansion of the untapped timber reserves in the upper reaches of the Mezen River, with the west Karelian line running north of Souyarvi parallel to the Kirov line associated with the expansion of the Karelian timber industry.

The pipelines for the transport of oil and gas from the Komi ASSR and elsewhere in the USSR to Yaroslavl, Cherepovets, Leningrad and other consuming centres have been noted above (*see* p. 121).

The deep-water Baltic-White Sea waterway, an important water transit route completed in 1933, enables merchant ships to ply between the White and Baltic Seas with bulk freights such as timber, apatite, iron ore and granite. Naval vessels also pass along this route from the major naval base at Leningrad and others on the Baltic to the strategic base at Murmansk and thence to the Arctic and Atlantic Oceans beyond.

Rivers have long provided routes through the northlands. Richard Chancellor's discovery of the White Sea in the sixteenth century opened up an important water route to Moscow via the Northern Dvina, the Sukhona and Vologda rivers, and inaugurated a flourishing trade between England and Russia through the Muscovy Company (*see* p. 140). This route was eclipsed when the Baltic outlet via St Petersburg (Leningrad) was opened in the eighteenth century, but it attained a new importance with the rising demand for timber. The Northern Dvina River system now provides a most valuable means of transporting timber from the otherwise inaccessible *tayga* to the coast.

The few roads that exist are generally unmetalled or poorly surfaced, and are usually impassable in winter and spring. They carry little or no long-distance traffic.

Manufacturing

The North-West Economic Region is basically a supplier of timber, paper, cellulose, ferrous and non-ferrous minerals to other regions. Lumbering and wood-working industries are important everywhere. There are major centres of the timber-sawing industry at Leningrad, Arkhangelsk, Onega, Mezen, Kem, Kotlas, Vologda, Belomorsk and Kovda, of the furniture industry in Leningrad and Petrozavodsk and of the pulp and paper industry in Kondopoga and Segezha. About a third of the total paper production of the USSR takes place in the North-West Region, with Karelia especially important. The large integrated plant at Cherepovets on the Rybinsk Reservoir using long-haul raw materials, coking coal from Vorkuta and iron ore from the Kola Peninsula, provides the iron and steel needs of

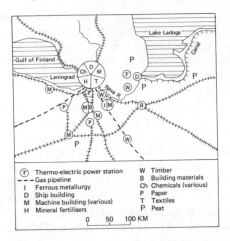

Fig. 116. Leningrad industrial region.

the region, including the steel converters in Leningrad. Vyartsila in Karelia makes high-grade steel by the electric arc process. Aluminium refining is undertaken at Volkhov, Kandalaksha and Nadvoitsy. However it is the light-to-medium, high quality manufacturing that sets the keynote and it is in this context in particular that Leningrad is the supra-dominant centre (*see* Fig. 116).

With a long history of manufacturing, related to the city's role as capital of the Russian Empire from the eighteenth century until 1918, a skilled labour force and a large market, Leningrad provides a range of high value, precision manufactures. The *Elekstrosila* plant is one of the biggest producers of electrical equipment in the world (turbines, turbogenerators, alternators, etc.) and absorbs nearly half of the entire labour force of the city. The remainder are largely employed in the Lenin Plant for machine tools, in the Red Triumph rubber works (the biggest in Europe), in chemicals (providing half of the Russian output of fertilisers, plastics, paints and synthetic rubber), textiles, food-processing, shipbuilding, light industries (clothing, footwear, porcelain) and printing. Leningrad is also the largest centre for book production in the Soviet Union. The bulk of the goods is manufactured from raw materials imported into the city either from abroad or from within the Union, e.g. timber from Karelia, apatite from Kola.

Metal products from iron and steel works at Cherepovets on the shore of the Rybinsk Reservoir, derived from Kola Peninsula iron ore, and are sent to Leningrad for fabrication. Chemical industries (superphosphate and nitrogenous fertilisers) also at Cherepovets, based initially on Kola apatite and coke-oven gases, are now fed by natural gas from Ukhta in the Komi ASSR and from Tyumen Oblast in the north of West Siberia. Engineering, transport equipment, barge-making and shipbuilding are located at Arkhangelsk and Murmansk, while high technology types of industry requiring highly skilled and adaptable manpower are found in small industrial centres, e.g. machine tools (Vologda), tractors (Petrozavodsk), telephone equipment (Pskov), chemicals (Novgorod).

POPULATION AND CITIES

The Leningrad-Novgorod region has long been a meeting-place for Russians of Slavonic speech, Scandinavians of Teutonic speech and Karelians of Finnish speech. It is also transitional between the land-based cultures of interior USSR and the sea-based cultures of the Baltic SSRs. In the Middle Ages both Novgorod and Pskov were flourishing centres on the "Water Road" (*see* p. 000) when Moscow was comparatively isolated and unimportant. However, both were eclipsed when, after the acquisition of the Neva area from the Swedes, St Petersburg (Leningrad) was founded at the beginning of the eighteenth century.

Over 46 per cent of the 13.3 million of the North-West Economic Region live in Leningrad Oblast. Rural populations are sparse and vast areas in the Kola Peninsula, Karelia and northern European Russia are virtually uninhabited. In the northern areas, there is a mixed population of Russians and Karelo-Finns (215,000), the latter speaking their own non-Russian languages. In the north-east the scanty population consists of Nentsy (an intrusive Mongoloid people (30,000)) in the tundra areas and Komi (a Finno-Ugrian group (322,000)) in the *tayga*. There are, however, large numbers of Russians living among them, attracted by the excellence of the timber resources, mineral deposits and fisheries, so that they are continually assimilated with the Russian culture and adopting the Russian way of life. In Arkhangelsk Oblast and the Komi ASSR 60 to 70 per cent of the population live in towns or urban-type settlements; densities are no more than 2 to 3 persons per km^2 in the northlands, 13 to 15 persons in the southern fringe of the region.

Leningrad (population: 4,073,000)
A city of national as well as regional significance, Leningrad is sited on a marshy swamp within three distributaries of the Neva River and between the Gulf of Finland and Lake Ladoga (*see* Fig. 117). The city is laid out to generous standards with long wide streets such as the Nevsky Prospect, and boulevards, huge squares (*see* Fig. 118) and spacious parks, interwoven by canals. Buildings such as the Winter Palace of the tsars (now the Hermitage, home of one of the finest art collections in the world (*see* Fig. 119), St Isaac's

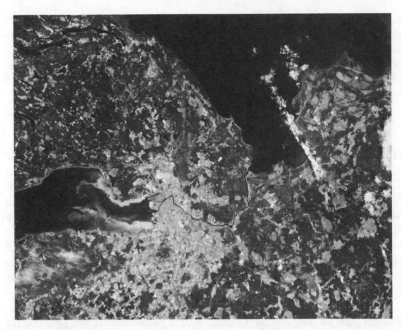

Fig. 117. Landsat photograph of Leningrad on 11th July, 1975, taken from a height of about 900 km. The city stands at the head of the Gulf of Finland and is traversed by the 75 km long Neva River which issues from the south-west corner of Lake Ladoga. Note the railway line to Moscow which runs absolutely straight from the south-east of the city, and the island of Kotlin with the important Soviet naval base of Kronstadt.

Cathedral (*see* Fig. 120) and the Admiralty stand in striking contrast to mammoth modern blocks of flats and sports stadia (e.g. Kirov Stadium) built during the Soviet regime. The blocks of flats are essentially utilitarian and have contributed to the solution of an appalling shortage of houses which was precipitated by the widespread damage inflicted by the Germans during a siege in the Second World War which lasted more than two and a half years (1941-44).

> I love you, Peter's creation,
> I love your severe, graceful appearance,
> the Neva's majestic current,
> the granite of her banks,
> the tracery of your cast-iron railings,
> the transparent twilight, the moonless gleam
> of your still nights,
> when I write and read in my room without a lamp,
> and the huge sleeping buildings in the deserted streets
> are clearly seen, the Admiralty spire is bright,
> and one dawn hastens to succeed another, not letting

Fig. 118. Leningrad: Victory Arch (so named after the defeat of Napoleon in 1812) and the semi-circular complex of the former headquarters of the tsarist military staff fronting the Palace Square, site of the "bloody Sunday" massacre in 1905.

Fig. 119. Leningrad: the Winter Palace, one time winter home of the tsar and his family in what was then called St Petersburg. It is now the State Hermitage Museum, one of the most important art galleries in the world.

Fig. 120. Leningrad: the Cathedral of St Isaac (designed by A. Montferrand in 1818-48) and the equestrian statue of tsar Nicholas I. Leningrad was laid out to generous standards with long wide streets, boulevards, huge squares and spacious parks, interwoven by canals.

> the night's darkness rise to the golden heavens
> and leaving a bare half-hour for the night.
> I love the still air and the frost of your severe winter,
> the sleighs racing on the banks of the wide Neva . . . .*
>
> A.S. Pushkin

Besides its important industrial functions (*see* Fig. 116), Leningrad's admirable position ensures a continuing role as an important point of contact with Western Europe. Although ice-bound for seven months, it is the chief port of the USSR and handles upwards of 700 ships each year. It is also a focal point for road and rail links from the Baltic Republics, Poland, the Ukraine, Moscow, the Urals, Vorkuta, Arkhangelsk and Murmansk.

Leningrad's two and a half centuries' history has been turbulent; of several memorable events, the massacre of 1905, when strikers from the Putilov works (now the vast Kirov metal foundries) were fired on, the "February Revolution" of 1917 and the Bolshevik Revolution of 1917 were outstanding (*see* Fig. 121). Leningrad has been an intellectual and cultural centre since its foundation, and

*This prose translation of *The Bronze Horseman* is taken from the Penguin book of Russian verse.

Fig. 121. The cruiser *Aurora* moored on the Greater Nevka embankment, Leningrad. A cannon shot from the *Aurora* triggered off the storming of the Winter Palace on 7th November, 1917.

continues to house the great national academies, several institutes, schools, libraries and museums.

Arkhangelsk (population: 385,000)
Situated at the mouth of the Northern Dvina River, Arkhangelsk is an important point for shipping connections with the northlands of the Soviet Union and is especially important for the export of timber and wood materials (*see* Fig. 116). Besides its port functions, which date from the end of the sixteenth century, it has timber, fishing, shipbuilding, textile (sacks) and engineering industries.

It is claimed that the port, and that of neighbouring *Severodvinsk* (population 180,000) where submarines are constructed, can be kept open by ice-breakers throughout the severest winters, although the shipping season normally lasts from early May to the end of November only. Nearby *Novodvinsk* is a pulp and paper-milling town. Arkhangelsk is the terminus of the railway from Moscow via Vologda, Konosha and Obozerskiy.

Murmansk (population: 381,000)
At 69° N Murmansk is the USSR's most northerly port and the world's largest polar city (*see* Fig. 115). Its latitude is comparable with those of Jan Mayen Island, central Greenland, Baffin Island and the north coast of Alaska. Warm waters from the Atlantic Drift pass round the north of Norway and keep the port ice-free the year

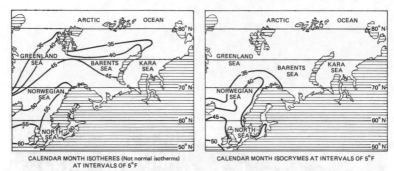

CALENDAR MONTH ISOTHERES (Not normal isotherms)   CALENDAR MONTH ISOCRYMES AT INTERVALS OF 5°F
AT INTERVALS OF 5°F

Fig. 122. Surface sea water temperature conditions affecting the north-west of the USSR: calendar month isotheres and isocrymes.

NOTE: The two charts are based on "Maximum and minimum monthly sea surface temperatures charted from the World Atlas of Sea Surface Temperatures" by Louis W. Hutchins and Margaret Scharff. (*Sears Foundation Journal of Marine Research,* Vol. VI, No. 3, 15th December 1947.)

Individual isotherms were plotted for each month and all twelve plottings superimposed on one chart. The whole area occupied at any time during the year by a particular mean temperature was thus delimited. On drawing the envelope around the area, the equatorial boundary provides the "isocryme" which is the isotherm for the temperature in question at the time of greatest cooling, irrespective of the month in which this occurs. In the same way the poleward boundary provides the "isothere" or isotherm or maximum warming.

The designations "Calendar Month Isotheres" and "Calendar Month Isocrymes" are appropriate, since nominal calendar months are the basis of all calculations rather than the warmest and coldest thirty-day periods. It should be emphasised that the two charts give monthly means: absolute maximum and minimum temperatures of any locality could be several degrees more extreme.

round (*see* Figs. 122 and 123). For this reason Murmansk has proved an important "back-door" from Russia to the West, summer and winter alike. Never was this function more amply demonstrated than during the Second World War, when the port was used to receive vital supplies from allies of the Soviet Union.

Murmansk is sited at the head of a long fiord, the only one on the north coast of the Kola Peninsula, and is the terminus of the railway from Leningrad. It is the principal Soviet fishing port of the western Arctic, base of the Soviet Northern Fleet and also a highly strategic amphibious base with well-equipped shipbuilding yards, repair yards and submarine pens.

Cherepovets (population: 266,000)
Situated at the northern end of Rybinsk Reservoir, Cherepovets has

Fig.123. Murmansk: 200 km north of the Arctic Circle on the shore of the Kola Fjord and the most northerly port in the USSR. Ice-free the year round it is the principal Soviet fishing port of the Western Arctic.

an important iron and steel complex providing steel for engineering industries in the Leningrad-Moscow-Gorkiy areas, and chemical industries based on natural gas from the Ukhta, north-west Siberian, Volga-Urals, Saratov and Central Asian fields (*see* Fig. 115). Population growth rates at this important industrial node have been spectacular since its foundation rising from a pre-war level of 32,000 to 266,000 in 1979.

Vologda (population: 237,000)
Founded in 1147, Vologda has a fine nodal position at the head of navigation of the Northern Dvina system of waterways and at the crossing point of the Moscow-Arkhangelsk Railway with that of the Leningrad-Perm line (*see* Fig. 115). It now functions as an important collecting centre for timber, dairy products and agricultural commodities such as oats, hemp, flax and linseed, and is a producer of machine tools.

Petrozavodsk (population: 234,000)
Situated on Lake Onega, Petrozavodsk represents a concentration of industrial population engaged in ferrous metallurgy and the lumber industry (*see* Fig. 115). Founded by Peter the Great in the early

eighteenth century, it manufactures iron and steel goods, including tractors for the lumber industry, is centre of the timber industry with important saw mills, and has the largest mica plant in the USSR.

Novgorod (population: 186,000)
In ancient Rus, Novgorod on the Volkhov was an important commercial entrepot and intellectual centre (*see* p. 131). Extensively damaged during the Second World War it has since been restored as a historical "monument". It has a nitrogenous fertiliser complex relying on natural gas brought in by pipeline. This industry in its turn has given rise to an appreciable increase in population, e.g. 45 per cent between 1970 and 1979.

Pskov (population: 176,000)
A "suburb" of Novgorod in Kiev Rus times and one of the oldest cities of Russia, Pskov has some light mechanical engineering and linen processing industries.

Syktyvkar (population: 171,000)
An old settlement on the Vychegda River, Syktyvkar is the administrative centre of Komi ASSR. It is a major timber-pulp-paper centre with ship-repair, food, leather and footwear industries.

3. BALTIC ECONOMIC REGION

This is a small but economically advanced region (*see* Fig. 124). It is generally agricultural, but has an expanding and sophisticated industrial zone along the Baltic coast. Embracing the three Baltic republics of Lithuania, Latvia and Estonia together with Kaliningrad Oblast, it stretches westwards to the Baltic Sea and to the international boundary with Poland, eastwards to the south-west boundary of the North-West Economic Region, southward to the northern boundary of the Belorussian Economic Region, and northwards to the Gulf of Finland (*see* Fig. 125). Invasions by Tatars, Teutonic Knights, Swedes, Poles, French and Germans have given the region a chequered history. Furthermore, it has suffered considerable mass movements of population. Lithuania, Latvia and Estonia were three fully independent countries between 1917 and 1940 before being annexed by the USSR (*see* p. 144), and continue to display much ethnic self-awareness. Kaliningrad Oblast (an outlying part of the RSFSR) represents the northern half of the former German province of East Prussia; the German town of Königsberg was renamed Kaliningrad (*see* Tables 35 and 36).

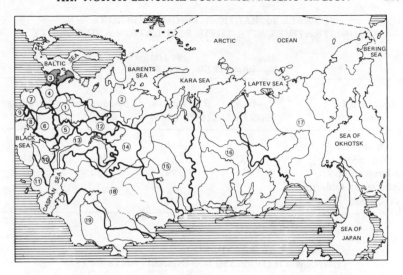

Fig. 124. Soviet Union: location of Baltic Economic Region.

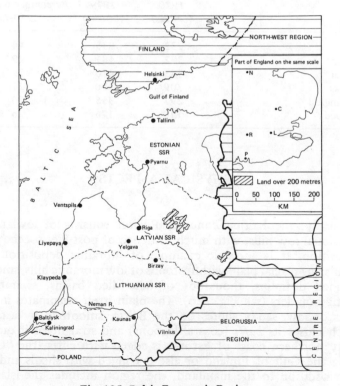

Fig. 125. Baltic Economic Region.

TABLE 36. BALTIC ECONOMIC REGION:
ADMINISTRATIVE UNITS, THEIR POPULATION AND DENSITY

Area: 189,100 km²
Population (1979): 8,149,000

Administrative unit	Area (000 km²)	Population (000, 1979)	Density (persons per km²)	Percentage urban
Estonian SSR	45	1,466	33	70
Latvian SSR	63	2,521	40	68
Lithuanian SSR	65	3,399	52	61
Kaliningrad Oblast (RSFSR)	15	806	54	77*

*1977

TABLE 37. BALTIC ECONOMIC REGION:
TOWNS WITH OVER 150,000 INHABITANTS IN 1979

Town	Population in thousands 1970 (census)	1979 (census)	Percentage increase 1970-79
Riga	732	835	14
Vilnius	372	481	29
Tallinn	363	430	19
Kaunas	309	370	21
Kaliningrad	297	355	20
Klaypeda	140	176	26

PHYSICAL ASPECTS

Relief
Physically, the Baltic Economic Region consists of lowland and occasional low hills, with much evidence of post-Pleistocene glacial deposition. It is a classic example of morainic deposition — an undulating glacial plain with festoons of low morainic hills, smoothly rounded drumlins, thousands of lake-filled basins, swamps and erratic boulders (*see* Fig. 126). The plain itself terminates in many miles of low, sandy shores on the Baltic, smoothed by a current which closes its *haffs* (coastal lagoons) and straightens it out. The rocky northern coast of Estonia is edged with cliffs (the "Glint") along the Gulf of Finland or else is fringed with shoals and reefs. In addition to the mainland, the region includes the islands of

(Novosti)

Fig. 126. A characteristic Latvian landscape — an undulating glacial plain with festoons of low morainic hills, smoothly rounded drumlins, swamps and erratic boulders.

Saaremaa, Hiiumaa and other of the Moonsund archipelago off the entrance to the Gulf of Riga.

Climate, natural vegetation and soils
By Soviet standards, winters in the region are mild. Average January temperatures vary from −3 °C to −1 °C in the Baltic coastlands to −8.5 °C to −7.5 °C inland (*see* Fig. 127). Occasional invasions of milder, moister air from the Atlantic during this season cause temporary thaws (*ottepeli*). Summers are cool, the average July temperature ranging from 14.5 °C to 15.5 °C in the north to about 19 °C in the south. Average annual precipitation is 500-600 mm with a slight summer (May-September) maximum. Winter precipitation comes in the form of snow, which lies for about four months, but depths are generally less than 30 cm.

The soils developed on both the glacial clays and the sands tend to be podzolised and are of varying degrees of fertility. Boulder clays and sediments deposited in ice-dammed lakes are reasonably fertile and well cultivated, but the sandy areas are usually wooded with pine, spruce, oak and maple. Areas of swamp and bog are large and increase in area and frequency towards the south.

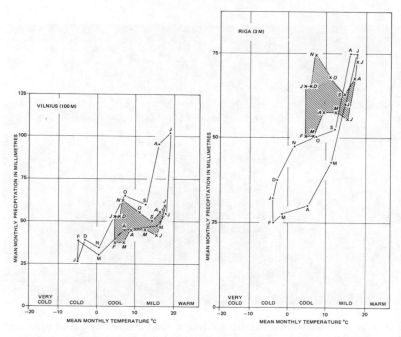

Fig. 127. Hythergraphs for Vilnius and Riga (Kew, London, shaded).

THE ECONOMY

Agriculture and forestry

Agriculture is limited to small, scattered, intensively cultivated fields within the forest, swamp and morainic hills. Main crops are rye, oats, barley, wheat, flax, hemp, potatoes, sugar-beet and also fodder (grass and clover) for cattle (*see* Fig. 128). This is one of the chief flax-growing regions of the USSR. The crop is grown in a six-year rotation with fodder crops. Flax-processing mills and linen mills are located in a number of towns such as Yelgava and Pyarnu but the greater part is sent to linen mills in the Yaroslavl and Kostroma districts east of Moscow. Cattle are raised for both beef and milk, and in recent years there has been an appreciable increase in the number of pigs and sheep. All parts, except the coastal zones, are important for dairy produce, particularly for milk and butter. Such activities as flour-milling, milk-processing, butter and margarine manufacture, meat-packing, fruit and vegetable canning and general food-processing are widely distributed. Much of the produce is sent to other parts of the Soviet Union, in particular to the Leningrad district.

Widespread deciduous and coniferous forests — occupying well

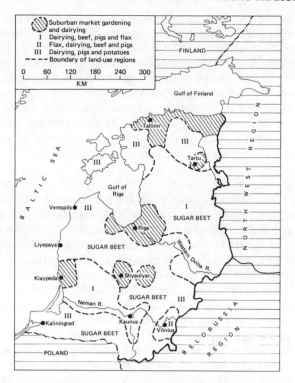

Fig. 128. Baltic Economic Region: agricultural land-use regions.

over a quarter of the total area of the region — have given rise to an important timber industry. Sawn timber, wood veneers, pulp, paper, furniture, matches and prefabricated houses are important products. Two thirds of the world's amber — a fossil resin from extinct coniferous trees — is found in Lithuania SSR and Kaliningrad Oblast.

Fishing industry
Unlike most other parts of the Soviet Union, the three Baltic republics have sea coasts, which are, moreover, less hampered by ice than those near the head of the Gulf of Finland. Leningrad is ice-bound for four or five months from December onwards, but the average duration of the winter freeze at Baltiysk, the outport of Kaliningrad, is only four weeks. With the help of ice-breakers, Baltiysk, Klaypeda, Liyepaya, Ventspils and Tallinn are open to shipping throughout the winter. Riga, at the southern tip of the Gulf of Riga, is ice-bound from the end of December until the middle of April, but the port is kept open for navigation with the assistance of ice-breakers.

People in the west of the region are more bound to the sea than those of other parts of the USSR — many gain their livelihood from fishing and from service in the merchant navy. Trawler fleets and accompanying factory ships from the Baltic ports operate within the Baltic itself, in the North Sea, and in the Atlantic Ocean (around Iceland, Newfoundland, Labrador and Greenland) and land catches of herring, cod and other species. Flatfish, pilchards, sprats and eels are taken in local waters. Smoking, drying, freezing and general fish-processing take place at the Baltic ports prior to long-distance distribution to consumers in the interior of the Union.

Trading and industrial activities
The Baltic republics are transit lands for goods from interior regions such as the industrial Centre and the Volga lands. Traditionally the republics are orientated towards foreign trade. Their ports are the best means of access to the North Atlantic and, for decades before the Revolution of 1917, they played a leading role in Russia's foreign trade. This necessitated good communications with the interior of the country and the railway network linking the ports with inland cities is impressive (*see* Fig. 129). The volume of trade with the non-Communist world (all trade with countries outside the USSR is arranged by the central authorities) and with the Soviet satellite countries of Comecon continues to grow. Riga, Tallinn, Klaypeda and Baltiysk are busy, well-equipped ports; Pyarnu, Ventspils and Liyepaya are smaller, with a more local trade, but they function also as service ports for the Soviet navy and air forces stationed on the Baltic.

The region lacks coal, but shale oil deposits in the north-east of the Estonian SSR are very important (*see* Fig. 130). Almost the entire oil shale production in the Soviet Union originates in Estonia and adjacent Leningrad Oblast. Heavy oil and gas distillation takes place at Kohtla-Järve and the gas is conveyed by pipeline westwards to Tallinn and eastwards to Leningrad. This gas is now supplemented by natural gas brought in from other parts of the USSR. The latter provides the base for a nitrogenous fertiliser industry at Kohtla-Järve. Power generation is supplemented by local peat and wood and by water at a hydro-electric station on the Narva River. There are no metal ores and raw material for industry is not plentiful.

Manufacturing industries tend to specialise in products that combine the application of skill with relatively small quantities of raw material imported from other countries or brought in from other parts of the Union. Many of the Baltic ports are producers of machinery (for food-processing, textiles and precision equipment), electrical and electronic equipment, machine tools, electric rail

Fig. 129. Baltic Economic Region: railways and industrial structure of towns.

coaches, diesel engines, optics and furniture. Despite the absence of local sources of raw material and local markets, there is also a significant production of chemical products such as dyestuffs, rubber goods and fertilisers, together with textile and leather goods. Industries directly related to the sea, such as shipbuilding (merchant and naval), equipment used in shipping, and fish-processing, are also found in these ports (*see* Fig. 130). As a group, the Baltic coast ports constitute a developing industrial area the result more of their maritime position, tradition of foreign trade, and government planning than of the local availability of supplies of energy or raw materials.

POPULATION AND CITIES

The Baltic Region supports 8.1 million people. In Estonia, Latvia and in Kaliningrad Oblast the urban populations are large and above the national average of 62 per cent. Everywhere else in the region the population is essentially rural. In the main, the countryfolk live

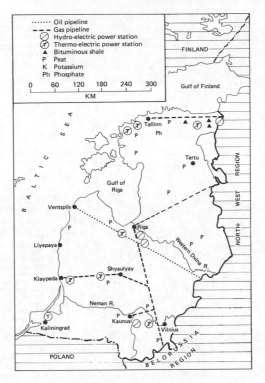

Fig. 130. Baltic Economic Region: mineral and power resources.

in dispersed wooden farmsteads, but with the gradual introduction of collective farms (*kolkhozy*) more and more are living in compact settlements. The region, following its incorporation into the USSR in 1940, experienced sizeable deportations of its indigenous Estonians, Latvians and Lithuanians, while considerable numbers of Russians have since settled there (33 per cent in Latvia, 28 per cent in Estonia and 9 per cent in Lithuania) motivated by higher living standards.

Riga (population: 835,000)
Capital of the Latvian SSR, Riga is the major outlet for western USSR (*see* Fig. 129). It is situated at the southern extremity of the Gulf of Riga above the mouth of the Western Dvina (Daugava) and connected by inland canals with the basins of the Dnieper and Volga Rivers. The city was once an important member of the Hanseatic League and has a long tradition of foreign trade. Exports include timber, flax, wooden goods and dairy produce; imports include sugar, industrial equipment, coal, fertilisers and raw materials for

Fig. 131. Yurmala: a strip of several small popular seaside resorts, backed by pine forest, between the Gulf of Riga and the lower reaches of the Lielupe River, 31 km west of Riga in the Latvian SSR.

local industries. Riga engages in shipbuilding, engineering, electrical and radio goods, buses, tractors, railway rolling stock, fish-processing and the manufacture of chemicals, and is a major rail and airport centre handling traffic with Scandinavia and Western Europe. It also has the famous Riga Yurmala seaside resort area (*see* Fig. 131). Unlike most other peoples of the USSR the majority of those living in Riga are Lutheran by religion.

Vilnius (population: 481,000)
Capital of Lithuanian SSR, Vilnius has experienced a rapid increase in population in recent years. It was once centre of a very much larger historic Lithuania which, shortly after the destruction of Kiev Rus, extended from the Baltic Sea to the Ukraine. The present city bears the imprint of Polish, Jewish, Russian, German and Lithuanian cultures, although its population is now largely Lithuanian and Russian. It is an important inland railway junction with a variety of light industry, devoted mainly to agricultural machinery, machine tools and electrical goods, e.g. computers (*see* Fig. 129).

Tallinn (population: 430,000)
Situated on the Gulf of Finland, Tallinn is the capital of Estonia SSR and a large seaport (*see* Fig. 132). Like Riga it was a member of the Hanseatic League and continues to have important trading

(Novosti)

Fig. 132. Tallinn (formerly Revel), the capital of Estonia SSR, is also its largest seaport. The view shows part of the old town with some of the best preserved examples of medieval urban architecture in the USSR.

functions. Exports from its large port, which serves also as winter outport for Leningrad, include timber, paper and cement; imports include cotton and coal. Local manufacturing industries include textiles, paper-making, cement, timber products, fish-processing, engineering and shipbuilding (see Fig. 129).

Kaunas (population: 370,000)

Like Vilnius, Kaunas has had a chequered history. It was founded in the eleventh century at the confluence of the Neris and Neman Rivers, since when it has suffered several attacks and occupations by Teutonic Knights, Poles, Russians and Germans. It is now the second town of the Lithuanian Republic, having been the temporary capital between the two World Wars, but has only limited administrative functions. Industries in Kaunas include synthetic fibres and textiles, electrical goods, chemical, flour-milling and meat-packing (see Fig. 129).

Kaliningrad (population: 355,000)

Kaliningrad and the oblast of that name were ceded to the Soviet Union by the Potsdam Agreement at the end of the Second World

War. The oblast represents the northern half of the former German province of East Prussia including the town Kaliningrad, the German Königsberg. Both form an outlying part of the RSFSR in which the German population has been replaced by Russians. Kaliningrad and its outport *Baltiysk* together form an important ice-free port and naval base. This most recent Soviet "Window on the West" combines shipbuilding, engineering, railway rolling stock, fish-processing, chemicals and wood-working with important commercial functions (*see* Fig. 129).

Klaypeda (population: 176,000)
An ice-free port on the Baltic coast of the Lithuanian SSR, it attracts a great deal of transit freight and serves as a winter outport for Leningrad and Arkhangelsk. Since 1945 the sizeable German element in its otherwise Lithuanian population has been replaced by Russians.

4. BELORUSSIA ECONOMIC REGION

Life has returned to normal in Belorussia (*see* Fig. 133) after the unprecedented devastation of the countryside, industrial enterprises, villages, towns and cities that occurred during the Second World War. Rebuilding, restoration and investment have provided the republic with fine new cities (*see* Tables 38 and 39), a diversified agriculture and expanding industry.

TABLE 38. BELORUSSIA ECONOMIC REGION:
ADMINISTRATIVE UNITS, THEIR POPULATION AND DENSITY

Area: 207,600 km²
Population (1979): 9,559,000

Administrative unit	Area (000 km²)	Population (000, 1979)	Density (persons per km²)	Percentage urban
Brest Oblast	32.3	1,363	42	45
Gomel Oblast	40.4	1,599	39	52
Grodno Oblast	25.0	1,131	45	42
Minsk City }	40.8	1,276 }	68	100
Minsk Oblast }		1,556 }		35
Mogilev Oblast	29.0	1,249	43	56
Vitebsk	40.1	1,385	35	56

PHYSICAL ASPECTS

Relief
The north-western part of Belorussia is hilly; the south-east has low-lying marshlands and the south is a flat to undulating lowland almost

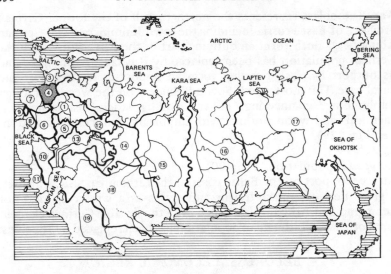

Fig. 133. Soviet Union: location of Belorussia Economic Region.

TABLE 39. BELORUSSIA ECONOMIC REGION:
TOWNS WITH OVER 150,000 INHABITANTS IN 1979

| Town | | Population in thousands | | |
		1970 (census)	1979 (census)	Percentage increase 1970-79
Minsk	proper	907	1,262	39
	with suburbs	917	1,276	39
Gomel		272	383	41
Vitebsk		231	297	29
Mogilev		202	290	43
Grodno		132	195	47
Bobruysk		138	192	40
Brest		122	177	46

entirely covered by forest and peat bog (*see* Fig. 134). Sandy moraines, the Belorussian Hills, extend from north of Brest to Minsk and thence eastwards as the Smolensk-Moscow Ridge. The Belorussia Hills represent the southern limit of the Valday glacial stage and constitute the main Baltic end moraine (*see* p. 19). These hills, 100-130 km wide and 200-300 m high (the highest point is only 345 m) barely interrupt the general flatness of the region but form an important divide between north-flowing (Baltic) and south-flowing (Black Sea) rivers. They also provide a "dry route" or "land

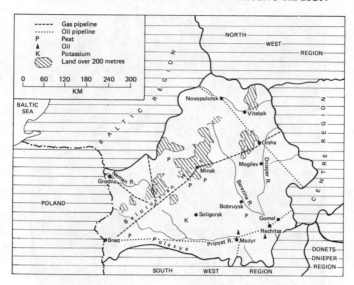

Fig. 134. Belorussia Economic Region: minerals and pipelines.

gate" for road and rail between the Polish People's Republic and the Soviet Union. Along this route, Napoleon's army moved in 1812 and Hitler's army in 1941. The area to the north of the hills is a classic example of morainic deposition — a swampy undulating glacial plain (the Neman-Polotsk Lowlands), with festoons of low morainic hills, smoothly rounded drumlins, thousands of lake-filled basins (the largest is Lake Naroch, 80 km²), swamps and erratic boulders.

South of the Belorussian Hills lie extensive areas of glacial out-wash sands. Along the upper Dnieper and Berezina there are culti-vated lowlands but within the broad shallow trough of the Pripyat River lies the swampy region of Polesye (Pripyat or Pripet Marshes) (*see* Fig. 135). Paustovsky wrote: ". . . . Polesye has remained in my memory as a sad and mysterious country".

Into the trough of Polesye there drained melt-water from the Pleistocene ice sheet, and with it great quantities of deposits of sands and clays, which in such a flat area have poorly developed drainage. This has led to the formation of very extensive swamps — the Pripyat Marshes — through which the streams wind sluggishly. Polesye forms the north-west section of the Dnieper Lowland (*see* p. 265).

Climate, natural vegetation and soils
The moderately continental climate is relatively cool and moist by Soviet standards. Winters usually last three months, with average January temperatures ranging between −4 °C in the south-west to

Fig. 135. Polesye, "land of forest clearing", along the Pripyat River in Belorussia. This is an area of swamp and extensive forests of pine, oak, willow and alder.

—8 °C in the north-east; there are frequent thaws (*ottepeli*). Summers last nearly five months and are cool with average July temperatures 17 °C in the north to 19 °C in the south. The average annual precipitation is between 500 mm in the south and 700 mm in the north with a slight summer (July-August) maximum which often interferes with the harvest (*see* Fig. 136). Winter snow lies for about four months at depths of about 30 cm.

Soils, mainly soddy-podzols (boralfs), are generally poor and there are over 7 million hectares of swamp and marshland. Concerted efforts are being made to drain and reclaim the boglands to provide additional productive land (*see* Fig. 137). Over 1.7 million hectares now have drainage networks, of which about a third have been turned over to cropping, the remainder to pasture.

About a quarter of the republic is covered with mixed forest and bush. Northern Belorussia abounds in fir trees interspersed with oaks and maples; pine and birch groves are also common. Further

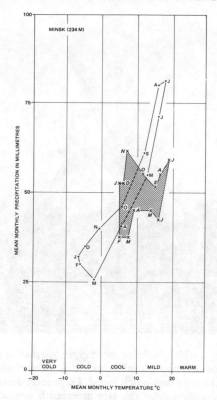

Fig. 136. Hythergraph for Minsk (Kew, London, shaded).

south the woodlands are mostly of pine, with deciduous trees such as oak, hornbeam, aspen, alder and ash. One large and ancient forest, the Belovezh Pushcha, is kept as a state preserve. It is the home of a rare animal, the auroch (i.e. the European equivalent of the North American bison), which has survived since Pleistocene times.

THE ECONOMY

Agriculture and forestry

Only a third of Belorussia is cultivated and agriculture is limited to small scattered fields within the forest, swamp and morainic hills. Main crops are rye, winter wheat, oats, barley and buckwheat (for which Belorussia is famous). This is one of the main flax-growing regions of the USSR, especially the Minsk-Mogilev-Vitebsk area (*see* Fig. 138). The crop is grown in a six-year rotation with fodder crops. Some flax-processing mills and linen mills are located in towns such as Orsha and Vitebsk, but the greater part of the flax crop is

(Novosti)

Fig. 137. The Polesye, which includes the Pripyat Marshes, is a shallow tectonic depression occupied by post-glacial lakes. It is characterised by numerous streams, lakes and swamps and much forest. Large-scale drainage of the marshlands has been proceeding since the late nineteenth century and many new farms have been established on the reclaimed land.

sent to linen mills in the Yaroslavl and Kostroma districts in the Centre Economic Region. There is increasing emphasis on the growing of sugar-beet and vast quantities of potatoes (12½-13½ million tonnes) for human consumption, starch, industrial alcohol, and fodder for pigs are harvested from the drier sandy soils.

There is an intense rearing of poultry, and animal husbandry is increasing. Dairying is important in the north and milk-processing, butter and margarine manufacture, fruit and vegetable canning and general food-processing are widely distributed. The forests provide material for sawn timber, wood veneers, pulp, cellulose, papermaking, furniture, matches and prefabricated houses. The wood products industries which include wood chemicals (turpentine, resins, ethyl alcohol, etc.) are expanding all the time in such centres such as Borisov, Gomel, Bobruysk, Rechitsa, Pinsk, Dobrush and Svetlogorsk.

Industrial resources

Non-agricultural raw materials for industry are in short supply. There

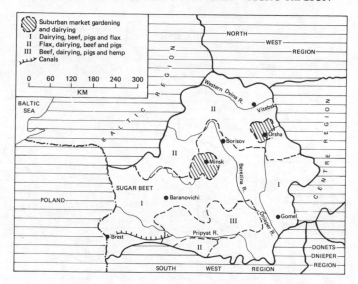

Fig. 138. Belorussia Economic Region: agricultural land-use regions.

are extensive reserves of peat which are used in thermo-electric power stations and for certain chemical products but the share of peat in the fuel budget is decreasing and is now no more than 20 per cent. Oil deposits were discovered near the towns of Ostash-kovichi and Rechitsa in the south-east of the Republic in the mid 1960s and by 1975 oil production had risen to near eight million tonnes. Though but a trifle compared with the vast West Siberian production, this oil has considerable locational value for the western regions of the USSR. Only modest increases are scheduled for this local oil production under the current Five-year Plan. The bulk of the oil requirements for the refineries and petrochemical complexes at Mozyr and Novopolotsk is supplied by West Siberia via the Druzhba ("Friendship") pipeline which extends to Czechoslovakia, Hungary, Poland and also to Germany via its Unecha-Ventspils branch. Major potash deposits in the Starobin area (Soligorsk) in south central Belorussia provide chemical raw material for the production of potassium salts and for a potash fertiliser industry supplying 35-40 per cent of the country's requirements. Though of lower grade than the Urals deposits (Solikamsk-Berezniki), the Belorussian potash deposits, because of their proximity to Eastern Europe, have become a significant export industry.

Industrial activities
Belorussia's appreciable and diversified manufacturing industry is located in a series of widely scattered nodes and centres (*see* Fig. 139).

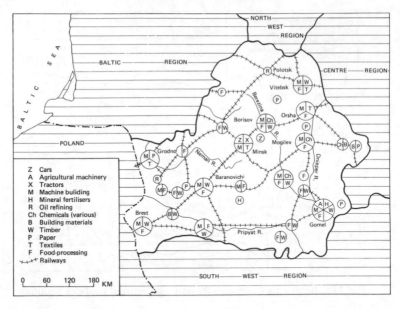

Fig. 139. Belorussia Economic Region: railways and industrial structure of towns.

The chemical industry is linked with the oil refineries at Mozyr and Polotsk and with the potash deposits at Soligorsk. Sulphuric acid, ethyl alcohol, polyethylene, plastics, detergents, synthetic rubber and tyres, and large quantities of fertilisers are produced. Raw materials for both the polyester fibre plants (which produce the fibre known as *lavsan* in the USSR) in Mogilev and the polyamide fibre plant (producing *kapon*, the Soviet nylon-type fibre) in Grodno come from Polotsk, but the nitrogenous fertiliser plant in Grodno is based on natural gas from Dashava in the Ukraine. Belorussia now produced one-sixth of all Soviet man-made fibres.

Machine building and metal working are major industrial developments which have taken place in Belorussia since the Second World War. Heavy duty lorries, tractors, electrical machinery, agricultural machinery, peat cutting machinery, lathes and machine tools are manufactured in Minsk, Vitebsk, Gomel and elsewhere. As in the Baltic Region, such industries rely on the availability of skilled workers, an adequate transport system, and proximity to markets in the Centre Region and other industrial regions of the USSR. Goods such as tractors (20 per cent of Soviet output) and metal-cutting lathes (12 per cent of Soviet production) claim an all-Union market together with markets in Eastern Europe.

POPULATION AND CITIES

The Belorussian Economic Region supports just over nine and a half million people. Over 80 per cent of this number are Belorussians, who, together with the Russians and Ukrainians who have migrated into the republic, constitute the eastern Slavs. Although traditionally agrarian and rural dwellers, ever increasing numbers are working in manufacturing industry and living in towns. Some 35 per cent are employed in industry and about half are now classified as urban dwellers.

Minsk (population: 1,276,000)
Located near the western frontier of the Soviet Union, Minsk is the largest city of the region (*see* Fig. 139). It is one of the oldest towns in Russia and has had a stormy history. It has changed more than once from Russian to Tatar, Polish, Swedish and Lithuanian control. It was situated on Napoleon's invasion route in 1812, and was occupied by the Germans from 1941-44. By the end of the Second World War, the city was in ruins but has since been completely rebuilt.

Minsk is the capital of Belorussia SSR and has enjoyed heavy capitalisation in industry. Among its numerous and varied industries are engineering (lorries, cars, motorcycles, tractors, cranes, machine tools, etc.), refrigerator and radio manufacture, instrument-making, textiles and leather goods. It is one of the fastest growing "million-aire" cities in the USSR (39 per cent increase between 1970 and 1979).

Gomel (population: 383,000)
Like Minsk, Gomel is now restored after complete destruction during the Second World War. It is a regional and commercial centre in south-eastern Belorussia with agricultural engineering, timber and fertiliser industries (*see* Fig. 139).

Vitebsk (population: 297,000)
Situated on the Western Dvina, Vitebsk is yet another town which was severly damaged during the Second World War. Its slow recovery from the degradation of 1944 has been based on timber, linen textiles, food and engineering industries.

Mogilev (population: 290,000)
Situated on the Dnieper, Mogilev was important during Kiev Rus times when the river was a recognised highway. Now its commercial functions are supported by chemical (synthetic fibre), engineering and food-processing industries.

Grodno (population: 195,000)
Situated on the Nieman River and near the Soviet-Polish border, Grodno is a machine-building (heavy duty lorries) and wool-textile centre. Its 47 per cent increase in population in the nine-year intercensal period 1970-79, doubtless the result of rural-urban migration, is noteworthy.

Bobruysk (population: 192,000)
Situated on the Berezina River, Bobryusk has machine-building, motor vehicle (tyre) and wood-working industries.

Brest (population: 177,000)
Situated on the Western Bug River, Brest is an important frontier port and transit point on the main road and railway line between USSR and Poland. It has food-processing, textile and light industries. The town has grown apace in recent years, largely the result of rural-urban migration.

CHAPTER XIII

South European Macro-Region

This macro-region consolidates seven basic economic regions, namely Central Chernozem, Donets-Dnieper, South-West, South, Moldavia, North Caucasus and Trans-Caucasus. With only 6.2 per cent of the total area of the USSR, it contains, nevertheless, 35 per cent of the total population living in urban or urban-type settlements. Aleksandrov *et al.* (1974) credit the macro-region with only 4 per cent of the country's potential fuel and energy, but 31 per cent of its iron ore reserves, 2 per cent of its timber resources and almost 17.5 per cent of its agricultural land. It is the most highly urbanised macro-region, particularly so in the Donets-Dnieper Region where one industrial node passes into another with no clearly defined boundaries. The macro-region is distinguished by an industrial-agrarian economy in which iron and steel, oil, gas, chemicals, machine-building and agriculture share. The economic linkages of the economy are shaped by the large-scale development of the iron and steel industry, machine-building, the oil-gas-chemicals cycle and agro-industrial complexes and integrated by good rail and road networks.

1. CENTRAL CHERNOZEM ECONOMIC REGION

This old region (*see* Fig. 140) of peasant farming has undergone a minor industrial revolution, notably since the Kursk Magnetic Anomaly began large-scale ore benefication and metallurgy has been introduced. The Kursk-Belgorod-Staryy Oskol complex has now developed to rival the Donbass. The highly productive agriculture devoted to the cultivation of cereals (especially wheat), sugar-beet, sunflowers and maize and also to dairying and stock raising is expanding and becoming more specialised.

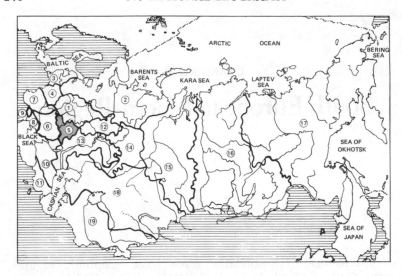

Fig. 140. Soviet Union: location of Central Chernozem Economic Region.

TABLE 40. CENTRAL CHERNOZEM ECONOMIC REGION:
ADMINISTRATIVE UNITS, THEIR POPULATION AND DENSITY

Area: 167,700 km²
Population (1979): 7,797,000

Administrative unit	Area (000 km²)	Population (000, 1979)	Density (persons per km²)	Percentage urban
Kursk Oblast	30	1,399	47	48
Belgorod Oblast	27	1,305	48	53
Voronezh Oblast	52	2,478	48	54
Lipetsk Oblast	24	1,255	52	55
Tambov Oblast	34	1,390	41	49

TABLE 41. CENTRAL CHERNOZEM ECONOMIC REGION:
TOWNS WITH OVER 150,000 INHABITANTS IN 1979

Town	Population in thousands 1970 (census)	1979 (census)	Percentage increase 1970-79
Voronezh	660	783	19
Lipetsk	289	396	37
Kursk	284	375	32
Tambov	230	270	17

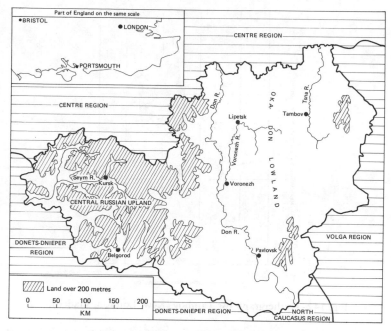

Fig. 141. Central Chernozem Region.

PHYSICAL ASPECTS

Relief and drainage

The western section of the region extends over a southern part of
the Central Russian Upland; the eastern section is part of the flat
Oka-Don Lowland (*see* Fig. 141). The Central Russian Upland
represents a broad upwarp of the Russian Lowland, which slopes
gently westwards to the valley of the Dnieper and more abruptly
eastwards to the valley of the Don. Summits between 250 and 300 m
are severely dissected by a considerable number of recent and
currently developing gullies, some reaching as much as 150 m below
the general surface level. The gullies and ravines are the result of
deforestation, the ploughing of slopes and overgrazing, aggravated
by the showery nature of the summer precipitation. South of Orel
the uplands were not subjected to glaciation and are entirely loess-
covered.

The Oka-Don Lowland is a flat, alluvial area filling the broad
(250 km) depression between the eastern slopes of the Central
Russian Upland and the Volga Heights. During Pleistocene times
it was occupied by a lobe of the ice sheet which extended as far
south as Pavlovsk. Broad river terraces covered with loess-like sandy

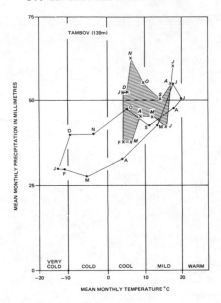

Fig. 142. Hythergraph for Tambov (Kew, London, shaded).

hills are the principal landscape forms. The watershed between the Don and the north-flowing Oka and its tributaries is an insignificant feature.

Most of the region is drained southwards by the Don and its tributaries. Part drains northwards via the Tsna to the Oka while the west of the Central Russian Uplands drains to the Dnieper. Like the River Volga to the east and the Dnieper River to the west, the River Don has a high, steep right bank, as much as 60-80 m above the river in places and a low flat left bank which is frequently flooded in spring.

Climate and natural vegetation
Tambov is at about the same latitude as London, but if taken as representative of the region, its summers are somewhat hotter (warmest month 20 °C) and its winters much colder (coldest month −10.6 °C) than those of London (*see* Fig. 142). Compared with the Centre Region, conditions are also drier; annual precipitation aggregates range from 500 mm in the north-west to less than 400 mm in the south-east (Tambov: 485 mm); maxima come late in spring. With decreasing aggregates comes increasing variability, aggravated further by the high evaporation losses of the summer and the desiccating effects of the occasional dry, hot south-east or south winds (*sukhovey*). Although the amounts are similar in the two seasons, summer precipitation is less effective than winter precipitation in

maintaining the flow of streams and the soil moisture reserve. Winter precipitation comes mainly in the form of snow, which lies for up to four months at mean depths of 30-45 cm. The insulating effect of this shallow snow cover is important for it keeps the soil warm enough to allow autumn-sown seeds to start germinating quite early in the spring.

The greater part of the region lies in the forest steppe (*leso-steppe*) zone, underlain by thick, though somewhat leached, borolls. The true steppe with borolls (chernozems) comes in south-east of Voronezh. Though large forested areas still occur, much forest has been removed and the land turned to agricultural use; practically all the steppe areas are under cultivation, except for occasional reserves like the Central Chernozem State Reserve near Kursk where an area of steppe and indigenous oak forest (*dubravas*) is protected and retained for scientific investigations.

THE ECONOMY

Agriculture

Well over half the region is farmed, with a wide range of crops. The region is transitional between the Centre Region, with its small-scale grain, flax and potato-growing, and the extensive grain and sunflower culture of the Ukraine. Crops include wheat, sugar-beet, maize, hemp, sunflowers (for oil seed), oats, millet, barley, rye, potatoes, vegetables, tobacco, fruits, together with fodder crops for the sheep, pigs and cattle that are kept practically everywhere. Market gardening and dairying form the chief agricultural occupations around all the large towns (*see* Fig. 143).

Under the 1981-85 Five-year Plan, considerable efforts are being made to increase agricultural production in the region by making use of poor quality land. Efforts are being made to improve the land by draining waterlogged areas and increasing the area under irrigation to over one million hectares.

Industrial activities

Agriculture-based industries, such as food- and sugar-processing, the extraction of sunflower oil, flour milling and alcohol production from grain and potatoes, rely on local raw materials; for heavy industry the only local source of importance is the Kursk Magnetic Anomaly (KMA) (*see* Fig. 144) which, accounting for 16 per cent of its total production, is one of the principal sources of iron ore in the Soviet Union. Here, rich bodies of iron ore of more than 50 per cent metallic content lie in pockets interbedded with ferruginous quartzites. Because of the wide extent of the deposits, only the high-grade ores were worked at first and the quartzites were left as spoil.

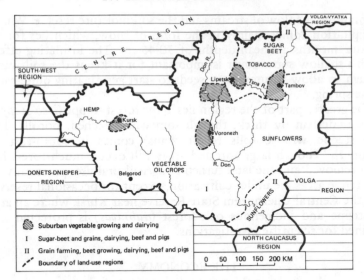

Fig. 143. Central Chernozem Economic Region: agricultural land-use regions.

Fig. 144. Opencast mining of iron ore near Zheleznogorsk (Kursk Magnetic Anomaly).This is one of the principal sources of iron ore in the Soviet Union.

Now, however, with the depletion of the richer ores increasing recourse is being made to the quartzite which is comparatively rich in iron (30-40 per cent). About 45 per cent of the current output consists of high-grade ore, which is available for direct shipping to the blast furnaces of the iron and steel works, and about 55 per cent is concentrate (pellets) derived from the iron quartzite. A planned doubling of ore output is dependent on the availability of more water. The two main centres of production are Gubkin near Staryy Oskol in Belgorod Oblast and Zheleznogorsk, 75 km northwest of Kursk in the oblast of that name, with a territorial-production complex in process of formation on the basis of the KMA. The exploitation of the ores of the KMA by both shaft mines and open-cast methods has revitalised steel production at the old works in Lipetsk and in the modern, integrated mills at Novo-Lipetsk. Relying also on coking coal from the Donbass and the Pechora Basin, these works together now seem destined to become the major producer of steel in European USSR. Ores from the KMA are also sent further afield to Tula, Cherepovets, the Urals, the Donbass and the Comecon countries (e.g. to the Katowice steel plant in Poland).

Manufacturing industry within the Central Chernozem Region was at one time limited, but now, with the availability of oil from the Volga-Urals fields and West Siberia via the Friendship Line, natural gas from the Ukraine, the northern Caucasus and West Siberia, Volga hydro-electricity and Donbass thermal electricity brought in by high voltage transmission lines, and the presence of nuclear power stations at Novovoronezh, 50 km south of Voronezh, and Kurchatov, 50 km west of Kursk, it seems likely that further industrial developments will occur (see Fig. 145). At present the region supplies an ever-increasing range of engineering equipment (railway rolling stock, tractors, lorries, mining machinery and plant for food, agricultural and chemical industries), organic chemicals (potato alcohol, fatty acids) and foodstuffs (flour, meat, sugar, butter). There is a pool of labour among the large rural population, and an intermediate location on a good transport system, orientated mainly north-to-south and converging on the Centre Economic Region in the north and the Ukraine in the south, is an additional advantage for industrial development. The high-grade cement from Belgorod Oblast, based on local supplies of chalk which overlie the iron ore, is already of importance throughout the Union (see Fig. 145).

POPULATION AND CITIES

For a long time the area that is now the Central Chernozem Economic Region was a frontier land peopled by semi-nomadic groups of horsemen, known as Don Cossacks, who had escaped southwards

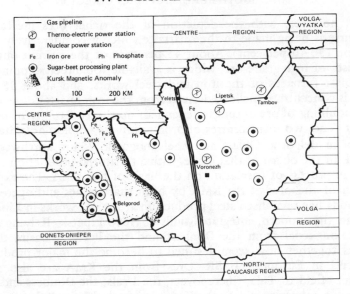

Fig. 145. Central Chernozem Economic Region: mineral and power resources.

from the oppression of Russian princes (*see* p. 135). The frontier zone was moved progressively southwards to the lower Don and Black Sea steppe and the lands to the north became settled and cultivated. Since the eighteenth century, the whole of the region has been a productive agricultural area supporting a dense rural population. It is unfortunate that past farming practices have led to widespread gullying and erosion, resulting in the loss of acres of precious soil every year. Considerable effort is now being expended to check this "rape of the earth" through erosion control and tile drainage.

The population in the forested area in the north lives mainly in log huts (*izba*), but in the steppe areas of the south adobe-filled frame huts (*khata*) are the usual habitations. Apart from Voronezh, the cities are comparatively small and widely distributed and are, in the main, administrative and commercial centres of the respective provinces or districts (oblasts) (*see* Fig. 146).

Voronezh (population: 783,000)

Chief city of the Central Chernozem Industrial Region, Voronezh is an important industrial centre which has experienced remarkable increase of population in recent years (19 per cent between 1970 and 1979). It was first established as a Khazar town and later became a Russian fort (sixteenth century) against the Tatars.

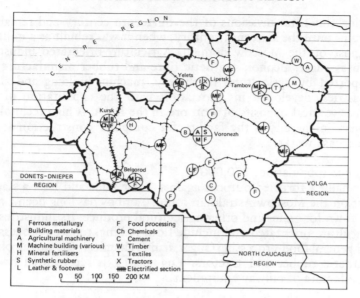

Fig. 146. Central Chernozem Economic Region: railways and industrial structure of towns.

> Your town stood as Russia's shield
> 'Gainst the nomadic Eastern horde.
>
> Konstantine Grusyev

During the Second World War, it was the scene of severe fighting and destruction and was riddled by mines left by the retreating Germans. Voronezh now functions as a collecting and processing centre for agricultural products and produces synthetic rubber (based on the use of natural gas), vehicle tyres, locomotives and railway rolling stock, aircraft and agricultural and earth-moving equipment (*see* Fig. 146).

Lipetsk (population: 396,000)
Trading in cattle, Lipetsk is a market town with a leather industry, flour mills and food industries, to which a large integrated iron and steel (Novo-Lipetsk) plant and machine-building works (tractors, farm machinery) have been added. Its metallurgical activities, which vie with those of Krivoy Rog and Magnitogorsk, seem destined to dominate in the future, and there has been a pronounced population increase in recent years (37 per cent between 1970 and 1979).

Kursk (population: 375,000)
First founded in the tenth century, Kursk was completely destroyed

during the Tatar invasions of the thirteenth century and remained in ruins until the sixteenth century, when it was rebuilt as a military outpost of the Moscow domain. Agriculture-orientated industries such as sugar, alcohol, synthetic fibre and rubber manufacture are supported by agricultural machinery, machine-building and allied industries, developed in association with the exploitation of the extensive local deposits of iron ore in the KMA. A high technology project in the city is the facility for computer construction at the Schermash works.

Tambov (population: 270,000)
Originally a fortified outpost against Tatar raids and later a staging post on the Moscow-Astrakhan route, Tambov has long been a market town for grains and other agricultural produce. Its industries are agriculture orientated and include flour milling, tobacco-processing, and general food-processing (sugar, fruit), chemicals (potato alcohol), synthetic rubber and tractors. Engineering is represented by the manufacture of railway equipment.

2. DONETS-DNIEPER ECONOMIC REGION

Although it has undergone a relative loss of dominance, the industrial eastern Ukraine, together with the Kharkov-Poltava area, is still the leading coal and metallurgical complex of the USSR. It is also one of its most highly urbanised regions (*see* Fig. 147). In recent years there has been a marked diversification of the economy into

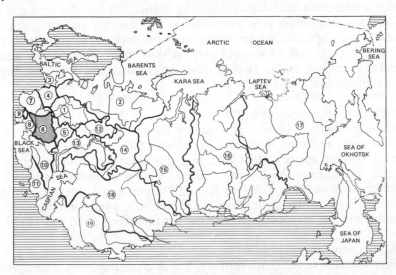

Fig. 147. Soviet Union: location of Donets-Dnieper Economic Region.

TABLE 42. DONETS-DNIEPER ECONOMIC REGION:
ADMINISTRATIVE UNITS, THEIR POPULATION AND DENSITY

Area: 220,500,000 km²
Population (1979): 21,045,000

Administrative unit	Area (000 km²)	Population (000, 1979)	Density (persons per km²)	Percentage urban
Dnepropetrovsk Oblast	32	3,640	114	80
Donetsk Oblast	27	5,160	191	89
Zaporozhye Oblast	27	1,946	72	71
Voroshilovgrad Oblast	27	2,788	103	85
Kharkov Oblast	31	3,056	99	75
Poltava Oblast	29	1,741	60	50
Kirovograd Oblast	25	1,251	50	52
Sumy Oblast	24	1,463	61	53

TABLE 43. DONETS-DNIEPER ECONOMIC REGION:
TOWNS WITH OVER 150,000 INHABITANTS IN 1979

Town	Population in thousands 1970 (census)	1979 (census)	Percentage increase 1970-79
Kharkov	1,223	1,444	18
Dnepropetrovsk	904	1,066	18
Donetsk	879	1,021	16
Zaporozhye	658	781	19
Krivoy Rog	573	605	13
Zhdanov	417	503	21
Voroshilovgrad	383	463	21
Makeyevka	429	436	2
Gorlovka	335	337	1
Poltava	220	279	27
Dneprodzerzhinsk	227	250	10
Kirovograd	189	237	26
Kremenchug	166	210	27
Sumy	159	228	43
Kramatorsk	150	178	19
Melitopol	137	161	18

chemicals, oil and gas industries, into industries associated with agriculture such as the extraction of sugar from beet and oil from sunflowers, and into the higher elements of industry. The whole region is characterised by a highly intricate system of economic linkages maintained by an efficient railway system.

Fig. 148. Donets-Dnieper Economic Region.

PHYSICAL ASPECTS

Relief and drainage

The Donets Ridge (Azov Heights) in the south-east of the region is the most prominent topographic feature (*see* Fig. 148). It is a deeply dissected rolling plateau, rising to heights of over 300 m stretching from west-north-west to east-south-east for over 300 km and extending about 160 km in width. It is a shield structure and represents an eastward extension of the Volyno-Podolian upland beyond the Dnieper. In this region the Volyno-Podolian Shield forms a slightly higher belt of country west of Kirovograd.

Its geologically recent emergence gave rise to an upland area and a 60 km long gorge and stretch of rapids on the Dnieper between Dnepropetrovsk and Zaporozhye where the river cuts through the crystalline rocks. At one time the rapids presented a serious hazard to river traffic and interfered with navigation on the Dnieper, but in 1932, following the completion of the Dneproges Dam, they were submerged beneath the deep Kakhovka Reservoir.

North-west of Dnepropetrovsk is a broad open low plain of the Dnieper extending for more than 150 km. In this stretch and upstream beyond Kiev the river takes on its characteristic aspect of steep and high bluffs on its right bank and low terraces on the left bank. A tongue of ice occupied this plain area during glacial times as far south as Dnepropetrovsk. With the eventual retreat of the ice, the lowlands were left extensively covered with sands and clays.

(Novosti)

Fig. 149. Part of the 410 km Dnieper-Donbass Canal designed to enhance the water supply of the industrial Donbass where local water resources have been inadequate to meet needs, and at the same time irrigate 165,000 hectares of arable ands in the Kharkov, Donetsk and Voroshilovgrad regions. The first stage was completed in 1981.

These have dried out long ago and have been reworked by the wind, covering much of the area with loess. Northward the Dnieper valley merges into the flat-to-undulating plain of Poltava, Kharkov and Sumy Oblasts. Southwards of Zaporozhye is a strip of monotonously flat coastal plain 50-150 km wide known as the Black Sea Lowland. This loess-covered region reaches the coast in cliffs up to 30 m high.

Climate, natural vegetation and soils

Here, as in the other economic regions of Ukraine-Moldavia, the climate is dominated by anticyclonic circulations, the Siberian high pressure during the winter and the Azores high pressure in the summer. The region is relatively far removed from its main source of moisture, the Atlantic Ocean, and suffers from some degree of moisture deficit much of the time (*see* Fig. 149). Kharkov, for example, suffers drought of varying intensity one year in every five. Characteristically the climate is continental with rapid changes in the temperature element between winter and summer. Spring is a brief and fleeting season; autumn tends to be somewhat more protracted.

January mean temperatures range from −5 °C in the south (note the ameliorating influence of the Black Sea in winter) to −8 °C in the north. July temperatures range from 20 °C in the north to 23 °C

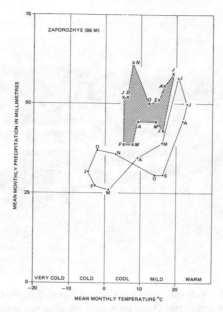

Fig. 150. Hythergraph for Zaporozhye (Kew, London, shaded).

in the south. Annual precipitation aggregates are 500-600 mm in the north of the region but no more than 200-400 mm along the Black Sea coast (*see* Fig. 150). Rainfall variability is such that in individual years aggregates may be anything between 70 and 125 per cent of the mean annual values. Maximum precipitation occurs in the summer half of the year (particularly in the first half of the summer). It takes the form of heavy rainstorms and gives rise to erosion of the soil and the formation of ravines. On the other hand, relative humidity in summer is low — about 40 per cent at noon in July and August — and evaporation rates are high. Droughts, often to the accompaniment of desiccating *sukhovey* from the east, are quite common. To some extent ley farming (*travopolye*) and irrigation (e.g. Dnieper-Donbass Canal) in association with multipurpose dams (e.g. at Zaporozhye, Kremenchug and Dneprodzerzhinsk on the Dnieper) help to supplement the limited precipitation of the growing season, but the dreaded *sukhovey*, which is especially frequent in May and August, can cause fruit blossoms to wither, vegetation to suffer irreparable damage, and the loss of an otherwise promising harvest. The pernicious effects of these hot, dry winds may be judged from the fact that, during the autumn of 1903, the *sukhovey* brought about the recession, through evaporation, of several square miles of the Sea of Azov for a period of five days. Winter precipitation is only slight and takes the form of snow, lying from forty to eighty days. As in the Central Chernozem Economic Region the slight snow cover (30-40 cm) is important in so far as it insulates the soil, which, in consequence, remains sufficiently warm to permit the early germination of grains sown in late autumn.

The zones of natural vegetation and soil types merge imperceptibly into one another from north to south. In the region of the forest-steppe and steppe, there are deep fertile borolls (chernozems) and ustolls (chestnut brown soils), both of which are loess-covered. In only a few comparatively small areas does grass remain in the steppe-lands; such areas are generally protected nature reserves.

THE ECONOMY

Agriculture
Much of the region which is not industrialised and urbanised has a vigorous agriculture almost to the extent that fields and orchards mingle with industrial towns and mining townships. Crop combinations change from north to south (*see* Fig. 151). In the northern oblasts, where conditions are less arid, flax, hemp and potatoes are grown, and dairying is intensively developed. Southwards, where conditions become progressively drier, wheat, barley, millet, buck-wheat, rye, flax, potatoes and sugar-beet seem to play an equal share in a general mixed type of farming. In the central zone, the concentration is on cash crops in which the extensive cultivation of sugar-beets and wheat predominates. Wheat and sugar-beet cover vast expanses of monotonous landscape and are produced in ever-increasing quantities, even though conditions tend to be rather dry for high yields of sugar-beet. Average annual output is 51-2 million tonnes of grain and 56-7 million tonnes of sugar-beet. The sugar-beet provides sugar for domestic use and also a valuable cattle feed. Southwards, in the drier steppelands, sunflowers form part of the crop combination. The oil extracted from their seeds is not only edible but is also used in the woollen industry and in the manufacture of fine paints and soaps. Potatoes provide food for humans and livestock, as well as industrial alcohol, starch and vodka. Lucerne (alfalfa), maize and fodder grasses support large herds of beef and dairy cattle. Around all towns both suburban market gardening and dairying are carried on.

Added to the proneness of the region to droughts, heavy thundery rains in summer (June especially) and strong winds are climatic hazards in the agricultural areas. Shelter belts to break the force of the winds (*see* Fig. 37), strip cultivation to reduce the extent of areas of exposed soil, contour ploughing to stop the downslope movement of soil, and brushwood dams to trap soils in gulleys are a few of the steps taken to attempt to reduce their ravages.

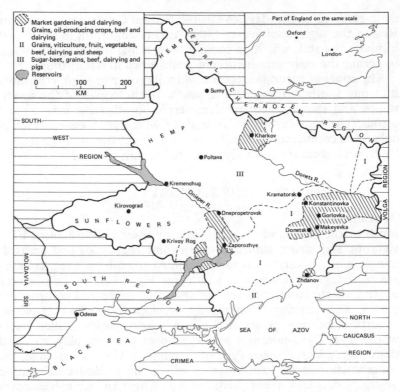

Fig. 151. Donets-Dnieper Economic Region: agricultural land-use regions.

Resources and industry

Agriculture-based industries such as flour-milling, sugar-refining and meat-packing are represented in the majority of cities and towns in the Donets-Dnieper Economic Region, but more especially in the western part (*see* Fig. 152). However, none of these is as important as the activities associated with the heavy industry of the Donbass. Here are to be found the oldest centre of coal production and the largest ferrous metallurgical region of the Soviet Union. Unlike the industries of the Centre Economic Region, which have to rely almost exclusively on imported raw materials, those of the Donbass are based on ample and varied local supplies (*see* Fig. 153).

The Donets Ridge contains the Donbass with its range of coals, including good coking coal (*see* p. 86). The relative importance of the Donbass in the USSR has declined as output from newer fields, such as those of West Siberia (Kuzbass), Kazakhstan (Karaganda, Ekibastuz) and the Pechora Basin (Vorkuta), has grown, but the 400 or so mines in the Donbass still produce, though at relatively

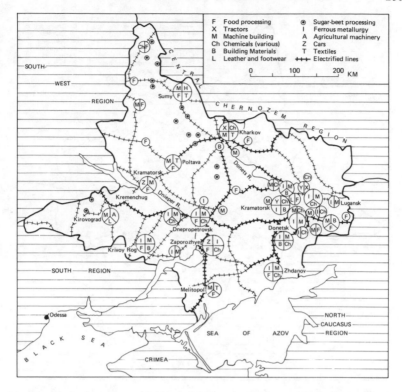

Fig. 152. Donets-Dnieper Economic Region: railways and industrial structure of towns.

high cost, more than half of the Union's coking coal and about 31 per cent of total coal production.

The presence of coking coals was an important factor in the early growth of metallurgy in this area. At Krivoy Rog, about 330 km from the Donbass on the west side of the Dnieper River (which compares with the distance between London and Middlesborough), is located the Soviet Union's largest iron ore producer (51 per cent) and largest single source of haematite ore, with a metallic content of between 54 and 64 per cent (*see* p. 98). High-grade ore and concentrated ores (derived from low-grade iron quartzites) are used locally or carried by rail to large, integrated iron and steel plants in the Donbass. For the return journey the railway wagons are loaded with coke for use in the iron and steel industry located at Krivoy Rog. The Kerch Peninsula provides a second source of iron ore, but its quality is not as high as that from Krivoy Rog. Nevertheless, its transport across the Sea of Azov is cheap, and a large integrated metallurgical plant has been built at the important port of Zhdanov.

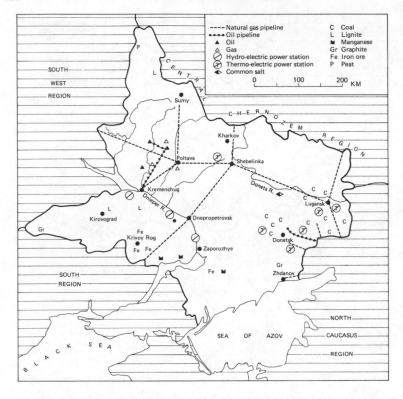

Fig. 153. Donets-Dnieper Economic Region: mineral and power resources.

The Kursk Magnetic Anomaly in the Central Chernozem Region (*see* p. 98) provides an additional source of iron ore.

At Marganets and Nikopol on the Dnieper, and lying between the Donbass and Krivoy Rog, is one of the world's major deposits of manganese (used in the production of special hard steels) and nearly 40 per cent of the USSR's reserves. A wide variety of other minerals used in the metallurgical and chemical industries is also available in the Donets-Dnieper Region, such as bauxite, mercury, salt, fireclay and limestone (for fluxing). The building of several nuclear power stations (Chernobyl, Yuzhno-Ukraine, etc.) and dams on the Dnieper has added an abundant supply of electricity to the energy resources of the region, and natural gas and oil from the northern oblasts (Kremenchug, Dneprodzerzhinsk, Zaporozhye) and beyond, are playing an important role in metallurgy. Indeed, few great industrial areas are as well endowed with locally available raw materials or power resources as is the Donets-Dnieper Region (*see* Fig. 153).

The geographical distribution of these resources has led to three territorial-production complexes or major concentration of heavy industry: *the Donets Basin, the Dnieper Bend,* and *the coast of the Sea of Azov.*

DONETS BASIN (DONBASS). Within the 300 km long Donets coalfield are to be found major producers of coal, pig iron, steel, chemicals and gases. Donetsk (formerly Stalino) on the western side of the coalfield is the main city. Originally known as Hughesovka (Yuzovka), it took its name from a Welshman, John Hughes, who, as head of the New Russia Metallurgical Company, founded the first ironworks (The Yuzovka Metal Factory) here in 1869. One-time mechanic at the Cyfarthfa Iron Works in Merthyr Tydfil in South Wales, and later manager of his own iron works at Newport, Hughes had been invited by Tsar Alexander III to help to develop the Russian iron and steel industry. He took several of his countryfolk with him to found what is now the oldest steel metallurgical town in the Donbass. Donetsk is a city of mine shafts, blast furnaces, steelworks, rolling mills, engineering works, chemical plant — and supports a population of 1,021,000 people.*

The Yuzovka I knew no longer exists. Today there is a prosperous industrial city in its place. In those days (before the Revolution) it was a slummy settlement ringed with wooden hovels and clay huts . . . . A startling crimson flame danced above the blast furnaces. Greasy soot dropped from the sky. Nothing in Yuzovka was white. Whatever had started out as white was a blotchy, yellowish grey — shirts, sheets, pillowcases, curtains, dogs, horses, cats. It rarely rained in Yuzovka and hot, dry winds swept the streets, stirring up the piles of dust, soot and chicken feathers into clouds . . . .

K. Paustovsky, from his *Autobiography.*

Other centres such as Voroshilovgrad, Makeyevka, Gorlovka, Konstantinovka and Kramatorsk have collieries and large integrated iron and steelworks and associated coke-chemical plants. Apart from Voroshilovgrad (Lugansk), these centres are situated on the western side of the coalfield nearest to the Krivoy Rog ores.

DNIEPER BEND. This area is located between the towns of Zaporozhye, Dnepropetrovsk and Krivoy Rog and its metallurgical industry is based on coal transported from the Donbass, iron ore from Krivoy Rog, manganese from Nikopol and bauxite from the Urals. Machine-building and chemical industries are also located there. Industrial growth is aided by supplies of electricity from hydro-electric

*Nikita Khruschev moved to Yuzovka with his parents in 1909 and worked as a metal fitter in the generator plants at the French-owned Rutchenkov and Pastukhov mines.

generating stations at Zaporozhye (Dneproges) and elsewhere along the Dnieper. The main centres are Dnepropetrovsk, Zaporozhye, Krivoy Rog, Dneprodzerzhinsk and Novomoskovsk.

COAST OF SEA OF AZOV. As would be expected, iron and steelworks have been built where Kerch iron ore is unloaded for transit to the inland steelworks of the Donets basin. This is at Zhdanov (population 474,000) (compare the Llanwern and Port Talbot-Margam works in South Wales) where the huge Azovstal works are but part of a major industrial complex which includes general machinery and shipbuilding industries. The port of Zhdanov, icebound for two and a half months in the year, exports coal and metallurgical products.

The iron and steel industry of the Donets-Dnieper Region produced, at high cost, about 36 per cent (48 million tonnes) of the pig iron and over 36 per cent (53.7 million tonnes) of the steel output of the USSR in 1980 and tens of millions of tonnes of rolled metal products of various kinds. Under the Eleventh Five-year Plan (1981-85) production of finished rolled steel in the Ukraine is to be increased by 14-16 per cent.

OTHER INDUSTRIAL CENTRES. Outside the three industrial areas, Kharkov is the most important industrial node. It has a complex of machine-building and mechanical industries.

Coal mining and iron and steel industries dominate the Donets-Dnieper Region but other heavy industries are important as are those associated with chemicals, oil (Poltava, Sumy and Kharkov Oblasts) and gas. Heavy engineering showing a close affinity with the main steel-producing districts is highly concentrated. For example, mining engineering is important in Donetsk, Kramatorsk, Gorlovka, and Voroshilovgrad; Kramatorsk and Kharkov are major centres for the production of machine tools and instruments. Diesel locomotives, electric motors, transformers and large turbo-alternators are built at Kharkov, Voroshilovgrad and Novocherkassk. Kirovograd is well known for the building of agricultural machinery. On the whole the engineering industries lack the sophistication of those in the Centre, North-West or Ural Regions.

Non-ferrous metallurgy is significant. Zaporozhye has an aluminium refinery, uranium is enriched around the town of Zheltyye Vody and several other branches of non-ferrous processing — nickel, tin and copper — are found.

By-products of the coke ovens, rock salt (Artemovsk) and local phosphate slag provided the initial basis for what is now a highly developed chemical industry. Now added to the ammonia, dyes, tars and fertilisers from these sources are synthetic plastics and resins, based on natural gas and oil from the petrochemical industry, and carborundum, tungsten-carbide and explosives from electro-chemical plant which use cheap electricity from the various Dnieper hydro schemes.

Light industries are particularly well developed in the Donets-Dnieper Region. They are based primarily on the local agricultural-pastoral resources and cater for the large consumer market both within the region and further afield.

Transport

The road and rail communications of the Ukraine-Moldavia Region are the densest and most highly developed in the Soviet Union. An arterial road via Zaporozhye and Kharkov links Sevastopol in the Crimea with Moscow, a distance of 1,300 km. There are also several other lesser roads, but it is on rail transport that the region depends most heavily. The railway system is particularly dense in the Donets coalfield (*see* Fig. 152). The Dnieper River (2,200 km long) is a major inland waterway for the region and, like the River Volga to the east, is being transformed by the construction of huge impound-ing dams. The dams are constructed primarily for electric power generation, but the reservoirs provide improved navigation. The reservoir at Novaya Kakhovka provides irrigation water for the Black Sea Steppe, northern Crimea (*see* Fig. 168) and lands further upstream. The six major installations, at Kremenchug, Dneprodzer-zhinsk, Zaporozhye, Kiev, Kanev and Kakhovka, have made the lower Dnieper a chain of lakes. Vital canal construction to convey much needed industrial water in this generally dry region is well underway between the Dnieper River, the Donbass and Krivoy Rog. This water will augment supplies currently obtained from the 125 km Northern Donets-Donbass Canal (*see* Fig. 149).

POPULATION AND CITIES

Over 21 million people (8 per cent of the total Soviet population) live in the Donets-Dnieper Economic Region. Practically three-quarters are Ukrainians and one fifth are Russian. Densities in the countryside are between 50 and 200 per km^2, but in parts of the Dnieper Lowlands and the Donbass they exceed 200 per km^2. With the exception of parts of the South-West Economic Region and Moldavia and certain of the oases in Soviet Central Asia, these rural densities are higher than anywhere else in the Soviet Union. Rural settlement, which was at one time dispersed, now takes on the form of single compact villages belonging to huge *kolkhozy*. The houses are generally constructed of prefabricated wood sections and the settlements are usually strung along routeways ("street villages"), near a watercourse, or in a gulley where water is available.

(Novosti)

Fig. 154. Kharkov. The city centre has characteristic tall blocks of modern buildings encircling Dzerzhinsky Square, one of the largest in Europe.

Kharkov (population: 1,444,000)
Founded in the seventeenth century as a military outpost on the southern frontier of Muscovy, its importance, however, dates from the nineteenth century with the rise of the Donbass as an industrial base. Kharkov functions as the gateway from Moscow to the Donets Basin and is a focal point for eight rail routes (*see* Fig. 152). Industrialisation has proceeded rapidly, but the city and its industries were severely damaged during the Second World War. Replanned and rebuilt by 1956, it is now the largest single industrial centre in the Donets-Dnieper Economic Region, with engineering works producing locomotives, tractors, aircraft, turbines, agricultural machinery, motor cycles and bicycles. Though a "million" city, it is growing more slowly than Kiev and its population increase in the nine-year period 1970-79 was 18 per cent, compared with 31 per cent in Kiev for the same period. Kharkov now ranks sixth in size in the Soviet Union (*see* Fig. 154).

Dnepropetrovsk (population: 1,066,000)
Two hundred kilometres south-south-west of Kharkov, Dnepropetrovsk is the chief centre of the heavy industry area of the Dnieper

(Novosti)

Fig. 155. Donetsk. Spoil heaps, pit towers and vast factory complexes characterise the city which is the principal economic, administrative, industrial and cultural centre of the Donets Basin.

Bend. It stands on the high right bank of the Dnieper River almost opposite its confluence with the Samara. The town was founded in the latter part of the eighteenth century when, under Catherine the Great, Russian territories were being extended to the west bank of the Dnieper. It was not until the construction of railway links with the Donbass, Moscow and Odessa that the town's industrialisation commenced and its population increased. It has developed steel industries (on the basis of Krivoy Rog iron ore, Donbass coal, Nikopol manganese, hydro-electric power from Dneproges, and thermal-electric power based on gas from the Shebelinka field to the north-east), heavy engineering (locomotives, rolling stock, bridge girders, mining machinery), vehicle tyres and chemical industries (*see* Fig. 152).

Donetsk (population: 1,021,000)
Within the Donbass there is a hierarchy of towns, at the peak of which stands Donetsk, surrounded by several satellite suburbs. It is the principal economic, administrative, cultural and industrial

centre of the Donets Basin, with coal mining, iron and steel, metal-working, machinery and chemicals as its main industries (*see* Fig. 155).

Voroshilovgrad (population: 463,000), *Makeyevka* (population: 436,000), *Gorlovka* (population: 337,000) and *Kramatorsk* (population: 178,000) are all industrial cities with individual specialisations. In addition to their coal mining and heavy industry they produce machinery, transport equipment (diesel locomotives) and chemicals.

In the urban hierarchy of the Donets Basin there follow exclusively iron and steel producing centres such as *Khartsyzsk, Kommunarsk* and *Yenakiyevo*, chemical centres such as *Rubezhnoye* and *Lisichansk*, and other centres of the coal industry such as *Krasnyy Luch*.

Zhdanov, the seaport for the Donbass, has already been mentioned (*see* p. 258).

Zaporozhye (population: 781,000)

Founded in 1770 as a fortress against the Crimean Tatars, Zaporozhye is now a major industrial centre well known for its alloy steel (based on cheap Dneproges electricity, local pig iron and alloys), rolled steel, engineering and chemicals. The local abundance of hydro-electricity was decisive in the developments in non-ferrous metallurgy and chemicals, e.g. siting of a plant at Zaporozhye to smelt clayey bauxite from north of Serov in the Urals.

Krivoy Rog (population: 605,000)

Krivoy Rog is an expanding steel and engineering centre, like Zaporozhye. The populations of both cities increased by 13 and 19 per cent respectively in the period 1970-79. The nearby reserves of high-quality iron ore provide the basis not only for the local iron mining and steel-making and engineering industries, but also for the well-developed metallurgical industries of the Donbass.

Poltava (population: 279,000)

Situated in the broad plain 140 km south-west of Kharkov, Poltava is of historical interest as the seventeenth-century centre of the Ukrainian Cossacks. Today it is a commercial town with food-processing, textile and engineering industries (machinery used in the food industries, chemical machinery, etc.). There is a natural gas field of industrial importance in the Poltava-Shebelinka area.

Dneprodzerzhinsk (population: 250,000)

Situated about 14 km upstream of Dnepropetrovsk on the Dnieper, Dneprodzerzhinsk is in many respects a suburb of the latter. It produces high-grade steels, chemicals, railway rolling stock and cement, using hydro-electricity generated near by. The city also has river port functions.

Kirovograd (population: 237,000)

Situated within the Volyno-Podolian Upland in the extreme west of the region, Kirovgrad has agricultural machinery and food industries.

Sumy (population: 228,000)

Like Poltava, Sumy is in a zone of intensive agriculture (especially of fruit culture) and dense rural populations. It has a chemical complex concentrating primarily on phosphate fertilisers.

Kremenchug (population: 210,000)

Situated on the Dnieper, Kremenchug is the site of a hydro-electric power station and oil refinery. It has a highly developed chemical industry and heavy motor vehicle plant.

Melitopol (population: 161,000)

Situated in the dry steppelands of the south of Zaporozhyy Oblast, Melitopol is an expanding town on the main Moscow-Sevastopol road and on the line of a major canal from the Kakhovka reservoir which is being built to irrigate the low-lying moisture deficient Black Sea steppe.

3. SOUTH-WEST ECONOMIC REGION

This western Ukraine and Kiev region (see Fig. 156) may be character-

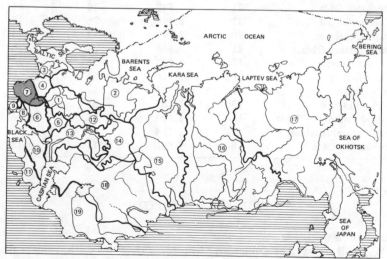

Fig. 156. Soviet Union: location of South-West Economic Region.

ised as an agricultural area with an admixture of related processing and consumer goods. Its western part has changed hands on several occasions in the twentieth century and much of it was not firmly in Soviet control until 1945. The region, therefore, is not so well integrated in Soviet life as is the Donets-Dnieper Region. Its proximity to the western boundary of the USSR has made it vulnerable strategically and until recently less attractive for investment in certain vital industries. Even so, it has considerable economic potential and in recent years electronics has become a rapidly developing sector. It is a region of dense rural settlement (*see* Table 44). A current problem is the need to expand labour-intensive industries to make use of the under-employed labour released through the mechanisation of agriculture. Drainage of the Polesye is considered vital to the future of the region.

TABLE 44. SOUTH-WEST ECONOMIC REGION:
ADMINISTRATIVE UNITS, THEIR POPULATION AND DENSITY

Area: 269,000 km²
Population (1979): 21,578,000

Administrative unit	Area (000 km²)	Population (000, 1979)	Density (persons per km²)	Percentage urban
Chernigov Oblast	32	1,502	47	44
Kiev City }	29	2,144 }	140	100
Kiev Oblast }		1,924 }		45
Cherkassy Oblast	21	1,547	74	44
Vinnitsa Oblast	27	2,046	76	35
Zhitomir Oblast	30	1,597	53	44
Khmelnitskiy Oblast	21	1,558	74	36
Rovno Oblast	20	1,121	56	36
Volyn Oblast	20	1,016	51	40
Lvov Oblast	22	2,583	117	53
Ternopol Oblast	14	1,163	83	31
Ivano-Frankovsk Oblast	14	1,333	95	36
Transcarpathia Oblast	13	1,154	89	38
Chernovtsy Oblast	8	890	111	38

PHYSICAL ASPECTS

Relief and drainage
The small arc of the Carpathian Mountains that lies within the region in the south-west is one of the lower sections of those ranges, where

TABLE 45. SOUTH-WEST ECONOMIC REGION:
TOWNS WITH OVER 150,000 INHABITANTS IN 1979

| Town | Population in thousands | | Percentage increase 1970-79 |
	1970 (census)	1979 (census)	
Kiev	1,632	2,144	31
Lvov	553	667	21
Vinnitsa	212	313	48
Zhitomir	161	244	52
Chernigov	159	238	50
Cherkassy	158	228	44
Chernovtsy	187	218	17

the highest peaks are less than 2,200 m (e.g. Mount Goverla, 2,058 m, Mount Petros, 2,020 m) (*see* Fig. 157). Slopes are generally heavily forested, with beech on the lower slopes, and pine and fir above. Beyond, in Ruthenia, is a small north-east section of the Hungarian Plain (formerly in Czechoslovakia) which is now Soviet territory and part of the South-West Region.

Along the foot of the Carpathians to the north-east flow the Prut and Dniester Rivers, which beyond the region to the south-east embrace between them the portion of the Podolian Upland that is now the Moldavian Republic.

> Here the azure skies shine long,
> Here the reign of cruel storms is brief.
>
> A.S. Pushkin

Between the Dniester and Dnieper Rivers lies the Volyno-Podolian Upland, an asymmetrical plateau, 150-300 m high, higher in the west and sloping gradually downwards to the east. It is composed of Tertiary deposits and loess, and is much dissected by ravines. Along the river valleys, e.g. the Bug, there are occasional outcrops of crystalline rocks which belong to the basal Podolian-Azov (Ukraine) crystalline shield.

Beyond the bounding escarpment of the Volyno-Podolian Upland in the north lies the Polesye Lowland, an extensive area of oak-pine forest and swamp (the Pripyat Marshes). Only the southern third of Polesye lies within the region (the remainder lies in southern Belorussia). The broad flat Polesye, with its sluggish winding rivers constitutes the north-western part of the Dnieper Lowland which, in its turn, merges eastwards into the Central Russian Uplands. In Pleistocene times, during the third (Dnieper) glacial stage (*see* p. 18), a lobe of the ice sheet occupied the Dnieper Lowland (compare the

Fig. 157. South-West Economic Region.

Don Valley to the east during the second or Oka glaciation), causing the formation of depressions and warping of the land surface. With the eventual retreat of the ice, the lowlands were left extensively covered with sands and clays, with swamps and a poorly developed drainage system. These conditions still prevail in the Polesye, but on the middle-lower Dnieper the lowland, which extends east of the river for more than 150 km, has long since dried out. The distinctive steep and high bluffs of the right bank of the Dnieper and the low terraces of its left bank are well displayed near Kiev.

Climate, natural vegetation and soils
The climate of the South-West Economic Region is dominated by anticyclonic circulations, the Asiatic anticyclone during the winter and the Azores anticyclone in the summer. Characteristically there is a continental climate with rapid temperature changes between winter and summer. Summers are relatively long and warm, winters cold and severe and last three to four months. Spring is everywhere short and fleeting; autumn is rather more protracted (*see* Fig. 158).

   January mean temperatures range from about −4.0 °C in the west (Lvov −3.8 °C) to near −6 °C in the east (Kiev −5.9 °C). July temperatures range between 18 ° and 20 °C throughout the region at this time.

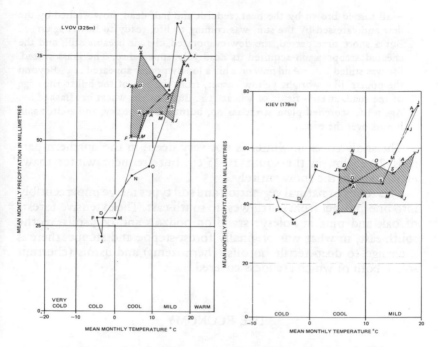

Fig. 158. Hythergraphs for Lvov and Kiev (Kew, London, shaded).

> the huge steppe sun shines evenly everywhere,
> without blinking, without losing itself among the trees.
>
> M. Prishvin

Annual precipitation aggregates are only light to moderate. In places, the Carpathian Mountains receive more than 1,500 mm of precipitation annually, but eastwards on the Dnieper Upland and plain it varies from about 700 mm in the west to less than 600 mm in the east. Maximum precipitation occurs in the summer half of the year (particularly in June). It takes the form of heavy rainstorms, giving rise to erosion of the soil and the formation of ravines. The effectiveness of the rainfall is much reduced by high evaporation rates in summer. Indeed, this part is consistently hampered by moisture deficits and is occasionally subjected to severe drought. The *sukhovey*, the hot dry type of weather that is very desiccating to crops and plants, can be particularly damaging, especially during the spring when crops are undergoing their most rapid growth.

Chekhov's description is evocative of the summer drought and the wide fields of this area:

In the meantime before the eyes of the travellers spread the wide, boundless plain, crossed by a chain of hills . . . reaped rye, tall grass, spurge, wild hemp

— all turned brown by the heat, reddish and half-dead, now washed by the dew and caressed by the sun, was coming to life, ready to flower again . . . But a short time passed, the dew evaporated, the air became still, and the cheated steppe again acquired its dead July appearance. The grass wilted, life was stilled . . . . And now on a hill a lonely poplar appeared . . . . Beyond the poplar, like a bright yellow carpet, from the top of the hill to the edge of the road, stretch fields of wheat . . . . But now the wheat has flashed by. Again the scorched plain stretches on, burnt hills, hot sky, and a kite again hovers over the earth.

The snow cover in winter is not very deep; in the northern part it is 20-25 cm, in the south 10-15 cm but frequent winter thaws may dissipate the snow entirely.

The zones of natural vegetation and soil types merge imperceptibly into one another from north-west to south-east. The extensive forests of oak and pine in Polesye stand on podzols and bog soils; to the south-east, in what was originally forest-steppe and steppe, there is a change to deep fertile borolls (chernozems) and ustols (chestnut soils), both of which are loess covered.

THE ECONOMY

Agriculture

The flat steppelands of the east and the rolling and dissected Volyno-Podolian Upland of the west have long been ploughed and given over to vast acres of cereals — wheat, barley and maize — and to industrial crops such as sunflowers, sugar-beet, flax and potatoes. Arable farming predominates and wheat is the chief crop.

Crop combinations change from north-west to south-east in relation to soil type and climate (*see* Fig. 159). In the north-west, on the "islands" of dry land among the marshes of Polesye, and in the lower valley of the Desna, flax growing and dairy farming are the main enterprises. Southwards, wheat, barley, millet, buckwheat, rye, flax, potatoes and sugar-beet seem to play an equal share in a mixed type of farming. In the central zone, the concentration is on cash crops in which the extensive cultivation of sugar-beet and wheat predominates. Wheat and sugar-beet cover vast expanses of monotonous landscape and are produced in ever-increasing quantities, even though conditions tend to be rather dry for high yields of sugar-beet (*see* Fig. 160). This is one of the most productive areas in the world for wheat and has long been known as the "Granary of Russia". The sugar-beet provides sugar for domestic use and also a valuable cattle feed. Southwards, sunflowers form part of the crop combination. The oil extracted from their seeds is not only edible but is also used in the woollen industry and in the manufacture of fine

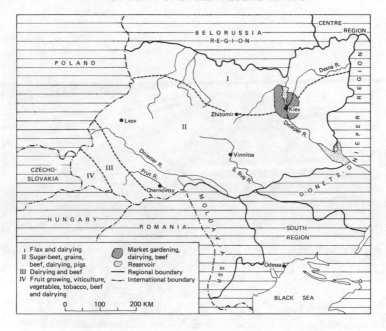

Fig. 159. South-West Economic Region: agricultural land-use regions.

paints and soaps. Potatoes provide food for humans and livestock, as well as industrial alcohol, starch and vodka.

Heavy thundery rains and strong winds are climatic hazards of the agricultural areas. As in the Central Chernozem Region, the Donets-Dnieper Region and elsewhere, strip cultivation to reduce the extent of areas of exposed soil, contour ploughing to stop the down-slope movement of soil, and brushwood dams to trap soils in gulleys are among the steps taken to attempt to reduce their ravages.

Lucerne (alfalfa), maize and fodder grasses support large herds of cattle. Around all towns both suburban market gardening and dairying are carried on. Along the foothills of the Carpathinas, crops are varied and include rye, wheat, maize, sugar-beet, flax, hemp, tobacco and sunflowers. Potatoes and other vegetables are grown in quantity and orchards abound. Large numbers of cattle, both dairy and beef breeds, are grazed on the Carpathian slopes.

Resources and industry
Agriculture-based industries such as flour-milling, sugar-refining and meat-packing are represented in the majority of the cities and towns of the South-West Economic Region (*see* Fig. 161). Mineral resources are limited. At Borislav and Drogobych, in the foothills of the Car-pathians, is a small but valuable oilfield which has been producing

(Novosti)

Fig. 160. Harvesting of winter wheat in the Ukraine, sown in the autumn and protected from the winter cold by a layer of snow. Winter wheat dominates the south-western part of European USSR.

for a long time. Oil refineries have been built in Drogobych and Lvov. New discoveries in Chernigov Oblast (as well as in the neighbouring Poltava, Sumy and Kharkov Oblasts in the Dnieper-Donets Region) now greatly overshadow the Drogobych production, which provided about 20 per cent of the republic's total production of about 8 million tonnes in 1980. Production is not great but it has locational value in a fuel-deficient region; it provides a useful supplement to the oil piped 2,000 km or more from the Caucasus, Volga-Ural fields and West Siberia. A branch of the Druzhba oil pipeline crosses the region *en route* to Czechoslovakia (*see* Fig. 162).

There is a source of natural gas in the west of the region at Dashava. At one time, this gas was sent to Leningrad and Moscow but this source has long since been superceded by supplies from bigger and more productive fields in West Siberia.

Deposits of sulphate of potash and magnesium salt in the Carpathian foothills in the Stebnik-Kalush area form the basis of a major potash-fertiliser industry at Kalush. At Rozdol near Yavorov in Lvov Oblast a valuable deposit of native sulphur is being developed.

Power needs provided by thermal-electric stations using local

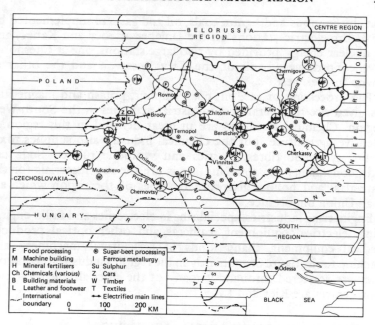

Fig. 161. South-West Economic Region: railways and industrial structure of towns.

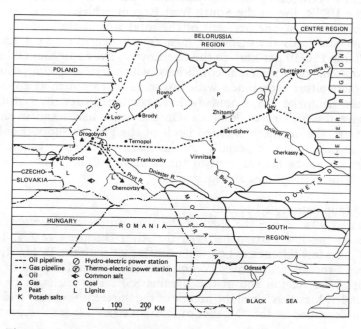

Fig. 162. South-West Economic Region: mineral and power resources.

peat, bituminous and lignite coals, oil and gas, are supplemented by the hydro-electric stations on the Dnieper at Kiev and Kanev, and by nuclear energy provided by two large stations, one at Chernobyl on the north-west bank of the Kiev Reservoir and the other at Rovno further west.

The processing of gas, oil, coal, sulphur, potash and magnesium has given rise to several new industrial activities in the South-West Region. Chemical fertilisers are in great demand in this region of intensive agriculture, but the chemical industry also supplies toxic sprays, synthetic fibres, plastics and synthetic rubber. Soda ash and good quality glass-making sands are the raw materials for the plate-glass and hollow glassware factories of the region which are of all-Union importance.

Engineering industries, specialising in electronics and radio engineering, electrical equipment, cameras and other optical products, medical equipment, many kinds of agricultural machinery and machine tools, figure prominently in the region's industrial economy. They are scattered throughout many of the cities although the two main centres are Kiev and Lvov.

POPULATION AND CITIES

About 21½ million people, or just over 8 per cent of the population of the USSR, live in the South-West Region, which itself makes up little more than one per cent of the total area of the country. By Soviet standards densities are high (mean density: 75 per km^2), attaining 110-30 per km^2 in the Chernovtsy, Lvov and Kiev Oblasts. Favourable environmental conditions, which encouraged a productive agriculture, combined with historical factors such as an early release from the Tatar nomads, have combined over the centuries to give the high rural densities. On the other hand, and in sharp contrast, the northern wooded lands of the Polesye support only a sparse population, especially in the marshy portions. Ukrainians make up about 80 per cent of the total; important minorities are the Belorussians, Poles and Bulgarians.

Kiev (population: 2,144,000)
Situated 90 m above the level of the river on the high western and also on the low eastern bank of the River Dnieper (*see* Fig. 163) and just a few kilometres below its confluence with the Desna River, Kiev is the administrative, commercial and cultural capital of the South-West Region and of the Ukraine SSR. This ancient city was capital of Kiev Rus*until the middle of the thirteenth century and has been described as the "Mother of Russian cities". It is an important

*Kiev celebrated its 1,500th anniversary in 1982.

(Novosti)

Fig. 163. Dnieper River at Kiev viewed from the high west bluff at Vladimirov Hill towards the low, sandy east bank.

focus of rail, river and road routes and of gas and oil pipelines. Local industries (both in Kiev itself and in the industrial suburb on the low left bank of the river) rely on raw materials and fuels brought in from other parts. Manufactures include machinery of several kinds, electronic calculating and automation machinery, machine tools, chemicals, commercial vehicles, motor cycles, river craft, aircraft, leather and footwear and general food products (*see* Fig. 161). Third largest city in the Soviet Union after Moscow and Leningrad, Kiev has experienced a remarkable increase in population since the end of the Second World War, e.g. 31 per cent between 1970 and 1979).

Lvov (population: 667,000) (Polish: *Lwow*; German: *Lemberg*)
A centre of Polish culture and Roman Catholicism until 1939 when, with the two south-eastern provinces of Poland (Volhynia and Galicia), it became part of western Ukraine, Lvov was a medieval city at the focus of routes from Volhynia and Podolia and along the Dniester River. Lvov and the surrounding area now make up a significant industrial complex producing chemicals, engineering goods, lorries, omnibuses, television and electronic equipment, textiles, timber and food products (*see* Fig. 161).

Vinnitsa (population: 313,000)
Founded in the fourteenth century, Vinnitsa stands on the Bug River. Like many other cities in western USSR, it suffered greatly while occupied by the Germans for two and a half years during the the Second World War. It has a chemical industry producing phosphate fertilisers and sulphuric acid and a meat-packing industry.

Zhitomir (population: 244,000)
Situated in the Dnieper Upland, 130 km west-south-west of Kiev, Zhitomir is the centre of the oblast of the same name. Fed by gas and oil pipelines it has a plant producing the polymide fibre *kapron* from caprolactum, a material associated with ammonia synthesis.

Chernigov (population: 238,000)
Situated on the River Desna, Chernigov was founded as early as the ninth century. It was the site of a bishopric which was once second only to Novgorod in importance. The town lost its early importance after being sacked by the Tatars in the thirteenth century. The town has been largely rebuilt after heavy bombing by the Germans in 1941. It is probably best known now for the manufacture of musical instruments, especially pianos, synthetic fibres and a variety of textiles.

Cherkassy (population: 228,000)
A famous Cossack centre as early as the fourteenth century Cherkassy played a part in the history of the Ukrainian liberation from the Polish feudal lords. Relying on natural gas brought by pipeline, it has now an important nitrogenous fertiliser industry.

Chernovtsy (population: 218,000)
Situated on the River Prut, Chernovtsy dates from the fifteenth century. It lies in an area famous for its beech trees. Previously capital of Bukovina, it was not until 1940 that it became a Soviet town. Its industries include food-processing, textiles and machine-building.

The remarkable increase in the urban population in the South-West Region is worthy of note. Both Zhitomir and Chernigov increased their populations by 50 per cent or more between 1970 and 1979; Cherkassy and Vinnitsa by 44 and 48 per cent respectively in the same period. Such increases reflect the natural growth in town populations, and also appreciable rural depopulation following the mechanisation of agriculture.

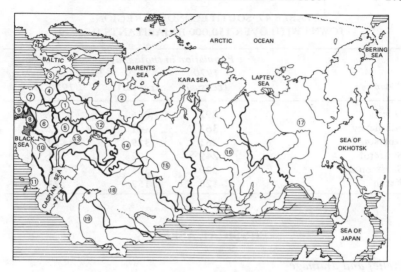

Fig. 164. Soviet Union: location of South Economic Region.

4. SOUTH ECONOMIC REGION

The South Economic Region (*see* Fig. 164), which includes the Crimea and north-western Black Sea coast, falls mainly in the steppe belt. This dry area, particularly in North Crimea, is limited in industrial resources, but has compensatory strength in agriculture. The port function, foreign trade and shipbuilding are very important at Odessa, Kherson and Nikolayev.

TABLE 46. SOUTH ECONOMIC REGION:
ADMINISTRATIVE UNITS, THEIR POPULATION AND DENSITY

| | Area: | 110,700,000 km² | | |
| | Population (1979): | 7,134,000 | | |

Administrative unit	Area (000 km²)	Population (000, 1979)	Density (persons per km²)	Percentage urban
Odessa Oblast	33	2,544	77	61
Nikolayev Oblast	25	1,242	50	61
Kherson Oblast	28	1,164	42	60
Crimea Oblast	27	2,184	81	67

TABLE 47. SOUTH ECONOMIC REGION:
TOWNS WITH OVER 150,000 INHABITANTS IN 1979

Town	Population in thousands		Percentage increase 1970-79
	1970 (census)	1979 (census)	
Odessa	892	1,046	17
Nikolayev	362	441	22
Kherson	261	319	22
Simferol	249	302	21
Sevastopol	229	301	31
Kerch	128	157	23

PHYSICAL ASPECTS

Relief and drainage
The region is made up of the low plain of the Black Sea steppelands extending from the mouth of the Danube River along the Black Sea to the north-western shores of the Sea of Azov, and includes the northern three-quarters of the Crimean Peninsula (*see* Fig. 165). The remainder is the southern rim of mountains — the Crimean Mountains — reaching to over 1,500 m and declining eastwards to the Peninsula of Kerch. The 6 km wide isthmus of Perekop links Crimea with the mainland.

The Black Sea Lowland, a monotonously flat and featureless plain, is interrupted here and there by ravine-like valleys of such rivers as the Dnieper, Southern Bug and Dniester and by a number of smaller streams. It presents to the sea a cliffed coast, sometimes broken by stretches of mudflats and lagoons protected seawards by sandspits and bars. The latter are the result of the reworking by long-shore currents of sediments brought down by heavily silted rivers. Sands are widespread on the lower left bank of the Dnieper River and its estuary and within other estuaries. The long Arabat sandbar (*Arabatskaya Strelka*, i.e. arrow) to the east of the isthmus encloses the stagnant waters (*liman*) of the Sivash Sea.

The Crimean Range forms part of the great belt of Tertiary (Alpine) folding which extends from Gibraltar, through the Alps, to the islands of Indonesia (*see* Fig. 166).

Climate
The climate of the South Region is continental, but tempered by the Black Sea and proximity to the Mediterranean. Winters range from relatively mild in the west to cold in the east. The mean temperature in January in Odessa is −2.8 °C, but in Zaphorozhye (*see*

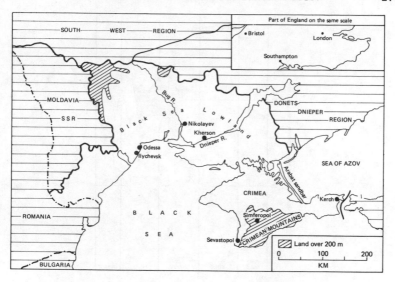

Fig. 165. South Economic Region.

(Novosti)

Fig. 166. Steep slopes of the limestone masses of the Crimean Mountains which dominate the Black Sea coast.

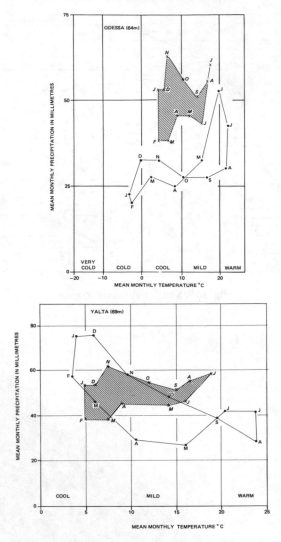

Fig. 167. Hythergraphs for Odessa and Yalta (Kew, London, shaded).

Fig. 167), which may be taken as representative of conditions near the eastern boundary of the region, it is −5 °C. Summers are relatively long and warm in the west, slightly colder in the east. Odessa has a mean temperature of 22.1 °C in July, Zaporozhye 22.8 °C. Precipitation is meagre throughout practically the whole of the region (380-500 mm) with maximum falling in early summer. Without the development of irrigation, agriculture is limited to drought-resistant crops (*see* Fig. 168). Strong winds (*sukhovey*) from the

(*Novosti*)

Fig. 168. Structure on the North Crimean irrigation canal. Precipitation is meagre in the southern part of the Ukraine and in North Crimea and the key to successful agriculture is the development of irrigation projects and the planting of drought resistant crops.

east are a notable feature of the climate of the treeless plains of the South Region. The winds cause duststorms in summer and blizzards in winter, and severe soil erosion at all seasons.

The climate of the south-east coast of Crimea is different from that of the northern three-quarters of the Peninsula and that of the mainland. Protected from cold northerly winds its winters are mild (a mean of 3.5 °C in Yalta in January). Summers are long and warm (23.9 °C in Yalta in July). Different from the regime of the remainder of the South, the south-east of Crimea has year round precipitation totalling 560 mm. Maximum comes in the winter half of the year, but there is also appreciable shower activity during the summer. Though similar, the climate of the area does not conform strictly to the classical "Mediterranean" type. Even so, its milder character compared with elsewhere in the USSR presents a powerful attraction for holiday-makers and the narrow strip of coast between Alushta and Yalta is a popular resort area. Of the several towns here, each with its quota of hotels and holiday homes (*sanatoria*), *Yalta* (population 73,000) is the best known through the world attention it achieved in 1945 when Churchill (UK), Roosevelt (USA) and Stalin (USSR) held a conference to discuss Allied policy.

The alkaline and loess-covered borolls (black earths) in the north of the region and ustolls (dark chestnut soils) in the south reflect the continental character of the climate of all but the south-east of Crimea. Originally these soils carried a steppe grassland vegetation, but a great deal has been removed and placed under cultivation.

Soils on the south coast of Crimea are poorly developed, but well suited for growing grapes and tobacco.

THE ECONOMY

Agriculture
The summer droughts and *sukhovey* conditions restrict agriculture in the South Region but a variety of crop combinations and animal husbandry practices have been successfully evolved to overcome the limitations imposed by the natural environment in these dry lands. Autumn-sown wheat, which matures before the available moisture gets less than potential evapo-transpiration, and drought resistant sunflowers and other oil-seed crops such as linseed, poppy and caraway, are grown extensively (*see* Fig. 169). There is really insufficient moisture for optimal growth but much maize is grown for silage. Sugar-beet, barley and tobacco (*makhorka*) are grown in favoured areas. Diversification is the key to successful agriculture and this has been facilitated by the development of irrigation projects in many large parts of the region. In the area south of the River Dnieper, for example, which is irrigated by the Kakhovka Reservoir,vegetables, rice, fruits and berries are grown. Where the general aridity is ameliorated by moisture-bearing winds from off the Black Sea and Sea of Azov, many types of intensive farming occur, e.g. water melons are grown on the sandy lowlands of the Perekop Isthmus. Elsewhere, the crops include early spring vegetables, salad crops and orchard fruits (*see* Fig. 170).

Pastoral activities, with which cattle, sheep and goats are associated, take over on the drier semi-arid steppelands, and on the pastures of the Crimean Range. In recent years cattle raising for meat and milk has become important along the coast of the Sea of Azov.

The South Region is second only to Moldavia in importance for viticulture. Black Sea and Crimean vineyards produce table grapes and vintage types. The Massandra-Magarach area is an important centre of the wine industry and responsible for the greater part of the wine production of the USSR. The provision of perishable high value products such as vegetables and milk are the main activities of farmers in the vicinity of urban agglomerations such as Odessa, Nikolayev and Kherson. Such activities represent a response to economic factors rather than to any particular advantages or conditions of soil and climate.

Industry
Intimately associated with the agriculture of the South Region are the food processing industries. Fruit and vegetable canneries, flour-

Fig. 169. A field of sunflowers in Mozdok Region, North Ossetian ASSR. Sunflowers are grown for their seeds which are pressed to extract vegetable oil or mixed with maize and peas for cattle fodder.

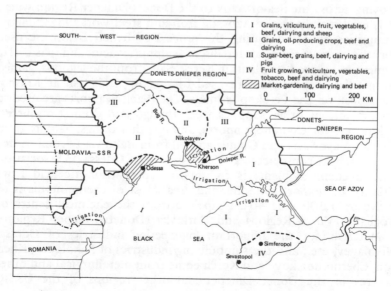

Fig. 170. South Economic Region: agricultural land-use regions.

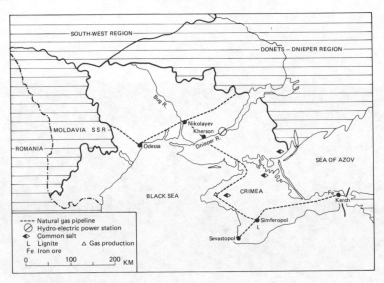

Fig. 171. South Economic Region: mineral and power resources.

milling, vegetable oil pressing, distilleries and wineries are among the more important of these industries.

Mineral resources are generally scarce. There is low-grade iron ore at Kerch and salts in lagoons such as the Sivash Sea and around the Sea of Azov (*see* Fig. 171). The iron ore undergoes beneficiation before moving across the Sea of Azov to the Donets-Dnieper Region where it is used mainly in the Azovstal iron and steel works in Zhdanov. Impurities collected during the process of beneficiation are used for the manufacture of fertilisers, sulphuric acid and basic slag cement in by-product plants in Kerch. Salts from the lagoons, gained from solar evaporation, are used for making soda ash at Krasnoperekopsk on the Perekop Isthmus. The Black Sea ports are used to import various other supplies from foreign and domestic sources. Nikolayev, for example, imports, among other things, bauxite from Greece, Yugoslavia and Guinea and oil from Baku via Batumi. A new chemical port constructed at Yuzhnyy east of Odessa (in association with a chemical plant) is to import superphosphoric acid from Florida and export ammonia and urea. Most of the ammonia is to arrive by 1,500 mile 40 cm pipeline from the chemical centre of Togliatti (Volga Region) and Gorlovka (Donets-Dnieper Region).

Materials for the important engineering industries of Odessa, Nikolayev, etc., and the shipbuilding industries of Nikolayev, Kherson, Chernomorskoye and Kerch come from metallurgical and other centres in the Donets-Dnieper and other regions of the USSR.

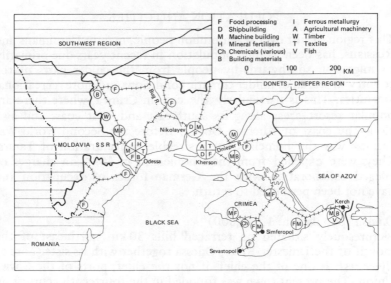

Fig. 172. South Economic Region: railways and industrial structure of towns.

Large-scale engineering includes the production of tractor-drawn ploughs, maize harvesters and other farm machinery, lathes, bull-dozers and other road-building equipment, oil mill presses and similar equipment. The shipbuilding industry provides ocean-going vessels of all kinds, including general cargo carriers, supertankers, container ships, bulk cargo ships, large roll-on/roll-off ships, whale factory ships and other fishing vessels (*see* Fig. 172).

Possibly the major resource of the South Region is its port facilities on the Black Sea and the foreign trade which these facilities generate. Ice forms in the northern Black Sea between mid-December and late February, but ice-breakers maintain year-round navigation in the ports. Rail connections inland from the ports to all parts of the Ukraine and beyond are also good. The facilities in the twin ports of Odessa and Ilyichevsk, for example, are the busiest in the USSR and are capable of handling special cargoes. Kherson has acquired great importance as the sea gates of the Dnieper waterway now navigable to beyond Kiev (following the construction of a cas-cade of dams and storage lakes and associated hydro-electric power stations). Izmail, on the Danube at the border with Romania, is both an important sea and river port handling Soviet trade with many Central European and Balkan countries along the River Danube. The current boom in foreign trade through the Black Sea ports compensates for the limited industrial resources in the South Region.

POPULATION AND CITIES

This region of just over seven million people, mainly Ukrainians and Russians, has been gaining population in recent years due primarily to migration southwards by people from the colder parts of the country in search of milder climatic conditions and more recreational amenities. This is particularly the case in Crimea, where there are popular resort areas along its south-east and west coast and also along the coast of Kherson Oblast. Before the Second World War Crimea was the homeland of a sizeable concentration of Tatars. They were expelled from their homeland in 1944 on charges of alleged collaboration with the German forces of occupation and have not been permitted to return.

Odessa (population: 1,046,000)
Picturesquely situated on terraced hills 30 km north-east of the mouth of the Dniester River, Odessa together with its sister port of *Ilyichevsk* is one of the chief, if not *the* chief, ports of the Soviet Union. The present town was founded in the fourteenth century by Catherine the Great in 1794, but during the course of its history it has undergone several vicissitudes at the hands of Lithuanians, Poles, Turks, Germans and revolutionaries, and suffered also from the effects of famines and diseases. It is a long established centre of market-oriented, labour-intensive industries, which include branches of the engineering industry (machine tools and instruments, etc.), industrial acids and alkalis, phosphate fertilisers, clothing and food industries (*see* Fig. 172). Its foreign trade functions have already been noted (*see* p. 283).

Nikolayev (population: 441,000)
Situated at the mouth of the Southern Bug River, Nikolayev was founded at the end of the eighteenth century as a shipbuilding centre and naval base. As previously noted (*see* p. 106), many ocean-going vessels of the Soviet Union are built here, and there are also agricultural engineering works, food and light industries. It has experienced a sizeable increase in population in recent years, growing by over a fifth between 1970 and 1979.

Kherson (population: 319,000)
Kherson was established at about the same time as Nikolayev and for the same purpose. The port, on the Dnieper River 24 km from its mouth, in addition to its trading functions, is concerned with building river vessels for the inland waterway along the Dnieper, the manufacture of agricultural implements (including combine harvesters for maize), textiles and food canning. Like Nikolayev, Kherson is gaining population rather rapidly — increasing by almost a quarter between 1970 and 1979.

Simferol (population: 302,000)
Situated on the northern slopes of the Crimean Ridge, Simferol is
the capital of the Crimean Oblast. It covers the site of the ancient
Scythian town of Neapolis (third to fourth century BC). In addition to its administrative functions it has industries based on
products grown in the local area such as fruit canning, and the curing
of tobacco.

Sevastopol (population: 301,000)
Standing on the south-west tip of the Crimean Peninsula near the
site of the ancient Greek colony, Chersonesus, Sevastopol is the
best harbour and chief Soviet naval base in the Black Sea. It is
famous in British history as the scene of the siege by the Anglo-
French armies during the Crimean War (1854-56). The battlefields
of Balaclava and Inkerman are near by.

Kerch (population: 157,000)
Situated on the extreme eastern end of the Peninsula, Kerch is a
port and centre of an iron mining and metallurgical district. It
occupies the site of the ancient Greek town of Panticapaeum.

5. MOLDAVIA

This region (*see* Fig. 173) equates with the Moldavian SSR, carved
out in 1940 from the Romanian province of Bessarabia and the
former Moldavian ASSR. It has not been granted the rank of a major

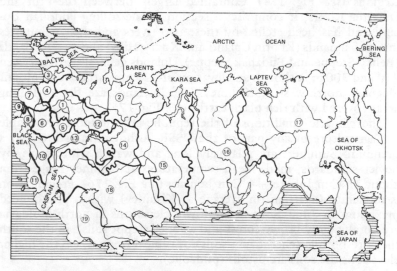

Fig. 173. Soviet Union: location of Moldavia Economic Region.

economic region and falls outside the eighteen-region scheme. It is, however, included as a basic economic region in the scheme of seven economic macro-regions of the USSR devised by Aleksandrov *et al.* (1974) for long-term planning purposes. The republic still retains its traditional agricultural base of vineyards, animal husbandry and maize, but is undergoing a gradual transition towards more light industry, including textiles, food, chemicals, and consumer durables. Irrigation investments along the Dniester River are expected to augment yields of fruit, grapes, sugar-beet and vegetables.

TABLE 48. MOLDAVIA: POPULATION, DENSITY AND TOWNS
WITH OVER 150,000 INHABITANTS IN 1979

Area:	33,700 km^2
Population (1979):	3,948,000
Density (persons per km^2):	116
Percentage urban:	39

Town	Population in thousands 1970 (census)	1979 (census)	Percentage increase 1970-79
Kishinev	357,000	503,000	41

PHYSICAL ASPECTS

Physically, Moldavia is a continuation of the South-West and South Regions (*see* Fig. 174). Contained largely between the Prut and Dniester Rivers, it comprises a section of the rolling Podolian Upland and has been etched by these two rivers and their tributaries into two uplands (Khotin Upland and Kodry Hills) and two lowlands (Beltsy Steppe and Budzhak Steppe). Uplands generally are between 250 and 300 m, although an elevation of 425 m is attained in Mount Meguray north-west of Kishinev. The lowlands are flat to rolling areas covered with rich black earths (*see* Fig. 175).

The climatic conditions of the republic are the most favourable for agriculture of any part of the USSR, although moisture is at a premium. Summers are relatively long and warm; winters are, by Soviet standards, mild. Mean temperatures at Kishinev range from about 21 °C in July to −4 °C in January (*see* Fig. 176). Precipitation is moderate (470 mm on average at Kishinev) with a pronounced maximum in June. Soils in the lower elevations in north Moldavia are boralfs (grey-brown forest and wooded steppe soils); in the south they are borolls (chernozem soils) of typical steppes. On the higher elevations the soils are ustolls (podzolic).

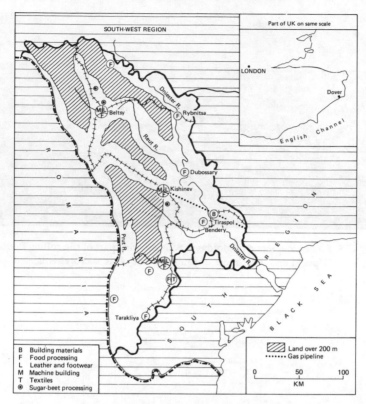

Fig. 174. Moldavia Economic Region.

THE ECONOMY

Agriculture

With its warm and relatively moist climate, Moldavia is particularly well suited to intensive agriculture and horticulture. Grain (maize and winter wheat) and livestock raising (cattle, sheep and pigs) are important throughout the republic, although it is the labour-intensive activities such as viticulture and the growing of fruits (apples, pears, cherries, plums), nuts, vegetables, tobacco and opium poppies which are typically associated with the area. Sunflowers and sugar-beet are also grown. Moldavia has about a third of the Soviet area of vineyards and is recognised as one of the chief wine districts of the country.

At present some 100,000 hectares of land are irrigated, in the Beltsy Steppe and Budzhak Steppe and along the lower Dneister

(Novosti)

Fig. 175. Landscape scene in Moldavia SSR showing part of the rolling Podolian Upland and the almost ubiquitous vineyards and orchards.

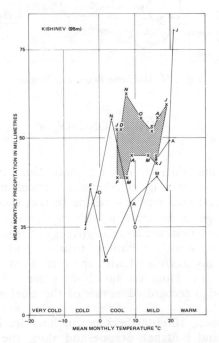

Fig. 176. Hythergraph for Kishinev (Kew, London, shaded).

valley. There are plans to irrigate a very much greater area along the River Dneister and in the Budzhak Steppe both to help avoid the hazard of summer drought and also to increase crop yields.

Industry
Devoid of significant mineral resources other than building materials, Moldavia is important mainly for its agricultural production, specialising in the production of wine, tobacco, fruits and vegetables, and in the food-processing industries. The republic takes third place in the USSR in the production of wine, tobacco and food-canning. Meat-packing and dairy products are growing industries. In percentage terms, industrial growth in the light industry sector during the last three decades has been appreciable. Innovations include food canneries, sugar refineries, tobacco factories, and fertiliser plant; revitalised industries include silk-throwing and woodworking.

POPULATION AND CITIES

With an over-all density of 116 people per km² Moldavia is the most densely populated republic in the entire USSR. It remains 61 per cent rural and pressure by the rural population on the available agricultural land is great.

After the Second World War about half a million of the Romanian population of Moldavia were resettled in the Astrakhan and Rostov provinces of the RSFSR and in Kazakhstan so that now, of the 3.9 million people of the republic, 64 per cent are Moldavians, 14 per cent are Ukrainians, 13 per cent are Russians, 3.5 per cent Gagauz, 2.0 per cent Bulgarians and 2.0 per cent Jews. The Gagauz, a Turkic ethnic group orthodox in religion and indigenous to the Balkans, moved into Moldavia early in the nineteenth century. An out-migration of Moldavians from their republic to the RSFSR since the 1970s has been balanced by an inflow of Russians into Moldavia.

Kishinev (population: 503,000)
Capital of the Moldavian SSR, Kishinev is centrally situated within the republic on a tributary of the Dniester River. It was severely damaged during the Second World War and at least half of the city has since been rebuilt. In addition to its administrative and cultural functions, it has light industries concerned with food, wine, leather and tobacco processing, chemicals, textiles and machine construction. The population of the city has increased markedly in recent years (e.g. 41 per cent between 1970 and 1979) due to natural growth of the city's population, people migrating from the countryside in search of work in industry and others moving from colder parts of the country in search of milder climatic conditions.

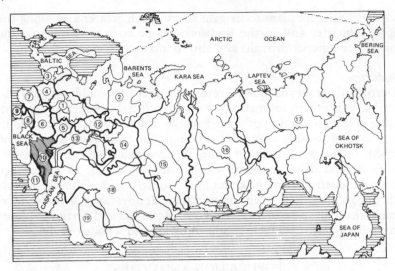

Fig. 177. Soviet Union: location of North Caucasus Economic Region.

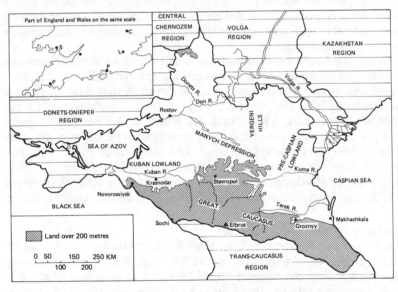

Fig. 178. North Caucasus Economic Region.

6. NORTH CAUCASUS ECONOMIC REGION

The North Caucasus Economic Region (*see* Fig. 177) extends from
the Great Caucasus Mountains in the south to the lower Don River
in the north, and from the Caspian Sea in the east to the Sea of

Azov and the Black Sea in the west (*see* Fig. 178). Including Rostov, Krasnodar, and Stavropol Oblasts and four ASSRs it lacks nodality as well as resource diversity (*see* Table 49). However, economic expansion is likely to continue because of the availability of natural gas and chemicals and the investment in irrigation.

TABLE 49. NORTH CAUCASUS ECONOMIC REGION: ADMINISTRATIVE UNITS, THEIR POPULATION AND DENSITY

Area: 354,700 km^2
Population (1979): 15,487,000

Administrative unit	Area	Population 1979	Density (persons per km^2)	Percentage urban
Rostov Oblast	101	4,081	40	69
Krasnodar Kray	84	4,814	56	51
(incl. Adyge AO)	8	404	52	47
Stavropol Kray	81	2,539	30	49
(incl. Karachay-Kherkess)	14	369	26	42
Kabardian-Balkar ASSR	12	675	56	47
North Ossetian ASSR	8	597	75	64
Chechen-Ingush ASSR	19	1,154	62	42
Daghestan ASSR	50	1.627	32	35

TABLE 50. NORTH CAUCASUS ECONOMIC REGION: TOWNS WITH OVER 150,000 INHABITANTS IN 1979

Town	Population in thousands		Percentage increase 1970-79
	1970 (census)	1979 (census)	
Rostov-on-Don	789	934	18
Krasnodar	464	560	21
Groznyy	341	375	10
Sochi	224	287	28
Ordzhonikidze	236	279	18
Taganrog	254	277	9
Stavropol	198	258	30
Makhachkala	186	250	35
Shakhty	205	210	2
Nalchik	146	207	42
Novocherkassk	162	183	13
Armavir	145	162	11
Novorossiysk	133	159	20

PHYSICAL ASPECTS

Relief
The most prominent physical features of the region are the northern ranges and slopes of the Great Caucasus Mountains and their northern foreland (*see* Fig. 179). Like the Ukrainian Carpathians and the Crimean Mountains to the west, and the Kopet-Dag and Pamirs to the east, this formidable range dates from the period of Alpine (Tertiary) folding. The area lay on the northern border of the great Alpine geosyncline. Earth movements caused by crustal pressures from north and south threw this zone into a series of anticlinal uplands and synclinal troughs. The mountains that now represent the evidence of these movements are a composite system of more or less parallel ranges with a crystalline backbone running west-north-west to east-south-east across the Caucasian isthmus and flanked by ranges running generally *en echelon*. During their relatively short history (in geological terms), they have undergone two major uplifts and suffered severe erosion, both by water and by ice. The zone of the Great Caucasus Mountains is in fact still unstable, as evidenced by the earthquakes, often locally disastrous, that disturb the area. The highest parts carry permanent mountain glaciers, the shrunken remains of Quaternary icefields and glaciers.

The Great Caucasus, extending nearly 1,300 km, form an effective mountain barrier between 80 and 250 km wide, right across the isthmus between the Black and Caspian Seas, with few readily negotiable passes. The watershed lies on the more southerly of the two principal parallel ranges; the highest peaks occur in the northerly range — Mount Elbrus, 5,642 m; Mount Koshtan-Tau, 5,210 m; and the Kazbek at about 5,040 m.

The northern foreland, lying beyond the Caucasus foothills, has two contrasting sections separated by the dome-shaped Stavropol Plateau. In the west is a steppe plain drained by the Kuban River to the Sea of Azov; in the east is a semi-desert plain drained by the Kuma-Terek Rivers to the Caspian Sea. The former is underlain by rich chernozems, the latter by sandy and salt-impregnated soils.

North of the Kuma-Manych depression — which in late Quaternary times connected the Black and the Caspian Seas — lies the elevated, though much dissected, plain of the lower Don and Donets Rivers. This plain is separated from the Caspian desert lowland by the Yergeni Hills, a southern extension of the Volga Heights.

Climate
The region as a whole is characterised by a continental climate which increases in severity towards the east. On the plains in the north the mean temperature of the warmest month (July) reaches

(*Novosti*)

Fig. 179. Summits of the Great Caucasus. The Great Caucasus, with peaks reaching 5,600 m and no low passes, presents a definite barrier to atmospheric movements and a formidable obstacle to transport links between the European part of the USSR and Trans-Caucasia.

21-24 °C, with maxima exceeding 38 °C. For the coldest month (January) the temperature is near −4 °C although cold waves accompanying north-easterly winds often cause it to drop to between −23 ° and −26 °C. At Stavropol (575 m), the January and July values are −5 °C and 20 °C respectively (*see* Fig. 180), and at Ordzhonikidze (625 m) they are −4° C and 20° C respectively. Annual precipitation on the plains diminishes from 460 to 500 mm in the west to less than 150 mm in the east. Intense surface heating on the plains in summer leads to the inflow of moisture from the Black Sea and the Sea of Azov, to frequent thunderstorms, and to a summer maximum of rainfall. Annual aggregates increase from 710 to 760 mm in the foothills to 2,039-2,550 mm in the mountains, with no dimunition of quantity from west to east. Above 1,000 m the mountains are permanently snow-covered.

Föhn winds from the mountains in spring cause rapid snow melt

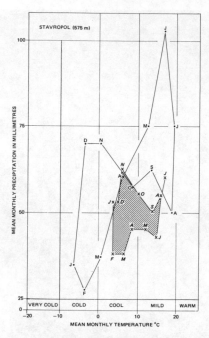

Fig. 180. Hythergraph for Stavropol (Kew, London, shaded).

and avalanches. During the summer the winds resemble the *sukhovey* and affect the sowing of crops and the harvesting of fruit.

THE ECONOMY

Agriculture

The steppelands of the lower Don are extensively used for growing wheat, sunflowers, millet and sugar-beet and for the grazing of cattle and sheep. Between Rostov and Tsimlyansk on the River Don, and along the lower Donets River, market gardening, dairying and fruit cultivation are carried on. The lowlands of the Kuban River to the west of the foreland resemble the better parts of the South-West Region, for they have fertile chernozem-like soils and a prosperous, intensive and progressive agriculture. A great variety of crops are grown: spring and winter wheat, oil seeds (especially sunflowers), sugar-beet, tobacco, maize, cotton and rice (in the swamp delta of the Kuban River). Along the shore of the Black Sea and in the shelter of the Caucasus, tobacco, tea, grapes, apricots, apples and pears are the main crops (*see* Fig. 181).

In the dry, eastern part of the foreland, crop husbandry takes second place to cattle and sheep herding. There is some irrigation

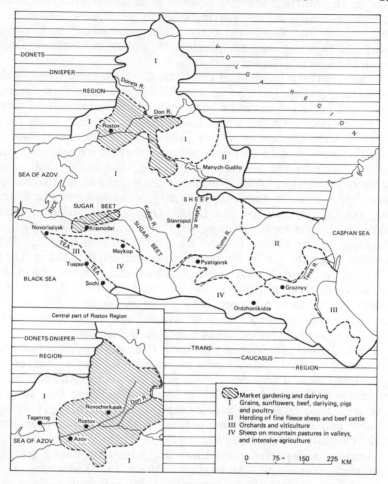

Fig. 181. North Caucasus Economic Region: agricultural land-use regions.

agriculture in the Kuma, Terek and Sulak river valleys, and more particularly in the better-watered foothills south of the Terek River where winter wheat, maize, vines, cotton, rice and fruits are grown. Within the Great Caucasus Mountains transhumance is widely practised, the stock making good use of mountain pastures during the summer.

Fuels, raw materials and industry
The extreme eastern end of the Donets coalfield lies in the valleys of the lower Don and Donets Rivers (i.e. in the western fringe of Rostov Oblast). Though separated by Gosplan from the Donets-

Dnieper Region there are thus obvious links between the two areas. Anthracite coal is mined, particularly around Shakhty, Kamensk-Shakhtinskiy and Koksovyy, there is heavy metallurgy at Krasnyy Sulin and Taganrog, and engineering takes place in Rostov-on-Don, Novocherkassk and Taganrog.

In the northern foothills of the Great Caucasus there are oilfields and natural gas deposits. The oilfields have been known from earliest times and exploited since the latter half of the nineteenth century. By comparison with the Volga-Ural and West Siberian fields they are small and their output, though significant (19 million tonnes in 1980), is now rivalled in importance by that of natural gas. The main oil centres are Neftegorsk, Maykop, Malgobek, Gudermes, Groznyy and Makhachkala. Refineries are located at Makhachkala, Groznyy, Krasondar and Tuapse with pipeline links to the Black Sea, the Caspian Sea and the Donets-Dnieper Region. A pipeline takes natural gas from Groznyy to Tbilisi and from Groznyy and Stavropol to the Centre Region via Rostov-on-Don (see Fig. 58). Another takes the gas via Krasnodar to Novorossiysk (see Fig. 182).

Non-ferrous metals such as molybdenum and tungsten (found in the Kabardian-Balkar ASSR), zinc and lead (Sadon and Ordzhonikidze) are mined and refined, and Novorossiysk on the Black Sea has a large production of concrete. Within the Great Caucasus there is a large reserve of timber and of potential water power.

The industrial activities of the North Caucasus Region reflect the availability of coal, petroleum and gas supplies and a prosperous agricultural base. There are metallurgical and engineering industries in Rostov Oblast and oil refining, machine-building (for the oil industry), flour-milling, vegetable oil production, distilling, tanning, tobacco manufacture and meat-packing in the Kuban Lowland and in the Caucasus foothills (see Fig. 183).

Tourism is important and there are numerous inland resorts. Pyatigorsk, Yessentuki, Mineralnyye Vody and Kislovodsk have mineral springs, some radio-active, in a volcanic region along the northern foothills of the Great Caucasus.

Yesterday I arrived in Pyatigorsk, rented a flat on the outskirts of the town, at its highest point, at the foot of the Mashuk: during thunderstorms the clouds will be coming down to my roof. Today, at five o'clock in the morning, when I opened the window, my room was filled with the scent of flowers growing in the modest little garden at the front. The branches of the flowering cherry-trees look into my window, and sometimes the wind covers my writing desk with their white petals. I have a wonderful view on three sides. To the west the five-headed Beshtu look blue, like "the last cloud of a spent storm"; to the north rises Mashuk, like a shaggy Persian hat, and covers all that part of the skyline; to the east the view is gayer: below and before me glitters the clean, new little town, the healing springs roar,

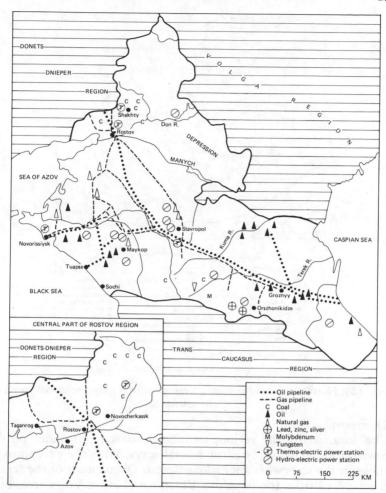

Fig. 182. North Caucasus Economic Region: mineral and power resources.

there is the sound of voices from the multilingual crowd, and there, further still, mountains are rising like an amphitheatre, bluer and mistier, and on the edge of the horizon stretches a silver chain of snow-clad mountain tops, beginning with a Kazbek and ending with the two-headed Elbrus. It is a pleasure to live in such a land!

M. Yu Lermontov, from *The Hero of our Time*

There is a popular seaside holidaying area along the Black Sea shores near Novorossiysk and also between Tuapse and Sochi, with numerous resorts, sanatoria and summer homes.

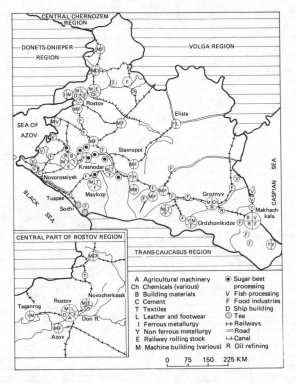

Fig. 183. North Caucasus Economic Region: railways and industrial structure of towns.

Transport

The location of the region, peripheral to the remainder of the Soviet Union, is expressed in several ways. With the exception of those in the somewhat anomalous Rostov Oblast most of the region is separated from the populous Ukraine and lower Volga areas by a thinly-populated tract of rather poor soils and low rainfall, and from the Trans-Caucasia Region by the high mountain barrier of the Great Caucasus. The Rostov-Makhachkala Railway was the only rail link between the south and the north of the region for over half a century, up to 1890. Now it has been supplemented by railways linking Volgograd-Tikhoretsk-Krasnodar-Novorossiysk, and Astrakhan-Kizlyar-Gudermes (see Fig. 183). The only railways connecting the North Caucasus Region with the Trans-Caucasian Republics pass along the shores of the Black and Caspian Seas at the extremities of the Great Caucasus. The former is the link between the rest of the Soviet Union and the Black Sea resorts. A recently completed line between Krasnodar and Tuapse through rugged mountain terrain provides a valuable short-cut between Rostov-on-

Don, the Black Sea resorts and Trans-Caucasia. The only road links across the Great Caucasus are the Georgian (Ordzhonikidze-Tbilisi), Sukhumi (Cherkessk-Sukhumi) and Ossetian (Alagir-Kutaisi) Military Roads. Mamison Pass on the Ossetian road is at 2,910 m and the highest point on the Georgian road is 2,380 m. The roads are tortuous and traffic over them is light. Built originally for military purposes they are now employed principally in carrying tourist traffic.

POPULATION AND CITIES

The distribution of population reflects economic, orographic and climatic conditions in the different parts of the region. Population densities range from fewer than 25 per km² in the uplands of the Krasnodar Oblast to 75 per km² in North Ossetian ASSR. Other areas of localised high densities are near gas and petroleum reserves. Among the high mountains, there is preserved a sparse population of perhaps the most varied collection of peoples to be found anywhere in the world. They include Iranic-speaking Ossetians, Turkic-speaking Balkars and Caucasic-speaking Kabardians, some of whom have autonomous republic status. Dagestan ASSR, for example, has one of the most complex ethnic situations in the world with as many as 30 ethnic groups identified. The inhabitants of the plains to the north of the Great Caucasus are largely the descendants of settlers, many of whom were Cossacks, who were given lands here in the eighteenth century. The region as a whole has experienced rapid population growth in recent years; the increase between 1970 and 1979 was over 1.2 millions or 8.4 per cent.

Rostov-on-Don (population: 934,000)
Situated on the right bank of the River Don 45 km from the Sea of Azov, Rostov-on-Don was founded in the eighteenth century as a frontier fortress against the Turks. It is now an important route focus, port and industrial centre. The town is also a collecting and assembly point for commodities and goods from the rich agricultural lands of the Kuban, the oil producing Caucasian foreland, the Donets coalfield, and, since the opening of the Volga-Don Canal in 1952, from the Volga Basin. Rostov port, closed by ice for three months in the year, exports wheat, petroleum and manufactured goods (*see* Fig. 183). *Azov* and *Taganrog* act as outports. Industries include engineering works (such as "Rosselmash" which specialises in tractors, combine harvesters and other agricultural machinery), aircraft, shipbuilding, electro-mechanical equipment, footwear and the processing of tobacco and fish.

Krasnodar (population: 560,000)
Situated on the navigable Kuban River 225 km from its mouth,

Krasnodar is the chief administrative, commercial and industrial centre of the rich Kuban agricultural area. Its industries include flour-milling, the manufacture and processing of butter, margarine fats and other foods, petroleum refining, and engineering (machine tools, petroleum machinery and spare parts for agricultural machinery). The town is the focus of routes from Novorossiysk, Rostov, Volgograd and Stavropol, and the Krasnodar Oblast has a major natural gas deposit (*see* Fig. 183).

Groznyy (population: 375,000)
Groznyy was founded in the late nineteenth century following the exploitation of nearby surface deposits of oil. Oil refinery, petrochemical and petroleum machinery industries are located here. Oil pipelines link the town with Makhachkala and Rostov, gas pipelines with Tbilisi, Novorossiysk and Rostov.

Sochi (population: 287,000)
Situated on the eastern shore of the Black Sea, Sochi is the most important spa and seaside resort (*kurort*) in the Soviet Union. It has a range of sanatoria (i.e. rest homes, *putyovkas*), hotels and camps, and access to sea-bathing and mud and mineral-water baths. Sochi serves the recreational and health needs of visitors from all parts of the country. Testimony as to its popularity with holiday-makers is given by the notable 28 per cent increase in population in the nine-year inter-censal period 1970-79.

Ordzhonikidze (population: 279,000)
Capital of the North Ossetian ASSR, Ordzhonikidze lies at the northern entrance to the Georgian Military Road (*see* p. 299). There are lead and zinc industries, engineering works and chemical plant.

Taganrog (population: 277,000)
Situated on the Sea of Azov 65 miles west of Rostov, Taganrog is a coal port and steel-making centre. The heavy industries include tube-, pipe- and boiler-making, and agricultural machinery.

Stavropol (population: 258,000)
Situated on the plateau of the same name, Stavropol is a centre of agriculture-based and subsidiary industries. It experienced a 30 per cent growth rate between the census of 1970 and 1979.

Makhachkala (population: 250,000)
An oil transhipment port on the Caspian Sea, Makhachkala had a 35 per cent increase in population in the inter-censal period 1970-79 suggesting rapid urban expansion.

Shakhty (population: 210,000)
This old anthracite coal-mining town lies in the eastern part of the Donbass where it extends into the Rostov Oblast. It has leather, textile and food industries. Shakhty's population has tended to stagnate in recent years (a mere 2 per cent increase during the inter-censal period 1970-79) whereas growth in other major cities in the region in the same period has ranged from 10 per cent to 30 per cent.

Nalchik (population: 207,000)
Located within the foothills and northern slopes of the Caucasus, Nalchik is capital of the Kabardian-Balkar ASSR. It has factories processing agricultural raw materials, engineering plant and some light industry. Natural increase and rural-urban migration have resulted in a rapid increase in the size of the town in recent years (e.g. 42 per cent between 1970 and 1979 censuses).

Novocherkassk (population: 183,000)
Situated 35 km north-east of Rostov-on-Don, Novocherkassk was founded in 1805 when the inhabitants of old Cherkassk were com-pelled to leave the original site because of frequent inundations by the Don. Onetime administrative centre of the Don Cossacks (*see* p. 245-6), the town now manufactures electric locomotives, machine tools, heavy machinery, plastics and synthetic fibres.

Armavir (population: 162,000)
Situated in a rich agricultural region Armavir has developed from an Armenian *aul* into an industrial town with food-processing plant, meat-packing, fruit and vegetable canning, milk-processing, butter-making, engineering, wood-working and light industries (e.g. syn-thetic rubber).

Novorossiysk (population: 159,000)
Novorossiysk on the Black Sea claims to have the highest port turnover in the USSR. Pre-1914 it was second only to Odessa as a grain exporting port. Its exports now are dominated by cement from rich local deposits of high-grade marl. Local industries include engineering and fish processing.

7. TRANS-CAUCASUS ECONOMIC REGION

The Trans-Caucasus Economic Region (*see* Fig. 184) lies south of the main crest of the Great Caucasus Mountains. It comprises three non-Slavic republics: Georgia (Gruziya) SSR, Azerbaydzhan SSR and Armenia SSR, and is a multi-nodal region (*see* Fig. 185). While maintaining its traditional economic profile it is also undergoing a continuing process of urbanisation and industrialisation.

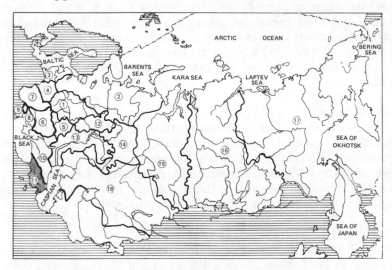

Fig. 184. Soviet Union: location of Trans-Caucasus Economic Region.

TABLE 51. TRANS-CAUCASUS ECONOMIC REGION:
ADMINISTRATIVE UNITS, THEIR POPULATION AND DENSITY

Area: 186,100 km²
Population (1979): 14,075,000

Administrative unit	Area (000 km²)	Population (000, 1979)	Density (persons per km²)	Percentage urban
Azerbaydzhan SSR	87	6,028	67	59
Georgian SSR	70	5,016	72	48
Armenian SSR	30	3,031	98	50

PHYSICAL ASPECTS

Relief and drainage
Though few parts of the Soviet Union display such variety of land-scapes as occur in this region, in essence there are three main relief regions. From north to south these are: the Great Caucasus south of the main crest-line (*see* p. 292), the Rioni-Kura depression, and the Lesser Caucasus. South of the southern foothills of the Great Cau-casus lies a sheltered tectonic depression which is drained to the

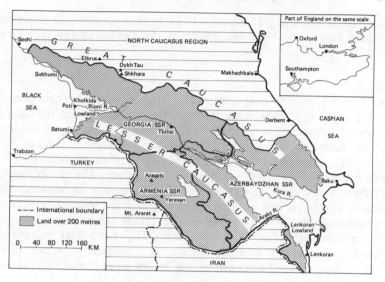

Fig. 185. Trans-Caucasus Economic Region.

TABLE 52. TRANS-CAUCASUS ECONOMIC REGION:
TOWNS WITH OVER 150,000 INHABITANTS IN 1979

| | Population in thousands | | |
Town	1970 (census)	1979 (census)	Percentage increase 1970-79
Baku, with suburbs	1,266	1,550	22
Tbilisi	889	1,066	20
Yerevan	767	1,019	33
Kirovabad	190	232	22
Leninakan	165	207	25
Kutaisi	161	194	21
Sumgait	125	190	53

Black Sea by the River Rioni and to the Caspian Sea by the River Kura. This depression is not a simple structural trough. Between the alluvial valleys of the Rivers Rioni and Inguri in the West and of the Lower Kura and Araks Rivers in the east, lies a belt of hilly, even mountainous country whose broken relief sometimes rises to over 600 m. This belt, called the Suram Uplands, links the Great Caucasus with the Lesser Caucasus and the Armenian volcanic plateau. The area west of the Suram Uplands, together with the Black Sea coast south of the Great Caucasus, is the Kolkhida Lowland (*Colchis* of the ancient Greeks). East of the Suram Uplands is the larger and very flat Kura-Araks Lowland; its extension southwards along the Caspian coast to the Iranian border is the Lenkoran (*Talysh*) Lowland.

Climate

The Great Caucasus is an important climatic divide, constituting a high barrier to atmospheric movement and sheltering the Trans-Caucasus Region from bitterly cold northern air during the winter.

The Kolkhida Lowland has a humid subtropical climate (*see* Fig. 186). Summers are warm (21-24 °C), winters are mild (4-7 °C) and, by Soviet standards, rainfall is very heavy. The rainfall varies between 1,500 and 2,540 mm and comes mainly in autumn and winter. This area, the south of Crimea and the extreme south of Turkmenia, are the only parts of the USSR where mean January temperatures are above freezing level. The Kura-Araks Lowland, with a steppe and semi-arid climate, is climatically an outlier of Central Asia. Near the mouth of the River Kura the annual rainfall is no more than 25 mm.

Borisov describes graphically the climate of Baku as follows.

Dry dusty winds are especially characteristic of the Baku district where the local "norther" is an "Egyptian death". It occurs at any time of the year, but particularly in summer. The average wind velocity is fairly high — 7.6 meters per second — but individual gusts reach twenty or even forty metres per second. The strong, dry and dusty wind blows for two or three days in succession, or at times even for nine days or more without interruption.

The Lenkoran Lowland, facing the Caspian Sea and sheltered by the Talysh Mountains, has a subtropical climate, but is less humid, (1,000-1,300 mm) than the Kolkhida Lowland.

THE ECONOMY

Agriculture and forestry

The warm moist climate of Kolkhida promotes a luxuriant vegetation. Where the land is not swampy, or has been drained, conditions are ideal for oranges, lemons, grapefruit and tangerines, tea (*see* Fig. 187), maize and tung oil. Ginger, bamboo, tobacco and mulberries (for the silk industry) are also grown. Farther east, in the warm dry valleys of eastern Georgia are some of the most important commercial vineyards of the Soviet Union and there is a flourishing wine industry. The well-drained terraces along the Iori and Alazani valleys are particularly important for vines, tobacco and fruits (*see* Fig. 188).

The southern slopes of the Great Caucasus west of the Suram Uplands are forested and fir, spruce, pine and beech are felled. In

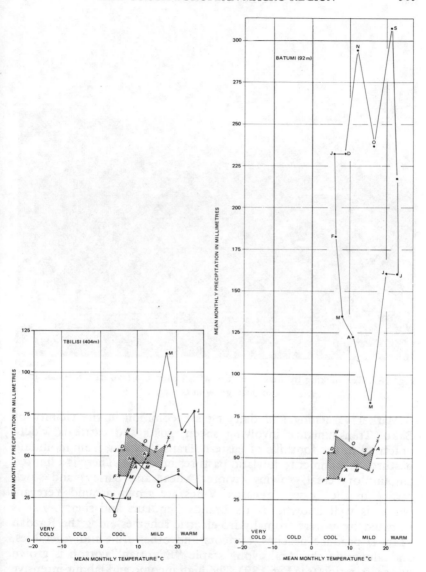

Fig. 186. Hythergraphs for Tbilisi and Batumi (Kew, London, shaded).

the east, on the lower reaches of the River Kura, lies an unhealthy swamp, but in the irrigated areas there is large-scale growing of cotton, rice and lucerne (alfalfa). Mulberry trees grown along most of the irrigation canals provide the basis for silk-worm culture and a silk industry. Southwards, in the Lenkoran Lowland, citrus fruits, tea, olives, wheat and barley are important.

(Novosti)

Fig. 187. Tea picking by machine. Tea with lemon is a favourite Russian drink and both grow in Georgia.

Market gardening and dairying are common in the vicinity of Baku. Transhumance involving sheep, goats and cattle is widely practised in the foothills of eastern Trans-Caucasia, from mountain pastures in summer to lowland pastures in winter. There is a limited amount of cereal growing (winter wheat and barley) and stock raising in the Lesser Caucasus. Vines are grown around Yerevan, which is well known for its brandy, liqueurs and sherry. Lands irrigated by waters from hydro-electric schemes along the Razdan (Zanga) produce peaches, apricots and other fruit and vegetables, and alongside the Araks long staple "Egyptian" cotton is grown under irrigation (*see* Fig. 189). The high income and labour-intensive sectors of agriculture (grapes, citrus fruits, tea, cotton, etc.) compensate for the shortage of fertile level land in this generally mountainous region.

Raw materials and industry
Citrus fruits, grapes, tea, tobacco, cotton, silk and wool provide the bases for some industries, but petroleum (with which Baku and district have long been virtually synonymous) is the single most

(Novosti)

Fig. 188. Vineyards and windbreaks on the Samgora *sovkhoz*, Georgia SSR.

important resource of Trans-Caucasia or, more specifically, of Azerbaydzhan. The oil occurs in Oligocene grits and sandstones beneath a capping of younger limestones and clays where the Kura depression adjoins the eastern end of the folds of the Great Caucasus. Exploitation began in the 1860s and, by the turn of the century, the Baku field was producing half of the world's petroleum, the bulk being exported abroad. Baku's position as chief oil-producing area of the USSR was eclipsed after the Second World War by the Volga-Urals field (then called "Second Baku"), but its production, though declining, is still significant. The main producing area, for both heavy and light oils, is within the Apsheron Peninsula, but as the search for oil continues, more wells are being drilled from off-shore platforms in the Caspian Sea. Some wells are 80-100 km from the shore and in some cases houses, flats, offices, cinemas and shops have been built on the platforms which are linked to land by causeways. Smaller oilfields occur near the mouth of the Kura

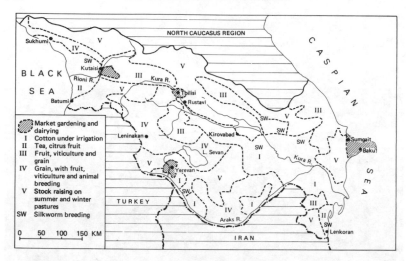

Fig. 189. Trans-Caucasus Economic Region: agricultural land-use regions.

River. Most of the oil is sent out of the region by tanker from the port of Baku, or by pipeline to the refinery at Batumi on the Black Sea coast.

Manganese (with Chiatura and Kutaisi districts producing about 22 per cent of the total USSR output), copper (at Alaverdi and Kafan), alunite (at Alunitdag), and salt (at Beyuk Shor and Nakhichevan) are of all-Union importance. Huge quantities of natural gas, found at Bakhar, 40 km south-west of Baku, are piped to five thermal-electric stations at Ali Bayramly, Tbilisi, Yerevan and Nevinnomyssk (each with a capacity in excess of half a million kW) and supply the large and growing chemical industry (see Fig. 190). Hydro-electric power is being actively developed; the dam and reservoir at Mingechaur on the Kura River, a multipurpose scheme involving hydro-electricity, irrigation, flood protection and river transportation, is the largest of the region. There is another series of dams and reservoirs on the small Razdan River that drains Lake Sevan to the Araks River (see Fig. 191).

Oil is not only a major source of energy but is also a raw material for a whole range of petrochemical industries. In addition, the need to provide turbo-drills, pipes, compressors, storage tanks, machinery and similar equipment for the oil industry has stimulated their manufacture within the region. Such industries and a wide range of ancillary ones are to be found in Baku. Steel, using Dashkesan iron ore, and Georgian and Donbass coal, is obtained from Rustavi, near Tbilisi. Sumgait, near Baku, is another steel centre, with aluminium works and a plant for making synthetic rubber. With new alumina

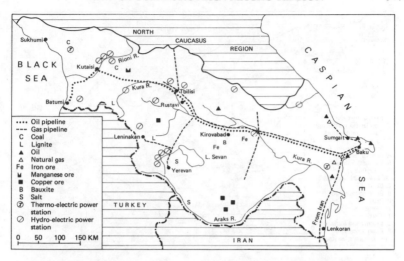

Fig. 190. Trans-Caucasus Economic Region: mineral and power resources.

(Novosti)

Fig. 191. Lake Sevan in the Armenian SSR, 1,900 m above sea level. Note the bare mountain slopes and the ninth century monastery on the rocky peninsula.

plants at Kirovabad and Razdan and aluminium ones at Sumgait and Yerevan, the Trans-Caucasus has become a major aluminium-producing region.

In recent years several new light industries (electrical and electronic equipment, microprocessors, colour TVs, computers, etc.,

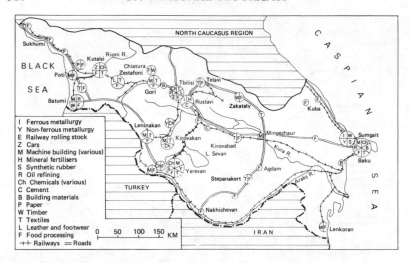

Fig. 192. Trans-Causasus Economic Region: railways and industrial structure of towns.

have been introduced into the larger cities of Trans-Caucasia. Planners are also endeavouring to integrate the whole region into a single territorial-production complex.

Transport

Difficult physical conditions hindered the construction of railways in Trans-Caucasia, and it was not until the turn of the century that the local system was linked to the railways of what is now European USSR. The Suram Uplands provided a particularly formidable obstacle to longitudinal communications along the Trans-Caucasian Lowlands and it was not until 1883 that the link between Tbilisi and Baku was achieved. The gradient on the line through the Suram Uplands is reported to be 1 in 50. No railway crosses the Great Caucasus and the classical land route, now followed by a railway, by-passes the mountains by traversing the Caspian shore via Derbent (*see* Fig. 192). It was not until after considerable difficulty that a road and railway were built along the Black Sea shore. The narrow coastal land routes on the west and east offer the simplest methods of negotiating the barrier of the Great Caucasus. A railway follows the Araks valley through the Lesser Caucasus, along the boundary with Iran and Turkey and joins Baku with Tbilisi via Leninakan. A branch of this line to Yerevan provides a link with Tabriz and Tehran in Iran, and Erzurum in Anatolia (Turkey).

Pipelines afford valuable means of transporting oil and natural gas out of the region (*see* Fig. 191).

POPULATION AND CITIES

The 14 million people living in Trans-Caucasia are mainly non-Russian and speak a variety of languages. They are of diverse ethnic origin, many with civilisations far older than that of the Russians. The three major groups — the Georgians, Armenians and Azerbaydzhanis — are numerous enough to form Union Republics. The Georgians and Armenians belong to the Caucasian ethnic group. The Georgians, highly concentrated in their republic, are Orthodox (except near Batumi); the ubiquitous Armenians belong to one of the oldest Christian churches, the Armenian Church, centred on Echmiadzin 20 km west of Yerevan. The Azerbaydzhanis, who migrated to the Caucasus from around the southern end of the Caspian Sea, belong to the Turkic ethnic group and are traditionally Moslem in religion. They differ from the Armenians and Georgians by a high rate of natural increase that resembles that of the Moslem groups in Soviet Central Asia.

The surge in development of power production, iron and steel-making, metallurgy, engineering, chemicals, building materials and in food and light industries has been widespread. Consequently, new towns have been set up in mining areas, near hydro-electric stations and around factories processing agricultural produce. Half the population of Armenia and Azerbaydzhan now lives in towns (mainly in the republic capitals) although there are several other localised high densities of population in all three republics. The humid Black Sea littoral and Kolkhida Lowland support more than 100-200 persons per km^2, as does the thickly-settled country around Baku. The drier eastern parts, notably in the steppe of the Kura Lowlands, have fewer than 20 persons per km^2, although here, too, there are some localised high densities, particularly in areas of irrigated farming. The sparse population of the Great Caucasus is generally found in nucleated villages. The Armenian Plateau has a sparse nomadic population, but irrigated farming areas along the Rivers Razdan (near Yerevan) and Araks (Nagorno-Karabakh AO) are thickly settled.

Baku (population: 1,550,000)
Capital of the Azerbaydzhan SSR, Baku lies on the western shore of the Caspian Sea on the southern side of the Apsheron Peninsula (*see* Fig. 193). When the several oil town of the Apsheron Peninsula, together with the oil settlements built on piles or stilts in the Caspian Sea are included, Greater Baku has a population of one and a half million. It is the fourth largest city of the USSR and the most important industrial city in Trans-Caucasia. Baku's great importance lies in its nearby petroleum resources which have been exploited since 1873. Oil derricks, refineries, processing plant, pipelines and

Fig. 193. Baku: capital of Azerbaydzhan SSR, the fourth largest city of the USSR.

other industrial paraphernalia jostle with Moslem mosques and a Shah's palace in what was formerly a ninth-century fortress town. The port, much troubled by silting and by strong northerly winds in winter exports petroleum across the Caspian and up the Volga River. Oil is also exported by pipeline to Batumi on the Black Sea. In addition to its oil refining, it has petrochemical, engineering, cotton textile, leather, meat-packing, flour-milling and timber industries (*see* Fig. 192).

Tbilisi (Tiflis) (population: 1,066,000)

Capital of the Georgian SSR and centre of Georgian culture, Tbilisi is an attractive city in a fertile basin of the upper Kura River, within the lower slopes of the Suram Uplands (*see* Fig. 194). Its foundation dates from the fourth century, but its history has been chequered, with several plunderings at the hands of Byzantines, Arabs, Iranians, Mongols and Turks. Oriental markets, bazaars and buildings of historical and architectural interest in the old part of the town stand in

(Fotokbronika Tass)

Fig. 194. Tbilisi: formerly Tiflis, capital of Georgia SSR. The view shows the Molekhi Fort (thirteenth century), the oldest part of the town on the right bank of the Kura River, and Mtatsminda Mountain topped by a television mast and restaurant.

stark contrast to the more modern geometrical layout of the Russian part. It is also an important rail focus and southern terminus of the Georgian Military Road from Ordzhonikidze via the famous Dariali Gorge. Industries in the city produce textiles (especially silk), hosiery, leather goods, tobacco, vegetable oils, wines, foods, machinery (for the tea, citrus and vine growing of Trans-Caucasia), electric locomotives and plastics (in association with its oil refining).

Yerevan (population: 1,019,000)
Lying on the Armenian Plateau where historic and relatively easy passes lead to Iran and Anatolia, Yerevan is the capital and cultural centre of the Armenian SSR (*see* Fig. 195). It is located on the Razdan (Zanga) River, a tributary of the Araks River, over 900 m above sea-level and dominated by the majestic peaks of Mount Aragats (4,094 m) in the north-west and Mount Ararat (5,156 m) on Turkish territory immediately to the south. The city has had a long and stormy history dating from the eighth century BC. It was incorporated within the Russian Empire in 1828 after a war with Persia, and attained capital status in 1920. In addition to its administrative

Fig. 195. Yerevan: with the monument of Lenin in the city centre. Most of the buildings in Yerevan are constructed of pink or mauve tufa stone which gives the city a distinctive character.

functions it has several important industries. Chemicals are represented by plastics and synthetic rubber, and engineering by cables, machine tools, turbines, lamps and generators. An aluminium works here uses alumina hauled 2,000 km or more from the Urals. Textiles, clothing, footwear, tobacco, wines, foodstuffs, chloroprene rubber, leather and woodwork are also produced (*see* Fig. 192). Local supplies of hydro-electricity and Azerbaydzhan natural gas provide the energy used in the manufacturing industries.

Kirovabad (population: 232,000)
Situated in the middle Kura valley, Kirovabad has an important alumina industry (using Zaglik alunite) and supplies the aluminium reduction plants at Sumgait and Yerevan. This is in addition to its earlier butter-making and cotton textile industries.

Leninakan (population: 207,000)
Situated on the western edge of Armenia in a mainly stock-raising area, Leninakan has a meat packing plant. It also manufactures carpets, textiles and light machinery.

Kutaisi (population: 194,000)
Situated in the Kholkida Lowland, Kutaisi was the ancient capital of western Georgia. It is now the centre of an important fruit and

(Fotokhronika Tass)

Fig. 196. Pitsunda: a modern seaside resort on the Black Sea coast, 90 km
north-west of Sukhumi.

vine-growing district with a variety of associated industries. Textiles
(particularly silk) and motor-car assembly plants are also located
here. The nearby Tkibuli bituminous coal mines supply much of the
local coal requirement.

Sumgait (population: 190,000)
This is a steel and petrochemicals complex on the Caspian Sea north
of the Apsheron Peninsula. It specialises in steel pipes for the oil
industry and also produces synthetic rubber from by-products of
its oil refineries. Its population underwent a spectacular 53 per cent
increase in the nine-year intercensal period 1970-79.

Other important cities
Rustavi (129,000), southeast of Tbilisi, has ferrous metallurgical
industries using Dashkesan iron ore and Tkvarcheli (Georgia) and
Donbass coking coals. *Batumi* (124,000) on the Black Sea is an oil
refining centre and oil and tea exporting port. Also on the Black
Sea are a number of popular holiday resorts including *Sukhumi, Gagra*
and *Pitsunda* (*see* Fig. 196).

CHAPTER XIV

Volga-Urals Macro-Region

As with the six other economic macro-regions of the USSR, the Volga-Urals Macro-Region is a consolidation of existing basic economic regions, namely the Volga-Vyatka (which might also be included in the North-Central European Macro-Region), Volga and Urals regions, all in the RSFSR. The macro-region is a recognition of homogeneity in such key parameters as manpower, fuels, land, water and transport geography in the basic economic regions. It contains 7.3 per cent of the total area of the USSR, 17 per cent of its population and 18.5 per cent of the urban population. Its potential fuel and energy resources are but 1.6 per cent of the country's total, but it has 10.5 per cent of the predicted iron ore reserves, 7.0 per cent of the timber resources and 15.7 per cent of the agricultural land. The higher level of economic development in the Volga-Urals Macro-Region (as also in the North-Central European and South European Macro-Regions) compared with the eastern macro-regions is reflected in lower labour and transport costs, whereas in the east (*see* p. 359) labour and transport costs are high while the costs of natural resources are at a minimum.

1. VOLGA-VYATKA ECONOMIC REGION

Volga-Vyatka (*see* Fig. 197), with just over 3 per cent of the total population and slightly more than 1 per cent of the total area of the USSR, contains two major industrial nodes — Gorkiy and Kirov-Slobodskoy — and several smaller cities (*see* Fig. 198). The two major nodes play a key role in the over-all integration of the region with economic linkages based on machine-building, transport equipment, chemical and wood-processing industries. Agriculture in the region continues to struggle against marginal soils and a short growing season.

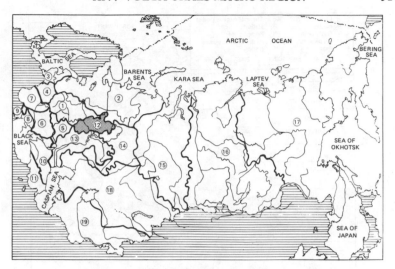

Fig. 197. Soviet Union: location of Volga-Vyatka Economic Region.

TABLE 53. VOLGA-VYATKA ECONOMIC REGION:
ADMINISTRATIVE UNITS, THEIR POPULATION AND DENSITY

Area: 263,200 km²
Population (1979): 8,343,000

Administrative unit	Area (000 km²)	Population (000, 1979)	Density (persons per km²)	Percentage urban
Gorkiy Oblast	74	3,695	50	73
Kirov Oblast	120	1,662	14	64
Mordov ASSR	26	990	38	47
Mari ASSR	23	703	31	53
Chuvash ASSR	18	1,293	72	46

PHYSICAL ASPECTS

The region lies astride the upper-middle Volga River and the upper reaches of its tributary the Vyatka River. In the south it encroaches on the northern part of the Volga Upland (Volga Heights); elsewhere it occupies the eastern margins of the Russian Lowland south of the morainic ridge known as the Shiboli Upland. Parts of the region are heavily forested — in the north coniferous (*tayga*) underlain by vast expanses of bog and marsh, in the south mixed deciduous. Soils are spodosols (aquods, podsols) of indifferent quality and needing much drainage and fertilising to improve the flax crops and cattle pastures.

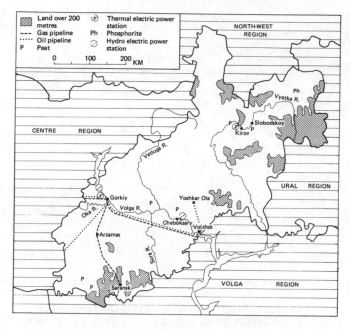

Fig. 198. Volga-Vyatka Economic Region.

TABLE 54. VOLGA-VYATKA ECONOMIC REGION:
TOWNS WITH OVER 150,000 INHABITANTS IN 1979

| Town | Population in thousands | | Percentage increase 1970-79 |
	1970 (census)	1979 (census)	
Gorkiy	1,170	1,344	15
Kirov	332	390	17
Cheboksary	216	308	43
Saransk	191	263	38
Dzerzhinsk	221	257	16
Yoshkar-Ola	166	201	21

The change from mixed deciduous forest to *tayga* reflects the change in climate from the somewhat warmer and drier conditions of the south to a moister and colder climate in the north. The mean January temperature in the south-west (Saransk) is −11 °C and −14 °C in the north-east (Kirov) (*see* Fig. 199). July mean temperatures are 18 °-20 °C throughout the region. Precipitation increases from 460 mm in the south to 560 mm in the north.

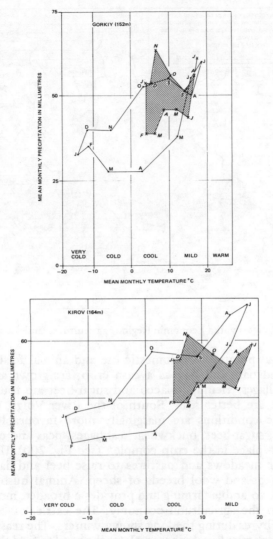

Fig. 199. Hythergraphs for Gorkiy and Kirov (Kew, London, shaded).

THE ECONOMY

Agriculture and forestry

At first sight, agriculture in Volga-Vyatka appears not to be significant. Only 40 per cent of the total area is cultivated and yields are among the lowest in the country for both crops and livestock products. This is due largely to an unfavourable environment. However,

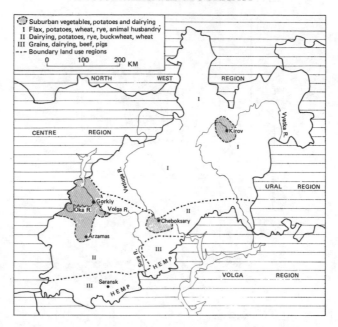

Fig. 200. Volga-Vyatka Economic Region: agricultural land-use regions.

crops such as potatoes for domestic use and animal feed, together
with rye and oats and flax as a cash crop, are grown around the
scattered villages. Hemp, tobacco and sugar-beet are found locally
where there are better soils. South of the River Volga, where soil
and climatic conditions are marginally more favourable, millets,
hemp, hops, sugar-beet, buckwheat, cabbages, peas and other vegetables find a place in the crop complex (*see* Fig. 200). Use is made
also of river meadows and pastures to raise beef and dairy cattle,
pigs, and meat and wool breeds of sheep. Animal husbandry is a
complement to arable farming and provides a broader, more diversified base to the agricultural economy. The cattle, of course, are
confined to byres during the long snowy winters. The reason for this
activity in the agricultural sphere reflects the need to feed the growing
populations of Gorkiy, Kirov and other large towns, all of which
have market gardening, and dairying in their immediate vicinity.

Forests, mineral and power resources
The timber wealth (12 million hectares) is important with Kirov
and Gorkiy Oblasts and the Mari ASSR the main forest areas. Unfortunately there has been over-exploitation, but there are still
extensive forested areas. Overcutting continues to greatly exceed
replanting and reserves are becoming depleted. Even so, the output

of milled timber, house frames, plywood, pulp and paper and matches is considerable, and timber is transported down the Volga and Vyatka Rivers to the treeless steppe country in the south. Transport by timber rafts pulled by tugs is no longer possible because of the several dams that have been constructed on the Volga. The wood chemical industry at Ryava, Vakhtan and Shumerlya, producing cellulose, turpentine and wood alcohol, has been enlarged in recent years to utilise in addition natural gas, oil and phosphorites as raw materials. The timber resources are continuing to play a definite role, but on the whole the woodworking industry can no longer be considered a major branch of the economy.

Mineral resources are limited to some phosphorites in the upper Kama area which are used, together with other imported raw materials, in the chemical centre of Dzerzhinsk, a satellite town of Gorkiy.

Oil and gas brought in by pipeline provide the thermal energy and raw materials for manufacturing industry in the region, while the Volga which passes through the centre is a source of hydro-electric power. There are two major hydro schemes, one at Gorodets, 55 km upstream of Gorkiy, the other at Cheboksary, 200 km downstream of that city.

Manufacturing
The region is one of the least industrialised and least urbanised in the European part of the USSR. Indeed, were it not for the inclusion of the highly-industrialised Gorkiy Oblast in the region (which is itself essentially an easterly extension of the Centre Region) the remainder would be predominantly rural territory much of it still heavily forested. Industrial ouput in Volga-Vyatka during the last quarter of a century has lagged well behind that for the USSR as a whole.

The greater part of the manufacturing industry is located in the Gorkiy area, though timber-based industries, for which the region is probably best known, are widely scattered. Metallurgy and machine construction, particularly of railway locomotives and rolling stock, motor vehicles (cars and lorries) and river vessels for use on the River Volga and its tributaries, submarines, tanks, aircraft industries, machine tools, oil refining and petrochemicals, and the making of plastics, synthetic fibres and fertilisers are among the several industries in Gorkiy and its environs (*see* Fig. 201).

The Volga River and its far-reaching tributaries continue to be of considerable importance as a means of transporting bulk goods, manufactured and otherwise, from, to and through the region. The reservoirs constructed along its length have converted the river into a deep main waterway navigable by large vessels. However, this "Mother of Rivers", historic highway and artery of communication

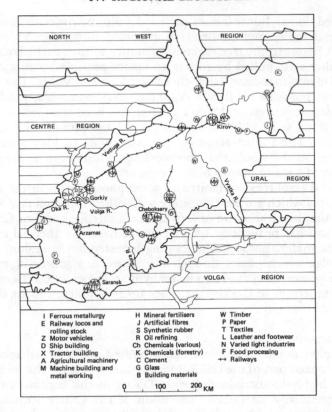

Fig. 201. Volga-Vyatka Economic Region: railways and industrial structure of towns.

I   Ferrous metallurgy
E   Railway locos and rolling stock
Z   Motor vehicles
D   Ship building
X   Tractor building
A   Agricultural machinery
M   Machine building and metal working

H   Mineral fertilisers
J   Artificial fibres
S   Synthetic rubber
R   Oil refining
Ch Chemicals (various)
K   Chemicals (forestry)
C   Cement
G   Glass
B   Building materials

W   Timber
P   Paper
T   Textiles
L   Leather and footwear
N   Varied light industries
F   Food processing
↔   Railways

0   100   200 KM

over the centuries has lost pride of place to the railways and pipelines which now serve the region.

POPULATION AND CITIES

Gorkiy and Kirov Oblasts are peopled primarily by Russians, but the three ASSRs are political units based on non-Russian nationality groups. Mordov and Mari ASSRs are based on Finnic-speaking, Russian Orthodox groups, descendants of ·people migrating southeastwards from the Scandinavian region. The people of Chuvash ASSR are of Turkic nationality, descendants of peoples who migrated north-westwards into the region from Central Asia. Apart from the Chuvash, the non-Russians are minority groups in their respective republics.

In 1979, the population of the region was 8,343,000 and the

(Novosti)

Fig. 202. Confluence of the River Volga (right) and the River Oka (left) at Gorkiy. Gorkiy, once called Nizhni-Novgorod, is a major industrial node in the Volga-Vyatka Region.

over-all density 31.5 per km². There are however considerable variations within the region. In Kirov Oblast, the average density is only 14.0 per km² but in Chuvash ASSR it rises to 72.0 per km². The degree of urbanisation also varies from 46-7 per cent in Chuvash-Mordov ASSRs to 73 per cent in Gorkiy Oblast.

Gorkiy (population: 1,344,000)
Previously called Nizhni-Novgorod, Gorkiy owed its early importance to a favourable position on the River Volga at its confluence with the River Oka (*see* Fig. 202). It was also an advance post from which ancient Muscovy penetrated the lands of Finnish and Tatar tribes towards Kazan, then key to the middle and lower Volga. Local forests provided timber for shipbuilding, supplying as early as the sixteenth century a yearly "caravan" of boats which carried products of the Moscow region to the Caspian and returned laden with products from the south and east. Shipbuilding is still carried on at Gorkiy, as are trading activities that originated in the exchange and barter of an early trade fair located there. Today, the city and its neighbourhood have become a major industrial area, the

focal point and dominant centre of the Volga-Vyatka Region, and yet in many respects bound up with the Centre Region and the Moscow industrial area. The major industries of Gorkiy have already been mentioned.

Nearby *Bogorodsk* has a specialty in leather-working industries, while *Pravdinsk* and *Balakna* have a major newsprint and paperboard complex.

Kirov (population: 390,000)

Formerly called Vyatka and, before 1780, Khlynov, Kirov is capital of the predominantly rural oblast of the same name. Founded in 1181 as a colony of Novgorod, it later became capital of a medieval principality. Sacked by Tatars in the fourteenth and fifteenth centuries, it eventually came under the rule of the Principality of Moscow (1489). A flourishing trading centre on the road to Siberia during the seventeenth and eighteenth centuries, Kirov now functions as an important industrial centre and railway junction with links with Arkhangelsk, Leningrad, Moscow, Perm and Sverdlovsk. Its industries and products include machine tools, railway rolling stock, agricultural implements, leather and footwear, fur-processing and woodworking (furniture, matches, prefabricated houses, etc.). Together with the town of *Slobodskoy,* 40 km to the north-east, Kirov is the second most important industrial node in the Volga-Vyatka Region (*see* Fig. 202).

Cheboksary (population: 308,000)

Capital of the Chuvash ASSR, Cheboksary has a major hydro-electric plant nearby (1.4 kW capacity), together with piped oil and gas supplies from outside the region providing the power for industries manufacturing heavy duty tractors, cotton textiles, electrical equipment and chemicals. The rapid increase in population in recent years (43 per cent between 1970 and 1979) reflects the decision to invest industrial capital to build up industry in the city.

Saransk (population: 263,000); Yoshkar-Ola (population: 201,000)

Respectively capital cities of Mordva ASSR and Mari ASSR, both are centres enjoying the benefits of recent injections of industrial capital and are experiencing rapid expansion of population in consequence. Saransk produces cars, lorries, earth-excavating machinery, electronics and electrical goods; Yoshkar-Ola specialises in automation equipment and precision machinery.

Dzerzhinsk (population: 257,000)

Situated 30 km west of Gorkiy, Dzerzhinsk is one of the most important centres of the chemical industry in the USSR. Local phosphate rock, apatite concentrate from the Kola Peninsula, oil and natural gas brought by pipeline, and coal are used in the manufacture of phosphatic and nitrogenous fertilisers, primary chemicals, inorganic acids, tar distillates, insecticides and feed stock for cellulose and synthetic fibre plant.

2. VOLGA ECONOMIC REGION

The Volga Region (*see* Fig. 203) comprises lands 100-300 km on either side of the Volga River from near Kazan to the Caspian Sea, and the lower Don and Belaya valleys (*see* Fig. 204). It contains six Russian oblasts — Ulyanovsk, Kuybyshev, Penza, Saratov, Volgograd and Astrakhan — and three ASSRs based on Tatar, Bashkir and Kalmyk (i.e. non-Russian) nationality groups respectively (*see* Table 55). Industrial centres arranged in linear fashion along the Volga River — Ulyanovsk, Kuybyshev, Saratov, Volgograd and Astrakhan — display an intensive and diversified series of north-south and east-west linkages. The region has a reputation for highly developed agriculture (grain, meat, wool and selected horticultural crops), while oil refining machines, precision tools and farm machinery are leading industrial specialities. Water for irrigation and industry is a major current problem in this region.

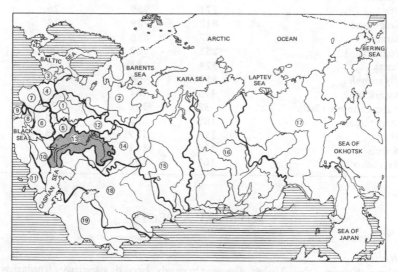

Fig. 203. Soviet Union: location of Volga Economic Region.

TABLE 55. VOLGA ECONOMIC REGION:
ADMINISTRATIVE UNITS, THEIR POPULATION AND DENSITY

Area: 680,000 km²
Population (1979): 19,393,000

Administrative unit	Area (000 km²)	Population (000, 1979)	Density (persons per km²)	Percentage urban
Tatar ASSR	67	3,436	50	51
Ulyanovsk Oblast	37	1,269	33	63
Kuybyshev Oblast	54	3,093	57	78
Saratov Oblast	101	2,560	25	72
Volgograd Oblast	113	2,475	22	72
Astrakhan Oblast	44	915	21	68
Bashkir ASSR	144	3,848	27	48
Penza Oblast	43	1,504	35	53
Kalmyk ASSR	76	293	4	34

TABLE 56. VOLGA ECONOMIC REGION:
TOWNS WITH OVER 150,000 INHABITANTS IN 1979

Town	Population in thousands 1970 (census)	1979 (census)	Percentage increase 1970-79
Kuybyshev	1,045	1,216	16
Kazan	869	993	14
Ufa	771	969	26
Volgograd	818	929	14
Saratov	757	856	13
Togliatti	251	502	100
Penza	374	483	26
Ulyanovsk	351	464	32
Astrakhan	410	461	12
Naberezhnyye Chelny	38	301	692
Sterlitamak	185	220	19
Syzran	173	179	3
Engels	130	161	24
Balakovo	103	152	47

PHYSICAL ASPECTS

Relief

Near Kazan, the Volga flows through broad swampy lowlands, but southwards from here to Volgograd its valley is dominated on its west side by high, cliff-like slopes; its left bank gives onto a

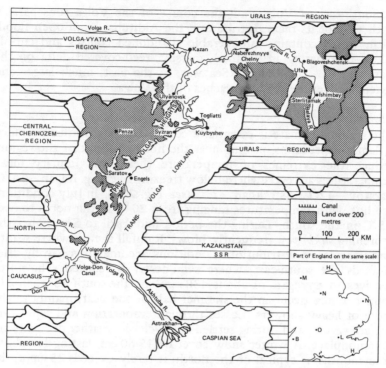

Fig. 204. Volga Economic Region.

plain to low relief. The western side of the valley is formed by the east-facing slopes of the asymmetrical Volga Heights which, rising gently, eastwards from the Don valley to heights of 150-200 mm and occasionally to over 300 m (as in the Zhiguli Hills within the Samara bend of the Volga near Kuybyshev), drop suddenly to the Volga. For the most part the Heights are unglaciated, but sub-aerial erosion of sandstones, clays and chalk under semi-arid conditions has produced many deep ravines and gorges. This dissection is particularly evident along the slopes facing the Volga where the Sura, Syzran and other tributaries have cut back deeply into the Heights. The Yergeni Hills are a lower, southerly extension of the Volga Heights, forming a divide between the Volga and the Don. At Volgograd, however, the Volga turns suddenly away from its bounding ridge in a pronounced bend to the south-east to debouch into the Caspian Sea some 500 km to the south-east.

The lowland on the eastern side of the Volga, the Trans-Volga Lowland, is broken only by the much dissected Belebei Upland of Bashkir ASSR north-east of Kuybyshev. This eastern side of the valley is generally featureless and marshy, and an alluvial plain stretches south-eastwards to the Caspian-Turanian Lowland.

South-east of Volgograd, the course of the Volga runs parallel with that of its main distributary, the Akhtuba, in an open flood-plain which contains innumerable abandoned courses and cut-off lakes, terminating in a broad, marshy, reed-covered delta on the Caspian Sea. The Caspian Sea was, in the past, much larger and extended over these lower reaches of the Volga.

Climate
The regional climate is essentially continental. Occasional occluded Atlantic depressions, passing near the northern limit of the region, reduce the extremes of temperature there, but January mean temperatures are everywhere below freezing level, e.g. Kazan −14 °C; Saratov −12 °C; Astrakhan −7 °C (*see* Fig. 205). In July conditions are hot, with temperatures ranging from 20 °C in the north to over 25 °C in the south. During the period mid-April to September the scorching *sukhovey* frequently blows. Rainfall is everywhere scanty and irregular in distribution. Conditions become progressively drier towards the south-east, where semi-desert is reached. The north receives an aggregate of about 430 mm and the south less than 230 mm. Maxima occur in the summer half of the year, mainly in the form of heavy showers. Losses through evaporation and rapid run-off are severe, and during settled anticyclonic weather droughts are commonplace. A winter snow cover of 45-60 cm, lasting for about four months, is typical of the north; it rarely exceeds 25 cm in the south and lasts no more than a month.

Natural vegetation and soils
Because conditions on the high, west side of the Volga are cooler and more humid than on the low eastern side, there is a difference in the natural vegetation. The *tayga* in the extreme north of the region gives way southwards to deciduous mixed forest which extends farther south on the Volga Heights than in the Trans-Volga (Zavolzhye) area. On the east side, natural steppe and chernozem begin to appear just south of Kuybyshev, but on the west woodland and wooded steppe, overlying brown earths, continue south to near Saratov. Similarly, the change from steppe to semi-desert occurs near latitude 51° N on the east side of the Volga, nearer 48° N on the west. Saline soils (*solonets*) are frequently associated with ustolls or chestnut soils in the lower reaches of the Volga.

Throughout the region ploughing has led to the breakdown of the soil structure and loss of friability, with consequent extensive soil erosion and gullying. Since drought is a constant threat (according to Borisov one in every three or four years during the past seventy years has been a drought year), agriculture has formidable

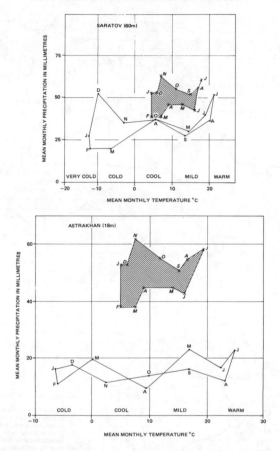

Fig. 205. Hythergraphs for Saratov and Astrakhan (Kew, London, shaded).

problems, and every effort has to be made to alleviate the adverse effects of the droughts that are inevitable in the continental climate of the region. Ley farming (*travopolye*) as practised here offers one method of improving soil structure and conserving soil moisture; it involves a regular alternation on the same land of a number of years under grass-legume mixtures and a number of years of arable cropping. The roots of grasses and legumes and manure from grazing stock build up the organic matter of the soil, improve its cohesion and increase its moisture-holding capacity. The planting of large shelter belts of deciduous trees, often hundreds of kilometres long, and irrigation offer other means of counter-acting the effects of drought.

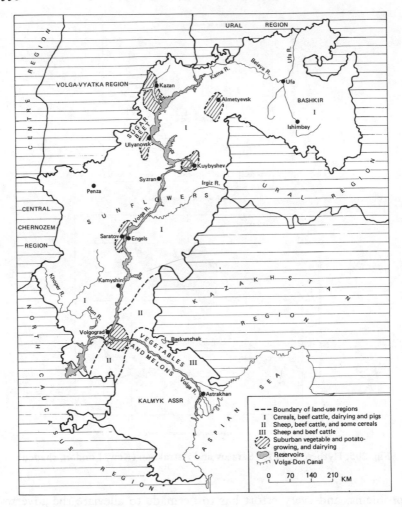

Fig. 206. Volga Economic Region: agricultural land-use regions.

THE ECONOMY

Agriculture

Despite the climatic hazards and the dangers of crop failure, the Volga Region is a leading producing area of spring wheat, winter rye, oats, flax, hemp, oil seeds (especially sunflower seed) and maize. Beef cattle, pigs, sheep, horses and poultry are raised and dairying is common near the towns (*see* Fig. 206). In the areas of more mixed farming in the north and west, potatoes and sugar-beet are important. Semi-tropical fruits, rice, melons and vegetables are grown in the floodplain of the lower Volga valley below Volgograd; peaches, apricots and vines thrive along the drier margins. In the semi-desert beyond the Volga-Akhtuba valley sheep are raised for meat and wool on an extensive system; there is barely enough vegetation for grazing so seasonal movement between pastures is necessary.

Agriculturally-based industries include flour-milling, meat-canning, cheese- and butter-making, soap manufacture, candle-making, leather and felt boots production, and cotton spinning.

Fuel and mineral resources
Until the early 1930s, the lands along the middle and lower Volga and along the lower Don seemed destined to remain essentially agricultural. The Volga functioned as an important and historic highway, but the extent of its power potential and the resources of the neighbouring lands were not appreciated. Since then the river has been harnessed for hydro-electric power generation and for irrigation water, and the great riches of oil and natural gas of the Volga-Urals field ("Second Baku") have been fully exploited (*see* Fig. 207). The region as a whole has undergone a very rapid growth of industry, trade and settlement.

This late industrial revolution of the region followed the construction under "The Great Volga Scheme" of a series of multi-purpose barrages throughout the course of the river. These dams were intended for hydro-electricity generation and for water conservation for irrigation, the control of seasonal differences in water level and of soil erosion, and for improved navigation. There are, upstream in the Centre Region, three relatively small stations at Ivankovo, Uglich and Scherbakov (now Rybinsk) and in the Volga-Vyatka Region two larger ones at Gorodets and Cheboksary. Those in the Volga Region are at Kuybyshev (2.5 million kW), Balakovo (1.3 million kW) and Volgograd (2.6 million kW). Together with one other station under construction on the Kama River at Naberezhnyye Chelny, they make the valley of the Volga outstandingly important in hydro-electricity production. Some of the power is used locally, but most is sent westwards to European USSR and to Moscow in particular.

The reservoirs formed by the dams on the Volga extend hundreds of kilometres upstream and cover several hundreds of square kilometres, and have transformed large areas through the inundation of valuable alluvial land. Some settlements have had to be re-sited. Reservoirs in the European part of the USSR have flooded more than four million hectares of low-lying land, much of which was agriculturally highly productive. The dams also block fish runs and prevent nutrient material from reaching the fisheries in downstream regions. On the other hand they also provide great quantities of

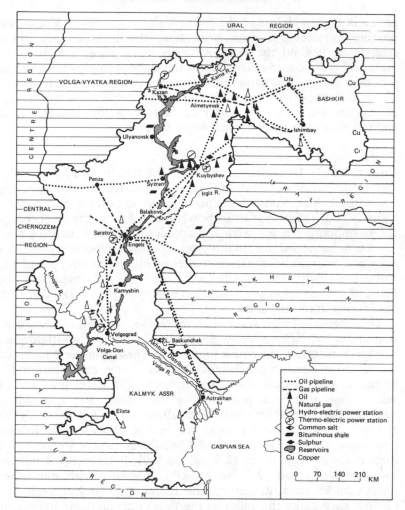

Fig. 207. Volga Economic Region: mineral and power resources.

water to farm lands nearby. Such vast water surfaces are naturally subject to high evaporation rates during the summer and the Volga system loses tremendous volumes of water thereby. In consequence the water level of the Caspian Sea is being lowered and there have been adverse effects on the fishing industry, on the shipping facilities and on the Kara-Bogaz-Gol sodium sulphate industry. To offset the water losses, a grandiose scheme — the Pechora-Vychegda Diversion Project — has been evolved (but not yet implemented), to divert northern waters from the Pechora River into the Volga.

Although the Volga-Urals oilfields had been known for several decades, serious prospecting began only during the 1930s, and large-scale development took place after the Second World War. In the late 1960s well over sixty per cent of the Union's output of oil came from this oil province, but with the continuing upsurge in production from the West Siberian fields during the 1970s (now accounting for 52 per cent of the national output) the contribution of the Volga-Urals fields has fallen to 25 per cent. The fields which produce the cheapest oil in the USSR are exploited in an area north and east of Volgograd, through Saratov, Syzran, Kuybyshev and Almetyevsk to Ufa and Perm (the last two being in the Urals Region (*see* p. 351). Drilling is concentrated in relatively few areas, e.g. Almetyevsk (Romashkiro field), Shugurovo, Syzran, Volgograd (together with Oktyabrskiy and Perm in the Urals Region) but the bulk of the field's production comes from an area within 250-300 km of Almetyevsk; indeed, this represents the greatest part of the region's total production. Production from the margins of the field is relatively limited (*see* Fig. 207). Refineries are located at Kazan, Kuybyshev, Syzran, Saratov and Volgograd, and there are pipeline links with consuming areas in the Urals and Siberian towns as far east as Irkutsk, westwards to central European USSR, East Germany, Poland, Hungary, Czechoslovakia, and to an oil-loading terminal at Ventspils in Latvian SSR.

Natural gas is exploited west of the Volga in western Saratov and Volgograd Oblasts at such centres as Yelshanka (linked with Saratov and Moscow), Kotovo (linked with Kamyshin) and Frolovo (linked with Volgograd). Production is 7 to 8 per cent of the total production of the USSR.

The region has no meaningful coal resources, but has some oil shale deposits in the south-west of Kuybyshev Oblast which are processed in Syzran. Annual production is little more than a million tonnes. Common salt (Lake Baskunchak), phosphate (Ulyanovsk Oblast) and sulphur (Kuybyshev Oblast) are important resources for the fishing and fertiliser industries.

Manufacturing

The location of the region's resources of hydro-electricity, petroleum and natural gas in relation to the Union's other industrial regions and to the over-all distribution of population is of great economic value to the USSR as a whole. It is also a factor that attracted industries into the region. Oil and gas serve as raw materials within the region for a wide range of petrochemical industries producing synthetic fibres, synthetic rubber, plastics, fertilisers, ethylene and alcohol, while the abundant supplies of electricity are important to the location of engineering industries. The resulting complex includes industries engaged in the manufacture of oil-drilling equip-

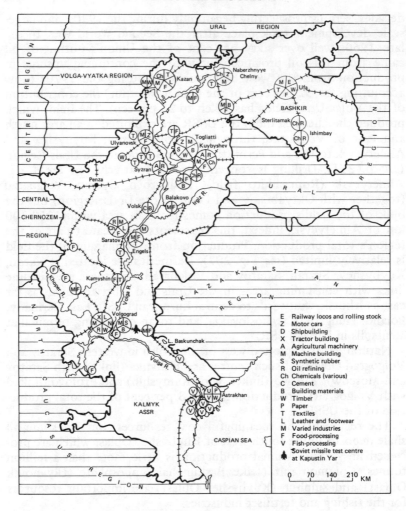

Fig. 208. Volga Economic Region: railways and industrial structure of towns.

ment, motor vehicles, machine tools, marine engines and boilers, ball-bearings, tractors and other agricultural machinery (*see* Fig. 208).

A temporary switch to a consumer-oriented economic policy (though now seemingly partially reverted to the previous emphasis on the heavy industrial sectors) led to the construction of a major motor car plant at Togliatti during the eighth Five-year Plan (1966-70). The plant, Europe's largest, was designed by Fiat of Italy and completed in 1970. It is fully integrated and combines all the basic processes on one site (*see* p. 340). Another vehicle plant — the KamAZ — has been built at Naberezhnyye Chelny to supply heavy duty lorries. About three-quarters of all the machinery equipment and technology for the plant (which started production in 1977) was provided by Western suppliers. Since 1980 Togliatti and Naberezhnyye Chelny have respectively accounted for over half of the national car (720,000) and half of the lorry production.

Oil refining, machines, precision tools, motor vehicles and farm machinery are leading specialities on the Volga Region. They are the modern industrial developments which now vie in importance with the more traditional agriculture-based manufacturing and with the grain, meat, wool and selected horticultural products of the region.

Transport

The Volga is an economic link both within the region and with other parts of the USSR; it is estimated that the Volga system carries about 45 per cent of the inland water transport tonnage of the entire Union (*see* Fig. 72). Its sphere was extended westward after the completion of the Volga-Don Ship Canal south of Volgograd (*see* Fig. 209) in 1952, giving free access to the Sea of Azov and the Black Sea.

The highly irregular regime of the Volga, with flood levels in April and May followed by low-water levels during the summer, has been much modified by the barrage constructions along its course, the chain of deep reservoirs and the locks that now exist greatly aid navigation. Despite the fact that the river is frozen over for several months during the winter, its huge carrying capacity for bulk cargoes makes it a vital part of the Soviet transportation system. At the mouths of the Volga, distributaries, sandbars and the falling water level of the Caspian Sea make it necessary to tranship cargoes from Caspian steamers to shallow draught Volga river steamers at "Twelve-Foot Roads", an artificial island port in the Caspian Sea, 200 km from Astrakhan.

Downstream traffic on the Volga system is mainly milled timber (but no longer as log rafts because of the numerous locks), refined petroleum products, salt and grain; upstream traffic is mainly coal, pig iron, cotton, salt, fish products, cement and building materials.

Formerly north-south communication through the region was virtually brought to a halt when the river was frozen or at low-water level. A railway now runs parallel to the river along the right bank, from near Kazan to Volgograd, and thence along the left bank to Astrakhan. Railway traffic is less affected by seasonal changes than is waterway traffic, but this advantage is offset by rail costs, which are more expensive per tonne kilometre than those for water traffic.

Not all transport movement within the region is latitudinal; the

Fig. 209. Near the entrance to the Volga-Don Canal.

former frontier-like character of the Volga Region has long been dispelled by the construction of railways running across the region from east to west, and the regional character is now more that of a transit zone, with five main trunk lines crossing the Volga (*see* Fig. 208). Wherever railways cross the river, considerable river ports have grown, e.g. Kuybyshev, Ulyanovsk, Saratov-Engels and Kazan. Freight traffic densities on these lines are very high, especially between Kuybyshev and Syzran (*see* Fig. 70) with a general preponderance of westbound traffic, particularly of oil, iron, steel, coal, timber and grains.

Petroleum production, mainly in the Tatar and Bashkir ASSR, has prompted the construction of many pipelines. Pipelines radiate

out, mainly from Almetyevsk and Kuybyshev, to all other parts. At
one time Volga-Urals oil was transported eastwards as far as Irkutsk,
but this flow has been reversed and with the phenomenal increase
in oil production in West Siberia, West Siberian oil destined for
European Russia and elsewhere passes through the region via the
existing pipeline corridor and via new routes constructed to Novorossiysk on the Black Sea and to Lisichansk, Kremenchug and Odessa
in the Ukraine.

Hydro-electricity generated along the Volga is moved to European
USSR by means of high-voltage transmission lines. The Soviet Union
is actively engaged in research in electricity transmission technology
in order to resolve the problem of moving surplus electricity long
distances from the Volga Region and Siberia Regions to consumers
in the western part of the country.

POPULATION AND CITIES

The lands along the Volga were the meeting place of Tatar and
Muscovite cultures. Bulgars who had settled near the Kama-Volga
confluence in the ninth to twelfth centuries succumbed to Mongol-
Tatars of the Golden Horde in the thirteenth century. These Tatars
copied the culture and settled way of life of the Bulgars and established a breakaway Khanate centred on Kazan. In 1552, that city
fell to Ivan the Terrible and the way was opened for a rapid Russian
advance down the Volga to Astrakhan. Ulyanovsk (formerly
Simbirsk), Kuybyshev (Samara), Saratov and Volgograd (Tsaritsyn)
were founded during the sixteenth and seventeenth centuries purely
as military establishments. Russian colonisation proceeded slowly
and full Russian political control over the Volga lands was not
achieved until the end of the eighteenth century when, under
Catherine the Great, links between the middle Volga Tatars and the
Tatars of Crimea and Constantinople were severed. At this time,
colonists from central Europe, and from Germany in particular
(Catherine was herself German), were settled on the right bank of
the Volga. During the Second World War members of this Volga
German community, like the Tatars of Crimea (*see* Fig. 91), were
dispersed eastwards throughout the RSFSR, Kazakhstan and Central
Asia.

Tatars are widely scattered through the Soviet Union with only
26 per cent living in their ASSR. Bashkirs, like Tatars, are Moslems
but they differ in that 72 per cent of them live within their ASSR.
They also have a much higher rate of natural increase. The Kalmyks,
occupying the right bank of the lower Volga, are a Mongolic-language
people. Accused of war-time subversion or collaboration, they were
exiled in 1943-44, but now with Kalmyk ASSR restored they are
mainly returned from their place of deportation.

The large number of Russians who have moved into the Volga-Don Region (and particularly into the large cities) during recent phases of economic development have greatly diversified the ethnic variety of the region. Intermarriage between Russian and non-Russian groups such as the Tatars, Bashkirs and Kalmyks has diluted the individuality of the latter, who are being increasingly assimilated into the Russian way of life.

With practically 19.4 million people, the Volga Region has an over-all population density of 28 persons per km². However, the density ranges from 57 persons per km² in Kuybyshev Oblast to 4 persons per km² in the Kalmyk ASSR. Seventy-eight per cent of the population is urbanised in Kuybyshev Oblast and more than half the population is classified as urban in the other oblasts of the region. Kalmyk and Bashkir ASSRs are still largely rural.

Kuybyshev (population: 1,216,000)
Temporary capital of the Soviet Union during the Second World War, Kuybyshev is the most important city of the region. Situated on the left bank of the Volga at the most easterly point of the river loop to the east at its confluence with the Samara River, the city holds a strategic and focal position (*see* Fig. 208). Functioning first as a defence outpost, then as a trading point for the exchange of goods brought overland from the east and via the Volga from north and south, it later acquired industries based on agriculture, such as food-processing and flour-milling. It is now a fully-developed industrial and commercial centre and the undoubted hub of the middle Volga, with important rail links to Siberia and the Soviet Far East via Ufa and Chelyabinsk, to Middle Asia via Orenburg and to European USSR via Syzran, a giant hydro-electricity generating station (2.3 million kW) nearby, oil refineries, petrochemical industries, engineering of many kinds, food-processing and wood-working. Kuybyshev increased its population by 16 per cent between 1970 and 1979 and now comes ninth in the urban hierarchy of the Soviet Union.

Kazan (population: 993,000)
An old Tatar trading and administrative centre, Kazan is the capital of the Tatar ASSR. First situated on a small left-bank tributary (Kazanka) of the Volga, it now stands by the "Kuybyshev Sea", the water dammed by the barrage at Kuybyshev. Kazan has excellent communications in the Volga waterway and the trunk rail link with Moscow and Sverdlovsk. It is a centre for oil refining, the Tatar ASSR being a major oil-producing area. To early-established manufacturing industries of soap, candles, woollens, leather and fur have been added petrochemicals and engineering — the latter diverse

enough to include the making of farm machinery, typewriters, calculating machines and computers (see Fig. 208). The Kazan *kremlin* is claimed to rival that in Moscow in its splendour and picturesqueness.

Ufa (population: 969,000)

On the navigable Belaya tributary of the Volga near its confluence with the Ufa River, Ufa is an important river port, focus of railways from Chelyabinsk, Ulyanovsk and Kuybyshev, and on the pipelines from the West Siberian and Volga-Urals oilfields. Capital of the Bashkir ASSR, Ufa is a major centre for petroleum refining, petrochemicals and the manufacture of aircraft and motor car engines. Other industrial products include mining and petroleum machinery, electrical and telecommunications equipment and, also, furniture veneers, prefabricated houses, etc., from a major timber combine. The city has experienced a remarkable increase in population in recent years — by over 26 per cent since the last national census in 1970.

Volgograd (population: 929,000)

Known as Tsaritsyn until 1925 and Stalingrad between then and 1961, Volgograd is sited on the high right bank of the Volga near the great river bend to the south-east. This point is only 70 km distant from the Don. The early fortress town established here in 1589 grew as a major transhipment point for goods portaged between the two rivers. Scene of a major engagement in 1918 during the civil war, and again in the Second World War when bitter fighting between Russian and German troops reduced it to rubble, the city has been completely rebuilt and repopulated. Its importance was greatly enhanced with the opening of the Volga-Don Canal in 1952 (*see* Fig. 209) and the completion of a giant barrage and hydroelectricity station (2.5 million kW) nearby in 1960. The industrial functions of Volgograd include steel-making (using pig iron from the Donbass), heavy metallurgy, engineering (especially tractors), shipbuilding, oil refining, petrochemicals, aluminium reduction (using alumina from the Urals and Hungary), sawmilling and timber working, together with food products, leather goods and footwear. Year-round navigation is prevented by ice, which forms here early in December and does not break up until the first week in April, but there are direct rail links with Moscow, Saratov, Astrakhan and the Donbass. Though it is an important southern gateway to the Volga region, Volgograd lacks strong functional connection with the middle reaches of the river, and it is becoming increasingly related to the steel producing areas of the Ukraine (*see* Fig. 208).

Fig. 210. The barrage and 1.4 million kW hydro-electricity generating station at Balakovo, 125 km upstream of Saratov. The barrage is one of a series constructed on the Volga River to generate electricity, improve navigation and provide irrigation water.

Saratov (population: 856,000)
Founded in 1590 on the left bank of the Volga, Saratov was moved to its present site on the right bank in the seventeenth century. Situated at the lowest bridging point of the Volga (*see* Fig. 145), it is an important rail junction. Traditional distributing functions (for grain, timber, salt, tobacco, fish, tallow and skins) and industries such as flour-milling and tobacco manufacturing draws on Caucasus oil (brought by pipeline from Astrakhan) and Tatar crude oils. Engineering includes agricultural machinery, aircraft and ball-bearings. One of the Union's natural gas resources lies just north of the city and there is a 1.4 million kW hydro-electric station on the Volga at Balakovo 125 km upstream of Saratov (*see* Fig. 210). Opposite Saratov on the left bank stands *Engels* (population: 161,000), former capital of the Volga Germans (who were expelled from the area in 1942). It has railway wagon workshops and supplies most of the trolley buses operating in the USSR.

Togliatti (population: 502,000)
Situated on the Volga about 80 km upstream of Kuybyshev and near the dam of the Lenin HEP station, Togliatti is an important river port and site of a major motor car plant (*Volzhskiy avtomobilnyy zavod*, VAZ). The plant, built and equipped in co-operation with the Italian firm Fiat, is the largest in the USSR. Other industries

XIV. VOLGA-URALS MACRO-REGION

include a factory making equipment for the cement industry, synthetic rubber production and phosphorous and nitrogenous fertilisers. Togliatti recorded the sixth highest average annual city growth rate for the USSR cities for the years between the censuses of 1970 and 1979 — namely 8.0 per cent — and in that time doubled its population.

Penza (population: 483,000)

Capital of Penza Oblast (previously considered to be part of the Central Chernozem Region), Penza was founded as a military centre on the Sura River in the seventeenth century. It now serves as an administrative centre and has light industries including engineering (diesel-engines), food and wood processing.

Ulyanovsk (population: 464,000)

The city marks an important rail crossing of the Volga. It is a river port as well as an industrial centre in a generally agricultural area. The remarkable increase in the population of Ulyanovsk in recent years (32 per cent between 1970 and 1979) is noteworthy. Ulyanovsk was the birthplace of Vladimir Ilyich Ulyanov or Lenin, founder of Bolshevik Communisim and the greatest single driving force behind the Soviet Revolution of 1917.

Astrakhan (population: 461,000)

Standing on an island in the delta of the Volga on the left bank of the main distributary and 70 km from the Caspian Sea, Astrakhan is an important river port. It has a dredged channel to the sea and, despite the need for transhipment of cargoes (noted above), transport movements continue to be focussed on the city. World-renowned sturgeon fisheries are centred here; *vobla* (Caspian roach), salmon, whitefish and herring are also caught, though the fishing industry has been adversely affected by industrial pollution and the falling water level of the Caspian Sea caused by the upstream use and control of the Volga waters. The river at Astrakhan is frozen over from about the third week in December until the second week in March, but railways across the semi-desert that surround the northern Caspian maintain all-season links northwards to Volgograd and southwards to Kizlyar and the Caucasus (*see* Fig. 211).

Naberezhnyye Chelny (population: 301,000)

Situated on the Kama River, Naberezhnyye Chelny had a phenomenal 25.8 per cent average annual growth rate in the inter-censal period 1970-79. It is the site of the Kama lorry (truck) complex

Fig. 211. Astrakhan, showing the Kremlin and Lenin Square.

(KamAZ), the Soviet Union's major project for increasing its output of motor vehicles, which is destined to be the largest lorry manufacturing complex in the world.

Sterlitamak (population: 220,000)
Situated in Bashkir ASSR, Sterlitamak is an oil refining and chemicals centre.

Syzran (population: 179,000)
Like most other industrial nodes in the Volga Region, Syzran is an important rail crossing point on the Volga.

Balakovo (population: 152,000)
One of the rapidly growing cities of the Volga Region (47 per cent increase in population in the period 1970-79), this eighteenth century town now boasts a hydro-electricity generating station (*see* Fig. 210), a viscose rayon mill using Siberian wood pulp to manufacture tyre cord, a phosphatic fertiliser complex and a rubber-fabricating plant. A factory for the manufacture of bulldozers, earthscrapers and heavy road-building machines is under construction.

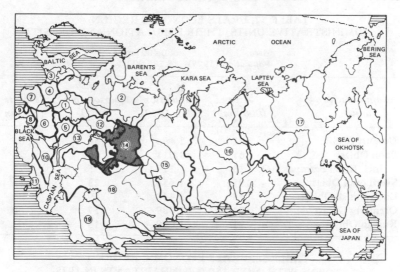

Fig. 212. Soviet Union: location of Urals Economic Region.

It is perhaps salutory to appreciate once again the scale of the USSR and that the distances which separate cities such as Astrakhan, Volgograd, Saratov and Kuybyshev are of the order of 300 km, i.e. greater than the distances in England which separate, say, London and Plymouth or London and Middlesborough.

3. URALS ECONOMIC REGION

The Urals Economic Region (*see* Fig. 212) does not cover the whole of the Ural Mountains region but only the southern part — the Central and Southern Urals, with their foothills — along with parts of the adjoining West Siberian Lowland on the east and the Kama Lowlands on the west. Administratively it embraces Perm, Sverdlovsk, Kurgan, Chelyabinsk and Orenburg Oblasts and Udmurt ASSR (*see* Fig. 213). Beneficiation of local iron ore and imports from Kazakhstan, oxygen converters and conversion from coal to liquid fuels have maintained the heavy industrial sector of the region and especially its pre-eminence in metallurgy and mining. To its early function as a maker of raw steel the Urals Region has added machinery machine tools, oil, chemicals, wood and food products.

PHYSICAL ASPECTS

Relief and drainage
The boundless Russian-West Siberian Lowland is interrupted by a meridional intrusion of ridges extending some 2,300 km from the

TABLE 57. URALS ECONOMIC REGION:
ADMINISTRATIVE UNITS, THEIR POPULATION AND DENSITY

Area: 680,400 km²
Population (1979): 15,185,000

Administrative unit	Area (000 km²)	Population (000, 1979)	Density (persons per km²)	Percentage urban
Udmurt ASSR	42	1,494	36	65
Perm Oblast	161	3,011	19	74
incl. Komi-Permyak AO	33	173	5	24
Sverdlovsk Oblast	195	4,454	23	85
Chelyabinsk Oblast	88	3,440	39	81
Orenburg Oblast	124	2,089	17	60
Kurgan Oblast	71	1,080	15	51

TABLE 58. URALS ECONOMIC REGION:
TOWNS WITH OVER 150,000 INHABITANTS IN 1979

Town	Population in thousands 1970 (census)	1979 (census)	Percentage increase 1970-79
Sverdlovsk	1,025	1,211	18
Chelyabinsk	875	1,031	18
Perm	850	999	17
Izhevsk	422	549	30
Orenburg	344	459	33
Magnitogorsk	364	406	11
Nizhniy Tagil	378	398	5
Kurgan	244	310	27
Orsk	225	247	10
Zlatoust	180	198	10
Kamensk-Uralskiy	169	187	10
Berezniki	146	185	27
Miass	131	150	14

Arctic to the Mugodzhary Mountains. These are the Ural Mountains, which are not particularly high — often not over 900 m — though they have long been considered a boundary between the European and the Asiatic territories of the Soviet Union.* The mountains lie

*For theoretical-academic purposes the Moscow section of the All-Union Geographical Society recommended in 1958 that the border between Europe and Asia should be drawn along the eastern flank of the Ural, the Mugodzhary Mountains, the Emba River, the north shore of the Caspian, the Kuma-Manych depression and the south coast of the Sea of Azov to the Kerch Straits. The Sea of Azov belongs to Europe, as do the Urals; the Caucasus lies wholly in Asia. Such a conventional division is not recognised in the organisation of Soviet life or in the facts of Soviet geography.

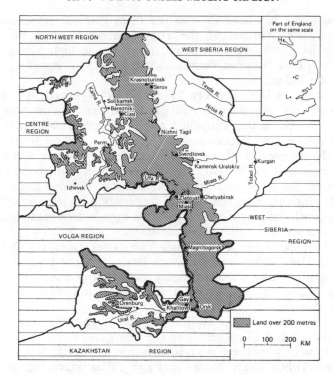

Fig. 213. Urals Economic Region.

on the western edge of a broad belt of Palaeozoic folding of which the greater part is buried beneath the Tertiary deposits of western Siberia. Folding, along a longitudinal axis, was asymmetrical and slopes are steep on the east and gentle on the west. The water divide is towards the eastern side.

Four parts of the Ural Mountains are recognised: The *Polar Ural* and the *Northern Ural* (which form the boundary between the North-West Region and the West Siberian Region) run southwards from near the head of Kara Bay to latitude 61° N. They form a distinct range 25-30 km wide, with summits above 900 m. Occasionally the main range is flanked on the west by two or three other ranges. Between 61° N and 64° N the summits assume a gently rounded appearance and several broad, flat, marshy, transverse valleys cross the mountains.

The *Central Ural*, from latitude 61° N to 55° N, is lower in altitude than the ranges to the north. Broad swellings, 300-600 m high, are cut by a multitude of transverse valleys, gorges and enclosed basins and the whole range is not more than 80 km wide. It cannot be described as "mountainous", for it is no barrier to east-west movement and has been used as the main gateway to Siberia for centuries. The branches of the Trans-Siberian Railway that pass this way have gentle gradients and there are no high passes to be negotiated; that between Perm and Sverdlovsk, for instance, never rises above 365 m.

The *Southern Ural*, between 55° N and 51° N, broadens to about 160 km and is composed of several parallel ranges. The most easterly of these which is the watershed rarely exceeds 750 m in height; those to the west have occasional summits over 1,500 m. Southwards the Urals assume the character of a dissected plateau 300-450 m high, terminated in the south by the great westward bend of the Ural River. South of this (in the Kazakhstan Region) the Mugod-zhary Mountains form the natural termination of the Urals; these are two gently sloping ridges 250-350 m high, which grade beneath the Kazakh Steppe south of latitude 40° N.

The most extensive of the Pleistocene glacial stages, the Oka, did not reach the Central and Southern Urals, and the present relief, the vestigial remains of a once mighty mountain system, is the result of the age-long processes of sub-aerial erosion and the depositional activity of rivers.

On the western flanks of the Urals drainage is by way of the Kama, Belaya and Ufa Rivers into the Volga and thence to the Caspian Sea. Drainage of the eastern Urals is into the Arctic Sea, through the Rivers Tobol, Miass, Nitsa, Tura and Tavda which join the Ob. The Ural River takes the waters of the Southern Urals to the Caspian Sea.

Climate and natural vegetation

The climate of the Urals Region is continental and severe, but with a considerable range of regional and local variations caused by the diversity and complexity of the relief, the wide range of latitude covered by the region and the contrasts in the aspects of its several parts. Winters are everywhere cold; the January mean temperature at Perm is −17 °C and at Zlatoust −16 °C (*see* Fig. 214). Sub-freezing temperatures persist for over five months. Winter conditions in the Southern Ural are as cold as in the Pechora area, some 1,000 km farther north. Snow, 60 cm or more deep, lasts for five to seven months. Summers are mild to warm with temperatures ranging from 16 °C in the north to 20 °C in the south. The July mean temperature at Perm is 18 °C and at Zlatoust 16 °C. Winds often bring intense heat and thick dust to the south of the region during this season. Annual precipitation is slight (600-700 mm) though it may attain 750 mm in the north-west and fall to less than 250 mm in the south-east. Aggregates on the western slopes of the mountains exceed those on the east by 100-150 mm. Thus the mountains have local

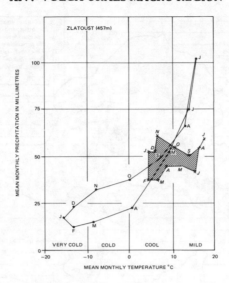

Fig. 214. Hythergraph for Zlatoust (Kew, London, shaded).

contrasts of climate, but do not constitute a sharp climatic divide between European and Asiatic USSR.

Spring and autumn are brief transitional seasons lasting no more than four to six weeks. During these seasons the north tends to be cloudy, but in the south clear weather generally results in frequent temperature inversions, which are reflected in inverted zonation of vegetation.

The Central Urals area carries a coniferous forest (*tayga*) of the spruce-fir type with admixtures of birch, aspen and pine. Soils are boralfs (i.e. podzolic). In the Southern Urals the forest gradually gives way to wooded steppe (with outliers of deciduous forest), thence to open steppe, overlying borolls (chernozem). In this area the normal vertical zonation of vegetation may be reversed (in response to temperature/humidity inversions), with pine-birch concentrated in the foothill valleys, oak forests on the lower slopes and lime, maple and elm on the higher slopes — the trees requiring higher temperatures growing at the higher altitudes.

THE ECONOMY

Forestry

Despite exploitation by an early charcoal-smelting iron industry, 70 per cent of the Urals Region remains forest-covered and a most valuable source of timber, providing about 15 per cent of the total timber output of the Soviet Union. Perm and Sverdlovsk Oblasts

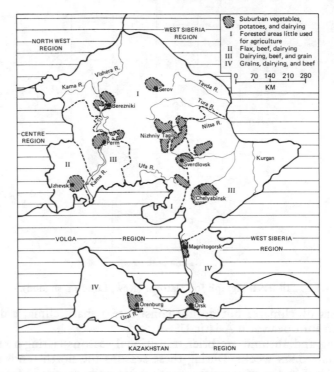

Fig. 215. Urals Economic Region: agricultural land-use regions.

account for most of the output. Novaya Lyalya, Krasnokamsk, Krasnovishersk and Berezniki are well known centres for paper, pulp and cellulose manufactures; Krasnokamsk, Nizhniy Tagil, Zlatoust and Chernikovsk are important for sawmills. Much of the timber exported is floated or transported along the Kama to the Volga, for distribution downstream.

Agriculture
The extent of arable agriculture is limited by forest cover and by the generally adverse physical environment. In the vicinity of large towns, such as Perm, Sverdlovsk and Chelyabinsk, market gardening (vegetables and potatoes) and dairying are the main activities, related to urban markets rather than to favourable conditions of soil and climate. In some favoured areas in the north and along the southern fringes of the forest, fodder crops (clover, lucerne), grains (barley, oats, rye and wheat, in the north-south sequence), flax and pasture occupy most of the available arable land (*see* Fig. 215). The steppe-lands of the Southern Ural lie within what was the area of the "Virgin and Long Idle Lands Project", which was ploughed up in

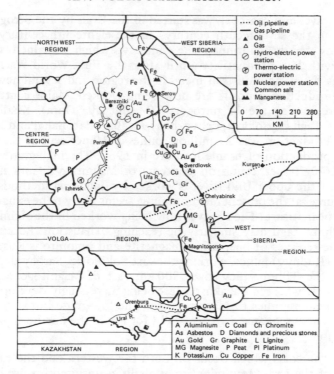

Fig. 216. Urals Economic Region: mineral and power resources.

1954-55 by workers on large *sovkhozy* and planted to spring wheat. The initial wheat monoculture in this southern region has been gradually replaced by a more mixed form of agriculture, embracing other crops, such as maize and sunflowers, and the raising of cattle (beef and dairy) and sheep.

Mineral resources and manufacturing industries
The role of agriculture in the economy of the region is secondary to mining and industry. The Urals Region is well endowed with metals and minerals (*see* Fig. 216) which supply the raw materials for ferrous and non-ferrous metallurgy, engineering, machinery, machine tools, chemicals and a range of allied industries. Iron, copper, bauxite, manganese, nickel, cobalt, tungsten, chrome, titanium, vanadium, gold, potash and precious stones are all found in the Urals Region, more particularly on the eastern slopes of the Ural Mountains. The discovery of petroleum on the western slopes (Volga-Urals field) led to the development of what was, until the discovery of the West Siberian fields, the premier oil-producing region in the Soviet Union.

IRON ORE. The manufacture of pig iron, using local resources of ore, water power and charcoal, was started in the Urals by the Strogonov family in the seventeenth century. In the eighteenth century, the Demidov family continued the industry, which remained small-scale, with low productivity until after the First World War. Iron remains the basic industrial metal in the region and several new and more productive deposits are now being worked. Major centres of iron ore mining are Magnitogorsk (Magnitnaya Gora), Khalilovo, Nizhniy Tagil (Vysokaya, Lebyazhka), Mt Blagodat, Bakal and Kachkanar. Production was 24 million tonnes or 10 per cent of the total Soviet production of usable iron ore in 1980. The high-grade magnetite (40-70 per cent iron content) of Magnitnaya Gora in the valley of the upper Ural River is worked by open-cast methods, but this source, at the present rate of mining, seems likely to be exhausted in the near future. The reserves now being worked in the vicinity of of Nizhniy Tagil may similarly be reaching exhaustion. Because of this, the reserves of haematite, magnetite and limonite is Kustanay Oblast (Rudnyy) mines, working the vast Sokolovka-Sarbay deposits astride the Tobol valley, over 300 km east of Magnitogorsk, and reserves elsewhere in Kazakhstan, are being increasingly developed to supplement supplies to Magnitogorsk. The low-grade but very large deposits at Kachkanar are earmarked for use in the northern part of the region.

COAL. The coals which occur on both the western and the eastern slopes of the Ural Mountains are of qualities unsuited for use in the metallurgical industry. The Kizel field produces low-quality coal (used in thermal electricity generating stations) and lignite; the latter can be used as blast furnace fuel after mixing with better grade coals from the Kuzbass (to reduce the sulphur content). South of Chelyabinsk lies the important Korkino-Kopeysk lignite-peat field, producing fuel for thermal electricity stations. There is also a small deposit of good-quality coal at Dombarovskiy near Orsk, in the extreme south of the region. Other scattered deposits of low-grade coal occur, but the region lacks good-quality coking coal, a deficiency that is a hindrance to the full exploitation of the rich mineral wealth, particularly the iron ore, of the region. Suitable coal is imported from Karaganda and the Kuzbass to make up the deficiency.

In 1930, Stalin said: "Our industry, like our national economy, relies in the main on our coal and metallurgical base in the Ukraine. Our task is this, that while continuing to develop this base in every possible way for the future, we must at the same time begin to create a second coal and metallurgical base. This must be the Ural-Kuznetsk Combine, the combination of Kuznetsk coking coal with the ores of the Urals." In the period up to the beginning of the

Second World War, this second coal and metallurgical base was created, involving two-way traffic — coking coal in one direction and iron ore in the other, to support iron- and steel-producing centres 1,600 km apart. Since then, the pattern of fuel supplies has changed: Ekibastuz and Karaganda in Kazakhstan now provide coking coal for the Ural. Despite the shorter haul involved in this traffic (over 900 km), the greater quantity of coal is still imported to the Ural from Kuzbass.

OIL AND GAS. Oil from the Kama valley (Udmurt ASSR), Belaya valley (Bashkir ASSR) and West Siberia is conveyed by pipeline to Perm, Ufa, Ishimbay and Orsk. Oil is used in large thermal power stations located in Nizhniy Tagil, Troitsk and Yuzhnouralsk which are linked together through a powerful grid system. Oil refining and the petrochemical industry now lead in the economy of the western Urals, with Perm as the most important centre.

Natural gas is imported from the Volga-Urals Region, the West Siberia Region and from the Gazli-Kagan area in the Central Asian desert near Bukhara. Probably more important than these distant sources is that of the large Krasnyy Kholm deposit, south-west of Orenburg. The gas found here has a hydrogen sulphide content and is rich in liquid petroleum fractions and helium. It is processed locally and also piped to a thermal power station at Zainsk (Tatar ASSR), and to petrochemical plants at Salavat (Bashkir ASSR) and Kuybyshev, and further afield to Czechoslovakia. Gas, a cheap fuel for thermal power production, may well, through its availability to the Urals Region, reduce the quantity of coke needed by the iron- and steel-producing plants. The use of natural gas for industry and domestic equipment has eased the pressure on Soviet oil which is now being made available to Eastern Europe, Finland, Germany, France, Italy, Austria, and Yugoslavia.

IRON AND STEEL PRODUCTION. Raw materials being immediately available or readily imported (though over long distances e.g. iron ore from Rudnyy in north-west Kazahkstan and from the Kursk Magnetic Anomaly), the Urals Region is now outstanding as containing one of the USSR's two great concentrations of iron, steel and rolled steel production. The region now produces about 25 per cent of the Union's pig iron and 30 per cent of its crude steel (although the Urals steel costs only half the cost of that of the Ukraine mills). A northern production area, centred on Nizhniy Tagil, Sverdlovsk and Serov (the last two are 320 km apart), is supplied with coal from the Kuznetsk Basin and the Kizel field; it may eventually be supplied from the Pechora Basin. For iron ore it increasingly relies on the Kachkanar field. Two hundred kilometres to the south, centred on

Chelyabinsk, Zlatoust, Magnitogorsk and Orsk-Novotroitsk (Chelya-binsk to Orsk is over 480 km) a southern production area is becoming increasingly reliant on Karaganda-Ekibastuz (Pavlodar Oblast) coal and Kustanay Oblast iron ore; this area has the prospect of receiving increasing natural gas supplies from West Siberia and from Soviet Central Asia.

Heavy engineering is closely integrated with steel production. Nizhniy Tagil specialises in railway rolling stock; Sverdlovsk pro-duces mining machinery, steel-rolling equipment, machine tools, railway wagons and coaches and electrical equipment. Chelyabinsk-Kopeysk, besides having huge tractor works, also supply agricultural machinery, bulldozers, earth scrapers, oil-drilling equipment and electrical goods. Miass produces lorries and Zlatoust high-grade stainless steels. Specialisation on metallurgy and engineering and intensive and intricate economic linkages is a feature of the north-south industrial nodes along the eastern flank of the Urals.

NON-FERROUS METALS. Bauxite, copper, lead, zinc and platinum are especially plentiful in the Urals Region. Bauxite, found generally widespread but in particularly large deposits as Severouralsk near Krasnoturinsk, is converted into alumina — an intermediate product — and aluminium — it takes two tonnes of alumina to make one tonne of aluminium — there and at Kamensk-Uralskiy; it is also exported to Yerevan and Sumgait in Trans-Caucasia and, until replaced by imported Greek bauxite, to Zaporozhye in the Ukraine. There are copper deposits in Chelyabinsk (Karabash), Sverdlovsk (Krasnouralsk) and Orenburg (Gay) Oblasts and there are important copper smelters at Krasnouralsk, Kirovgrad, Kyshtym and Karabash (65 and 80 km north-west of Chelyabinsk respectively) and at Gay (30 km north-west of Orsk). A decline in ore production in the Urals has meant that these smelters have become increasingly reliant on ores from Kazakhstan. The zinc foundaries at Chelyabinsk are supplied from nearby sources of zinc sulphides derived from copper concentration plants. Platinum and gold are mined in the mountains west of Serov.

OTHER MINERALS. The largest deposit of high-grade asbestos in the Soviet Union is found at Asbest (the former Baxhenovo) on the eastern slopes of the Urals, 65 km north-east of Sverdlovsk. About 70 per cent of the total Soviet output comes from this site. Com-mercial gold mining began in the Urals over a century and half ago and there are rich deposits of diamonds and other precious and semi-precious stones. Jewel cutting and polishing are crafts traditionally associated with Sverdlovsk; emeralds are particularly important.

Some of the world's largest deposits of salts lie in the Urals Region. In the upper Kama valley, north of Perm, the twin cities Solikamsk and Berezniki have huge deposits of potassium and magnesium salts

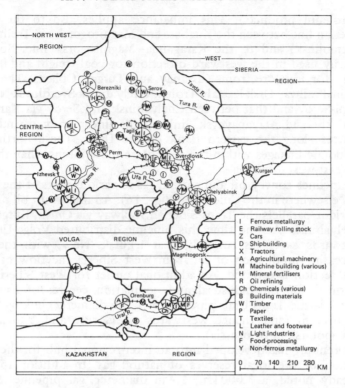

Fig. 217. Urals Economic Region: railways and industrial structure of towns.

and of sodium chloride. These resources are the basis of one of the largest centres of heavy chemicals production in the Soviet Union, with enterprises devoted to the production of potash, soda, sulphuric acid, synthetic ammonia, dyes and mineral fertilisers. The contrasting industrial structures of the zones on the west and east sides of the Urals — basically chemicals and heavy metallurgy respectively — are largely a reflection of the differing resource bases of the two flanks.

Transport
Although five west-east trunk lines traverse it, the several industrial areas of the Urals Region have, as yet, no completely integrated railway intercommunicating system (*see* Fig. 217). The Trans-Siberian Railway between Chelyabinsk and the Kuznetsk Basin, and its offshoot from Sverdlovsk to Omsk, have some of the highest freight densities in the USSR (*see* Fig. 70). There is, however, a marked imbalance on these sections, westerly traffic (coal, grain and timber) being greatly in excess of easterly traffic (iron ore and

petroleum products). This imbalance applies also to the South
Siberian line between the Kuzbass and Magnitogorsk via Tselinograd
(Akmolinsk) and to the Karaganda—Magnitogorsk line. Both are
heavily used in the westward direction for coal freight and increasingly for iron ore from Kustanay and Turgay Oblasts. The longitudinal railway Orsk-Kartaly-Troitsk-Chelyabinsk-Sverdlovsk-Nizhniy
Tagil-Serov and that between Chelyabinsk and Serov via Kamensk-
Uralskiy and Alayapayevsk, link up the linear array of industrial
centres along the eastern flank of the Urals. These north-south
economic linkages within the region are more intense than those in
the east-west direction.

Pipelines convey oil and natural gas to various parts of the region
and elsewhere in the Union (see Fig. 216). An important oil pipeline
corridor parallels the Trans-Siberian Railway via Omsk, Kurgan and
Chelyabinsk. At one time this pipeline distributed Volga-Urals oil
eastwards as far as Angarsk, near Irkutsk. Now, with the ever-
increasing production of oil from West Siberia the flow of oil in
this section is reversed. An additional outlet for West Siberian oil,
destined for the industrial and population centres of European
USSR is the Trans-Urals pipeline (of 1.2 m diameter) linking Surgut
with Perm (and thence westwards via Gorkiy and Yaroslavl to
Novopolotsk in Belorussia).

Orenburg has developed into an inter-regional hub for the distribution of the local reserves of natural gas. In addition to those
already noted, a 3,000 km, 1.4 m diameter, gas pipeline (Soyuz,
Alliance) has been laid as a joint Comecon countries project from
Orenburg to near Uzhgorod on the Soviet-Czechoslovak border. To
accommodate the growing gas transmission needs of West Siberian
fields to western consuming areas large diameter pipelines now link
Medvezhye and Perm and another is planned to Chelyabinsk. The
eastern flank of the Urals is already served by a double string
transmission corridor from Central Asia and from Western Siberia.

POPULATION AND CITIES

With 15.6 million or about 6 per cent of the population and 680,400
km² or three per cent of the area of the USSR the Urals Region
ranks seventh among the nineteen basic economic regions (including
Moldavia SSR) in terms of population and area. Its over-all density,
no more than 23 persons per km², makes it the most sparsely populated economic region after Siberia, the Far East, Middle Asia and
the North-West Region. Practically three-quarters of the population
live in towns or urban-type settlements; the forested countryside
of much of the north of the region is only sparsely populated.

During and following the Second World War industrial growth in the Urals Region was well above the national average and the population of cities like Sverdlovsk and Chelyabinsk increased rapidly. Since the early 1950s, however, the rate of growth has slowed down. Energy resources, always notoriously deficient in the region, have to be imported. Many of the traditional resources are nearing exhaustion and there is increasing reliance on regions to the east. Most of the region is experiencing out-migration and in practically every city there is a much reduced growth rate.

Ethnically, the people of the Urals Region are overwhelmingly Russian, though there are sizeable concentrations of non-Slavic speaking groups. In particular there are the Udmurt (714,000, 69 per cent in Udmurt ASSR) and Komi-Permyak (146,000, 81 per cent in Komi-Permyak AO) who speak Finnic languages. These non-Slavs are being increasingly assimilated into the Russian way of life ("Russianised") as more and more Russians migrate to the region. Administrative boundaries based on ethnic differences are rapidly losing validity in the Urals Region.

The main concentrations of population are at Sverdlovsk, Chelyabinsk and Magnitogorsk on the eastern slopes of the Urals and at Perm and Ufa on the west. There are, moreover, scores of workers' settlements and clusters of population associated with mines and oil wells.

Sverdlovsk (population: 1,211,000)
Founded when copper mining started nearby in 1721, the town was called Ekaterinburg in honour of Catherine I, wife of Tsar Peter the Great. Located within the *tayga* in the eastern foothills of the low Central Urals, Sverdlovsk has since developed as an important route focus and industrial centre. Railway lines converge on the city from seven directions. Its industries include the manufacture of iron and steel, heavy engineering (e.g. Uralmash), woodworking and chemical and copper enterprises (*see* Fig. 217). The city is the largest in the Urals Region and is regional capital of the northern part. Its population increased by 80 per cent between 1939 and 1959, and by 32 per cent between 1950 and 1979. In terms of population Sverdlovsk ranks eleventh among the cities of the Soviet Union.

Chelyabinsk (population: 1,031,000)
Capital of the southern part of the region, Chelyabinsk, like Sverdlovsk, is an important route focus and industrial centre. As the starting-point, in 1891, of the Trans-Siberian Railway, it has long been considered the gateway to Siberia. It has extensive ferrous, ferro-alloys and non-ferrous metal-working industries, heavy engineering (rolling stock, tractors, etc.), chemicals and food-processing

(*see* Fig. 217). Its population increased by 150 per cent between 1939 and 1959, and by 27 per cent between 1959 and 1979.

Perm (population: 999,000)
Situated on the Kama River below its confluence with the Chuso-vaya River (which provides an important route through the Urals to Sverdlovsk), Perm is the focus of the upper Kama industrial area. It has chemical, fertiliser and pulp-making industries based on local salt and timber supplies and engineering works which utilise steel processed on the eastern flank of the Urals. Perm developed early as an oil-refining centre on the Volga-Urals field and is now the chief centre for refining and petrochemicals; nowadays local production of oil has to be supplemented by imported oil and natural gas. A possible increase in hydro-electricity generation at a station sited just upstream from Perm could arise from the projected Pechora-Kama diversion scheme. The present population, over three times that of 1939 (largely the result of in-migration), increased by 17 per cent in the period 1970-79.

Izhevsk (population: 549,000)
Capital and economic and cultural centre of the Udmurt ASSR, Izhevsk possesses steel sheet and rolling mills, motor vehicle and metal-working industries and an old-established firearms factory. The population of the city has grown rapidly since the late 1950s and by as much as 30 per cent since the 1970 census.

Orenburg (population: 459,000)
Founded in 1737 as a Russian fortress against Kazakh nomads, Orenburg stands at the point where the railway from Kuybyshev to Tashkent crosses the Ural River. It is the centre of an important agricultural region (spring wheat, sheep, etc.) with food-processing and engineering industries specialising in agricultural machinery. The discovery and development of the huge Krasnyy Kholm natural gas deposit south-west of the city has resulted in a rapid growth in population in recent years (33 per cent between 1970 and 1979 largely through natural increase), and has made it an inter-regional hub for natural gas distribution within the USSR. A 2,700 km (*Soyuz*) pipeline also conveys gas to the western border of the Soviet Union.

Magnitogorsk (population: 406,000)
Situated on the banks of the Ural River and within the steppelands, Magnitogorsk is one of the foremost of the Soviet metallurgical centres (*see* Fig. 218). It relies on ores from nearby Magnitnaya

Fig. 218. Magnitogorsk, on the banks of the Ural River, is one of the foremost metallurgical centres in the Soviet Union.

Gora and from Kustanay Oblast, and on coking coal from Karaganda. The city was not founded until 1931, but boasted a population of 146,000 by 1939, 311,000 by 1959 and 364,000 in 1970. The speed of growth has fallen off markedly in recent years (11 per cent increase between 1970 and 1979).

Nizhniy Tagil (population: 398,000)
Situated in a valley on the eastern side of the Ural a few kilometres from the point where the Tagil River debouches on to the West Siberian Lowland, Nizhniy Tagil is a metallurgical centre with one of the largest integrated iron and steel works in the Soviet Union. Urals ores mainly from Kachkanet and local and imported (Kuzbass) coals provide the basis for the industry, with which are associated coal by-products, industrial chemicals and engineering (largely railway rolling stock construction). Local forest supply lumber and raw materials for paper, pulp and cellulose industries.

Kurgan (population: 310,000)
Regional centre of Kurgan Oblast, Kurgan is a river port and industrialised market town in a rich farming area. It lies at the intersection of the Trans-Siberian Railway and the Tobol River, where a branch line leads to Sverdlovsk. Precision instruments, omnibuses and agricultural machinery (especially grain combines) are made here, and there are also other agriculture-based industries. Surprisingly its population increased by over a quarter in the period of 1970 to 1979.

Other towns

Though smaller in the urban hierarchy than the foregoing, the following towns also deserve mention.

Orsk (population: 247,000) and *Novotroitsk* (population: 90,000) are twin towns in the steppe country of the extreme south of the region, associated with oil refining (oil from the Guryev/ Baku, Volga-Urals and Mangyshlak fields), petrochemicals, high quality chrome and nickel alloy steels, engineering (farm machinery and rolling stock), nickel refining (using Svetlyy and Batamshinskiy nickel) and meat-packing.

Zlatoust (population: 198,000) and *Miass* (population: 150,000) have steel works relying on local Bakal ore and increasingly on ores hauled 300 km from Rudnyy in Kazakhstan. Zlatoust is known for its production of high grade steel and Miass for motor vehicle assembly.

Kamensk-Uralskiy (population: 187,000) has a combined alumina-aluminium plant using thermal electricity, powered by low-grade coals from the vicinity of Chelyabinsk, and Severouralsk bauxite.

Berezniki (population: 185,000) has chemical industries based on local potassium and magnesium salts, and titanium and magnesium metal production. Magnesium, when alloyed with aluminium, produces light, extremely tough and stress-resistant metals used in the aircraft and spacecraft (e.g. *Salyut, Soyuz, Cosmos, Molniya, Prognoz*) industries, including intercontinental ballistic missiles (IBMs).

CHAPTER XV

Siberia Macro-Region

This macro-region consolidates the West and East Siberia basic economic regions of the RSFSR. It contains 29.22 per cent of the total area of the USSR but only 8.6 per cent of the population and 8.8 per cent of the urban population. Estimates (Aleksandrov *et al.*, 1974 – *see* Table 31) suggest there are 56 per cent of the country's potential fuel and energy resources, 45.5 per cent of the predicted iron ore reserves, and 48.4 per cent of the timber resources in the region. It has only 11 per cent of the agricultural land of the USSR. A surplus of fuels and energy, water and timber resources is a characteristic of the Siberia macro-region in contrast to the European macro-regions (*see* Chapters XII-XIV), which are distinguished mainly by the large scale of development of industry, agriculture and transportation and also, at present, an adequate supply of manpower.

Siberia is still in the early stage of economic development. This is reflected in high labour and transport costs – costs for natural resources are minimal. In the eyes of Russian planners and economists this Asiatic part of the USSR is looked upon as the Soviet "El Dorado" and vital to the economic future of the country. The principal industrial centres, where energy-intensive and heat-intensive industries are significant and transport links are strongest, are concentrated in the most highly developed southern parts, although rapid industrial growth is currently taking place in association with the continuing upsurge of production from the gas and oilfields in the Tyumen Oblast and Yamal-Nenets AO.

1. WEST SIBERIA ECONOMIC REGION

The vast West Siberia Region (*see* Fig. 219) extends eastwards from the Urals to the Yenisey River. Politically it comprises the huge Tyumen Oblast (which includes two national *okrugs*), Omsk, Tomsk, Novosibirsk and Kemerovo Oblasts and the Altay Kray in the southeast (*see* Fig. 220). It is poorly integrated and transport linkages are

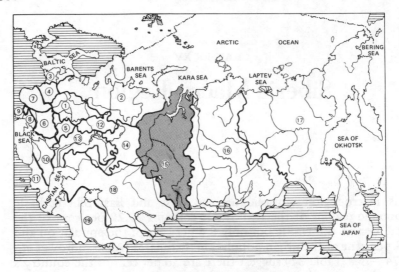

Fig. 219. Soviet Union: location of West Siberia Economic Region.

Fig. 220. West Siberia Economic Region.

not well developed. Nevertheless, new railways are under construction, and pipelines are acquiring an important role in association with the important developments taking place in the new oil- and gasfields in the north and north-west of the region. The greatest industrial concentration is in the Kuznetsk Basin, although Novosibirsk, known as the "gateway to the Kuzbass", appears to be losing its predominant regional influence to such towns as Omsk, Tyumen and Surgut.

TABLE 59. WEST SIBERIA ECONOMIC REGION:
ADMINISTRATIVE UNITS, THEIR POPULATION AND DENSITY

Area: 2,427,000 km^2
Population (1979): 12,959,000

Administrative unit	Area (000 km^2)	Population (000, 1979)	Density (persons per km^2)	Percentage urban
Altay Kray	262	2,675	10	52
(incl. Gorno-Altay AO)	93	172	2	28
Kemerovo Oblast	96	2,958	31	86
Novosibirsk Oblast	178	2,618	15	72
Omsk Oblast	140	1,955	14	63
Tomsk Oblast	317	866	3	65
Tyumen Oblast	1,435	1,887	1	61
(incl. Khanty-Mansi AO)	523	569	1	78
Yamal-Nenets	750	158	(0.2)	51

TABLE 60. WEST SIBERIA ECONOMIC REGION:
TOWNS WITH OVER 150,000 INHABITANTS IN 1979

Town	Population in thousands 1970 (census)	1979 (census)	Percentage increase 1970-79
Novosibirsk	1,161	1,312	13
Omsk	821	1,014	23
Novokuznetsk	499	541	8
Barnaul	439	533	21
Kemerovo	385	471	22
Tomsk	338	421	24
Tyumen	269	359	34
Prokopyevsk	274	266	−3
Biysk	186	212	14
Rubtsovsk	145	157	8

PHYSICAL ASPECTS

Relief and drainage
The region embraces the West Siberian Plain together with a north-western extension of the Altay Mountains in the extreme south-east. The former, covering an area practically ten times that of Britain, is an almost perfect plain in which the landscape stretches flat and unbroken to an endless horizon. This is one of the world's largest areas of unbroken flat land with only an almost imperceptible gradient northwards. The latter comprises a complex of mountains which skirts the West Siberian Plain and the Central Siberian Plateau. The Altay are characterised by high eroded plateaus topping the summits. They culminate at heights in excess of 2,000 m on the Kazakh-Siberian border, where they are known as the Rudnyy (mining) Altay. What are probably two northern continuations of the Altay, the Kuznetsk Ala Tau and the Salair Range, enclose a hilly, rolling land which gradually merges northwards into the West Siberian Plain. This is known as the Kuznetsk Basin which contains the vast Kuzbass coal reserves.

Drainage is northwards to the Arctic by means of such sluggish, branching and tortuous rivers as the Ob, Irtysh, Ishim and Tobol. On the plain the interfluves seldom rise more than 10 m above the surrounding countryside. Widespread flooding in the middle and lower reaches of the rivers is an annual event after the spring thaw which is earlier in the upper reaches (for example, record floods in Tyumen in May 1979 forced the evacuation of 3,000 people from low-lying areas and necessitated the urgent construction of 40 km of temporary embankments to protect the city against rising water). Waterlogging of the soils is common and there are extensive areas of bog, marsh and shallow lake. West Siberia is recognised as the world's largest contemporary centre for the development of swamp forming processes. The Vasyuganye Swamp between the Ob and Irtysh Rivers is the largest in the world. It includes a vast tract of bog and moss-covered land with few trees. In fact about 50 per cent of West Siberia is swamp.

During Quaternary times, the West Siberian Plain was affected by three glacial advances, the Samarovo (Dnieper stage), Taz (Moscow sub-stage) and Zyrianka (Valday). Novaya Zemlya—the Polar Urals in the north-west—and the Putoran Mountains in the north-east were the ice sources for the first (Samarovo) continental glaciation which extended southwards to near what is now the confluence of the Ob and Irtysh. The ice blocked the north-flowing rivers to form vast lakes in the area now occupied by the Baraba, Kalunda and Ishim Steppes. A depression in the Turgay tableland formed an overflow channel to the Aral Sea. Sediments laid down

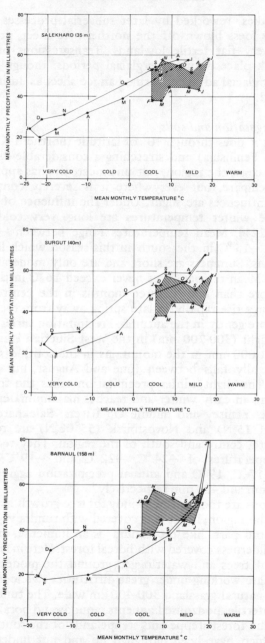

Fig. 221. Hythergraphs for Salekhard, Surgut and Barnaul (Kew, London, shaded).

in these lakes, reworked by later subaerial processes and supplemented by loess blown off the northern ice sheet, provided what are now very flat fertile lowlands. Transgressions of the Arctic Ocean took place during interglacial periods, though none of the subsequent glacial advances formed an ice sheet as during the Samarovo period.

Climate, vegetation and soils
Ranging as it does through 30° of latitude (northern Kazakhstan to the Yamal Peninsula) and stretching a considerable distance along the Arctic coast the region, not unexpectedly, has appreciable variations in climate, but everywhere it is severely continental, and maritime influences are slight. Under the influence of the Siberian anticyclone winter temperatures are long, very cold and severe (*see* Fig. 221). Mean temperatures range between −30 °C in the north and −15 °C in the south in this season which lasts seven to nine months. Summers are short and are only moderately warm in the south. Mean temperatures never exceed 16 °C in the north and for no more than one to three months in the centre and south. Temperatures rise rapidly in late spring away from the north coast, but fall more gently in the autumn. Precipitation varies appreciably, but it is slight (300-700 mm) in the West Siberian Plain, increasing to about 1,000 mm in the mountains in the south-east. The maximum generally falls between June and August, but droughts are frequent. The slight winter precipitation takes the form of snow which forms in early winter and reaches maximum depths between the middle Yenisey and middle Ob Rivers. Salekhard (66°32′N), Surgut (61°15′N) and Novosibirsk (55°02′N) are representative of the north, centre and south of the region. They record January mean temperatures of −24 °C, −22 °C and −19 °C, July means of 14 °C, 17 °C, 19 °C and annual precipitation aggregates of 464 mm, 492 mm and 425 mm respectively.

Conditions are too cool and windy for tree growth in the northern fringe of the region; hence it is covered with tundra vegetation. The broad central part, like the tundra, is an immense, virtually uninhabited wilderness covered with boreal forest. Here in an inextricable mingling of trees and waterlogged ground the modern oil and gas industries are working under great difficulties, while in the south is a zone of natural grassland 300-400 km wide. The tundra and *tayga* soils are infertile, podzolised aquepts, aquods and boralfs with much peat but the forest-steppe and steppelands of the south have fertile borolls which have been ploughed up and put under cultivation. Vertical zonation of soils and vegetation occurs in the southern mountains. The southern limit of perenially frozen ground (permafrost) extends southwards to a latitude just north of Samotlar at varying degrees of depth.

THE ECONOMY

Agriculture
Climatic and soil conditions favour a highly-developed and diversified agriculture in the south-west of the region, so much so that it is one of the most important farming regions of the whole of the USSR. Between Tyumen and Omsk has been a major dairying area since the nineteenth century, producing a surplus of milk,

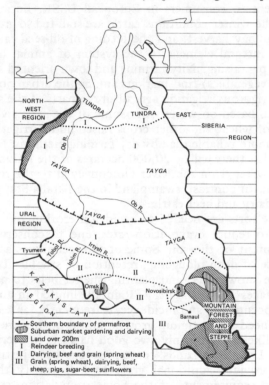

Fig. 222. West Siberia Economic Region: agricultural land-use regions.

butter and cheese (*see* Fig. 222). In 1954, the Soviet Government started to develop further the agricultural potential of this region and contiguous northern Kazakhstan under the "Virgin and Long Idle Lands Project" whereby vast areas of wild steppe, overgrown with feather-grass and couch-grass (virgin and fallow lands), were ploughed up. Between 1954 and 1962 over 23 million hectares in south-west West Siberia and northern Kazakhstan were brought under the plough and cultivated for spring wheat.

The agricultural south-west contains some 20 million hectares of ploughland (9 per cent of the country's total) and 15 million hectares of permanent and improved pastures. Spring wheat is the main crop, although rye, oats, millet, maize (for silage), rape, sunflowers, sugar-beet, linseed, hemp, flax and potatoes are grown. Drought, hot winds, dust storms, late spring frosts, danger of flooding and cold *purga* winds are, however, serious physical hazards to which all crops are exposed. Traditionally, cattle are raised for milk and meat and sheep for both meat and wool. West Siberia has a considerable surplus of these animal products which, like the grains and industrial crops, are sent to consumers in European USSR. Because of the severity of the winter conditions cattle are stall-fed so great store is placed on the hay harvest, and the feeding of oil-seed cake concentrates is an integral element in the system of animal husbandry. Poultry and pig raising, dairy farming and town-oriented agriculture (fresh green vegetables) find markets among the urban populations.

There is a vigorous irrigation agriculture in parts of the south-west of the region, based on water from some of the main rivers. Yields and output of wheat and other crops raised under irrigation are far greater and more reliable than by dry farming methods. By 1980, it is expected that there will be 20,000 hectares of the Kalunda Steppe irrigated by water from the River Ob conveyed to the region via a 180 km canal. In contrast, swampland in the Baraba Steppe is being drained for dairy and beef cattle.

Constant efforts are needed to avoid soil erosion and dust bowl conditions, to reduce evaporation rates, and to conserve the low moisture content of the soil. Some of the techniques adopted are the avoidance of deep ploughing, retention of stubble after harvest to retain the snow cover, and planting shelter belts to protect the exposed surfaces from *sukhovey*. Rainfall, limited in amount and irregular in occurrence and incidence, is frequently far less than the crops really need for optimum growth, and droughts are common. Despite the likelihood of only two good harvests in every five, the "Virgin and Long Idle Lands" enterprise has been justified: first, because it provides additional grain to help satisfy the rapidly growing food requirements of the Soviet population; secondly, it helps alleviate food shortages following harvest fluctuations elsewhere in the country (e.g. 1972, 1975, 1981 and 1982 when the overall harvests were disastrous); and thirdly, it enables such regions as the Ukraine and the North Caucasus to switch over to maize and other fodder crops in what is considered to be an even more urgent drive to increase meat and milk production in the country. The eventual achievements of the enterprise as yet remain to be seen.

Resources and industry
The natural resource base of West Siberia is rich and varied. The timber stands, covering about a third of the region, contain many

different types of tree, reflecting the variations in climate: conifers, aspens (used for matchsticks), birch, elder and large stands of larch (used for railway sleepers and telegraph poles). Much of the forest cover in the Ob River Basin is of poor quality or else is too remote for extraction. Currently, the main timber lands are in Tyumen and Tomsk Oblasts but others are being opened up by branches of the Trans-Siberian Railway or by lines like the Tyumen-Tobolsk-Surgut link which was built to facilitate the development of the oil and gas industry (*see* Fig. 223).

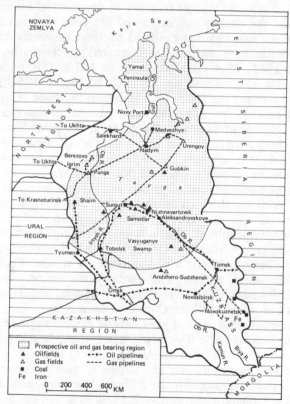

Fig. 223. West Siberia Economic Region: mineral and power resources.

Mineral resources are overwhelmingly mineral fuels. Coal, oil and natural gas occur in great abundance. The Kuzbass coalfield is the second largest producer in the USSR and is thought to have the largest reserves in the Asiatic part of the country. The coals include a large proportion (about 40 per cent) which are of excellent coking quality. Their low sulphur and ash content and high calorific value make them eminently suitable for use in blast furnaces. The coal seams are exceptionally thick (6-14 m and occasionally as much as 20-25 m) and lie near the surface. They thus afford excellent opportunities for mechanised working by open cast and strip methods. Further south, the seams are thinner and their steep dip makes them difficult to work. In 1979 the output of coal from the Kuznetsk Basin was 150 million tonnes with 167 tonnes planned for 1985. Much is used locally in thermo-electric generating stations, in steel mills, and smelters, but the bulk serves such distant industrial areas as the Urals, the Centre and Kazakhstan.

One of the world's great reserves of commercial oil and natural gas underlie the marshy wilderness of the West Siberian Plain. Discovered in the mid 1950s the oilfield started commercial production in 1964. Since then output has increased spectacularly, 1 million tonnes in 1965, 31.4 million tonnes in 1970, 148 million tonnes in 1975 and 312 million tonnes in 1980. Some 385-395 million tonnes are planned for 1985, by which time the share of the national total will be close to sixty per cent. Almost all the West Siberian output originates in Tyumen Oblast, from the giant Samotlar field in the Nizhnevartovsk district and a number of medium-size fields. The development of new fields is proceeding northward from *Nizhnevartovsk* (population: 76,000) and *Surgut* (population: 74,000), the two principal oil towns and more recently at Vartovsk-Sosnino, Vakh and the Vasyuganye swamp district in Tomsk Oblast, but access through the sandy, swampy and flooded forest terrain presents serious problems. The oil is moved out by 76-cm and 100-cm diameter pipes to refineries at Omsk, Kurgan and Anzhero-Sudzhensk (Kuznetsk Basin). There are also links with the Trans-Siberian oil pipeline which extends eastwards to the refinery at Angarsk, near Irkutsk and with the Druzhba (Friendship) line which conveys oil across European USSR to Comecon countries.

The West Siberian natural gas fields lie in even more remote areas in the far north of the Tyumen Oblast. Here, largely in the difficult permafrost zone within the Arctic Circle at Medvezhye, Urengoy, Vyngapur and elsewhere, are the largest known gas deposits in the world. Active exploitation is taking place and production has increased at a phenomenal rate — 2.5 billion m^3 in 1965, 9.3 billion m^3 in 1970, 97 billion m^3 in 1978, 156 billion m^3 in 1980 and 330-370 billion m^3 planned for 1985. In 1980 West Siberia's gas production was 36 per cent of the national total (*see* Table 61). In addition to this dry gas there is a significant component of wet gas associated with the oil production in the more southerly fields. The natural gas liquids are being used as petrochemical feedstocks.

The pipelines for transporting the gas out of the region whether operating, under construction or planned, involve very difficult construction and technological problems associated with the severe,

(*Novosti*)

Fig. 224. A 2,120 km trunk pipeline conveys natural gas from remote areas in the far north of Tyumen Oblast, West Siberia, to consumers in European USSR and Eastern and Western Europe. Pipelines, whether operating, under construction or planned, involve difficult constructional and technological problems related to the severe adverse environment.

TABLE 61. NATURAL GAS PRODUCTION IN WEST SIBERIA
(dry gas in billion m^3)

Area	1970	1975	1977	1978	1980	1985 (planned)
USSR	198	289	346	372	435	600-640
West Siberia	9.3	35.7	71	—	156	330-370
Medvezhye	—	30	63	71	[65]	
Urengoy	—	—	—	12	[60]	
Vyngabur	—	—	—	—	[15]	
Punga—Igrim	9.3	3.5	—	—	—	

Source: in part, *Soviet Geography* XX (4), (1979).

NOTE: dashes indicate no production in these years.

adverse natural environment (cold, bogs, forests, lakes, etc.) (*see* Fig. 224). Pipelines are currently conveying gas to consumers in

European USSR and Eastern Europe from Nadym, the collecting point near the Medvezhye field to Punga, and thence via Serov and Perm or else via Ukhta and Torzhok (Northern Lights line). Another transmission system is planned for Urengoy gas to run through Surgut to Chelyabinsk.

The human problems associated with the exploitation of the oil-gas reserves are proving formidable. Housing and domestic amenities are lacking, food and goods supplies are unsatisfactory; there is a paucity of cultural facilities and living conditions generally are poor. Substantially higher pay scales than are obtained in European USSR (though these are often inadequate in terms of local costs) do not compensate for unsatisfactory living conditions and there is a large turnover of labour.

Electrical energy is obtained from a number of thermal stations, large (e.g. Tomusa, 1.3 million kW; Belovo, 1.2 million kW) and smaller units. There are also small hydro-stations on the River Ob at Novosibirsk (400,000 kW) and at Kamen (630 kW). The latter generates power and also serves the Kalunda Steppe with irrigation water.

Flour mills, dairies, tanneries, meat-packing factories, oil-pressing plants and canneries apart, industrialisation of the region began with the construction of the first big metallurgical plant at Novokuznetsk (formerly Stalinsk) in 1929, which processes iron ore from the Urals and was the eastern limb of the Urals-Kuznetsk Combine. It now works on ores from deposits at Gornaya Shoriya (Temir Tau, Tashtogol) to the south of the Kuzbass, from the Minusinsk Basin (in Khakass AO, Eastern Siberia), from Zheleznogorsk on the Ilim River, and iron ore pellets (compact iron concentrates) from Kustanay Oblast are now used to enrich the fuel charge of blast furnaces and steel-making open hearths. Novokuznetsk has two large integrated works and the Kuzbass ranks third after the Ukraine and Urals as a heavy metallurgical area. There are also small steel-making or re-melting plants in Novosibirsk, Omsk, and Guryev (Kuzbass). The products of the metallurgical industry have fostered the growth of industries devoted to heavy metal structures, equipment for mines, and other metal-consuming items, but a sizeable proportion of the region's iron and steel is transported to other parts in a raw or semi-finished state for fabrication into various machines, machine tools, turbines, and agricultural machinery in such centres as Novosibirsk, Omsk, Tomsk and Barnaul.

Coke oven by-products associated with the ferrous metallurgy laid the basis for chemical industries in the Kuzbass. These now produce nitrogenous fertilisers, analine dyes, various coal-tar derivitives and the polyamide fibre *kapron* (produced from caprolactum, a material associated with ammonia synthesis).

No less significant is the development of non-ferrous metallurgy. The first enterprise in this field was the zinc smelter at Belovo using zinc found in the Salair Ridge (now exhausted) followed by the aluminium plant at Novokuznetsk, utilising bauxite found near Angarsk, and alumina from the Urals, and Arkalyk and Pavlodar in Kazakhstan.

Two large petrochemical projects based on the region's oil and gas reserves are now in operation. That at Tomsk produces a wide range of plastics including ethylene, propylene and polypropylene; the other at Tobolsk specialises in synthetic rubber.

Transport

Railways integrate the territorial-production complex of the Kuznetsk Basin with the Trans-Siberian line at Novosibirsk and at Yurga, and with the Turk-Sib Railway at Barnaul (*see* Fig. 225). Another east-west connection is afforded by the South Siberian Railway which provides a link between the southern Urals (Magnitogorsk), Barnaul and Novokuznetsk. This line has been extended eastwards to Abakan in Eastern Siberia and thence northwards to Achinsk and north-eastwards to Tayshet, both on the Trans-Siberian line. The Trans-Siberian Railway, running through the wooded steppe, is the undoubted lifeline of Siberia, and between the Kuzbass and the Urals is probably the most heavily-used section of railway in the world.

Feeder railways northwards from the Trans-Siberian main line have facilitated the northward movement of the important logging industry. In Tyumen Oblast improved access to timber reserves was fostered by the building of a spur from the Kotlas-Pechora railway across the northern Urals to Labytnangi on the lower Ob River opposite Salekhard. Further south, the line from Ivdel in the northern Urals to Serginy on the Ob River has also opened up a vast new forest region of high grade timber as did the completion of a spur in the east from Tomsk on the Trans-Siberian to Asino and beyond Belyy Yar on the Ket River.

The Tyumen-Tobolsk-Surgut-Nizhnevartovsk railway, completed in 1976, provides a year-round overland transport link for the West Siberian oilfields with the rest of the USSR. Together with its extension northwards to Urengoy (planned to be completed during the period 1981-85) it will assist in the development of additional oil resources in the north and provide a link with the great gasfields near Urengoy.

The pipelines which transport the oil and gas from the Tuymen Oblast have been mentioned (*see* Fig. 93 and p. 128).

POPULATION AND CITIES

A Slavic amalgam of Russians, Ukrainians and Belorussians, displaying a brash, tough frontier spirit, attracted by mineral and industrial development form the vast majority of the population; the native Altay (60,000), Khanty (21,000), Mansi (7,600) and Nentsy (30,000) groups of nomadic herdsmen and hunters are small and are being progressively assimilated into the Soviet economy. The West Siberian Region as a whole provides a home for almost 13.0 million people. Forty-one per cent live in Kemerovo and Novosibirsk Oblasts, which are 86 per cent and 72 per cent urbanised respectively. Densities are practically 31 persons per km^2 in the urbanised, industrialised Kuzbass (Kemerovo Oblast), but in the vast Tyumen Oblast only a little over one person per km^2. The average density for the region as a whole is 5 persons per km^2, but there are vast tracts of swamp and forest which are uninhabited. Until the late 1950s, the region was one of in-migration, but since then — and despite the oil and gas developments — the net movement of people appears to have been outwards to European USSR.

Novosibirsk (population: 1,312,000)
Novosibirsk, called Novonikolayevsk in 1893 when it was founded in honour of the new Tsar Nicholas II, has more than trebled its predominantly Russian population during the last forty years and is now the eighth largest city in the USSR. This metropolis of West Siberia (further from Moscow than is London) with several industrial satellite towns set in a wheat and dairy cattle region has frequently been dubbed the "Chicago of Siberia" to express its rapid growth and industrialisation. Located at the intersection of the River Ob and the Trans-Siberian trunk line, Novosibirsk is a natural focus of routes and a leading transportation centre (a train passes through every four minutes). Though not strictly within the Kuznetsk coal basin, its diversified industries are important. They include steel rolling mills (based on Kuzbass and Urals steel), tin smelting, machine tools, tractors, farm machinery, electrical equipment, motor vehicles, river boats (ships carry goods more than 1,600 km down the Ob to towns and regions of the north), chemicals, flour-milling, meat-packing and other food industries, oil refining, textiles, clothes, soap, footwear and furniture (*see* Fig. 225). At present, the city appears to be losing its predominant regional influence in favour of Omsk, Tyumen and Surgut.

Thirty kilometres south of Novosibirsk is the township of *Akademgorodok* ("Academy town"). Akademgorodok (*see* Fig. 226) is the focal point of a sociological experiment in that it has been designed to induce the country's top-rank young scientists and economists to leave Moscow and other cities in the western part of the Soviet

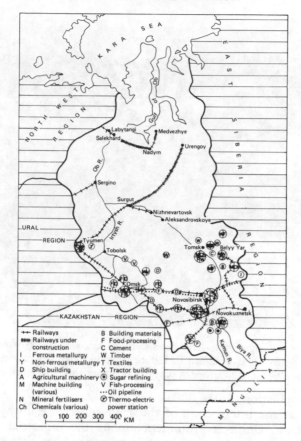

Fig. 225. West Siberia Economic Region: railways and industrial structure of towns.

Union and work in Siberia. The purpose-built town, founded in 1957, contains eleven major scientific institutes, a university, an "experiment factory", generous accommodation and a wide range of social services for the whole community. Here, and in Irkutsk (*see* p. 392), the country's most illustrious brains, under the aegis of the Siberian Branch of the Soviet Academy of Sciences, mastermind the future of the former "virgin lands" of West Siberia, test the likely climatic and other effects of such colossal development projects as the diversion of north-flowing rivers into Central Asia, and plan territorial-production complexes along the route of the Baykal-Amur Mainline (BAM). The town is also the site of one of the few new and highly experimental boarding-schools for exceptionally gifted, scientifically inclined children from the whole of the Asiatic part of the USSR.

(Novosti)

Fig. 226. Akademgorodok. This township, 20 km south of Novosibirsk, is a scientific centre. It is designed to induce top-rank scientists to leave Moscow and other cities in the European part of the Soviet Union to work in Siberia.

Omsk (population: 1,014,000)

Located at the intersection of the Trans-Siberian Railway and the Irtysh River, Omsk is prominent among the industrial nodes in West Siberia and, as a result of in-migration, has shown a quite remarkable increase in population in recent years (up 23 per cent between 1970 and 1979). It grew in the first place directly after the Trans-Siberian line reached it in 1895, but its rapid growth in recent years is partly a reflection of manufacturing plants evacuated here from centres in European USSR threatened by the German advance during the Second World War, and of its fast growing hinterland. The city functions as a commercial and industrial focus. It has major engineering enterprises (e.g. railway equipment, farm machinery), a large oil refinery, several petrochemical factories, textiles and agriculture-orientated industries such as flour-milling and meat-packing (see Fig. 225).

Novokuznetsk (population: 541,000)

Centre of the Kuzbass and site of well-developed heavy industry, Novokuznetsk has two integrated iron and steel works, heavy engineering and locomotive works, coke-chemical industries and an aluminium reduction works. The city pioneered the production of aluminium when equipment was evacuated there in 1943 from the Volkov works in Leningrad.

Barnaul (population: 533,000)
Barnaul is an important railway focus with five lines — the Turk-Sib via Semipalatinsk, the South Siberian via Tselinograd and the Middle Siberian via Kokchetav, a link with the Trans-Siberian and another with the Kuzbass — all meeting at this point. The city, sited on the left bank of the Ob River within the agriculturally rich Kulunda Steppe, is the administrative centre of the Altay Kray. Its industries produce spun cotton and clothing (raw cotton from Central Asia), rayon fibres, agricultural machinery, motor vehicle tyres (synthetic rubber from Omsk petrochemical plant and artificial fibre), milled grain and wood products.

Kemerovo (population: 471,000);
Prokopyevsk (population: 266,000)
Situated within the Kuznetsk Basin, Kemerovo and Prokopyevsk are primarily concerned with the mining of coal and associated chemical industries, but also have a variety of metal-working and food industries. While the population of Kemerovo continues to grow, that of Prokopyevsk has declined in recent years.

Tomsk (population: 421,000)
One of the oldest Siberian cities and once the only Siberian city with a seat of higher learning (dating from the 1880s), Tomsk is now an important centre of woodworking, engineering (electric motors, cables, calculating machines, etc.), food-processing and other industries. It is also the site of a giant petrochemical complex producing a wide range of plastics (including 75 per cent of all Soviet polypropylene and 28 per cent of Soviet methanol), based on the great development of gas and oil to the north. It lies on the high right bank of the Tom River, a tributary of the River Ob at the southern edge of the *tayga*. It is served by a branch line from the Trans-Siberian Railway which, extending to Asino and Belyy Yar on the Ket River, also fosters the logging industry. There has been a notable increase in population in Tomsk in recent years (24 per cent between 1970 and 1979).

Tyumen (population: 359,000)
Situated on the Tura River near the western head of navigation of the Ob-Irtysh system, Tyumen was the first permanent Russian settlement in Siberia. An *ostrogi* (stockaded wooded fort) was built here in 1586 on the site of a former Tatar settlement. In the eighteenth century, it was at the eastern end of the Siberian Highway and

became the terminus of the nineteenth-century Trans-Urals (Perm-Tyumen) Railway. The town has long functioned as the gateway to Siberia. It is a shipbuilding centre and river-rail transfer point (mainly for timber and wheat), but is above all else the gateway and supply base for the northern oil and gas region with which it now has a rail link. The oil boom has led to several new industries connected with the oil industry being located in Tyumen and also to an exceedingly rapid growth of population as a result of in-migration of able-bodied age groups (34 per cent between 1970 and 1979). The great Torman peat bog serves as the source of fuel for the Tyumen power station.

Biysk (population: 212,000)
Terminus of the tortuous 620 km long Chuya *trakt* from Outer Mongolia and of a branch line southward from the Trans-Siberian Railway, Biysk was an eighteenth-century outpost in the wooded steppes of the Altay. It is a trading centre in a rich agricultural area processing grains, meat, wool, flax and other farm products, and also manufactures farm machinery. It also possesses a match combine.

Rubtsovsk (population: 157,000)
Situated in the extreme south of the region in the Altay Kray, Rubtovsk is notable for its production of tractors and tractor-drawn implements and electrical equipment, located here following the evacuation of machinery before the German advance during the Second World War.

2. EAST SIBERIA ECONOMIC REGION

In contrast to the general plain character of West Siberia, the vast territory of East Siberia (*see* Fig. 227) is made up of plateaus and mountains. Still in an early stage of economic development, it is distinctive on account of its huge forest resource base, enormous hydro-electric surplus and specialisation in power-intensive industries such as aluminium and pulp processing. The largest industrial centres are situated along the Trans-Siberian Railway; the north remains largely underdeveloped (*see* Fig. 228).

PHYSICAL ASPECTS

Relief and drainage
East Siberia includes much of the Central Siberian Plateau, together with a complex of high mountains skirting it on the south. The

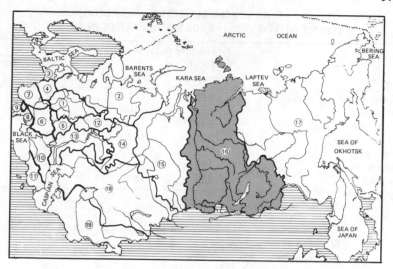

Fig. 227. Soviet Union: location of East Siberia Economic Region.

TABLE 62. EAST SIBERIA ECONOMIC REGION:
ADMINISTRATIVE UNITS, THEIR POPULATION AND DENSITY

Area: 4,123,000 km²
Population (1979): 8,158,000

Administrative unit	Area (000 km²)	Population (000, 1979)	Density (persons per km²)	Percentage urban
Krasnoyarsk Kray:	2,402	3,198	1	69
incl. Khakass AO	62	500	8	68
Taymyr AO	862	44	(0.05)	64
Evenki AO	768	16	(0.02)	36
Irkutsk Oblast:	768	2,560	3	77
incl. Ust-Orda AO	22	133	6	20
Chita Oblast:	432	1,233	3	63
incl. Aga AO	19	69	4	29
Buryat ASSR	351	901	3	45
Tuva ASSR	170	266	2	38

Central Siberian Plateau is an extensive dissected upland of ancient rocks. Within it the Pre-Cambrian crystalline rocks of the Siberian Platform (Angaraland, the Asian counterpart of the Russian Platform) are exposed in worn-down mountain ranges, or masked by virtually horizontal marine deposits of Palaeozoic age. The plateau has a generally mountainous character, particularly in the Putorana Mountains in the north (over 1,500 m), but in general it is 500-600 m

TABLE 63. EAST SIBERIA ECONOMIC REGION:
TOWNS WITH OVER 150,000 INHABITANTS IN 1979

| Town | Population in thousands | | Percentage increase 1970-79 |
	1970 (census)	1979 (census)	
Krasnoyarsk	648	796	23
Irkutsk	451	550	22
Ulan-Ude	254	300	18
Chita	241	302	25
Angarsk	203	239	18
Bratsk	155	214	38
Norilsk	135	180	33

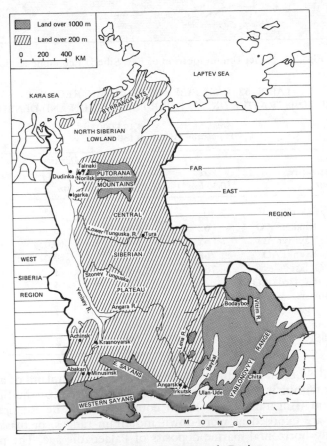

Fig. 228. East Siberia Economic Region.

high and surfaces are usually flat. In contrast to the Russian Lowland, which did not become dry land until Quaternary times, the Central Siberian Plateau achieved this state towards the end of Palaeozoic times. This probably accounts for the high degree of erosion in and dissection of the Siberian Plateau.

The north-east extension of the West Siberian Plain along the northern edge of the Central Siberian Plateau is known as the North Siberian (or Taymyr) Lowland. This sedimentary plain of comparatively dissected relief is practically twice the size of the United Kingdom. The Byrranga Mountains of the Taymyr Peninsula to the north is made up of two, and sometimes three, parallel and flat-topped ranges, 1,500-2,500 m high and separated by shallow lowlands. This plateau displays considerable evidence of glaciation.

Severnaya Zemlya (North Land) is a group of four large islands composed of ancient Palaeozoic rocks, but the northernmost, Komsomolets, shows only Pleistocene deposits and is largely ice-covered. Ice covers 40 per cent of the total area of the islands, and where glaciers reach the sea, small icebergs continually detach themselves.

In the southern part of East Siberia elevations become much higher. The Western and Eastern Sayan Mountains to the west of Lake Baykal enclose the Minusinsk Basin on the south and north-east respectively. Though described as of Tertiary origin, it would seem that the ranges were formed at a much earlier date. After a period of erosion, which had almost reduced many of them to pene-pleins, they were again uplifted by Tertiary earth-movements. Consequently, the Western Sayans show flat, eroded surfaces, even on their summit levels. The Eastern Sayans, oriented north-west/ south-east between the Yenisey and Angara Rivers, reach their highest elevation at about 3,300 m and then continue eastwards as a series of high plateau blocks, at somewhat lower altitudes, to Lake Baykal.

The east-west oriented Western Sayan Mountains, extending east-wards from the Altay system separates the Minusinsk Basin in the north from Tuva ASSR to the south. This autonomous republic is a highland area, 450-600 m above sea-level, enclosed by mountains rising to over 2,400 m.

East of Lake Baykal the Yablonovyy Range, one of the more prominent of the south-west/north-east oriented mountains in this area, cuts the Trans-Baykal region into two parts. The Yablonovyy themselves rise to 1,200-1,600 m above sea-level, though their broad, rounded summits rarely rise more than 300 m above the floors of the intervening valleys. West of the Yablonovyy is a complex of mountain ranges and basins. The mountains, like the

Yablonovyy, are flat or round-topped, but exceed 1,800 m. They are the remnants of ancient, uplifted and eroded peneplains (compare the Sayan Mountains west of Lake Baykal). The Khamar-Daban Range skirting the south-eastern shores of Lake Baykal has a pronounced drop to the lake, but gentle, step-like, slopes to the south. East of the Yablonovyy are a series of heavily glaciated mountains which include the Cherskiy, Borshchovochnyy, Gazimurskiy and Nerchinsk ranges. These run north-east to south-west, at 1,200-1,800 m, and are seamed by several deep river valleys and gorges.

Lake Baykal, 640 km long and 80 km wide at its widest part covers an area of 31,500 km² (equivalent to a quarter of England). Its bed, formed by the collapse of adjacent troughs or rift valleys (fault graben), is at least 600 m deep and at one point reaches 1,620 m. Baykal, "Pearl of Siberia", the deepest fresh-water lake in the world (with 20 per cent of the world's surface fresh water resource) and ninth largest in area, discharges near the south-western end via the Angara River (1,826 km), a fast flowing tributary of the Yenisey River. The Angara (Upper Tunguska) for a few kilometres does not freeze in winter and its discharge (6,181,000 m³ h), regulated by the waters of Lake Baykal, is not subject to seasonal variations in supply. Passing through a series of treacherous rapids this river has tremendous hydro-electric potential.

The majestic Yenisey River (3,350 km long, not including headwater streams which have different names — i.e. the Kemchik and Ulug-Khem Rivers of the Tuva Region) and its tributaries drain practically the whole of East Siberia. The main stream begins in Tuva ASSR, collects the waters of the Minusinsk Basin, flows within 12 km of the Chulym tributary of the River Ob before flowing east and then northwards through Krasnoyarsk to the Arctic Ocean two thousand or more kilometres away. Its left bank is part of the West Siberian Plain and rises to heights of no more than 45-50 m. The marshiness and slow-flowing nature of the small left bank tributaries contrast markedly with the higher right bank and abundant rapid-ridden streams associated with the sharp western edge of the Central Siberian Plateau. The Yenisey River is navigable for steamers below Minusinsk for five months in its lower course. A shallow-draught ice-breaker is in service on the lower reaches of the Yenisey River.

The Yenisey takes from the east three large tributaries: the Angara (already mentioned), the Stony Tunguska, and the Lower Tunguska River. The Stony Tunguska, like the Angara is noted for its rapids and hydro-electric potential.

Climate, natural vegetation and soils
East Siberia has probably the most continental climate on earth.

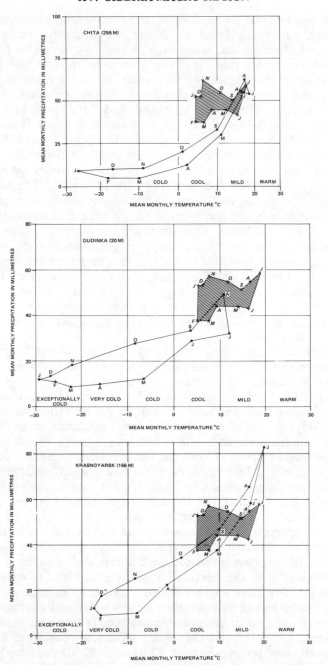

Fig. 229. Hythergraphs for Chita, Dudinka and Krasnoyarsk (Kew, London, shaded).

Winters are everywhere prolonged and very severe, summers short and cool, and precipitation is slight. The latitudinal range, areal extent and diverse relief, however, give rise to appreciable regional variations in climate (*see* Fig. 229). In winter, the southern part is dominated by the Siberian high pressure. Skies are clear, winds are absent, and extremely cold conditions are experienced. Average January temperatures in the Minusinsk and Tuva basins and in the vicinity of Irkutsk are below −20 °C. Further north at Turukhansk on the middle Yenisey they are about −28 °C, but Tura (130 m) on the Central Siberian Plateau experiences frequent inversions of temperature and records −37 °C. The north-east comes under the influence of the Aleutian low pressure in winter. The weather generally is unsettled and stormy with violent winds, overcast skies and heavy snowfall. "The wind is so icy here that even the pine trees feel cold" (V. Inber). Conditions are not quite so cold as nearer the centre of the region: January temperatures average −30 °C.

In the summer the whole of the region is under the influence of a shallow low pressure system. Temperatures at this time tend to vary latitudinally, from a July average of 18° to 20 °C in the south to near 4 °C along the coast of the Kara Sea in the north. A sudden transition from the long severe winter to spring and summer conditions is characteristic.

Precipitation throughout the whole of East Siberia is generally less than 600 mm, except for precipitation of 700-1,000 mm on the Putoran Mountains which, rising to heights of 2,000 m east of the Yenisey River, present an elongated obstruction to the air flow across Eurasia from the west. Maximum occurs rather regularly in August in the north, July in the south; minimum comes late in winter. Though precipitation in winter is slight and snowfall modest, the length and extreme cold of the winter means that snow accumulates to give a relatively thick (50-100 cm deep) and persistent cover for anything from six and half to eight months each year.

East of Lake Baykal, the climate is transitional between that of the Mongolian steppe and the Siberian *tayga*, complicated by the effects of appreciable variations in relief and by the water mass of Lake Baykal. Summers are warm and dry; winters are cold and snowless. Temperature inversions are frequent and, as in the southern mountains and in the north of East Siberia, there is widespread permafrost. Dry clear weather is characteristic of all seasons, especially in winter and there is hardly ever any really bad weather. Sixty to seventy per cent of the possible sunshine is experienced, and the cloudless air is exceptionally clear. Winter temperatures are low (mean January temperature at Chita is −27 °C), but with clear skies, bright sunshine and absence of winds, conditions generally are far less trying than they are in the European part of the country, where, though less cold, winters are damp and windy and skies are overcast for long periods. Annual precipitation in Trans-Baykalya is meagre. At Chita the average is 310 mm a year, with about 220 mm or 70 per cent coming in summer, usually in the form of heavy showers.

The heavy summer downpour of 1897 on the Yablonovyy Range during the construction of the Trans-Siberian Railway is well known. In the words of Imshenetskii: "a colossal wall of water about 4 m high destroyed the construction works in twenty-four hours and swept away hundreds of villages and tens of thousands of cattle along the Ingoda, Onon, Shilka and Amur rivers causing losses worth millions. The rivers changed their channels in places, villages had to be reconstructed and the railway was laid in a totally different location."

Baykal is a cold lake. Even in August, the temperature of the surface waters averages only 9-10 °C. At depths of 240 m and below, the temperature is fairly constant at about 3.1 °C. Freezing usually occurs in December and lasts until May. Depending on location the ice may persist on the lake for between three and a half and eight months. In the area where the Angara River flows out, neither the lake nor the river freezes. In its immediate vicinity the lake has the effect of reducing summer temperatures, prolonging the autumn, and ameliorating the winter cold, but, because it is surrounded by high mountains, these mollifying influences do not extend very far into the surrounding countryside.

> . . . I sailed across Baykal and drove through Transbaykal region. Baykal is amazing, and it is not for nothing that the Siberians call it the sea and not a lake. The water is incredibly transparent, so that one can see right through it, as if through air; its colour is delicate turquoise, pleasant to the eye. The shores are mountainous, covered with forests; wilderness around is impenetrable. There is an abundance of bears, sable, wild goats and all kinds of other wild life.
>
> Letter from Chechov to N.A. Leiken, June 20, 1890.

The vegetation in the far north of the region — Severnaya Zemlya, Byrranga Mountains, North Siberian Lowland — is tundra type with mosses, lichens, sedges and dwarf bushes and shrubs and flowering perennials on better-drained sites. Except for a wedge of steppe and forest steppe around Minusinsk-Krasnoyarsk and in Khakass AO and foothill steppes in the eastern hinterland of Irkutsk, the remainder of the region is *tayga*. Siberian fir, eastern (Dahurian) larch and stone pine are the most common tree species; Irkutsk Oblast has some of the best stands.

Soils are poor with leached aquepts and boralfs in the tundra and *tayga*, and permafrost is widespread. In the steppe and wooded

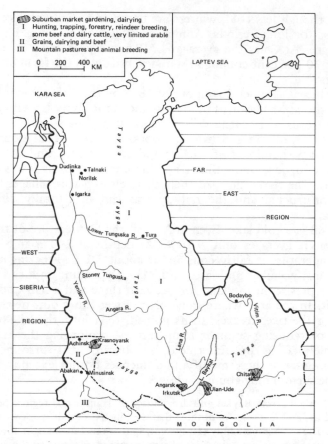

Fig. 230. East Siberia Economic Region: agricultural land-use regions.

steppe areas in the Minusinsk Basin and certain parts of Irkutsk Oblast they are good with deep borolls which grow spring wheat, some sunflowers and pasture grasses.

THE ECONOMY

Agriculture, hunting and fishing

Agriculture throughout the greater part of the region is obviously very limited on account of the adverse environmental conditions. In the southern steppe basins, where soils are fertile borolls and ustolls, daily mean temperature during the short summer is about 10 °C, accumulated temperatures amount to 1,600°-2,200 °C and rainfall amounts to between 150-400 mm. Conditions are suitable for the cultivation of some crops, particularly grains. Spring wheat, rye, oats, barley, sunflowers, potatoes and other vegetables are grown, but livestock farming is of greater importance (*see* Fig. 230). The farms in the vicinity of towns such as Krasnoyarsk, Irkutsk and Chita send market garden produce into the urban areas. Potatoes, cabbages and other vegetables and some hardy small grains are grown in the forest clearings in the north.

Outside the southern cultivated areas, there is a semi-nomadic pastoral economy with stock raising on the steppelands of the intermontane basins of the southern borderland. Sheep, goats and beef cattle are kept and dairying is practised near the towns. East Siberia, and especially Krasnoyarsk Kray, Khakass AO and Trans-Baykalya, is one of the leading cattle-breeding and meat-shipping regions of the Soviet Union. Horses and camels are kept in the semi-arid steppe of the south-east. In many instances the *yurta* (felt-covered tent) of the semi-nomadic Buryats has been replaced by more substantial timber houses within permanent *kolkhozy*.

Reindeer breeding, fur dressing, hunting and fishing are important elsewhere in the region. Reindeer husbandry is a non-Russian concern, carried on by people such as the Nentsy and Chukchi; much the same may be said for cattle farming. The indigenous peoples also predominate in the hunting and fishing activities. Sable, ermine, squirrels and arctic fox are hunted throughout the region (*see* Fig. 231) and the lower reaches of the major rivers are fished. Whitefish and sturgeon are the main catches. Walrus and seals are present along most of the coast. Fishing in Lake Baykal is also important. The lake has an unique endemic fauna which includes the Baykal hair seal (*Phoca sibirica*), a fresh water seal called the *nerpa* by the Russians which is related to similar types in the Arctic Ocean (*Ph. hispida*) and in the Caspian Sea (*Ph. caspia*) (*see* Fig. 232), the *omul* (of the salmon family) and the Baykal carp. Fishing is organised by fishing *kolkhozy* and by the State and there are several lakeside settlements engaged in the canning of fish. Reports suggest that there is overfishing of the commercially important *omul* and serious pollution of the waters of the lake arising from industrial effluent from pulp-mills and lumbering operations.

Lumbering
Although production lags well behind the potential of the huge timber stands of East Siberia (one-half of the Soviet total), lumbering is an important industry, particularly along rivers, roads, and railways and even around towns and cities. Total wood production for the region is second only to that of the North-West Economic Region with heaviest concentrations currently in the Krasnoyarsk and Irkutsk areas. Krasnoyarsk Kray has vast reserves of unexploited timber stands but seemingly the Irkutsk forests are

(Novosti)

Fig. 231. For many people of North Siberia, furs constitute the main source of cash income. The Soviet Union is the world's greatest exporter of furs, but excessive hunting has depleted supplies of ermine, silver fox and other valuable species. Supplies are now supplemented by fur-breeding *sovkhozy*.

threatened with exhaustion through overfelling (*see* Fig. 230). In the more remote forested areas the industry is handicapped both by inaccessibility (lack of railways, roads and other forms of transport) and by adverse environmental and living conditions for the timber workers. Harvested timber is floated down the Yenisey and other rivers as roundwood to mills (Krasnoyarsk, Yeniseysk, Lesosibirsk) for subsequent export, either via the Trans-Siberian Railway or else through the port of Igarka and the Northern Sea Route. The practice of floating timber to mills results in an inevitable residue of sunken logs in rivers, the polluting of the river water by timber bark and the consequent poisoning of fish. It also leads to the neglect of the larch stands, the most common species in East Siberia, because

(*Fotokhronika Tass*)

Fig. 232. Baby seals. The seals (*Phoca sibirica*) of Lake Baykal — called *nerpa* by the Soviets — are related to similar types in the Arctic Ocean and in the Caspian Sea.

larch is too dense for floating. Industrial effluent from mills (e.g. the pulp mill on the shores of Lake Baykal) is an additional source of pollution.

The big industrial timber complex at Bratsk is a major producer of wood pulp, containerboard, fibreboard, timber chemicals and sawn timber. Maklakov, south of Yeniseysk on the Yenisey is a wood-processing complex, as is the major pulp and paper mill at Krasnoyarsk. The completion in 1980 of the pulp plant at the hydro-electric site at Ust - Ilimsk on the Angara downstream of Bratsk added yet further strength to the expanding East Siberia wood-processing industry. The shipping out of roundwood, with little processing, to markets in the western parts of the USSR continues to increase steadily with the building of feeder branches from the Trans-Siberian Railway. With the availability of cheap hydro-electricity at such places as Krasnoyarsk, Bratsk and Ust-Ilimsk and large forest reserves, there have been spectacular developments in the wood-processing (especially pulp) industry of the region and, during the last two decades, in power supplies.

Mineral resources and industry
The Kansk-Achinsk Basin in the south of East Siberia, thought to contain about 40 per cent of the lignite reserves of the USSR, figures importantly in Soviet coal-expansion plans for the 1980s.

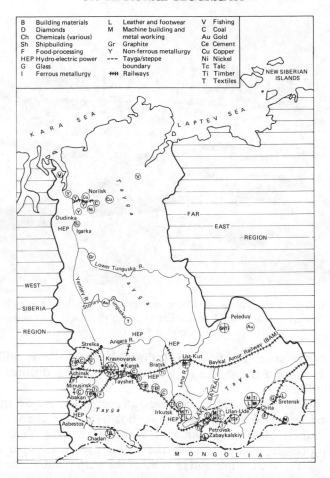

Fig. 233. East Siberia Economic Region: mineral and power resources, railways and industrial structure of towns.

The lignite is readily accessible in a wide band running alongside the Trans-Siberian Railway for over 650 km (*see* Fig. 233). The lignite is too brittle for long-distance transport and is used locally in thermal power stations. Production in the Kansk-Achinsk Basin, planned to rise to 42 million tonnes a year by 1980, was 33 million tonnes in 1979. The good quality coals of the Minusinsk Basin are used in the same way as those from the Kansk-Achinsk Basin. The massive deposits of the Cheremkhovo field on the Angara are not of coking quality, but find increasingly important outlets in thermal power stations and in chemical plants. Coal seams, as much as 7 m thick and dispersed horizontally, are worked by open-cast and deep mine methods.

The hydro-electric power resources of East Siberia are enormous and their development has been such that the region now has a surplus for "export" to the European part of the USSR. The first rivers to be harnessed for this purpose were the Yenisey and its tributaries. The Angara tributary, fed by Lake Baykal, has a regular flow throughout the year and one station on the river near Irkutsk, with a capacity of just over half a million kW, has been in operation for several years. However, it does not compare with stations downstream, at Bratsk, Ust-Ilimsk and Boguchany, which have capacities of 4.0, 3.6 and 4.0 million kW respectively, or with the Krasnoyarsk (capacity 6.0 million kW) and Sayan-Shushenskoye* (capacity 6.4 million kW) hydro stations on the Yenisey River. These two stations have the largest capacities in the world.

Electric power is the principal interlinking element in the East Siberia Region, accounting for its specialisation in power-intensive and heat-intensive industries. Territorial-production complexes (TPCs) have been constructed (at, for example, Kansk-Achinsk and Sayany) on the basis of these power centres† all linked by high-voltage transmission lines and the availability of local or imported raw materials. Aluminium reduction takes place at Shelekhov (20 km from Irkutsk) and Bratsk (both relying on long-haul alumina from the Urals, Pavlodar and Achinsk), Krasnoyarsk (dependent on alumina from Achinsk), and Sayanogorsk (near the Sayan-Shushenskoye power station) using alumina moved 4,800 km from Nikolayev on the Black Sea. Special steels and ferro-alloys, mechanical engineering, chemicals and a wide range of manufacturing are planned for the Sayan territorial-production complex.

In the *tayga* in the north of the region is the isolated but highly significant Norilsk territorial-production complex. A large copper-nickel sulphide ore deposit here, together with more recently discovered copper deposits in the Taymyr Peninsula (Talnakh area), provide nickel, cobalt, copper and platinum. Primary production and smelting are carried on at Norilsk. Natural gas piped from West Siberia is used in Norilsk power stations and smelters, and electricity needs are further supplemented by two hydro stations sited 150 and 300 km to the south. Norilsk is connected by rail with Dudinka on the Yenisey River. From Dudinka cargoes are taken along the Northern Sea Route during the brief summer shipping season. In recent years, the shipping season in the Barents and Kara Seas has been extended by the use of nuclear ice-breakers.

Gold is scattered widely throughout Eastern Siberia. Placer gold in the Vitim River valley near the town of Bodaybo (Irkutsk Oblast)

---

*Lenín was exiled to the village of Shushenskoye in 1897-1900.
†This development lends meaning to the statement made by Lenin that Soviet power plus electrification equals Communism.

is extracted by means of huge dredges floating on the river. The town of Petrovsk-Zabaykalskiy has the only steel works in the immediate region. It obtains coal from Tarbagatay and Khalyarta both in the Khilok Valley and relies on pig-iron railed in from the Kuzbass for its steel and rolled products.

POPULATION AND CITIES

Of the nineteen basic economic regions, East Siberia is second only to the Far East Region in size but ranks thirteenth in terms of population. Over 8.1 million people inhabit the 4.1 million km^2 giving an overall density of about two persons per km^2. Densities vary considerably and there are vast areas which are sparsely populated or virtually uninhabited. About 60 per cent of the population live in cities, towns and urban-type settlements. In spite of the fact that there are a number of native groups and nationality-based political units such as Khakass (71,000), and Evenki (28,000), Russians are in the majority everywhere except in Tuva ASSR where the Tuvans (165,000) make up about 60 per cent of the population. The Tuvans are Lamaist Buddhists who form a distinctive non-Russian community in an isolated homeland south of the Sayan Mountains. They were incorporated officially into the Soviet Union in 1944, and it seems only a matter of time before they will be "Russified" and fully integrated into the Soviet economy. The Buryats (353,000) of Southern Siberia are the most northerly of the major Mongol peoples. They are closely related to the Mongols of the Mongolian People's Republic and make up about 22 per cent of the population in Buryat ASSR. Traditionally they are nomadic pastoralists, but more and more are they adopting a sedentary life and foresaking their felt tents (*yurta*) for the log hut (*izba*). The Evenki are a Tungus-Manchu strain; the Khakass like the Tuvans, are Turkic. Taymyr Autonomous Okrug has two quite different native groups, Samodian Nenets and Turkic Dolgans. With ever-increasing Russian inroads and settlement in the national units, and inter-marriage between Russians and indigenous peoples, ethnographic distinctions are becoming very blurred.

Krasnoyarsk (population: 796,000)
Situated at the point where the Trans-Siberian Railway crosses the Yenisey River, Krasnoyarsk is regional centre for Krasnoyarsk Kray (*see* Fig. 234). It is a fast-growing city (23 per cent increase between 1970 and 1979) with considerable industrial potential. Hydroelectricity from a nearby barrage on the Yenisey is in generous supply and power-orientated industries such as aluminium smelting (using nepheline from Achinsk, 150 km to the west) are being

(Fotokhronika Tass)

Fig. 234. Krasnoyarsk: view of the river station on the Yenisey. This fast growing city is benefitting from fuller use of local resources of coal and hydro-electricity from a 6 million kW station nearby which powers modern electric steel mills, aluminium smelters and a range of other industries.

attracted to this site. In addition there are wood-based industries, including synthetic rubber production (ethyl alcohol derived from wood cellulose), agricultural and mining machinery, railway repair works, machine tool industries, oil refining, petrochemicals and food industries (*see* Fig. 234).

Of Krasnoyarsk, Chekhov wrote (taken from his letters):

> . . . Siberia is a cold and long country. I am travelling and travelling and there is no end in sight . . . . I fought the overflowing rivers, the cold, impassable mud, and hunger . . . . On the whole I am pleased with my journey and am not sorry I went . . . . The mountains near Krasnoyarsk surround the town like high walls . . . Yenisey is a wide, fast, curving river; a beauty, better than the Volga . . . . On Yenisey life began with a groan, and will end in splendour such as we never dreamed of. So at least I thought, standing on the banks of the wide Yenisey, and looking eagerly into its waters, which with frightening speed and force were rushing into the severe Arctic Ocean . . . . On this bank is Krasnoyarsk — the best and most beautiful of all the Siberian towns, and on the other — mountains, reminding me of the Caucasus, just as misty and dreamy. I stood and thought: what full, clever and fine life will light up these shores in the future.

Irkutsk (population: 550,000)
One-time fortress, trading and administrative centre of Siberia, Irkutsk with nearby Shelekhov is now developing as the centre of a rapidly-growing industrial area. It is located at the confluence of the Irkut and Angara Rivers, about 65 km from Lake Baykal; the Trans-Siberian Railway passes through the city on the left bank of the Angara. Ample power is provided by the Cheremkhovo coalfields and hydro-electricity comes from a nearby station on the Angara River. Thus, as with Krasnoyarsk over 1,000 km to the west, power-hungry industries are attracted to the site. At present chemicals (using local salt deposits and the by-products of the oil refinery at Angarsk), aluminium smelting (at Shelekhov), saw milling and wood-working industries, insulation elements (using East Siberian mica), food products, general machinery (especially gold-, coal- and iron-mining machinery) and motor vehicles are the main industrial enterprises, but others are expected to be located here in the future (*see* Fig. 233). Population growth in Irkutsk is more the result of natural increase than of net in-migration.

The Sverdlovsky district of Irkutsk houses eight research institutes of the Siberian Branch of the Academy of Sciences (cf. Akademgorodok near Novosibirsk).

Chita (population: 302,000)
Situated 560 km east of Ulan-Ude, Chita is capital of Chita Oblast, and has administrative and commercial functions. Locomotives and rolling stock are repaired here and there is flour-milling, meat-packing and sawmilling. Chita is well known for its furs and leather products.

Ulan-Ude (population: 300,000)
Capital of the Buryatskaya ASSR, Ulan-Ude lies at the Uda-Selenga confluence. It was once a great centre for the Chinese tea trade, but is now an administrative and industrial centre and rail junction. It has locomotive and rolling stock works, plant for the processing, preserving and packing of meat, sawmills, glass works, shipbuilding and repair yards, and factories for the treatment of furs (*see* Fig. 233), which are obtained by hunting (chiefly squirrel and sable) or from breeding farms (silver fox and racoon). The city is characterised by a low annual growth rate of less than 2 per cent.

Angarsk (population: 239,000)
West of Baykal at the eastern terminal of the trunk pipeline carrying oil from the West Siberian fields, Angarsk has petrochemical industries associated with oil refining, machine building (especially mining equipment for the Cheremkhovo coalfield) and pulp and paper

(Fotokhronika Tass)

Fig. 235. Norilsk, Lenin Avenue. This highly significant copper-nickel mining and smelting town lies well within the Arctic Circle near the mouth of the Yenisey River.

industries. It is one of the larger of many industrial centres (e.g. Shelekhov, Cheremkhovo) which have sprung up along the line of the Trans-Siberian Railway in recent years.

Bratsk (population: 214,000)
Only a workers' settlement in 1955, Bratsk is now the centre of a large territorial-production complex with aluminium, metallurgical and timber-processing industries, all capitalising on the nearby source of hydro-electric power. It is one of the fastest growing towns in East Siberia, having increased its population by over one third between 1970 and 1979. Growth is largely the result of a net in-migration of able-bodied groups — mainly single and male.

Norilsk (population: 180,000)
Lying 100 km east of the Yenisey on the fringe of the tundra at latitude 69° N, Norilsk is the northernmost town in the Soviet Union (*see* Fig. 235). It was founded in 1935 and, until the mid 1950s, was one of the principal concentration camp areas for political and war prisoners. The prisoners were employed in building the town and its industries, and working in the nickel, platinum,

copper, cobalt and coal mines. Norilsk is an important modern territorial-production complex for the smelting of non-ferrous metals such as copper and nickel, and by-product metals obtained from the copper-refining process which include platinum, titanium and vanadium. As noted earlier, the outlet for these metals is along the railway to Dudinka and thence via the Northern Sea Route.

CHAPTER XVI

Far East Macro-Region

The Far East Macro-Region (*see* Fig. 236) is the largest in area, but the most sparsely populated of all the nineteen basic economic regions of the USSR. It includes the vast Magadan Oblast (practically 1.2 million km²), together with Amur and Sakhalin Oblasts, the Khabarovsk and Maritime Krays and the huge Yakut ASSR (3.1 million km²). It occupies an area equal in size to Australia. The

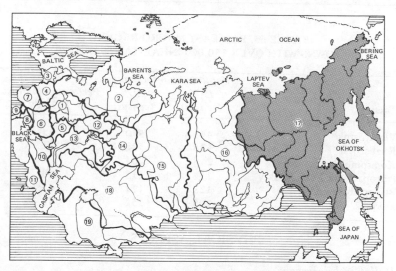

Fig. 236. Soviet Union: location of Far East Macro-Region.

average over-all density of population is only about one person per km², but huge areas are only sparsely populated or else completely devoid of population. Practically three-quarters of the population are classified as urban dwellers, concentrated mainly in industrial centres along the southern fringe and near the Trans-Siberian Railway. The specialisation of the Far East Region is provided by the fishing industry, machine building and the forest industry.

TABLE 64. FAR EAST MACRO-REGION:
ADMINISTRATIVE UNITS, THEIR POPULATION AND DENSITY

Area: 6,215,900 km²
Population (1979): 6,819,000

Administrative unit	Area (000 km²)	Population (000, 1979)	Density (persons per km²)	Percentage urban
Maritime (Primorskiy) Kray	166	1,978	12	76
Khabarovsk Kray	825	1,565	2	79
(incl. Jewish AO)	36	190	5	68
Amur Oblast	364	938	3	65
Kamchatka Oblast	472	378	(0.8)	83
(incl. Koryak AO)	302	34	(0.1)	38
Magadan Oblast	1,199	466	(0.4)	78
(incl. Chukchi AO)	738	133	(0.2)	70
Sakhalin Oblast	87	655	8	82
Yakut ASSR	3,103	839	(0.3)	61

TABLE 65. FAR EAST MACRO-REGION:
TOWNS WITH OVER 150,000 INHABITANTS IN 1979

Town	Population in thousands		Percentage increase 1970-79
	1970 (census)	1979 (census)	
Vladivostok	441	550	25
Khabarovsk	436	528	21
Komsomolsk-na-Amure	218	264	21
Petropavlovsk-Kamchatskiy	154	215	40
Blagoveshchensk	128	172	35
Yakutsk	108	152	41

PHYSICAL ASPECTS

Relief and drainage

The greater part of the region is mountainous, remote and generally inaccessible; flat land suitable for agriculture is confined to the Yakutian Basin, the valleys of the Amur and Ussuri and to small coastal and river plains (see Fig. 237).

In the extreme north-east is a complex of ancient mountains, generally with denuded summits. The Verkhoyansk folded mountain system and the Kolyma Highland (Gydan Range) form a great semi-circle facing the East Siberian Sea, and encircle parallel ranges such

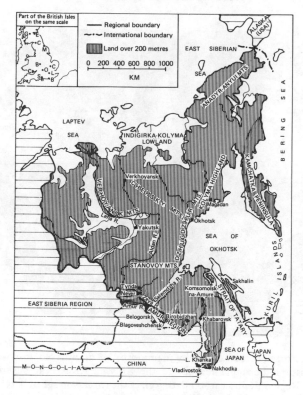

Fig. 237. Far East Economic Region.

as the Cherskiy Mountains and enclose the Indigirka and Kolyma Lowlands. The highlands have elevations in excess of 2,000 m, although Gora Pobeda (Victory Peak) in the Cherskiy Mountains attains 3,149 m. They are all heavily dissected, severely glaciated and extremely difficult of access. The Anadyr-Anyuy or Chukotsk Mountains which parallel the shores of the Chukchi Sea as far as the Bering Strait are generally 600-1,000 m above sea level although peaks rise above 1,700 m. They form a watershed between the Anadyr River, which flows to the Bering Sea, and the Anui River draining to the East Siberian Sea.

The Dzhugdzhur Mountains, separated from the Stanovoy Mountains by the Maya tributary of the Aldan, run along the coast of the Sea of Okhotsk. The main range of the Stanovoy Mountains forms the divide between Pacific drainage via the Zeya and Amur Rivers, and Arctic drainage via the Aldan River.

Within the broad arc of the Verkhoyansk-Dzhugdzhur-Stanovoy Mountains and the eastern margins of the Central Siberian Plateau

(Soviet Weekly)

Fig. 238. Frozen carcass of a baby mammoth, 7-8 months old, discovered in the permafrost in the upper reaches of the Kolyma River near Susuman in the Magadan Region. Radio carbon dating gives the carcass an age of between 39,000 and 44,000 years. It is hypothesised that the mammoth died of exhaustion and fell into a muddy pool which froze and never thawed again.

is the large tectonic Yakutian Basin. This comprises a series of flat to gently rolling plains associated with the middle reaches of the Lena River and the middle reaches of the Vilyuy and Aldan Rivers.

North-east of the Lena delta are the New Siberian Islands (*Novosibirskiye Ostrova*) comprising four main islands and a number of islets. They are virtually uninhabited. A climatic amelioration in these latitudes has laid bare a great wealth of fossil mammoth remains which have proved a valuable source of ivory (*see* Fig. 238). Wrangel Island in the Chukchi Sea is dry and barren and devoid of glaciers (*see* Fig. 239).

The valley of the Amur River is restricted in the extreme north-west of Amuria. It lies between the Great Khingan Mountains of China in the south and the Olekminsk-Stanovoy Mountains of the Soviet Far East in the north. Eastwards of the latter lie the east-west Tukuringra and Dzhagdy Mountains. The Tukuringra Mountains are breached by the River Zeya which taps an enclosed upland basin that lies to the north. The lower Zeya River divides the wide plain

(*Fotokhronika Tass*)

Fig. 239. Wrangel Island: mosses, lichens, dwarf shrubs and bushes are among the perennial plants which appear in summer in the better-drained sites of the tundra.

of the middle Amur into two parts: the Amur-Zeya Plateau 240-50 m high to the west, and the alluvial upper Amur-Zeya-Bureya Plain to the east.

The Bureya Range separates the valley of the Bureya River and the lower Amur River. Below the confluence of the two rivers, the Amur flows between sheer rocky banks through the mountains for a distance of 140 km. Where breached by the Amur, altitudes are only 200-450 m, but near the source of the Bureya River these mountains rise northwards to 2,000 m.

The Ussuri-Khanka Plain and the part of the Amur valley that lies downstream from Khabarovsk together form an elongated trough. It represents the subsided portions of a fault block between, on the one side, the Little Kingan and the Bureya Mountains, and on the other the Sikhote-Alin Mountains.

Below Khabarovsk the lower portion of the Amur Valley is a flat, marshy lowland. It is about 500 km long and expands in width to become very broad indeed, with numerous channels and islands. Only occasionally do the mountain ranges close in on the river from both sides and force it into a single individual channel. The left bank is mainly flat and marshy; the right bank is hilly and drier. Though the lower reaches of the river are hemmed in by mountains, it is 5-10 km wide in places. At Lake Bolshie Kizy, the Amur comes within 14 km of the sea and it is possible that its mouth may once have been located here. Its present outlet is blocked by a massive sandbank over which ocean-going vessels are unable to pass, having to be unloaded into river craft on the open ocean. The Ussuri valley section in Soviet territory is narrow, widening only where tributary valleys meet the main valley. Conditions along the Ussuri valley are very boggy. Lake Khanka is shallow, with a maximum depth of about 9 m but covering over 4,000 km². It is surrounded by large moors and marshes and is being rapidly silted up.

The much eroded Sikhote-Alin Mountains represent the uplifted edge of a submerged fault block, or *horst*, and consist of as many as eight parallel ranges, generally between 600 and 900 m high and oriented north/north-east. The submerged eastern slopes of these mountains provide a ria-type coast in the south, but further north the coastline is regular and has relatively few bays.

Sakhalin Island is composed of a double range of mountains 1,800 m high, separated by a longitudinal depression extending the length of the island and drained by the Tym and Poronay Rivers. It extends more than 950 m from north to south, having a steep rocky coastline in the west and a low coast in the east.

Kamchatka Peninsula, 1,200 km in length, comprises a double line of Tertiary fold mountains with volcanic peaks and an intervening depression drained by the Kamchatka and Elovka Rivers. Relief is everywhere accentuated. The central range reaches over 3,000 m in the Ichinskaya Sopka (volcano), the only active volcano in this range; the lower eastern range has eighteen volcanoes active at the present time. Klyuchevskaya Sopka, which reaches 4,776 m is the highest and the world's most grandiose symmetrical cone (*see* Fig. 240).

Climate, vegetation and soils

Climatic conditions are almost completely dependent upon seasonal changes in the major air masses. Under the influence of the Siberian high pressure system average winter temperatures in the northern part of the Far East are below −18 °C. At the "pole of cold" in the vicinity of Oymyakon and Verkhoyansk mean temperatures in January are between −48 °C and −50 °C (*see* Fig. 241). Mean temperatures in January are −14 °C in Vladivostok, −12 °C in Petropavlovsk-Kamchatskiy and −24 °C at Nikolayevsk-na-Amur. Cold waves and temperature inversions are frequent and an absolute minimum temperature of practically −70 °C has been recorded at Oymyakon and Verkhoyansk. Rivers are frozen over for more than six months. The East Siberian, Okhotsk and Bering Seas are frozen over for up to ten months of the year but they maintain air temperatures over the ice surfaces 20-40 °C above those on the adjacent land mass (*see* Fig. 242). There is in consequence a steep temperature gradient with associated strong winds from the "pole of cold" to

(*Leonid Poseniuk*)

Fig. 240. Kamchatka Peninsula. The peninsula is notable for its volcanoes, a number of which are still active. The crater in the foreground is that of the volcano *Besymiannyi*.

the coasts. Different from the calm, clear sky and stable conditions of the interior, the strong atmospheric movement combined with low temperatures make the coastal areas extremely severe with exceptionally low "sensible" temperatures (i.e. extreme windchill).

Winter cold in the interior is more bearable than is widely supposed because of the extreme dryness of the atmosphere. Nevertheless, it has obvious economic consequences such as the need for additional building and heating requirements and the difficulty and slowness of all operations in winter. On the other hand, there are minor compensations in that many waterways and tracts on open land can be used for sledge or vehicle transport while they are hard. Even so, "King Frost is far more cursed than blessed".

Winter lasts for practically eleven months in the Chukotia area in the far north-east of the region, ten to ten and a half months in Kamchatka, eight and a half to nine months in the Aldan-Okhotsk area, six to eight months in the Amur basin and Maritime Kray (*Primorskiy*), seven and a half to eight months in Sakhalin and six to seven months in the Kuril Islands.

In the high latitudes within the Arctic Circle, the sun does not rise above the horizon for about three months in winter and does

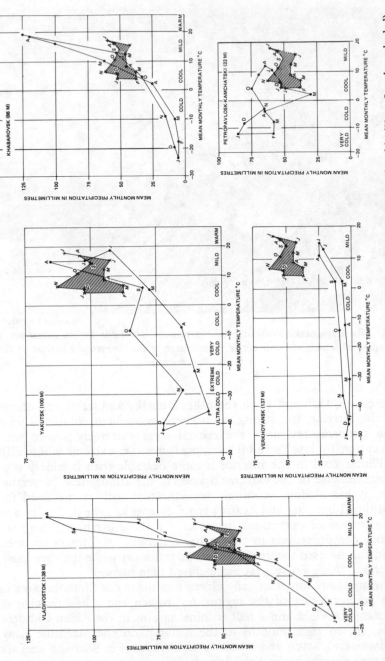

Fig. 241. Hythergraphs for Vladivostok, Yakutsk, Verkhoyansk, Khabarovsk and Petropavlovsk-Kamchatskiy (Kew, London, shaded).

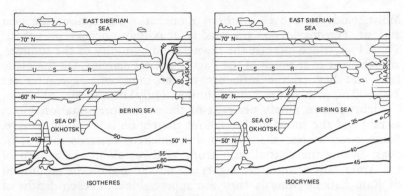

Fig. 242. Surface sea-water temperature conditions off north-east Siberia: calender month isotheres and isocrymes (*see* NOTE to Fig. 122).

not descend below it for about three months in the summer. These pecularities of daylight, or lack of it, introduce new concepts of such climatic phenomena as the diurnal range or the annual march of temperature.

Heating by solar radiation, together with the effects of local topography causes a sudden rise in temperature during May so that spring is scarcely recognisable as a separate season. The relatively high temperatures of the short summer (19 °C in Yakutsk in July) follow swiftly upon the extreme cold of the long winter. Barometric pressure is low over the mainland at this time of the year and high over the Pacific. By April, the direction of the wind changes from mainly north and north-west to south and south-east. These monsoon-like winds bring comparative cool and moist air and much cloud northwards to about 60° N.

Summers in the coastal region of Primorskiy exhibit all the characteristics of a maritime climate — damp and foggy, and with frequent drizzle and rain. The air masses moving towards the mainland from the sea are cooled during their passage over the Okhotsk current. July temperatures are 8-10 °C in coastal Kamchatka, 12-14 °C along the Gulf of Tatary, nor more than 18-20 °C at Vladivostok and near the mouth of the Amur, and 20-21 °C in Amuria. Along the northern fringe of the region they are about 10 °C.

Precipitation varies greatly according to position and the general relief of the land but, in association with a mainly south-easterly air flow, aggregates decrease significantly away from the Pacific. The maritime slopes of the Sikhote-Alin Range, Sakhalin Island, Kamchatka Peninsula and the Kuril Islands are very wet (1,000 mm and more per annum). Maximum rainfall comes in August and September, often in association with typhoons, but there is also precipitation in spring and summer from East Asia depressions.

Moist winds blow over southern Kamchatka throughout the year and at Petropavlovsk-Kamchatskiy maximum occurs in winter. Thick fogs, which increase the rawness and humidity of the summer, are frequent over much of the Pacific coastal margins. On the mainland and beyond the influence of the monsoon, aggregates are 300-600 m, with a pronounced summer (July) maximum.

Eighty-five to ninety per cent of the annual precipitation comes as rain and the snowfall throughout the region is generally meagre. Snow cover is less than 50 cm, but thickens towards the Pacific coast. Along the coastal strip from Vladivostok to the mouth of the Amur falls of snow are slight; in Sakhalin and on the mountains of Kamchatka Peninsula they are appreciable and reach depths of more than 60 cm. Because of the long cold winter snow persists for a long time, from about the end of September until early May in the south and until early June in the north. Central Yakutia is, however, an exception. Because of this initial snow cover, clear air and intense solar heating in spring, the snow cover disappears earlier than elsewhere in the Far East and despite its northerly position the 24-hour daylight at this period makes Arctic agriculture possible. In Kamchatka, on the other hand, blizzards are common.

> Kamchatka may be called the country of blizzards. Nowhere else, save perhaps in the extreme north-east of Siberia and on the western shores of the Sea of Okhotsk, do they attain such intensity and duration, nowhere else are they observed so often.
>
> K.A. Vlasov

The north of the region is a zone of tundra; south of this lies a zone of forest tundra which gradually gives way to dense *tayga*. The *tayga* belt is immense and extends through twenty or more degrees of latitude. The more humid and warmer Amur and Ussuri valleys in the southern part of the Far East have *tayga* with Siberian types of fir, pine and larch and also broad-leaved species such as oak, elm, maple, cedar, ash and lime. In the Ussuri valley there is an extraordinary variety of flora which includes characteristic southern forms such as vines, walnuts, cherry and lilac. There has been some ruthless felling of trees in the more accessible areas of the Sikhote-Alin Range which has resulted in serious soil erosion. Elsewhere there are vast and rich timber reserves awaiting exploitation. The logging industry is well developed in Amur Oblast along the main Trans-Siberian Railway and its various branches, and also in Khabarovsk Kray, but more extensive stands of *tayga* will be open to exploitation by the construction of the Baykal-Amur Mainline (BAM) railway (see p. 412).

The aquepts of the tundra and aquods of the *tayga* are not of high grade. The soils of the black-earth-like pockets in the Zeya-Bureya and Lake Khanka areas are rather better. In the Khanka area soils tend to be peaty, drying out, shrinking and cracking in the spring but becoming over-moist and soggy after rain. Though known locally as chernozem (borolls), the rich black soils of the Zeya-Bureya area have no underlying loess or carbonates, and lack the granular structure of typical chernozems, but they have a high organic content. In the lowland between Khabarovsk and Komsomolsk-na-Amure, there are thick impermeable clays and extensive areas of boggy grasslands.

THE ECONOMY

Agriculture, hunting, lumbering and fishing
The only area of real agricultural significance in the north of the region is the centre of Yakut ASSR where 100,000 hectares of arable land are concentrated. Hardy strains of wheat, rye and barley, that ripen within about two months, are grown under very marginal conditions. Reindeer are bred on collective farms by the indigenous population, particularly in Magadan and Kamchatka Oblasts. Sable, ermine, squirrels, arctic fox and other fur-bearing animals have long been hunted and trapped and in many places to near extinction. There is therefore now a very large development of fur-farming, which, like the reindeer breeding, is a non-Russian concern. The lower reaches of the major rivers are fished; whitefish and sturgeon are the main catches. Walrus and seals are present along most of the coast and there are whales in the Bering Sea. Overhunting has resulted in serious depopulation of the walrus and whale, the numbers of which are considered low enough to warrant special attention to their protection.

Lumbering is an important industry and there are vast forest reserves. To date, felling has been confined to river regions and alongside routeways within the *tayga,* particularly in the Amur Oblast and Khabarovsk Kray, the Maritime Kray and Sakhalin. The region now accounts for about 50 per cent of the roundwood output of the USSR. Much is for export, particularly to Japan. Major saw-milling plant are located in Vladivostok, Khabarovsk, Birobidzhan, Ussuriysk; Southern Sakhalin has mills for pulp, paper and paper board. Expansion of roundwood extraction and of the wood-processing industry is expected with the completion of the BAM railway.

It is in the Zeya-Bureya Plain and in the Suifun-Khanka Lowland that soils and climatic conditions are best suited to agriculture. Dry periods in spring and early summer and humid conditions in late summer and autumn present difficulties for sowing and harvesting the wheat, oats and rye crops. Wheat is the main crop. Sunflowers, soybeans, sugar-beet, rice, maize, potatoes and millet are grown and cattle, pigs and sheep are raised. Practically the whole of the Soviet

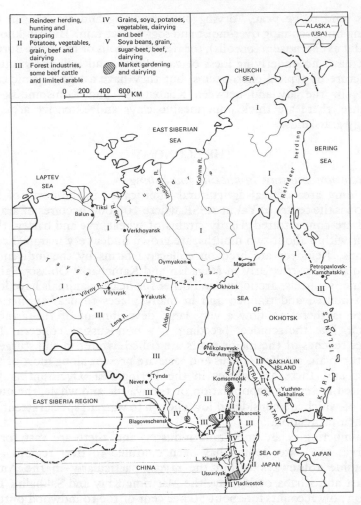

Fig. 243. Far East Economic Region: agricultural land-use regions.

Union soybean production comes from the Amur Oblast and the Maritime Kray which also carry 90 per cent of the cows and 80 per cent of the pigs of the whole of the Soviet Far East (*see* Fig. 243).

South of Lake Khanka and more particularly in the Suifun valley there is fertile land where wheat, oats, barley, millet, soybeans, perilla, rice, sugar-beet, potatoes, fruit and vegetables are grown and cattle are raised.

Of far greater importance than either agriculture or forestry in the economy of the Soviet Far East are the fisheries and fish-processing industries. The seas around Kamchatka, the Kuril Islands and Sakhalin and in the Strait of Tatary are, after the Caspian Sea, the second most important fishing area of the Soviet Union. The marine fisheries here represent one of the best developed in the world. The meeting, off-shore, of the warm waters of the Kuro Siwo current (literally: *Blue Salt*) and the cold waters of the Okhotsk current provides a rich supply of plankton which provide food for and assures abundant supplies of many species of fish and marine animals. Each year the rivers of Kamchatka are visited by large shoals of valuable species of salmon (especially pink salmon) and large king crabs (up to ½ m long) thrive around the coasts. Coastal waters only are fished; high-seas fishing for salmon in Soviet waters is prohibited by international agreement. Other species caught include cod, herring, mackerel, tunny, sole, smelt and sardines. Walrus, seals and sea otter are taken for their furs.

While practically every settlement on the coast is a fishing village and the larger ones have canneries, a special feature is the mother or factory ship to which boats deliver their catches for the complete process of cleaning, processing and canning. Tinned crab and salmon prepared in both floating factories and shore-based canneries are sold on the world market. The largest fishing fleet is based on Vladivostok where there is a large fish-canning industry. Vladivostok is also the home port of one of the Soviet Antarctic whaling flotillas. Nikolayevsk-na-Amure is the centre of the lower Amur fishing area where the Keta salmon (which also provide red caviar) and the Garbusha salmon spawn.

Fuel, power and mineral resources
The Far East abounds in coal resources, especially in the basin of the Lena River in Yakutia (*see* Fig. 244). To date, only in the south, near most of the population, has coal been produced in any significant amount. However, in October 1978, the first coal was moved out from the Neryungri mine in south Yakutia. The Neryungri deposits of steam and coking coals are being developed by Japanese credits. Most of the mined coal is earmarked for export to Japan. The coal is shipped out along a north-south branch railway to the Trans-Siberian Railway (cutting BAM at Tynda) and thence to the port Nakhodka-Vostochnyy. Total production in the Far East is currently about 5 per cent of the total for the whole of the USSR. Lignite is produced in the lower Bureya valley at Raychikhinsk and Svobodnyy-Nygla (Amur Oblast), at Luchegorsk in the Ussuri valley, at Artem near Vladivostok, and at Novoshakhlinskiy and Rettikhova north of Ussuriysk; bituminous coal is worked at Lipovtsy and Partizansk (formerly Suchan) near Vladivostok, at Urgal on the upper Bureya (Khabarovsk Kray) and on Sakhalin Island at Gornozavodsk and Vakhrushev.

Lignite is too friable for long distance transport and has to be

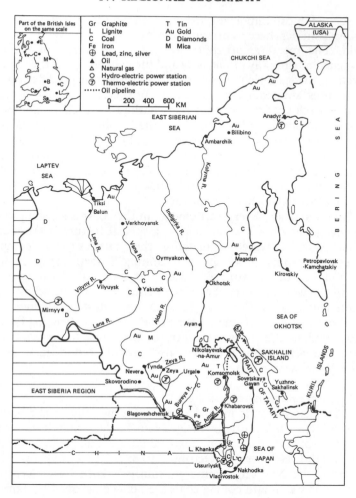

Fig. 244. Far East Economic Region: mineral and power resources.

used locally, but the bituminous coals can be transported. Currently both the lignite and brown coals are used for generating electricity in thermal stations at Luchegorsk (Maritime Kray), Artem, Partizansk, Ussuriysk, Raychikhinsk, and Vostok (near Vakhrushev, Sakhalin). The mainland power stations, including the hydro-stations near the town of Zeya and at Talakan on the Bureya River, are linked by a transmission grid. There are small thermal- and hydro-electric developments designed to meet power needs in isolated mining districts, e.g. at Myaundzha, Magadan, (Kolyma HES), and Mirnyy (Vilyuy HES).

Oil in the north-east of Sakhalin near the towns of Okha, Ekhabi

(Novosti)

Fig. 245. Mirnyy, within the dense *tayga* of Yakutia, is the diamond capital of Siberia. The USSR is believed to be self-sufficient in diamonds which are exported for valuable foreign currency.

and Katangli is sent by pipeline beneath the Tatary Strait to the mainland for use in the refineries in Nikolayevsk-na-Amure, Komsomolsk-na-Amure and Khabarovsk. Sakhalin output amounts to about 3 million tonnes or less than 0.5 per cent of total Soviet production. This is sufficient to meet about 30 per cent of the regional needs of the Soviet Far East. Much of the gas found in association with the oil is used to stimulate the dwindling flow of oil. Vast gas reserves are inferred for the Vilyuy basin in Yakutia (thought to rival West Siberia), but they have yet to be demonstrated.

The region makes a significant contribution in diamonds. Kimberlite pipes in a tributary valley of the Vilyuy River in Yakutia yield these gem stones from mines at Mirnyy, Aykhal and Udachnyy. Mirnyy, within the dense *tayga*, was formerly a penal camp but is now "diamond capital of Siberia" with a population of 26,000 (*see* Fig. 245). The traditional placer gold deposits of the Kolyma basin (first worked by Dal-Stroy, an organisation notorious as an employer of convict labour), the Aldan, Bodaybo and Vitim valleys are now seriously depleted and recourse is being made to lode mining and to the use of floating dredges and power shovels to reach buried placer deposits. The focus of activity appears to have shifted to the

Chukchi Autonomous Okrug with the main centres at Bilibino and Leningradskiy within the Arctic Circle. Important new gold-mining operations have taken place in Armenia (Zod) and Central Asia (Zarafshan and Altynkan), but the Far East Region remains the major producer of gold in the Soviet Union.

Tin is mined at Solnechnyy, 65 km west of Komsomolsk-na-Amure, Kavalero (Maritime Kray), Khingansk (Jewish AO) and Omsukchan (Magadan Oblast) and destined, after concentration, for the tin smelting plant in Novosibirsk. Lead and zinc are found at Dalnegorsk (Maritime Kray). The lead is smelted locally, but the zinc is shipped by sea to Konstantinovka in the Donets-Dnieper Region.

Industry

Industry other than that associated with timber and fish seems to have been determined more by the application of the Soviet principle of regional self-sufficiency rather than any inherent assets of raw materials and/or power sources in the region. The Second World War had an effect also, as several factories which were moved into the region at that time have remained.

The small steel works at Komsomolsk-na-Amure, opened in 1943, provides support for local metal-using industries (*see* Fig. 246). It is not independent, but relies mainly on local and imported scrap, and pig iron from the Kuzbass. Its steel products and tinplate are used in engineering (the region accounts for about a third of all casting equipment produced in the Soviet Union, 17 per cent of the gantry cranes and substantial portions of the nation's diesel engines (Shabad, 1977 (p. 56)), in machine and metalworking industries and in shipbuilding. Chemical industries are important at Komsomolsk-na-Amure and Khabarovsk, the refining centres for Sakhalin oil.

The high cost of bringing in manufactured goods from other parts of the USSR has made it expedient to produce them locally, even on a small scale. The Soviet Far East therefore has diverse, but generally minor industries, dispersed among the various regional centres concentrated along the railways. A second system of industrial centres, associated with the fishing industry, is located along the Pacific coast. Being a relatively young economic region, the Far East lacks established territorial-production complexes, but one such is in process of formation in South Yakutia.

Transport

Most traffic in the Soviet Far East is carried by rail and the main artery is the Trans-Siberian Railway (*see* Fig. 246). However, the main traffic from the Soviet Union west of Trans-Baykalya to Vladivostok uses the line from Chita through China via Harbin (the route

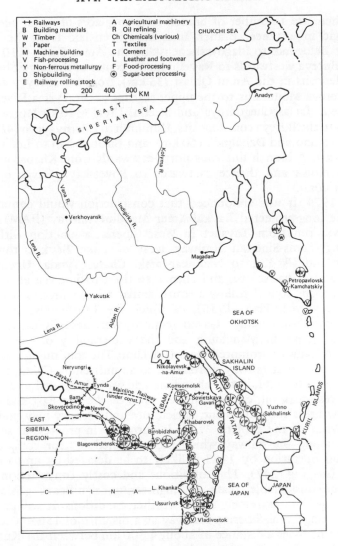

Fig. 246. Far East Economic Region: railways and industrial structure of towns.

is about 950 km shorter than by the all-Union route via Khabarovsk); the Amur and Ussuri sections of the Trans-Siberian line tend to be of secondary and local importance. Nevertheless, they are strategically safer though vulnerable in times of tension in Sino-Soviet relations. The insistence on the employment of only Russian labour at the time of the building of the track of the Trans-Siberian Railway indirectly assisted in the colonisation of the Far East Region.

The Trans-Siberian line passes through the more important towns and there are a number of branch lines to places of economic and strategic importance. Branch lines have been laid from the main line at Belogorsk to Blagoveshchensk on the Amur River (110 km), from Bureya westwards to Raychikhinsk, centre of the largest brown coal deposits in the Amur Oblast (35 km), from Izvestkovyy across the Bureya Mountains to the upper reaches of the Tyrma River and thence as far as Chegdomya and Stredni Urgal (320 km), providing access to the Bureya coal deposits, Ushumun to Chernyayevo (48 km), Skovorodino and Dzhalinda (60 km), and Birobidzhan to Leniskoye (150 km). A branch line runs north-eastwards from Khabarovsk to Komsomolsk and thence eastwards to Sovetskaya Gavan on the Pacific coast.

In 1974, it was announced that construction would commence on the long-projected Baykal-Amur Mainline railway (BAM). This line will run from Tayshet in West Siberia, a junction with the existing Trans-Siberian Railway west of Lake Baykal, through Bratsk and Ust-Kut to Nizhneangarsk, Chara, Tynda, Urgal and Komsomolsk-na-Amure, and thence to the Pacific coast at Sovetskaya Gavan. It will follow a route similar to that proposed in the Third Five-year Plan (1938), of which the Tayshet-Ust-Kut, and Komsomolsk-Sovetskaya Gavan sections, were actually completed. Fear of Japan in Manchuria and the vulnerability of the Trans-Siberian Railway prompted the original line. The continuing strategic weakness of that railway in relation to an unfriendly China, as well as a desire to exploit the abundant and varied mineral and other resources (coal, oil, copper, timber, etc.) of the Far East and open up new areas for settlement, agriculture and forestry may underlie the revival of the project. Work is currently in progress at several places along the railway which though scheduled for completion and full operation by 1983 is likely to be delayed by up to three years (*see* Fig. 247). This ambitious and costly construction will involve considerable feats of engineering, significant geological difficulties and extremely harsh weather conditions. It will parallel the existing Trans-Siberian Railway at a distance of 150-480 km to the north, cover a distance of about 4,300 km between Ust-Kut and Sovetskaya Gavan and play a key role in further integration of the Far Eastern economy.

The only important roads in the Far East are those between Khabarovsk and Vladivostok, Never and Yakutsk (the Aldan Highway), Yakutsk, Kolyma and Magadan (the Kolyma Highway) and Yakutsk and Ayan. They, and the local roads focussed on the Trans-Siberian Railway, are mainly unmetalled or poorly surfaced and in winter and spring are frequently impassable quagmires. The *corduroy* road — a log structure covered by grit and suitable for lorries — is common in the permafrost area. Hardening of pneumatic tyres,

(Novosti)

Fig. 247. Track-laying for the Baykal-Amur Mainline railway (BAM). This ambitious and costly construction 150 to 480 km north of the Trans-Siberian Railway will link Ust-Kut with Sovetskaya Gavan via Komsomolsk-na-Amure. It will aid the exploitation of the varied mineral and forest resources of the Soviet Far East.

heat loss from engines and fuel viscosity are but some of the problems experienced by road transport during the intense cold of winter.

The Amur River, the Sino-Soviet boundary for 2,400 km, is the main waterway. It is especially important because both the main stream and its numerous large tributaries are navigable for ships and suitable for timber rafts. Traffic, in bulk cargoes of timber, oil, grain and building materials, is limited to the summer months since the river is frozen over in the winter half of the year, for 185 days at Khabarovsk and 170 days at Blagoveshchensk.

The Far East Region contributes about a quarter of the annual turnover in marine transport in the USSR. Vladivostok is the main seaport, but Nakhodka-Vostochny, 190 km to the east, and Posyet, 50 km to the south-west are serious rivals. The deep-water port of Vostochny is designed to handle container traffic for and from the Trans-Siberian Landbridge (*see* p. 121) and coal from south Yakutia. Sovetskaya-Gavan, linked by rail with Komsomolsk-na-Amure is another important port and one of the Soviet Union's major naval dockyards. Korsakov and Kholmsk are the main ports on Sakhalin, and Petropavlovsk on Kamchatka. The latter is also the eastern terminus of the Northern Sea Route.

Air transport is becoming increasingly important for passenger traffic. Khabarovsk is the main centre with a network embracing such places as Birobidzhan, Blagoveshchensk, Svobodnyy, Urgal, Komsomolsk-na-Amure, Nikolayevsk, Sakhalinsk, and Petropavlovsk in the Soviet Far East, and also with many external connections.

POPULATION AND SETTLEMENT

Fishing, forestry, rare metals and foreign trade would appear to hold out large potential for more settlement in the Far East and yet it has proved difficult to attract permanent migrants. During the 1939-59 period, the growth of population was particularly high in a narrow belt of settlement in the southern portion and along the Trans-Siberian Railway (e.g. Maritime and Khabarovsk Krays) which are reasonably well settled with farming communities, lumbering towns or mining communities. There was a further increase of about 19.5 per cent between 1959 and 1970 from 4.8 million to 5.7 million, and another 18 per cent or 1.1 million added up to 1979 when the total was 6.8 million. Even so, in relation to its size (over a quarter of the USSR) this population is very sparse; the average density is not much more than one person per km^2.

A startlingly large proportion (74 per cent) of the total population lives in towns or urban-type settlements. Eighty-two per cent of the population are classified as urban on Sakhalin Island and in Kamchatka Oblast, but only 38 per cent in the Koryak AO. The sparseness of the population in the outlands is very marked with vast areas uninhabited.

The present population of 6.8 million is small compared with the 1.1 billion or more in neighbouring and rival China, or the 90 millions in China's nearby North-Eastern Region (Manchuria). A vital requirement for both economic and strategic reasons is for the Soviet Union to raise the total population of its Far East Region and to improve its effective work force. The Soviet Government has adopted every effort to increase colonisation by the attraction of higher wages, tax exemptions, subsidised journeys and other benefits together with appeals to the patriotism of young Communists. The indigenous peoples (e.g. 328,000 Yakuts, 14,000 Chukchi, 8,000 Koryak) are completely dominated numerically and qualitatively by Russians and Ukrainians and their lives modernised, collectivised and "Russified".

Vladivostok (population: 550,000)
Situated 9,320 km from Moscow by the Trans-Siberian Railway, Vladivostok was founded in 1860 and two years later made the base of the Russian Pacific Fleet. At the end of the nineteenth century, the town developed as an important Pacific port (*see* Fig. 248). It is sited on the slope of a ridge of hills alongside a deep and well-protected bay (the "Golden Horn") at the southern end of the Muravyev Peninsula and opposite Russkiy Island. The Peninsula is separated from the island by the "Eastern Bosporus". The restricted site, sometimes likened to San Francisco for its scenic beauty, has given rise to closely packed business premises and high-density

(Fotokbronika Tass)

Fig. 248. Vladivostok: terminus of the Trans-Siberian Railway. Vladivostok owes its growth primarily to its function as the main Soviet port on the Pacific coast serving fishing and commercial vessels and also the Soviet Pacific Fleet.

building. The side streets which run up the hill slopes are sometimes too steep for vehicular traffic. Industries in Vladivostok include fish-processing and canning, wood-using industries (saw mills, plywood factories, matchmaking plant and the prefabrication of timber houses), general engineering, machine building and shipbuilding (*see* Fig. 246). There is ice in the port in winter but it is fairly easily kept open by ice-breakers. Vladivostok recorded a surprising 25 per cent increase in its population between the censuses of 1970 and 1979, largely as a result of in-migration rather than natural growth.

Khabarovsk (population: 528,000)
The administrative and economic centre of the territory (*Kray*) of the same name, Khabarovsk is located on the elevated eastern bank of the Amur River, at this point several kilometres wide, some 45 km below its confluence with the Ussuri River. Despite the fact that the river is frozen over from December until April, Khabarovsk is well placed on a large system of navigable waterways. It is the

terminus of the Ussuri section of the Trans-Siberian Railway and centre of all air traffic in the Soviet Far East. In addition, it has industries which include mechanical engineering, shipbuilding, oil refining, cable works, timber working and lumbering and food-processing (*see* Fig. 246). Its population of Russians, Koreans and Chinese continues to increase apace, by over a fifth in the nine years, 1970-79. Like Vladivostok, there is a large migratory component involved in this growth.

Komsomolsk-na-Amure (population: 264,000)
Built by Komsomols (Young Communists) in 1933 as a bulwark against the Japanese, Komsomolsk-na-Amure is the most diversified industrial centre in the Far East Region with a steel plant (Amurstal), shipyards, oil refinery, paper and pulp industries, chemical industries, lumber industry (from railway sleepers to furniture), fish-processing and canning plant. *Amursk* (pulp-paper) and *Solnechy* (tin-mining and dressing) are satellite towns. Previously trains from Sovetskaya Gavan and its adjacent port of Vanino were carried across the Amur by rail ferries and, in winter, when the river is firmly frozen, tracks were laid over the ice. Floating ice in spring and autumn severely hampered communication. Now the Amur is spanned by a 380 m railway bridge completed in 1975.

Petropavlovsk-Kamchatskiy (population: 215,000)
Capital of Kamchatka Oblast, the city is a major fisheries centre and important naval base on the south-east coast of Kamchatka Peninsula (*see* Fig. 249). Its principle industries are associated with fish-processing and canning, lumber milling and shipbuilding. Its population increased by as much as 80 per cent in the intercensal period 1959 and 1970, and by another 40 per cent between 1970 and 1979, largely as a result of in-migration.

Blagoveshchensk (population: 172,000)
With the smaller towns of *Belogorsk* and *Svobodnyy*, Blagoveshchensk is an engineering centre with flour-milling and other branches of the food industry, all closely connected with the agriculture of the Zeya-Bureya Plain.

Yakutsk (population: 152,000)
Lying well within the *tayga* and permafrost zone 1½ km from the west bank of the Lena (here 16-18 km wide) Yakutsk was founded by Cossacks in 1632 during their eastward advance through Siberia. The town is now capital of Yakut ASSR and has sawmills, small engineering works and maintenance yards for the Lena river fleet.

(*Fotokbronika Tass*)

Fig. 249. Petropavlovsk-Kamchatskiy, a major fisheries centre and Soviet naval base on the south-east coast of Kamchatka Peninsula. It plays a role in the Pacific analogous to that of Murmansk on the Atlantic. The vessel in the foreground is the floating cannery *Pyatdesyat Let Oktyabrya.*

Transport links are either by road along the Aldan Highway to Never on the Trans-Siberian Railway or along the Kolyma Highway to Magadan on the Sea of Okhotsk, or else by air. There is no railway.

CHAPTER XVII

Kazakhstan Macro-Region

Kazakhastan (*see* Fig. 250) has emerged as a strong economic region despite its generally low level of migration and lack of an internal focus. It is characterised by a series of sub-regional industrial clusters, namely heavy industry and mining in the centre, extensive grain farming and agricultural industries in the north, energy-intensive and non-ferrous metals in the north-east, irrigated agriculture, non-ferrous metals and chemicals in the south and petrochemicals in the west. Karaganda and Temirtau and the grain lands of northern

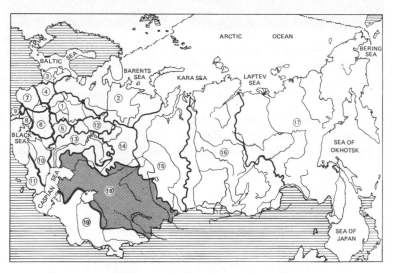

Fig. 250. Soviet Union: location of Kazakhstan Macro-Region.

Kazakhstan are linked to the Urals and West Siberia Regions, while the capital, Alma-Ata and southern Kazakhstan are isolated from the northern section by an extensive area of desert and semi-desert 400-480 km wide and are more akin to Central Asia (*see* Chapter XVIII). The space activity at the Baykonur cosmodrome and the traditional Soviet nuclear testing ground at Semipalatinsk are quasi-independent of the Kazakhstan economy.

TABLE 66. KAZAKHSTAN MACRO-REGION:
ADMINISTRATIVE UNITS, THEIR POPULATION AND DENSITY

Area: 2,717,300 km²
Population (1979): 14,685,000

Administrative unit	Area (000 km²)	Population (000, 1979)	Density (persons per km²)	Percentage urban
Aktyubinsk Oblast	300	629	2	47
Guryev Oblast	112	370	3	59
Uralsk Oblast	151	581	4	38
Kokchetav Oblast	78	617	8	35
Kustanay Oblast	115	939	8	47
Pavlodar Oblast	128	806	6	57
North Kazakhstan Oblast	44	570	13	44
Tselinograd Oblast	125	808	6	57
Dzhambul Oblast	145	933	6	45
Kzyl-Orda Oblast	227	566	2	63
Chimkent Oblast	116	1,567	14	40
Alma-Ata City ⎱ Alma-Ata Oblast ⎰	105	914⎱ 851⎰	17	100 / 19
Taldy-Kurgan Oblast	119	664	6	40
East Kazakhstan Oblast	97	877	9	61
Karaganda Oblast	86	1,253	15	85
Semipalatinsk Oblast	180	770	4	48
Mangyshlak	166.6	252	2	87
Turgay Oblast	111.9	268	2	31
Dzhezkazgan	313.4	450	1	77

PHYSICAL ASPECTS

Relief
An extensive area of separate hill ranges of subdued relief and less than 900 m high — the Kazakh Uplands — occupies the north-eastern core of the region (*see* Fig. 251). This is the water divide between drainage northwards to the Arctic and interior drainage to the Aral Sea. In the west is the monotonous and arid Turanian Lowland. Until the end of the Tertiary period this lowland and the low-lying lands surrounding the northern part of the Caspian Sea were part of the bed of a much greater Aral Sea which extended westwards to embrace both the Caspian and Black Seas. Now

TABLE 67. KAZAKHSTAN MACRO-REGION:
TOWNS WITH OVER 150,000 INHABITANTS IN 1979

Town	Population in thousands		Percentage increase 1970-79
	1970 (census)	1979 (census)	
Alma-Ata	733	910	24
Karaganda	523	572	9
Chimkent	247	321	30
Semipalatinsk	236	283	20
Ust-Kamenogorsk	230	274	19
Pavlodar	187	273	46
Dzhambul	187	264	41
Tselinograd	180	234	30
Temirtau	166	213	28
Petropavlovsk	173	207	20
Aktyubinsk	150	191	27
Uralsk	134	167	24
Kustanay	123	164	33
Kzyl-Orda	122	156	27

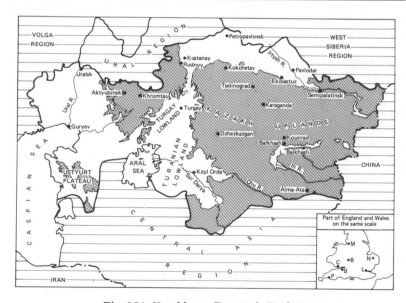

Fig. 251. Kazakhstan Economic Region.

the lowland is a vast basin of interior drainage, a region of arid steppe and clay and sandy (*kum*) desert.

Between the Caspian and Aral Seas is the semi-arid and partially dissected Ustyurt Plateau. This is a flat, barren upland of nearly

(*Novosti*)

Fig. 252. Drifting sand dunes (*barkhans*) in the Hungry Steppe, Kazakhstan.
Irrigation work under way in the background.

horizontal strata lying at an elevation of about 300 m. North of
the Aral Sea (which is generally little more than 12-18 m deep, and
a maximum depth of only 68 m) and between the Mugodzhar Hills
(a southerly extension of the Urals) and the Kazakh Uplands is a
sandy extension of the Turanian Lowland known as the Turgay Lowland. It is, in fact, a plain dotted with residual tablelands (*turtkulie*).
South of the Kazakh Uplands comes Bekpak-Dala (northern Hungry
Steppe or Golodnaya Steppe), a dry Tertiary plateau rising from a
scarp, 130 m high overlooking the Chu River in the south, to 450 m
in the north. Further south, between the Chu River and the Kara
Tau mountains, are the Muyunkum (Sandy Desert). They extend for
a distance of over 450 km and their highest elevations reach 380 m.
South, beyond the valley of the Syr-Darya, comes Kyzylkum
(Red Sands), a very dry alluvial plain with scattered dunes, its
centre deeply buried in loose sand within which dunes (*barkhans*),
varying in height up to more than 30 m, abound (*see* Fig. 252).
Apparently, all these sands are of alluvial origin from the Quaternary
times when large rivers, then numerous but now extinct, carried a
great deal of sand to the plains and lowlands of Turkestan.

Lake Balkhash occupies an area of 21,750 km², but it is very
shallow — 10-20 m in depth. Like its eastern extension, Lakes
Sasykkol and Alakol, it lies along the northern margins of a structural basin. In eastern Kazakhstan, between the central Tyan-Shan
(Dzhungarskiy Ala-Tau, rising to 5,000 m) and the Tarbagatay Range
is the low Dzhungarian Gate, the historic highway leading from
China across Mongolia to the Kazakh steppe and thence to the Volga.

North-east of the Kazakh Uplands lies the southern margins of

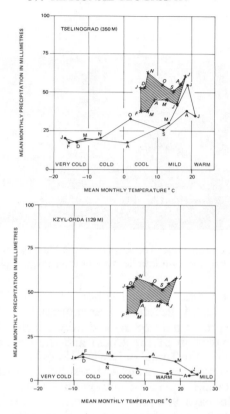

Fig. 253. Hythergraphs for Tselinograd and Kzyl-Orda (Kew, London, shaded).

the flat west Siberian Plain, through which flows the upper Irtysh River.

Climate, vegetation and soils
The entry of moist air masses into the region is prevented by its great distance from any oceans and by the screen of high mountains along the south. Precipitation over the plains is slight and most unreliable with aggregates less than 250 mm per annum (*see* Fig. 253). The meagre precipitation has different sources and different seasons of incidence. In the southern part it comes from cyclone storms which are more frequent in spring and winter. Along the northern border the precipitation is the result of summer cyclonic storms augmented by convection activity. The month of maximum precipitation changes progressively from south to north, from April in the south through to June and July in the north.

Northern Kazakhstan receives a slight winter snowfall, equivalent to 50-100 mm of rainfall, but the cover is of variable depth because of the drifting caused by violent blizzards. The snow establishes itself in November and usually disappears during the last fortnight of April with the sudden arrival of spring. During the winter the ground freezes to a depth of 80-100 cm.

Winter temperatures are low for the latitude, varying from a January mean of about −8 °C along the southern border of the region to −18 °C in the north. Mean minima may fall to as much as −38 °C in January (e.g. at Kzyl-Orda on the Syr-Darya) or even −49 °C (e.g. in Karaganda). Summer temperatures, on the other hand, rise to between 20 °C and 28 °C which is as high as those experienced in the Sahara or the interior of Australia. At Karaganda the July average is 21 °C, but the daily maximum temperature may rise to 39 °C, and the night minimum fall to 3 °C under clear skies and the resulting radiational cooling. At Kzyl-Orda the July mean temperature is 25 °C, the average daily maximum 46 °C and the night minimum 8 °C. Spring and autumn are brief seasons and pass virtually unnoticed.

The southern half of the region is desert or semi-desert with semi-shrub and desert tree-shrub but towards the north, where conditions are slightly more humid, there is a gradual transition to steppe. Along the most northerly fringe of the region come the beginnings of the wooded steppe. The soils have much the same east-west zones as the vegetation, with aridosols in the desert and semi-desert areas, entisols around the Aral Sea and on the Ustyurt Plateau, and mollisols underlying the steppelands.

THE ECONOMY

Agriculture
Kazakhstan has an estimated 34 per cent of the agricultural land of the USSR. In the steppelands of the north-east and north, climatic and soil conditions, though marginal, favour dry farming of grains, mainly spring wheat (*durum*) and millets, and the growing of industrial crops such as rape, flax, hemp and sunflowers (*see* Fig. 254). As previously noted, this northern part of Kazakhstan, together with the south-west of West Siberia was ploughed up during the mid 1950s as part of the "Virgin and Long Idle Lands Project", (*see* p. 365).   The object of the project was to maintain, or indeed expand, the nation's wheat production at a time when maize was being introduced as an animal fodder crop into the traditional granary lands of the Ukraine and North Caucasus. Grain *sovkhozy* in Kustanay, Tselinograd and Kokchetav Oblasts and North Kazakhstan now cover tens of thousands of hectares and they are highly

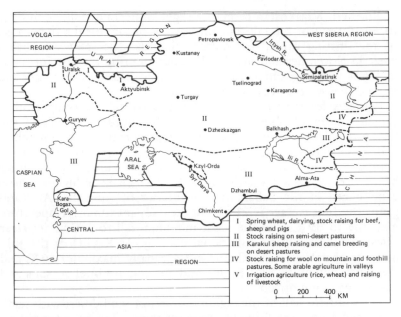

Fig. 254. Kazakhstan Economic Region: agricultural land-use regions.

mechanised. Their combined output accounts for about 14 per cent of the total grain production of the USSR (*see* Fig. 255). Under marginal conditions the vagaries of the climate are as likely to result in a disastrous crop failure as a bumper harvest. Fortunately, experience has shown that rarely does a drought occur in north Kazakhstan at the same time as there is a drought in the grainlands of the Ukraine or North Caucasus.

In the south of Kazakhstan, there is a long strip of irrigated land along the lower reaches of the Syr-Darya, centred on Kzyl-Orda, which is given over to rice growing. Kzyl-Orda is also the site of a large pulp and cardboard mill which utilises the reeds growing in the Syr-Darya. The Chu River — ostensibly a right bank tributary of the Syr-Darya though it disappears into the sands before reaching the main stream — supports another important area of irrigation agriculture. The area, centred on Frunze (Kirgiz SSR), is devoted to wheat, barley, tobacco and sugar-beet, the latter introduced by Russian and Ukrainian settlers. Eastwards, along the alluvial fans which foot the Tyan-Shan and towards and around the city of Alma-Ata, capital of Kazakhstan SSR, there is much fruit (especially apples) and vegetable growing under irrigation, together with dairying. Most of the irrigated land at Taldy Kurgan, south of the eastern end of Lake Balkhash, is under wheat, barley and rice.

(Novosti)

Fig. 255. Spring wheat growing on what used to be virgin or long idle land in Kazakhstan, Northern Kazakhstan and south-west Siberia, ploughed up during the mid 1950s as part of the Virgin and Long Idle Lands Project, now provide about 14 per cent of the total grain production of the USSR.

In addition to the dry farming and specialised irrigation agriculture there is also animal husbandry. Cattle, for meat and milk, and sheep for fine wool, are raised on the steppe and semi-desert pastures; there is also horse breeding. Cattle, sheep and yak are grazed on the mountain pastures of the east and south-east.

Power, mineral resources and industry
Kazakhstan plays a major role in the Soviet coal-mining industry. Karaganda coalfield is one of the main suppliers of coking coal to the metallurgical industries of the southern part of the Ural Region (*see* Fig. 256). Since the coals have a high ash content (20 per cent), and not all of the thirty coal seams of the field are of coking quality, Karaganda coal has to be mixed with the richer Kuznetsk coal before it can be used in blast furnaces. The latter is still hauled 1,600 km from the Kuzbass to the Urals, even though it is twice the distance the Karaganda coal has to travel.

Coal is worked also in the Ekibastuz Basin to the north-east of Karaganda. The coals here are non-coking and have a 40 per cent ash content. Worked by opencast methods they are more suitable

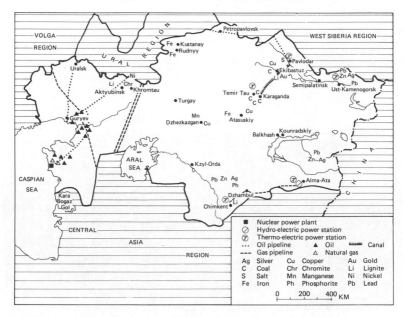

Fig. 256. Kazakhstan Economic Region: mineral and power resources.

for thermal-electric generating stations than for metallurgy and are used in generating stations locally and in adjacent parts of northern Kazakhstan, the Urals and West Siberia. The intention is to link the Ekibastuz stations with consumers in the European part of the USSR by means of high voltage (1,500 kV DC) transmission lines. Ekibastuz Basin surpassed Karaganda in volume of production in 1977 (67 million tonnes from Ekibastuz in 1980 compared with 49 million tonnes from Karaganda) and is now the third largest coal producer in the Soviet Union. A territorial-production complex, Ekibastuz-Pavlodar, is in the process of being developed.

Oil occurs in the Emba (Guryev) fields along the northern shore of the Caspian and further south, in the desert area of Mangyshlak Peninsula. Yields are relatively low in the Emba fields, but the deposits in the Mangyshlak fields (e.g. Buzachi Peninsula) hold out more promise. A new railway, road and pipeline have had to be constructed to link the Mangyshlak region with refineries in Guryev, Orsk and Kuybyshev, and with other parts of Kazakhstan. Most of the Kazakhstan production (23.9 million tonnes in 1975 and 18.4 million tonnes in 1980) now comes from Mangyshlak, though performance here has been disappointing owing to technical problems posed by the high paraffin content of the crude oil. Eastern and southern Kazakhstan obtain oil from West Siberia via a pipeline which links Omsk with refineries in Pavlodar and Chimkent.

Some gas is produced in conjunction with the oil (5.2 billion m³ in 1975 and 4.3 billion m³ in 1980) but what little there is is fed into the pipeline system which runs through Kazakhstan from Central Asia to European USSR.

Water and hydro-power is in short supply, but a number of important water construction projects have been undertaken. A series of hydro-electricity stations (Ust-Kamenogorsk, Bukhtarma) on the upper Irtysh River in eastern Kazakhstan facilitate the exploitation of this area's lead, zinc, copper and other non-ferrous metal resources. The serious water shortage, which at first inhibited industrial development in central Kazakhstan (annual precipitation at Karaganda 273 mm), has been relieved somewhat by the diversion of large quantities of water from the Irtysh River westwards via a gravity-flow canal, and then, by means of more than twenty pumping stations, to the Karaganda area which is at an elevation of over 500 m. *En route* the water is used for irrigation purposes to raise potatoes, vegetables and fruit for the urban markets. The plan to divert waters from the basin of the north-flowing Tobol River southwards via the Turgay Lowland into the Aral Sea has yet to be implemented.

Iron ore from Kustanay Oblast (Rudnyy, Lisakovsk, Kachar) not only supplies the blast furnaces of Magnitogorsk and other Urals iron and steel plants, and mills in the Kuzbass, but also the integrated iron and steel producing complexes in Karaganda and Temirtau which together produce upwards of 6 million tonnes of steel a year.

Copper ores are found in Dzhezkazgan Oblast, the Balkhash-Kounrad area and in East Kazakhstan Oblast. Dzhezkazgan Oblast claims to have the biggest copper reserve in the USSR and there is now a self-contained copper-producing complex at the town of Dzhezkazgan. The Balkhash plant processes Kounrad ores through the entire manufacturing cycle and there is a smelter in Gluboye for the refining of local and Orlovka deposits (*see* Fig. 257).

Lead, zinc, copper, gold, silver, cadmium and other non-ferrous metal ores occur east of the river in the upper Irtysh Basin in East Kazakhstan Oblast. With the assistance of the hydro-power provided by the Bukhtarma and Ust-Kamenogorsk stations these ores are smelted and refined at Leninogorsk, Ust-Kamenogorsk, Glubokoye and Ust Talorka. Chimkent in southern Kazakhstan also has a big lead smelter using local ores and ores and concentrates from numerous other mining districts of Central Asia. Kazakhstan now accounts for about three-quarters of the Soviet Union's total lead smelter output. This same general area, in the Kara Tau Mountains between Chimkent and Dzhambul, has the Soviet Union's second source of supply of phosphate raw material after the Kola apatite. Mining of the lower-grade phosphate rock takes place at Kara

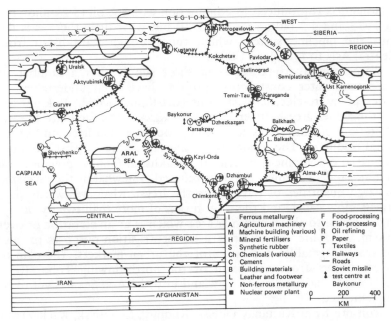

Fig. 257. Kazakhstan Economic Region: railways and industrial structure of towns.

(Chulak) Tau, Zhanatas and over a wide area nearby, and provides the ground phosphate used in a superphosphate plant at Dzhambul, in electric furnaces in Chimkent to yield phosphorus, and in fertiliser plant in Central Asia and Togliatti (Volga Region).

A major deposit of bauxite at Arkalyk in the Turgay Oblast of northern Kazakhstan and another at Krasnooktyabrskiy in Kustanay Oblast provide ore for the alumina and aluminium plant at Pavlodar and Ust-Kamenogorsk. The alumina is used locally and the surplus sent eastwards to energy-intensive aluminium plants using low-cost hydro-electric power at Bratsk, Shelekhov, Krasnoyarsk and Novo-kuznetsk.

POPULATION AND CITIES

Only the Central Asian Republics record percentage increases of population greater than Kazakhstan. Between 1959 and 1970, the population of Kazakhstan increased by 40 per cent to reach 13,009,000. In 1979, the population was 14,685,000, an increase of practically 13 per cent on the 1970 total. These totals reflected not only the high natural increase rates of the Moslems of Central

Asia but also net migration of other ethnic groups into the region. During the 1970s however, the migration trend was reversed resulting in a net out-migration of little short of half a million Russians, Ukrainians and Belorussians as well as ethnic Germans.

Russians and Ukrainians, the virgin-lands farmers and industrial workers, now make up practically 47 per cent of the total population whereas the Kazakhs represent about 36 per cent; the latter are now a minority in their own republic.

The core of Kazakhstan is a large, sparsely peopled desert region, except for its mining activities and related urban development. In the dry farming lands on the northern periphery of the region the number of villages that have administrative functions together with the low densities of population (6-8 persons per km^2) reflect the rural character of the area. Along the southern margins, in some of the intensively farmed, irrigated oases there may be as many as 300-400 persons per km^2, but they are still predominantly rural. Population densities in Kazakhstan are, in general, rather low, but there are appreciable regional and local variations.

Fifty-two per cent of the total population of Kazakhstan are classified as urban dwellers but there are considerable spatial variations. The farming oblasts in the north generally range from 30-50 per cent urban; Guryev and East Kazakhstan Oblasts are 62 per cent urbanised; Karaganda Oblast has as many as 86 per cent of its population living in towns or urban-type settlements. Between 1913 and 1972 the urban population of Kazakhstan increased from 9.7 per cent to just over 50 per cent; rapid urbanisation appears to be an integral element of the region's general economic upsurge. Urbanisation also embraces many of the rural areas where *kolkhoz* and *sovkhoz* settlements acquire urban features and their populations adopt an urban style of living.

Alma-Ata (population: 910,000)
Capital of the Kazakh Republic, Alma-Ata is an entirely Russian city and dates from the middle of the nineteenth century. It occupies an attractive site at an altitude of about 600 m within the foothills of the Chu-Ili mountains (*see* Fig. 258). The surrounding countryside supports the fruit-preserving, meat-packing, leather-making and wine and tobacco factories of the city, but engineering and wood textiles tend to dominate its industries (*see* Fig. 258). Rail communications via the Turk-Sib line provide links with other Middle Asian and Siberian cities. Russians outnumber Kazakhs in the population, which rose from 222,000 in 1939 to 456,000 in 1959, and to 730,000 in 1970. Its population of 910,000 at the 1979 census represented an increase of 24 per cent in nine years.

(Novosti)

Fig. 258. Alma-Ata, capital of Kazak SSR, showing government, ministry and office buildings in the spacious Lenin Square. This open, geometrically regular city has fine views of snow-capped mountains rising to 5,000 m.

Karaganda (population: 572,000)

The city was founded in 1926 as a mining centre to supply coal to the metallurgical industries of the Urals. These functions persist and continue to expand, but with the building of giant steelworks in nearby *Temirtau* and *Solonichka* and the opening of additional coal mines at *Saran,* Karaganda has become the centre of a sizeable mining-metallurgical complex with a population which now exceeds half a million. In addition to its coal, iron and steel, the complex provides constructional and mining machinery, chemicals, cement and foodstuffs. The lack of water associated with the semi-arid situation of the complex has been overcome by the construction of a canal from the Irtysh River, a distance of 480 km (*see* p. 427). The spectacular, almost four-fold, rise in population from 154,000 in 1939 to 572,000 in 1979 is noteworthy. It is largely the result of high natural increase.

Chimkent (population: 321,000)

Situated on the Turk-Sib line, 110 km north of Tashkent, Chimkent is known for its large lead smelting plant (the largest in the USSR), phosphatic fertiliser and chemical industries, textiles, pharmaceuticals and food industries. A new oil refinery constructed here receives oil from West Siberia via Omsk, Pavlodar, Karaganda and Karazhal. Its population has more than quadrupled in the last forty years.

Semipalatinsk (population: 283,000)
Semipalatinsk was founded in 1718 as one of a chain of forts to secure the Russian occupation during the advance against the non-Slav nomads of Central Asia. The Turk-Sib railway crosses the Irtysh at this point, which has become a food-processing (meat packing) and textile centre.

Ust-Kamenogorsk (population: 274,000)
Situated on the Irtysh River, Ust-Kamenogorsk is the centre of a non-ferrous metallurgical district. It processes local deposits of lead, zinc, copper and silver. Power is obtained from the nearby hydroelectric station and another at Bukhtarma.

Pavlodar (population: 273,000)
Also situated on the Irtysh River, Pavlodar has an alumina and aluminium plant using bauxite from the Arkalyk (Turgay Oblast) and Krasnooktyabrskiy (Kustanay Oblast) districts and cheap electric power from large thermal stations on the Ekibastuz coalfield. It also has an oil refinery using oil piped 450 km from Omsk in West Siberia, an associated petrochemical complex together with a tractor plant turning out heavy farm tractors for the grain-growing area of northern Kazakhstan. Its rapid increase in population in recent years is noteworthy (46 per cent between 1970 and 1979).

Dzhambul (population: 264,000)
Situated in the extreme south of Kazakhstan, Dzhambul is the site of a thermal reduction plant processing Kara Tau phosphorite for phosphatic fertilisers. Like other Kazakhstan towns, it has grown apace in recent years.

Tselinograd (population: 234,000)
Formerly Akmolinsk, centre of the "Virgin and Long Idle Lands" (*see* p. 423), Tselinograd has experienced a phenomenal rise in population. It has increased six-fold in forty years. It manufactures agricultural and transport equipment and processes grain.

Temirtau (population: 213,000)
Like Karaganda, Temirtau is a comparatively new town which arose exclusively as a result of the development of coal mining in the area. It now has a major metallurgical plant alongside a reservoir which provides essential process water for the blast furnaces and steel mills.

Petropavlovsk (population: 207,000)
Centre of North Kazakhstan Oblast and situated at a point where the Trans-Siberian Railway crosses the Ishim River, Petropavlovsk owes its growth to industries processing agricultural raw materials and transport organisations servicing the countryside.

Aktyubinsk (population: 191,000)
Situated in the north of Kazakhstan, Aktyubinsk is a centre of the chromium industry based on the Donskoye deposit 80 km east, and has a chemical complex producing superphosphate fertilisers from apatite concentrate from the Kola Peninsula.

Uralsk (population: 167,000)
Situated on the Ural River, Uralsk is a meat-packing centre. It also processes grains, wool and skins from the surrounding agricultural region.

Kustanay (population: 164,000)
Situated on the Tobol, Kustanay lies within the fertile grain-growing region of northern Kazakhstan and south-west Siberia. Its rapid growth has been promoted by the expansion of industries processing agricultural raw materials (flour-milling, millet stripping) and those associated with servicing the countryside.

Kzyl-Orda (population: 156,000)
An oasis city on the Syr-Darya, Kzyl-Orda is important for its large pulp and cardboard mill which utilises the reeds growing in the mouth of the river. It is served by the Tashkent-Orenburg railway.

CHAPTER XVIII

Central Asia Macro-Region

Central Asia comprises the four republics of Turkmenistan, Tadzhikistan, Kirgiziya and Uzbekistan (*see* Fig. 259). It is a vast area of deserts and high mountains, though with some densely populated oases. With practically 13 per cent of the agricultural land of the USSR, agriculture dominates the economy. Nevertheless, the region lags behind the nation in most agricultural branches other than

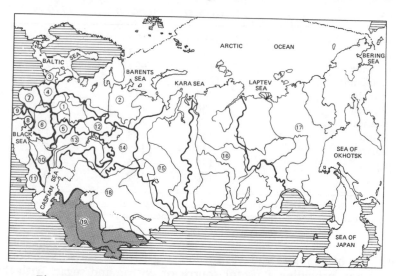

Fig. 259. Soviet Union: location of Central Asia Macro-Region.

cotton and market gardening. The oil-gas-chemicals complex is assuming a growing importance in the economy and the the availability of electric power will be greatly expanded from large hydro-projects at Dushanbe (Tadzhik) and Toktogul (Kirghiz), and the gas-fired Syrdarya thermal station at Shirin, south of Tashkent (Uzbek).

Before its annexation by Russia, the whole area comprised a

TABLE 68. CENTRAL ASIA MACRO-REGION:
ADMINISTRATIVE UNITS, THEIR POPULATION AND DENSITY

Area: 1,279,300 km²
Population (1979): 25,480,000

Administrative unit	Area (000 km²)	Population (000, 1979)	Density (persons per km²)	Percentage urban
Turkmen SSR	488	2,759	6	48
Uzbek SSR	447	15,391	34	41
Tadzhik SSR	143	3,801	27	35
Kirgiz SSR	198	3,529	18	39

TABLE 69. CENTRAL ASIA MACRO-REGION:
TOWNS WITH OVER 150,000 INHABITANTS IN 1979

Town	Population in thousands 1970 (census)	1979 (census)	Percentage increase 1970-79
Tashkent	1,385	1,779	28
Frunze	431	533	24
Dushanbe	374	493	32
Samarkand*	(267)	476	—
Ashkhabad	253	312	23
Andizhan	188	230	22
Namangan	175	227	30
Kokand	133	153	15
Bukhara	112	185	66
Fergana	148	176	19
Osh	120	169	40

* The boundaries of Samarkand were extended in May 1978 to include three outlying suburbs. For this reason no increase is given for the intercensal period 1970-79.

number of *khanates* and was for long regarded by Russia as colonial territory, providing a useful source of cotton and sugar. With the Second World War and the German occupation of the western parts of the Soviet Union, there was an influx of Russians and Ukrainians into Middle Asia. At the same time the region's economy was stimulated and further developed to meet the needs arising from the loss of the food and industrial resources in enemy-occupied territories. Central Asia is now an important region of specialised agriculture, particularly of cotton cultivation, and it supplies over two-thirds of the Union's total requirement of cotton. This is supplemented by

Fig. 260. Bukhara: cupolas of the bazaar.

Fig. 261. Bukhara: Mausoleum of Ismail Samanid, founder of the Samanid dynasty. Bukhara is a veritable museum town which takes pride in its magnificent monuments dating from the ninth century.

pastoral activities and diversified light industries. The irrigated oases, which, since time immemorial, have been the abodes of settled cultivators, include long renowned centres of Islam such as Samarkand,

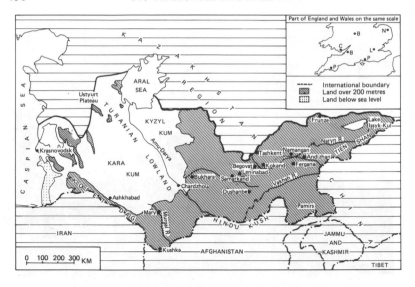

Fig. 262. Central Asia Economic Region.

Tashkent, Mary and Bukhara which can trace their history back to the beginnings of agriculture in the first millennium (*see* Figs. 260 and 261). The deserts, semi-arid lands and mountains are the home of nomadic pastoralists who range over seasonal pastures on the desert fringe, or else move between mountain pastures in summer and valley pastures in winter. The differences between the settled cultivator and the nomadic pastoralist were traditional until the beginning of the Soviet era, since when they have largely disappeared. The former cattle herders have been settled in permanent communities on large stock-rearing *sovkhozy* where increasing attention is devoted to cattle breeding and the raising of good-quality stock.

PHYSICAL ASPECTS

Relief

The monotonous and arid Turanian Lowland occupies the western part of the region; everywhere on the south and east is bounded by high rugged mountains (*see* Fig. 262). Until the end of the Tertiary period, the Turanian Lowland was part of the bed of a much larger Aral Sea which extended westwards to embrace both the Black and Caspian Seas. Now, the lowland is a vast basin of interior drainage, a region of clay and sandy desert and dry steppe. Between the Caspian Sea and the Amu-Darya (Oxus) is a vast area of sandy desert and clay depressions (*takyr*), known as Karakum (Black Sands). Kyzyl-kum (Red Sands), between the Amu-Darya and the Syr-Darya

(Iaxartes), is a dry alluvial plain with scattered dunes, its centre deeply buried in loose sand within which dunes (*barkhans*), varying in height up to more than 30 m, abound. This is how Vladimir Lugovski sees Turkestan in *A Ballad of a Desert:*

> And so day after day barkhans were rolling,
> Like silent waves of a stilled sea,
> There was only the shimmer of heat left in the world,
> In the yellow and blue of the glassy expanse.
>
> No sound, no water, no people, complete isolation,
> No wind, not a rustle, not a movement of air.
> Bent bushes and camel's bones,
> And the dull beating of heart and pulse.
>
> The horses are swaying, the rifles, like hot coals,
> The heat hands over, the knees are getting weak,
> Words die unspoken, and lips have swollen.
> Not a beast, not a bird, not a sound, not a shade.
>
> Is it possible that one day the might of man,
> Will rise up, conquering the solitude of the sands,
> Or will the barkhan sea, the grey desert
> Roll on from century to century?

Between the southern border of the Turanian Lowland and the high mountains of Central Asia is a zone of loess-covered piedmont plains at a height of 100-250 m. This zone includes the slopes of the Kopet-Dag and also the Fergana Basin.

A high mountain wall, extending from the east coast of the Caspian Sea to the Zaysan Depression, encloses Central Asia on the south and east. In the south, the Kopet-Dag ("Dry Mountains") and associated ranges lie mainly in Iran, where they reach heights above 2,700 m. Much the same applies to the ranges of the Hindu Kush to the east of the Kopet-Dag in that they lie almost entirely in Afghanistan.

In the south-east, wave after wave of high snow-capped mountains alternate with deep valleys. The Pamir-Alay mountains are a series of east-west orientated ranges fanning out from the Pamir massif ("Roof of the World") of Afghanistan and Pakistan. These are the highest mountains in the Soviet Union, where Mount Communism rises to 7,495 m, and Mount Lenin to 7,134 m. The Pamir-Alay mountains also contain the Fedchenko Glacier, reputed to be one of the most extensive mountain glaciers in the world. Earthquakes within these mountains often give rise to avalanches of snow and ice which dam existing streams and cause floods. The northernmost range of the Pamir-Alay mountains is known as the Trans-Alay Range.

The Tyan-Shan ("Heavenly Mountains") system is a complex of ranges, some of which are notoriously difficult to cross because of their great height (over 3,300 m) and infrequent passes. Individual ranges are aligned roughly west-east and enclose mountain basins. Of these, the Fergana Basin ("the gem of Central Asia"), 15-40 km wide and 160 km long, lying just north of the Trans-Alay Range, is the broadest. The basin containing the Issyk-Kul ("hot lake") is another.

Climate
The high mountain wall which borders Central Asia on the south prevents the entry of moist air masses from the south, and the Caucasus Mountains block any such movement from the west. The region is wide open to the north but distance precludes ameliorating influences from any ocean in that direction. Consequently this is the driest part of the Soviet Union. Precipitation over the plains is slight and very variable from year to year, and is on average less than 150 mm a year (e.g. Bukhara, 113 mm). It increases towards the southern mountains where some south-western slopes may receive 1,000 mm or more. Drought is the unifying factor over the plain and of Central Asia. Only the Amu-Darya, fed in the mountains by melting snow and ice, survives the journey through the deserts to the Aral Sea.

Winter temperatures are low for the latitude and, except in the extreme south, are below freezing level (January mean in Kzyl-Orda −9.6 °C, in Tashkent −1.1 °C). Mean summer temperatures rise to well over 30 °C on the plains and absolute temperature may be as much as 44-46 °C making this the hottest part of the USSR in this season (*see* Fig. 263). On the other hand, night temperatures in summer drop occasionally to 3-4 °C. The air is dry and clouds are absent, but daytime conditions are turbulent and windy.

> Because of the dry air in the summer heat is endured much more easily here than in the humid subtropics of Trans-Caucasia, but the midday hours are too oppressive for work in the open, even for those who live here always. The burden of the heat is increased by dry, scorching winds — the *harmsil*, which sometimes affect the harvest of cotton and grain adversely. It is interesting that temperature differences between the oases and desert are neglible in winter (0.2 °C-0.4 °C) but at the height of summer the desert is three degrees warmer than its oases.
>
> A.A. Borisov, 1965

Spring and autumn are fleeting seasons and pass virtually unnoticed. The climate generally is not unlike that experienced in the Great Basin of the USA, or the Gobi of Mongolia. The foothill belt, along the fringe of the desert and the valleys of the south and southeast receive rather more precipitation than the desert itself, and

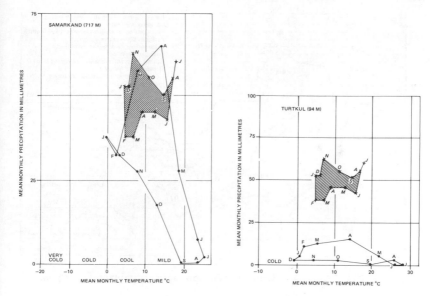

Fig. 263. Hythergraphs for Samarkand and Turtkul (Kew, London, shaded).

they are also watered by the mountain-fed streams. Irrigation agriculture in these areas provides spectacular results.

Of the Pamirs, Semenov writes:

> Little snow falls (in winter) in the Pamirs, but there are hard frosts there
> and terrible freezing winds rage. In quite sunny weather it often becomes
> so hot in the middle of the day that it is necessary to discard warm clothes
> but there is sometimes sufficient cloud or shade to blot out the sun's rays
> and chill one through with sharp cold. The side of one's face turned towards
> the sun is strongly heated; but the side in the shade almost freezes, and the
> skin sheds its outer layer several times and finally becomes dark and dry like
> parchment.

P.P. Semenov (-Tien-Shanski), 1903

THE ECONOMY

Agriculture

In southern Turkmen SSR, the Karakum merges into the loess-
covered piedmont plain 90-120 m above sea-level. The rivers and
small mountain streams that cross the plain have built up a series of
alluvial fans along the mountain front. Only the Murgab and Tedzhen
Rivers succeed in flowing any distance into the desert before drying
out through seepage and evaporation. The plain contains a line of
wonderfully fertile oases which have attracted man since Neolithic
times. The largest irrigated areas are at Ashkhabad in the west, in
the Tedzhen delta and valley, and in the Murgab valley (*see* Fig. 264).

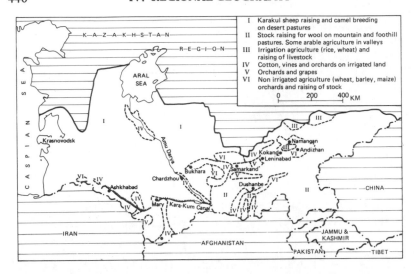

Fig. 264. Central Asia Economic Region: agricultural land-use regions.

(Novosti)

Fig. 265. Cotton harvesting in the Vakhsh valley, Tadzhik SSR.

(Novosti)

Fig. 266. Part of the Karakum Canal which conveys waters westwards from the Amu-Darya at Kelif through the oases of the Murgab and Tedzhen to Ashkhabad, a distance of 800 km.

The Ashkhabad area (*see* Fig. 265) is well known for its cotton, grains and lucerne (alfalfa), the Tedzhen valley for wheat, cotton and lucerne, and the Murgab for cotton. The Karakum Canal supplements local streams by conveying waters westwards from the Amu-Darya at Kelif through the oases of the Murgab and Tedzhen to Ashkhabad, a distance of 800 km (*see* Fig. 266). Over half a million hectares of thirsty lands of southern Turkmenistan are irrigated thereby. There are plans to extend the Karakum Canal to the vicinity of Krasnovodsk on the Caspian.

Irrigation has been practised in the basin of the Amu-Darya since ancient times. About 65 per cent of the irrigated land is in the delta region, 15 per cent along the west bank of the middle course (between the Soviet-Afghan frontier and the delta) and 20 per cent in the upper basin, primarily in the valleys of the Vakhsh, Surkhan-Darya and Kafirnigan. In the upper reaches of the Amu-Darya and

(*Fotokhronika Tass*)

Fig. 267. The Zeravshan River ("the river that sprinkles gold") before it debouches into the loess plains near Samarkand.

its tributaries long-staple cotton and grains are the chief irrigated crops, but there are also non-irrigated crops such as wheat, maize and other grains grown by dry farming methods.

In the lower reaches, downstream from Urgench, is the famous Khorezm oasis and Khiva city where the emphasis is on cotton in rotation with lucerne. The effects of the First World War, the civil war, and the 1917 Revolution on the delicate balance of these irrigated lands were disastrous and the Khorezm oasis was crippled. Irrigation works were re-established under the Soviet administration and Khiva is once again a rich area producing cotton and lucerne, maize, onions, grapes and fruits.

Though ostensibly a tributary of the Amu-Darya, the Zeravshan River dries out in the desert at Karakul (Black Lake) Oasis, about 100 km before it reaches the main stream (*see* Fig. 267). Fed by a glacier in the Alay Mountains, it has been the source of water for scores of oases along its banks from very ancient times; in its valley there arose one of the earliest river civilisations in Central Asia.

Fig. 268. The Ark, Bukhara. This 2½ hectare citadel 20 m above the level of the city is the oldest inhabited site in Bukhara. It was once the home of a long dynasty of Emirs.

The Zeravshan now irrigates an almost unbroken belt 15-30 km wide and 320 km long from near the ancient city of Samarkand to just beyond Bukhara (*see* Fig. 268). Though devoted chiefly to irrigated cotton (*see* Fig. 265), this area also produces wheat, rice, tobacco, grapes, fruit and vegetables. Like the Zeravshan, the Kashka-Darya peters out in the desert after having watered several oases which are given over to the cultivation of wheat, cotton, rice, tobacco and fruit.

The whole of the loess-covered piedmont zone between the Amu-Darya and the Kashka-Darya is celebrated for its fruit growing. The elaborate irrigation system was destroyed at the time of the Mongol invasions in the thirteenth century, but has been completely restored and extended under the Soviet administration.

The Kara-Darya (Black River), rising in the Tyan-Shan, and the Naryn River, rising in the Alay Mountains, join to form the Syr-Darya in the basin of subsidence known as Fergana (*see* Fig. 269). There is no rain during the period May-September but the Syr-Darya, tapped by the Great Fergana, North Fergana, Andizhan and Great Namangan Canals, irrigates all but the sandy and salty central portion of the area. Hot summers with temperatures up to 35 °C and fertile soils are conducive to excellent crops of cotton which are grown in rotation with lucerne; about a quarter of the Soviet Union's cotton production comes from here. Wheat, barley, rice, melons,

(*Novosti*)

Fig. 269. Fergana valley, Uzbek SSR. This wholly irrigated, densely populated basin enclosed by mountains is an important producer of cotton, grains, vines, fruits, vegetables and silk.

fruits (especially apricots) and mulberry trees (to provide leaves for silkworms) are also cultivated and there are numerous vineyards. The irrigation canals are provided with water from a series of dams built on the Naryn River. The largest is the site of the Toktogul hydro-station.

The Farkhad Dam and Kayrakkum Dam at the western end of the Fergana valley, besides generating hydro-electricity for local industries, provide additional irrigation water to the Pakhta Aral (Cotton Island) in the Golodnaya (Hungry) Steppe to the west. A long strip of irrigated land in the lower reaches of the Syr-Darya and centred on Kzyl-Orda is given over to rice growing. Tashkent, the most important cotton town in the USSR (Uzbekistan accounts for about 64 per cent of Soviet cotton production), is situated in the centre of a loess oasis, watered by the interlocking Chirchik and Keles tributaries of the Syr-Darya. Complex works on the Chirchik River provide not only irrigation and domestic water but also power for a series of small hydro-electric stations.

The Chu River — ostensibly a right bank tributary of the Syr-Darya, though it disappears in the sands before reaching the main stream — supports another important area of irrigation agriculture. The area centres on Frunze and is devoted to winter wheat, barley and sugar-beet. There is a strong European component in the population here, particularly Russians and Ukrainians who settled as farmers.

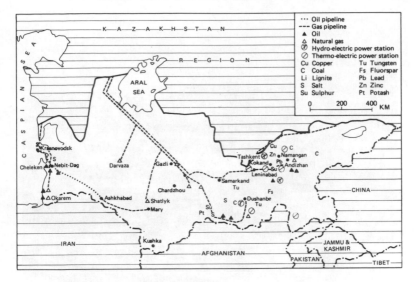

Fig. 270. Central Asia Economic Region: mineral and power resources.

In addition to the specialised irrigation agriculture of Central Asia (e.g. 5.9 million tonnes of raw cotton in 1980), there is also pastoralism. Although the natural vegetation of the desert and semi-desert is very limited, it is important for supporting migratory animal husbandry. The vegetation — ephemeral grasses, flowering herbs and some stunted trees (saxual) — helps to fix the moving sands. Stock raising has been the traditional mainstay of agriculture in the drier lowlands with sheep, goats, and camels predominating. Karakul sheep are admirably suited to desert conditions. The pelts of the new-born lambs have black curly wool and are especially valuable on the world market. In the mountain foreland areas trans-humance is practised. Stock are taken to mountain pastures for summer grazing and brought down to the valley pastures for the winter. Increased attention is being directed to livestock breeding and to the use of forage and hay crops, grown under irrigation, in rotation with cotton and grain; consequently most nomadic herds-men are now settled in permanent *sovkhozy*.

Power, mineral resources and industry

Central Asia is endowed with natural gas, petroleum, coal and non-ferrous metals (*see* Fig. 270). Outstandingly important are the natural gas deposits of Western Uzbekistan and Turkmenia. Until the comparatively recent finds in West Siberia, the deposits near Gazli, Uchkyr and Dzharkak in Bukhara Oblast were considered to be the largest single reserve of natural gas in the Soviet Union. They

(Fotokbronika Tass)

Fig. 271. Transporters carrying large diameter pipes over the Karakum desert for the construction of a pipeline which now conveys natural gas from the large deposits of the Shatlyk field.

were also cheap to exploit. These and other larger deposits near Mary (Shatlyk field) and at Okarem in Turkmenia, have added impeto the industrialisation process in Central Asia by providing valuable power for thermo-electric generating plant, such as the Syrdarya station at Shirin, south of Tashkent. Possibly more important, however, is the fact that the gasfields are linked by long-distance pipelines with European USSR, the Urals, and eastwards with Tashkent and Alma-Ata. Output from Turkmenia is now practically double that of Uzbekistan, about half of which comes from the giant Shatlyk field (*see* Fig. 271).

TABLE 70. NATURAL GAS PRODUCTION IN
TURKMEN AND UZBEK SSRs
(in billion m^3)

	1965	1970	1975	1977	1978	1980
USSR	128	198	289	346	372	435
Turkmen SSR	1.2	13	52	64	66	70.5
Uzbek SSR	17	32	37	36	35	39

Source: *Soviet Geography* XXII (4), (1981).

Until about 1976, Central Asia was primary producer of natural gas in the USSR. Since then it has been overtaken by the West Siberian fields. Production from the Uzbek fields is falling off, but that from the Turkmen fields continues to increase. Central Asia production was 109.5 billion m^3 in 1980, or about 25 per cent of that for USSR as a whole for that year.

Oil occurs around Nebit Dag on the Chelekan Peninsula in Turkmen, and there are small amounts in Uzbekistan (Fergana Basin), Tadzhikistan and Kirghizia, but Central Asia is likely to remain only a minor producer responsible for no more than 3 per cent of the total Soviet production. The oil is refined locally at Krasnovodsk, also at Goznyy in the North Caucasus Region, and at Volgograd in the Volga Region. There are plans for a further refinery and petrochemical plant at Chardzhou on the Amu-Darya in eastern Turkmen SSR.

The few small scattered deposits do not make Central Asia self-sufficient in coal, neither is the quality suitable for use in the small steel plant at Bekabad (Begovat). However, it can be used in thermal power stations and for steam raising in factories. Production (about 10 million tonnes a year) is no more than 1.4 per cent of the Soviet total, although it has considerable locational value. The best fields are at Angren and Kyzyl-Kiya in the Fergana valley.

Besides the natural gas, oil and coal, energy supplies are also provided by the rivers debouching from the Central Asian mountains. These are swift-flowing and there are many suitable sites for the installation of hydro-electricity generating stations. In fact, Central Asia is considered to have about a quarter of the potential hydro-electric power of the Soviet Union. The Toktogul station on the Naryn River has an installed capacity of 1.8 million kW. Small stations at the Farkhad and Kayrak Kum dams on the Syr-Darya supply electric power to the Bekabad steelworks and other local industries near Tashkent. The Nurek Station (2.7 million kW) and the giant Golovnaya station at Ragun (3.2 million kW), both on the Vakhsh, service the Yavan valley electro-chemical complex (sodium chloride, magnesium chloride, chlorine, etc.), and the aluminium reduction plant situated at Regar. Many of the installations are dual purpose in that the dams created for generating electricity also store irrigation water.

A number of lead, zinc, alumina, sulphur, copper, molybdenum and tungsten mines are functioning in Central Asia. The lead smelter at Chimkent (in Kazakhstan) relies on Central Asian sources such as Tekeli, Bordunskiy, Altyn, Topkan and Kugitang. The large electrolytic refinery at Almalyk in the Angren Valley has its lead and zinc from nearby mountains, and copper concentration refinery and rolling mill uses a local copper-molybdenum source. Alumina extracted from the kaolin overburden in the Angren coalfield is intended to provide the raw material for the aluminium plant at Regar (west of Dushanbe) and for a similar plant planned for Angren. The saline waters of the naturally evaporating pan of the east Caspian shore, Kara-Bogaz-Gol ("black-throat lake"), provide the world's largest deposit of Glauber's salt (mirabilite), sodium sulphate, magnesium sulphite, magnesium chloride and common salt.

Local iron ore is not available and the Bekabad steel plant 120 km south of Tashkent relies on pig iron brought in from Karaganda and the Urals and scrap from the region's engineering industries. Steel production from this source is inadequate for the region's engineering industries, and there have to be sizeable imports from other steel producing regions. Engineering in Central Asia places emphasis on agricultural machinery, especially tractors and combines, textile machinery and machine tools, at such centres as Tashkent, Frunze and Dushanbe.

Phosphates, gas, oil and a variety of raw materials support an expanding chemical industry. Superphosphate fertiliser plant, using Kara Tau phosphate, are located in Almalyk, Kokand, Samarkand and Chardzhou; plant using natural gas and oil for nitrogenous fertilisers are to be found in Fergana, Navoi and Chirchik. Sulphur is recovered from natural gas at Mubarek, 100 km south of Navoi. Petroleum refineries at Krasnovodsk, Fergana and Shagal (55 km north-west of Chardzhou) manufacture synthetic fibres and synthetic rubber.

Cotton textile manufacturing takes place in Tashkent, Fergana, Ashkhabad and Dushanbe, but most of the raw cotton continues to move to the Centre Region of European USSR, where 70 per cent of the country's cotton cloth is produced. The rearing of silkworms is a traditional activity and natural silk is produced at Ashkhabad, Chardzhou, Bukhara and other centres.

Agriculture-based industries are well represented and include fruit and vegetable canning, wine-making, meat-processing, flour-milling and sugar refining.

Transport
The exploitation of the natural wealth of Central Asia and of Kazakhstan has involved the laying of railway lines, oil and gas pipelines, the digging of irrigation canals, and the construction of hydroelectricity stations. The first railway, the Trans-Caspian line from Krasnovodsk on the Caspian to Tashkent via Ashkhabad, Mary, Bukhara and Samarkand, was mainly concerned with the transport of oil. The Kazalinsk line, leading directly north-west from Tashkent across the desert to Orenburg and beyond, conveys raw cotton to

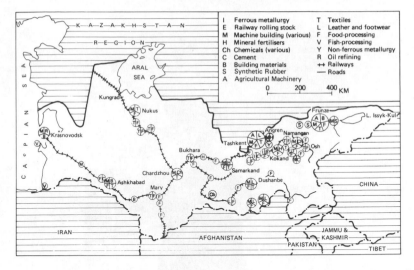

Fig. 272. Central Asia Economic Region: railways and industrial structure of towns.

the mills of Ivanovo and Moscow (*see* Fig. 272). The Turk-Sib line provides a link around the eastern end of Lake Balkhash between the cities of Central Asia and the Trans-Siberian Railway, and the Trans-Kazakhstan trunk line provides a direct route from the same cities northwards through the area of heavy industry around Karaganda, to the grain-growing areas of northern Kazakhstan and Western Siberia. The construction of these and other lines in the region has been accomplished in the face of very severe natural hazards, not least drifting sands.

Transport of another kind is present at the Soviet "cosmodrome" at Baykonur (near Karsakpay) in the desert of Kazakhstan between Karaganda and the Aral Sea. The Baykonyr site is used for the launching of spacecraft of various kinds (e.g. *Salyut 5* and *Salyut 6* unmanned orbiting space stations, *Soyuz 26* two-man spacecraft, *Meteor 2* weather satellite, *Molniya 3* communications satellite, *Ekran* television satellite etc.).

POPULATION AND CITIES

The population of Soviet Central Asia increased 44 per cent between 1959 (13.8 million) and 1970 (19.8 million). Almost 25.5 million now live in the region. i.e. a 29 per cent increase in nine years. Such growth rates and absolute population increases are a reflection of high birth rates among the indigenous Moslem peoples, and also of in-migration into the region on the part of the Russians and

Fig. 273. A young Uzbek.

Ukrainians. It would appear, however, that the net in-migration up to the 1960s has now given way to a net out-migration.

The bulk of this burgeoning and youthful population is of Turkic stock (*see* Fig. 273) traditionally Moslem in religion and Turko-Tatar in language, but there are also mixtures of indigenous and in-coming, mainly Slav, groups. Settlement, generally in the form of large nucleated villages (*kishlaks*), occurs in oases, the better watered areas and along the railways, and is highly concentrated and localised. Population densities range from 40 to 80 per km² in the oases, and in places (e.g. the Fergana Basin) may even reach 800 per km². The deserts are virtually uninhabited. Irrigation agriculture, the mining of mineral resources and the presence of developing and diversified industries related to the gas-oil-chemicals complex account for most of the main centres of population.

Tashkent (population: 1,779,000)
Tashkent is both capital of the Uzbek Republic and regional capital of Central Asia. The old Moslem town, situated in the oasis of the Chirchik tributary of the Amu-Darya, has been a centre of irrigation agriculture and the focus of caravan routes through the desert since its foundation in the seventh century AD. The Soviet city is now the dominant settlement. It is a thriving industrial centre and rail focus in the heart of a rich and densely populated cotton growing area. Cotton textiles, textile machinery and agricultural machinery are major industrial enterprises, but there are in addition leather works, sawmills, food-processing plant and tobacco factories (*see* Fig. 272). The natural gas piped from Gazli which fires the Syrdarya thermal station (3.2 million kW designed capacity) at Shirin, south of Tashkent, is a valuable source of power for the city's industries. Some indication of the dynamics of population growth in Tashkent is given by the following census figures:

1959 :   927,000
1970 : 1,385,000
1979 : 1,779,000

The population, chiefly Uzbeks and Russians has thus almost doubled in the last two decades. This is mainly a reflection of ethnic traditions stressing large families and many children. Tashkent now ranks fourth city in size in the Soviet Union.

Frunze (population: 533,000)
Capital of the Kirgiz Republic, Frunze stands 670 m above sea-level in mountainous country near the Chu River which flows from Lake Issyk-Kul and peters out in the desert. Originally a fortress and known as Pishpek, it became settled as the centre of a Russian colony in the latter part of the nineteenth century. Although it has been served by a branch of the Turk-Sib railway since 1924 which accelerated its economic development, the interests of the city remain primarily agricultural. It has one of the largest meat-packing plants of its kind in the USSR, and there are other food industries, textile and engineering (agricultural machinery, machine tools) factories. The mainly Russian population showed a remarkable increase of 24 per cent between 1970 and 1979.

Dushanbe (population: 493,000)
Capital of the Tadzhik Republic, Dushanbe occupies the site of an old Tadzhik village in the Gissar valley (tributary of the Vakhsh River) on the southern slopes of the Zeravshan Range (*see* Fig. 274). In 1926, when it was elevated to town status, its population was

(Novosti)

Fig. 274. Dushanbe: capital of Tadzhik SSR showing Privokzalnaya Square.

only 6,000. This has increased eighty-fold during the last half century, due to some thriving light industries, the presence of cotton and silk textile works and superphosphate plant, the administrative functions of a capital city, but not least to the fertility and natural increase of the population.

Samarkand (population: 476,000)
The ancient Maracanda, Samarkand is the oldest city of Central Asia, dating possibly from the fourth or third millenium BC. It lies in the fertile, irrigated, loess lands of the valley of the Zeravshan River, a cradle of civilisation in Central Asia. Samarkand, in the fourteenth century AD, was capital of the Mongol (Tatar) empire of Tamerlane (*Timur i Leng* − "the lame Timur") which extended over much of the Middle East. Ruins of many of its mosques (e.g. Bibi Khanum) and mausoleums remain, but several have been beautifully restored (e.g. Gur-Emir, Tamerlane's tomb) (*see* Fig. 275). The Registan, or central square, of the ancient Samarkand has been described by Curzon as "the noblest public square in the world" (*see* Fig. 276). But the modern Samarkand, established by the Russians in 1868, is an industrial city and has virtually engulfed the old town. Its broad, tree-lined streets and Soviet-style buildings contrast markedly with the intricate labryinth of narrow winding

Fig. 275. Samarkand, showing the Gur-Emir mausoleum with large turquoise dome built in the fifteenth century. Inside the mausoleum is the tomb of Timur (Tamerlane) the Mongol, his two sons and grandsons, including the famous Ulug Beg and Mohammed Sultan.

Fig. 276. Samarkand, showing minarets and tiled facade of the Ulug Beg mosque school (*medresseh*). This mosque school and those of Shir Dar and Till a Kari form an ensemble of great architectural symmetry and beauty enclosing the Registan (central square) of Old Samarkand. Capital of the empire of Timur in the fourteenth century, Samarkand is the oldest city of Soviet Central Asia.

streets of the Moslem part. The industries include engineering (tractor parts, cinema equipment), chemicals, footwear, fruit canning, cotton-processing and silk-weaving. Natural gas, piped from the Gazli area 290 km to the west, provides a valuable new source of industrial power. The Trans-Caspian Railway line links Samarkand with other parts of Central Asia and with the Soviet Russian world to the north, while the famous old "Silk Road" from China and India to Samarkand is now asphalted and bears heavy lorries instead of camels.

Ashkhabad (population: 312,000)
Capital of the Turkmen Republic, Ashkhabad is situated in the irrigated lands of the oasis of Akhal Teke between the foothills of the Kopet-Dag and the Karakum. It was founded as a fort and base for the construction of the Trans-Caspian Railway between Krasonvodsk and Tashkent. A serious earth tremor in 1948 destroyed much of the town, but this has been rebuilt according to the original radial plan. It is a centre for glass, food, textiles, leather, printing, metalwork and carpets, and its importance in the film-making industry accounts for the local manufacture of cinema equipment. The Karakum Canal (*see* Fig. 266 and p. 441) provides additional water for the Ashkhabad Oasis, and a pipeline carries refined oil products from the Krasnovodsk refinery 530 km to the west. The city is isolated from the main concentrations of people in Central Asia but its population increased by 59,000 (23 per cent) between 1970 and 1979.

Andizhan (population: 230,000); *Namangan* (population: 227,000)
Two of the largest towns of the Fergana valley, Andizhan and Namangan process cotton and foods grown locally, although Andizhan also has engineering and chemical plant and Namangan a viscose rayon plant. Both towns are surrounded by areas with exceptionally high densities of population (as much as 800 per km² around Andizhan) and are linked with each other and with other parts of the valley by the Fergana circular railway.

Kokand (population: 153,000)
Situated on the alluvial fan of the Sokh River on the southern side of the Fergana Basin, Kokand is an ancient city (one time centre of a *khanate*) serving as commercial centre for a rich agricultural (cotton, grains, fruit, vegetables, alfalfa) area.

Bukhara (population: 185,000)
Situated in the Zeravshan valley, Bukhara, like Samarkand, is one of the oldest centres of civilisation in Central Asia. It was, for many centuries, a major centre of Islamic learning and it still retains several

outstanding examples of Muslim architecture such as the Ismail Samani mausoleum (9-10th century) and the 60 m Kalyan minaret (12th century). These ancient monuments, together with the bazaars and flat-roofed houses of sun-dried brick, make Bukhara a veritable museum town holding great attraction to Western tourists. The industrial part of Bukhara contains plant processing the fur of Karakul sheep (Persian lamb) and spinning cotton. The remarkable 66 per cent increase in the town's population in the inter-censal period 1970-79 reflects a 5.7 per cent annual growth rate, due largely to natural increase (*see* p. 156).

Fergana (population: 176,000)
With Andizhan, Namangan, Kokand and Margilan, Fergana is one of an inner ring of towns within the irrigated and densely populated Fergana valley. Like them it processes locally produced agricultural raw materials, particularly cotton.

Osh (population: 169,000)
Situated at the eastern irrigated margins of the Fergana valley, Osh has a cotton *Kombinat* based on locally-grown cotton.

CHAPTER XIX

Soviet Economic Progress

In the preceding chapters, reference has been made to new coal, iron and steel, petroleum, natural gas, petrochemicals, electrical machinery, hydro-electric and other installations, and to a general expansion of heavy industry. Attention has been drawn to the mechanisation and reform of agriculture under the Soviets, to the construction and electrification of railways, the construction of waterways and irrigation canals, oil and gas pipelines, and to several other indicators of economic expansion. The expansion has taken place at a rapid pace since 1917 when the Communists secured a monopoly of power. In the (practically) two-thirds of a century under Communist rule the Soviet Union has been transformed from a backward agricultural country into an industrial giant capable of producing jet aircraft, hydrogen bombs, intercontinental ballistic missiles, manned and unmanned spacecraft, moon probes, electronic and precision instruments and consumer goods of the highest quality.

REASONS FOR ECONOMIC GROWTH

What is the explanation for this remarkable achievement in such a comparatively short space of time? How did it come about? In the first instance there are ample supplies of the basic raw materials for industry within the Union. Very often geographical locations that are inconvenient in relation to the main centres of population tend to impose a strain on the transport system, but the mineral deposits that have been found are usually fairly easy to work. It would appear that the Soviet Union is generously endowed with large quantities of coal, oil and natural gas, that iron ore is plentiful and that she is completely self-sufficient in most industrial materials.

A transfer of labour from the relatively over-populated country-side to the towns has helped to swell the industrial labour force. At first, former peasants, half-trained, were poor material and were liable to produce a high proportion of spoiled work, but with the passage of time the country has acquired a fairly large and skilled labour force. There is still not enough skilled labour available in the USSR, and priority is given to supplying heavy industries such as coal, engineering, ferrous and non-ferrous metallurgy and the oil, gas and petrochemical industries.

The urbanisation and "Sovietisation" which accompanied the movement of people from the countryside to the towns greatly increased the consumption of industrial goods and services, which in turn led to an increase in the number of bakeries, meat-processing plant and much else besides. While not necessarily reflecting improved welfare for the people, urbanisation tended to expand measurable industrial growth.

Productivity per worker in many branches of industry was brought quickly to a favourable level by the borrowing of technical ideas from industrially advanced countries. In the early days of her industrialisation the Soviet Union by-passed time-consuming "trial and error processes" to which new ideas are usually subject. For instance, technical assistance during the building of the huge iron and steel plant at Magnitogorsk in 1929 to 1933 was obtained from American experts. Several foreign firms acted as consultants for the Dnieper hydro-electric station (Dneproges) — the first of the large hydro-electric stations to be built in the Soviet Union — and most of the equipment for the station was supplied by the General Electric Company (UK).

A further and not unimportant factor accounting for the flattering pace of Soviet industrial achievement was the low point at which the country started. Nonetheless, Soviet industrial growth has been more rapid than that of other countries in a comparable stage of industrialisation.

Finally, probably the most significant factor in the industrial expansion of the country has been the Soviet political system — Communism. This political system facilitated the concentration of resources on capital goods rather than on consumer goods in a way which would have been impossible under any democratic form of government which, to remain in office, relies on the votes of the people.

FIVE-YEAR PLANS

The development of the Soviet economy is implemented through a series of plans. Within the framework of fifteen to twenty year long-term reference plans, more detailed Five-year medium-term and annual plans operate. In general, the targets of the long- and medium-term plans are relatively ambitious, while the annual plans are more realistic and their targets are usually achieved in most sectors. Responsibility for planning lies with the State Planning Commission, Gosplan and its subordinate organs representing the individual republics and the eighteen basic economic regions (plus Moldavia) (Chapters XII-XVIII), in conjuction with Ministries and other interested bodies.

The aim of the planning is a balanced development of the national economy. Such is the scale and structure of the Soviet economy and that of its numerous interdependent sectors, that it can be organised only on a nationwide basis. Centralised planning thus embraces the whole of the USSR. The balanced development of the economy requires that every industrial establishment, collective farm or state farm provides the goods, crops, products and services necessary to meet the need of the national economy and the population.

The economic plans are scientifically based and conform to objective plans. Each plan takes the form of a government decree and has the force of law. Under it everyone must strictly adhere to the planned assignments fixed by the state.

Under the first Five-year Plan, begun formally in 1928, stress was laid on the development of heavy industry, particularly in outlying areas rich in natural resources and inhabited by national minorities. The second Five-year Plan (1933-37) was aimed at strengthening the defensive capacity of the Soviet Union and about half of the total investment in new heavy industrial constructions was allocated to areas beyond the Ural Mountains. Some stress was given to increasing the output and improving the quality of consumer goods under this plan, but targets were not achieved. The third Five-year Plan, to run from 1938-42, was cut short in June 1941 when Germany attacked the USSR. Under the plan, stress was to be laid on war industries. Industrial output had been increasing appreciably in the Urals, the Volga, Siberia and Central Asian areas, but, following the German invasion, the whole of the national economy was switched to the war effort. The Supreme Soviet adopted a fourth Five-year Plan in 1946, a fifth in 1951 (containing measures to stimulate the development of agriculture, improve the output of consumer goods and expand internal trade), and a sixth in 1956 (demanding priority for further development of heavy industry and an increase in agricultural production). In consequence of changes made in planning methods (collective farms were given greater authority over planning their own output, and industrial establishments in various basic industries were turned over from Union to republic control), the sixth Five-year Plan was abandoned and a

Seven-year Plan for 1959-65 adopted. Under the plan, special attention was given to mechanisation of agriculture and arduous industrial labour, automation and new technological processes, and housing. In April 1966, the 23rd Congress of the Communist Party adopted "directives" for the eighth Five-year Plan for 1966-70. Under these, power output was to reach 830,000-850,000 million kW/h; oil 345-55 million tonnes; coal 665-75 million tonnes; steel 124-9 million tonnes; mineral fertilisers 62-5 million tonnes; machine tools 220,000-230,000; cars 700,000-800,000; tractors 600,000-625,000; paper 5-5.3 million tonnes; cement 100-105 million tonnes; fabrics 9.5-9.8 million m^2; leather footwear 610-30 million pairs; meat 5.9-6.2 million tonnes; butter 1.2 million tonnes; sugar 9.8-10 million tonnes. The average output of grain was to increase 30 per cent over 1964-65; 7,000 km of new railway line, 63,000 km of new motor roads and 35-40 new airports were to be built; marine tonnage was to be increased by 50 per cent.

The directives of the ninth Five-year Plan (1971-75) stressed as a main task ". . . a considerable rise of the people's material and cultural level on the basis of a high rate of development of socialist production, enhancement of its efficiency, scientific and technical progress and acceleration of the growth of labour productivity". In the event the Gross National Product (GNP) of the Soviet Union grew at an average annual rate of 3.8 per cent compared with the 5.5 per cent achieved in the eighth Five-year Plan (1966-70). Industrial output grew by 6.0 per cent per annum (6.8 per cent in 1966-70) but, largely as a result of two disastrous harvests in 1972 and 1975, agricultural output declined by 0.6 per cent per annum.

The objectives of the tenth Five-year Plan (1976-80) labelled the "Five-year Plan of efficiency and quality", were similar to those of the previous period. Industry (with emphasis on the heavy industrial sectors, particularly petrochemicals, electrical machinery and railway industries), and the armed forces were to maintain their prime claim on the nation's resources. Agriculture, subject to extreme fluctuations in output, was to be further stimulated by more efficient and intensive farming, greater use of chemicals and machinery and was to receive a quarter of the government's investment; improved technology and efficiency in both industry and agriculture were regarded as the key to increased productivity and there was renewed stress on the creation of territorial production complexes. Consumers were to enjoy a moderate increase in living levels, the "chief task" being "raising the people's material and cultural living standards". Despite mounting social pressure for better living standards the authorities appeared to have abandoned the pursuit of a consumer-oriented economic policy.

THE PRESENT-DAY ECONOMY

In the past, the central planning mechanism of the Soviet Union ensured steady economic growth by exploiting the vast reserves of raw materials and a large rural labour force. There was a rapid advance in material production rather than in any over-all improvement in living standards of the population. Coal, iron, steel, petroleum, cement, engineering, received proportionately more of the investment capital than other sectors of the economy and over the last sixty or more years these sectors have experienced spectacular expansion. Agriculture, in contrast, suffered until comparatively recently from under-investment. For many years there have been material inadequacies in virtually everything from rural roads to the production of ploughs and harrows. Farm workers, too, have been dissatisfied with their peasant and, seeming, second-class citizen status. The effects of vagaries in the weather constitute an ever present hazard to their conditions. Agricultural plans have hardly ever been fulfilled. The magnitude of the Soviet grain purchases from the USA, Canada and Australia in 1975 and the contracting to buy 6-8 million tonnes of wheat and maize from the USA under the tenth Five-year Plan* strongly suggests that the drought of that year was merely the culminating disaster in a long succession of failures in the agricultural front. Because of the lag in agricultural production, food and many light industries have fallen short of their targets.

Recent Soviet statistics suggest a slowing down in the pace of economic growth (*see* Table 71). Reasons suggested by foreign observers relate to a scarcity of skilled labour, difficulty and expense of obtaining raw materials, and low productivity (poor use is made of high technology imported from the west), a reduction in the length of the working week, and the high level of military expenditure. Possibly of equal if not greater significance is the central planning mechanism itself which seems reluctant to devolve authority. This results in bureaucratic delays and inefficiency, often preventing the swift incorporation of technological innovations into factory and farm production. It would appear that only by a more intensive and more efficient use of resources will continued growth be ensured.

Industrial output and growth reflect material production in the Soviet Union (*see* Appendix II), but they do not necessarily reflect any rise in the over-all standard of living of the Soviet population. Living standards have not risen commensurate with the industrialisation of the country; for the bulk of the population they are still far below those of industrialised nations in the West. Some consumer goods are still in short supply in the Soviet Union and the quality of

*Extended for one further year, i.e. until 1982.

TABLE 71. CHANGES IN ECONOMIC GROWTH 1951-80

| | Percentage increase over previous year | | |
	National income*	Gross industrial production	Gross agricultural production
1951	12.3	16.4	−6.7
1952	10.9	11.6	8.7
1953	9.5	12.0	2.9
1954	12.2	13.3	5.1
1955	11.9	12.5	11.0
1956	11.3	10.6	13.5
1957	7.0	10.0	3.1
1958	12.4	10.0	10.8
1959	7.5	11.4	0.4
1960	7.7	9.5	2.2
1961	6.8	9.1	3.0
1962	5.7	9.7	1.2
1963	4.0	8.1	−7.5
1964	9.3	7.3	14.5
1965	6.9	8.7	1.9
1966	8.1	8.7	8.7
1967	8.6	10.0	1.5
1968	8.3	8.3	1.5
1969	4.8	7.1	−3.3
1970	9.0	8.5	10.3
1971	5.6	7.7	1.1
1972	3.9	6.5	−4.1
1973	8.9	7.5	16.1
1974	5.4	8.0	−2.4
1975	4.5	7.5	−5.3
1976	5.9	4.8	6.5
1977	4.5	5.7	4.0
1978	4.8	4.8	3.0
1979	2.0	3.4	−4.0
1980	3.5	3.6	−3.0
1981	3.3	3.4	−2.0

*Soviet definition, i.e. material goods only; it includes construction, and also transport of and trade in goods.

Source: *Narodnoye Khozyaistvo SSSR v 1979*, Moscow 1980, and, *USSR v tsifrakh v 1980*, Moscow 1981.

others is low. There is a shortage of adequate living accommodation in most towns and there is chronic residential overcrowding. Good roads are all too few and rural roads are in a very bad state. Farms may be cut off from their neighbours and from the outside world for months on end during the traditional Russian spring and autumn *bezdorozhye* (roadlessness).

Private transport is still limited, though car sales to the population have increased considerably in recent years. Under the eighth Five-year Plan (1966-70), the Italian Fiat Company was contracted to build a major motor vehicle plant at Togliatti in the Volga Region (*see* pp. 340-1) and help reorganise the antiquated car production plant elsewhere in the USSR. By the end of the ninth Five-year Plan the Togliatti plant was producing 660,000 cars a year and 720,000 cars by 1980. Total USSR production of passenger cars that same year was 1,327,000. This compares with 3,530,000 for West Germany, 3,487,000 for France, 1,445,200 for Italy, and 923,000 for the UK in 1980. (In 1979 the USA produced 8,434,200 cars and Japan 6,175,000.) Current increases in output should soon take the Soviet Union into the age of the private car.

Under the recently announced eleventh Five-year Plan (1981-85) consumer goods are, for the first time, to be given priority over heavy industry, and food supplies are to be improved. It will be many years, however, before output increases to enable Soviet society to reap the full fruits of its labours.

World Production Data for Selected Commodities

Unless otherwise stated all figures are in thousands of tonnes (metric tonnes) for the years listed. (1 metric tonne = 0.984206 long ton.)

Source: *The Geographical Digest*, 1982; London, George Philip.

COAL (see also Lignite)	1979	1980	LIGNITE AND BROWN COAL	1979	1980
World	2,580,000	3,200,000	World	942,000	966,000
USA	703,752	714,468	East Germany	256,068	258,000
USSR	495,000	492,995	*USSR*	161,148	159,996
China (1977)	490,000	—	West Germany	130,584	129,828
Poland	201,000	193,116	Czechoslovakia	96,204	94,896
UK	122,808	130,140	Yugoslavia	41,676	45,444

CRUDE PETROLEUM	1979	1980	NATURAL GAS (thousand teracalories)	1979	1980
World	3,225,300	3,074,000	World	12,778	13,170
USSR	586,000	603,000	USA	5,056	4,875
Saudi Arabia	469,900	493,600	*USSR*	3,388	3,629
USA	480,000	483,600	Netherlands	729	666
Iraq	170,600	130,200	Canada	702	689
Venezuela	125,400	116,000	UK	367	352

IRON ORE
(Fe content)

	1979	1980
World	530,000	520,000
USSR	145,044	147,600
Australia	53,875	62,070
USA	53,129	42,946
Brazil	40,580	41,159
Canada	36,366	30,385

PIG-IRON AND
FERRO-ALLOYS

	1979	1980
World	540,000	538,000
USSR	120,000	—
Japan	85,728	88,908
USA	78,960	62,340
West Germany	35,352	34,056
China (1977)	30,000	—

CRUDE STEEL

	1979	1980
World	710,000	730,000
USSR	149,004	147,996
Japan	111,744	100,800
USA	124,272	111,408
West Germany	46,044	43,812
China (1977)	27,000	—

BAUXITE

	1979	1980
World	87,870	92,623
Australia	27,585	27,178
Guinea	12,199	13,311
Jamaica	11,505	12,064
USSR	6,500	6,400
Surinam	4,741	4,903

COPPER ORE
(Cu content)

	1979	1980
World	7,646	7,816
USA	1,114	1,168
USSR	1,150	1,150
Chile	1,062	1,068
Canada	636	708
Zambia	588	596

LEAD ORE
(Pb content)

	1979	1980
World	3,627	3,603
USSR	590	580
USA	526	550
Australia	422	398
Canada	342	297
Peru	184	189

ZINC ORE
(Zn content)

	1979	1980
World	6,345	6,248
Canada	1,204	1,059
USSR	1,020	1,000
Peru	491	494
Australia	528	531
USA	294	368

PHOSPHATE ROCK
(P_2O_3 content)

	1977	1978
World	115,920	125,370
USA	47,256	50,037
USSR	24,200	24,800
Morocco	17,572	19,273
China	4,100	4,400
Tunisia	3,615	3,712

POTASH (K_2O content)				CHROME ORE (Cr_2O_3 content)		
	1976	*1977*			*1977*	*1978*
World	25,440	26,669	World		4,200	4,260
USSR	8,500	8,500	South Africa		1,461	1,380
Canada	5,215	5,910	USSR		910	860
East Germany	3,161	3,244	Albania		370	390
West Germany	2,441	2,838	Zimbabwe		305	300
USA	2,177	2,229	Brazil		260	280

SALT				NICKEL ORE (Ni content)		
	1977	*1978*			*1979*	*1980*
World	172,500		World		679	748
USA	38,736	42,869	Canada		128	143
China	17,100	19,530	USSR		145	195
USSR	14,317	14,500	New Caledonia		83	86
West Germany	12,556	12,961	Australia		70	70
UK	8,202	7,310	Indonesia		36	41

MANGANESE ORE (Mn content)				SILVER (Ag content)		
	1977	*1978*			*1979*	*1980*
World	9,900	9,380	World		10,933	10,422
USSR	2,904	2,945	USSR		1,550	1,550
South Africa	2,338	1,950	Mexico		1,537	1,473
Brazil	900	—	Peru		1,332	1,232
Gabon	941	1,000	Canada		1,184	1,037
Australia	811	633	USA		1,164	974

TUNGSTEN ORE (WO_3 content)				WHEAT		
	1977	*1978*			*1979*	*1980*
World	51,800	55,500	World		428,095	445,123
China	11,300	11,300	USSR		90,211	98,100
USSR	10,340	10,700	USA		58,080	64,492
USA	3,436	4,320	China		62,803	54,158
Bolivia	3,759	3,997	India		35,508	31,564
Thailand	2,464	3,780	France		19,393	23,668

MILLET	1979	1980	SUGAR-BEET	1979	1980
World	27,295	28,968	World	261,652	266,446
India	8,216	9,500	*USSR*	76,000	79,600
China	6,004	5,803	France	26,444	26,347
Nigeria	3,130	3,200	USA	19,954	21,115
USSR	1,553	2,000	West Germany	18,358	19,122
Niger	1,246	1,371	Italy	13,465	13,521

BARLEY	1979	1980	RYE	1979	1980
World	158,990	162,327	World	23,725	27,324
USSR	47,954	44,500	*USSR*	8,103	10,200
France	11,228	11,758	Poland	5,233	6,566
Canada	8,460	11,041	West Germany	2,105	2,098
UK	9,620	10,300	China	2,000	2,000
			East Germany	1,830	1,900

POTATOES	1979	1980	OATS	1979	1980
World	284,471	227,307	World	42,909	42,667
USSR	90,300	66,900	*USSR*	15,162	14,200
Poland	49,582	26,400	USA	7,757	6,642
USA	15,768	13,737	Canada	2,978	3,028
China	12,536	12,537	West Germany	2,999	2,658
East Germany	12,540	9,214	Poland	2,199	2,245

COTTON (lint)	1979	1980	COTTONSEED	1979	1980
World	14,050	14,318	World	26,396	27,155
USSR	2,821	3,200	*USSR*	5,954	6,600
China	2,200	2,707	China	4,414	5,414
USA	3,163	2,422	USA	5,258	3,955
India	1,220	1,300	India	2,440	2,800
Pakistan	750	710	Pakistan	1,301	1,400

FLAX (fibre and tow)			HEMP (fibre and tow)		
	1979	*1980*		*1979*	*1980*
World	591	594	World	220	232
USSR	311	317	*USSR*	57	57
China	76	79	India	46	50
France	51	51	China	25	36
Poland	64	45	Romania	30	31
Egypt	25	35	Hungary	15	15

WOOL (clean)			FISH CATCHES		
	1979	*1980*		*1977*	*1978*
World	1,638	1,680	World	71,213	72,380
Australia	426	426	Japan	10,763	10,753
USSR	283	277	*USSR*	9,352	8,930
New Zealand	234	252	China	4,700	4,660
Argentina	92	106	USA	3,085	3,512
South Africa	86	91	Peru	2,541	3,365

ROUNDWOOD (coniferous) (million m^3)			ROUNDWOOD (broadleaved) (million m^3)		
	1978	*1979*		*1978*	*1979*
World	1,135.4	1,193.7	World	1,698.6	1,732.3
USSR	302.3	302.3	India	193.8	198.1
USA	256.1	260.7	Indonesia	153.1	158.0
Canada	143.1	146.8	Brazil	148.1	152.5
China	99.3	99.3	China	113.2	113.2
Sweden	41.3	52.9	Nigeria	84.9	87.3

WOOD PULP (chemical)			WOOD PULP (mechanical)		
	1978	*1979*		*1978*	*1979*
World	80,606	85,699	World	25,353	26,607
USA	34,105	36,073	Canada	7,545	7,588
Canada	10,952	11,411	USA	3,544	3,977
Japan	6,246	6,812	Finland	1,984	2,238
Sweden	6,227	6,558	Sweden	1,748	1,840
USSR	6,391	6,391	*USSR*	1,840	1,981

APPENDIX II

Soviet and World Production Data

Some comparisons between the Soviet Union and the European Economic Community (Federal Republic of Germany, France, Italy, Netherlands, Belgium, Luxembourg, United Kingdom, Ireland and Denmark), the United States of America, and the United Kingdom in 1979.

	USSR	EEC	USA	UK
Area (thousand km^2)	22,402.0	1,525.6	9,363.1	244.1
Population (000), mid 1979	264,108	260,435	220,584	56,001
Density per km^2	12	171	24	229
Projected population (000) 1985	279,558	261,156	232,880	56,298
Projected population (000) 1990	291,637	263,129	243,513	57,027
Crude steel production (000 tonnes, 1979)	149,087	140,195	126,111	21,472
Aluminium production (000 tonnes, 1979)	2,400.0	2,021.0	4,556.9	359.5
Refined copper production (000 tonnes, 1979)	1,480.0	934.0	1,981.3	121.7
Refined lead production (000 tonnes, 1979)	780.0	1,245.0	1,225.7	368.3
Zinc production (000 tonnes, 1979)	1,085.0	1,291.0	525.7	76.7
Refined tin production (000 tonnes, 1979)	18.0	19.0	4.7	11.4

	USSR	*EEC*	*USA*	*UK*
Sulphuric acid (000 tonnes, 1979)	22,411	19,501	35,970	3,453
Passenger cars (000)	1,314.0	10,597.0	8,434.2	1,070.5
Commercial motor vehicles (000)	859.0	1,385.0	3,046.6	408.4
Total cereal production (000 tonnes, 1977-79 average)	194,332	111,113	273,250	17,135
Wheat production (000 tonnes, 1977-79 average)	101,030	44,148	54,210	6,351
Meat production (000 tonnes, 1979)	15,511	22,704	25,656	3,154
Milk production (000 tonnes, 1979)	93,300	113,305	55,978	17,839

Source: *EUROSTAT*, 1981.

Glossary of Terms

Afganets	South-west wind in Middle Asia.
ASSR	Autonomous Soviet Socialist Republic: a nationality based division of a Union republic.
Aul	Mountain village (Caucasus).
BAM	Baykal-Amur Mainline railway.
Barkhan	Sand-dune, usually with a crescentic plan.
Basseyn	Basin — abbreviated to -*bass,* as in Donbass.
Batraki	Landless agricultural workers.
Biednyaki	Poor peasants.
Bolsheviks (bolshinstvo)	Russian for majority. Name, a misnomer, adopted by adherents of the radical left wing faction ("extremists") of the Russian Social Democratic Labour Party in 1903. Until 1952 part of official title of the Communist party of USSR.
Buran	Snowstorm.
CPSU	Communist Party of the Soviet Union.
Chernozem	Fertile black soil.
Comecon (CMEA)	Council for Mutual Economic Assistance: the body responsible for the co-ordination of economic development in the Soviet Union and the communist block of Eastern Europe, Cuba, Mongolia and Vietnam.
Derevnayas	Village.
Dolina	Valley.
Gavan	Harbour.
GAZ	Gorkiy motor works.
Glint	North-facing escarpment near the coast of the Gulf of Finland.
Goelro	State Commission for the Electrification of Russia.
Gora	Mountain.
Gorny	Baykal area wind.
Gorod (grad)	Town.
Gosplan	State Planning Committee (Commission).
Gryada	Ridge.
Harmsil (Turk)	Hot dry wind of Middle Asia (cf. *sukhovey*).
Izba	Log hut.

KamAZ	Kama River complex of motor-vehicle-building plants.
Karakul	Breed of sheep.
Kazaki	Cossacks.
Khata	Frame huts, adobe-filled.
Khrebet	Mountain range.
Kishlak (Turk)	Village.
Kolkhoz	Collective farm.
Kolkhoznik	Worker on a collective farm.
Kombinat	Industrial complex.
Kray	Territory: large, sparsely populated, administrative-area, usually in Siberia.
Kreml (Kremlin)	Fort.
Kulak	Prosperous peasant.
Kum (Turk)	Sand.
Kurott	Holiday resort.
Loess	Fine-textured loam, greyish-yellow in colour.
Makhorka	Low-grade tobacco.
Mensheviks (menshinstvo)	Russian for minority. Name given to right wing faction of the Russian Social Democratic Party in 1903. Usually associated with middle-class liberalism.
Mir	Village commune.
More	Sea.
Mys	Cape.
Neft	Petroleum.
Nizhniy	Lower.
Nizmennost	Lowland.
Novy (novaya)	New.
Oblast	Region or province: large administrative division of a Union republic.
Okrug	Autonomous area (AA): low status administrative area, part of a kray or oblast.
Ostrov	Island.
Ottepel	Unseasonal warm spell (temporary thaw) during winter cold.
Ovrag	Erosion gulley.
Ozero	Lake.
Permafrost	Soil or rock the temperature of which remains below 0 °C continuously for a year or more. The surface layer, which freezes and thaws seasonally, is called the active layer (*vechnaya merzlota*).
Podzol	Infertile acid soil, ash-grey in colour, beneath boreal forest.
Polesye	Forested land (lit. "land of forest clearing"): broad marshy depression in Belorussia. In English called Pripet or Pripyat Marshes.
Posyelok	Rural settlement in newly populated areas.

Povolzhye	Lands along the middle and lower Volga.
Prospect	Avenue.
Purga	Arctic blizzard.
Ravina	Plain.
Rayon	Area: lowest status administrative unit within a republic, kray, oblast, okrug or city.
Rasputitsa	Spring thaw (literally traffic stoppage), slush.
Reka	River.
Roundwood	Wood in its natural state as felled, or otherwise harvested, with or without bark.
RSFSR	The Russian Soviet Federative Socialist Republic.
Sarma	Baykal area wind (cf. *gorny*).
Serednyaki	Medium-placed peasants.
Serozem	Grey soil of desert and semi-desert areas.
Severnyy	Lower.
Solonchak	Saline soil, salt marsh.
Solonets	Alkali soil. Soil leached of soluble salts except sodium.
Sovkhoz	State farm.
Sredniy	Central.
SSR	Soviet Socialist Republic, one of fifteen comprising the Soviet Union.
Steppe	Dry grassland.
Sukhovey	Hot dry south or south-east wind in steppelands.
Syelos	Village.
Takyr	Clay flats.
Tau (Turk)	Mountain.
Tayga	Boreal — mainly coniferous — forest.
Travopolye	Grass-arable (*ley*) system of agriculture.
Tundra	Treeless sub-polar vegetation zone.
Ulitsa	Street.
Ustye	Estuary.
VAZ	Volga motor works at Togliatti.
Velikiy	Great.
Verkhniy	Upper, higher.
Vechnaya merzlota	Perenially frozen ground (*see Permafrost*).
Vozvyshennost	Upland.
Windchill	Cooling power of the combination of wind and temperature on human skin.
Xerophyte	A plant structure adapted for life and growth within a limited water supply.
Yurta	Felt tent.
Yuzhnyy	Southern.
Zavolzhye	Trans-Volga lands, i.e. to the east.
Zemlya	Land, earth.

Conversion of Metric Units to Imperial

TEMPERATURE: DEGREES CENTIGRADE TO DEGREES FAHRENHEIT

°C	°F	°C	°F	°C	°F
40	104.0	6	42.8	−28	−18.4
38	100.4	4	39.2	−30	−20.2
36	96.8	2	35.6	−32	−25.6
34	93.2	0	32.0	−34	−29.2
32	89.6	−2	28.4	−36	−32.8
30	86.0	−4	24.8	−38	−36.4
28	82.4	−6	21.2	−40	−40.0
26	78.8	−8	17.6	−42	−43.6
24	75.2	−10	14.0	−44	−47.2
22	71.6	−12	10.4	−46	−50.8
20	68.0	−14	6.8	−48	−54.4
18	64.4	−16	3.2	−50	−58.0
16	60.8	−18	−0.4	−52	−61.6
14	57.2	−20	−4.0	−54	−65.2
12	53.6	−22	−7.6	−56	−68.8
10	50.0	−24	−11.2	−58	−72.4
8	46.4	−26	−14.8	−60	−76.0

PRECIPITATION: MILLIMETRES TO INCHES

mm	in	mm	in
		800	31.50
2,000	78.70	750	29.53
1,000	39.37	700	27.56
950	37.40	650	25.59
900	35.43	600	23.62
850	33.46	550	21.65

mm	in	mm	in
500	19.69	250	9.84
450	17.72	200	7.87
400	15.75	150	5.91
350	13.78	100	3.94
300	11.81	50	1.97

DISTANCES: KILOMETRES TO MILES

km	miles	km	miles
1	0.6	20	12.4
2	1.2	30	18.6
3	1.9	40	24.9
4	2.5	50	31.1
5	3.1	60	37.3
6	3.7	70	43.5
7	4.3	80	49.7
8	5.0	90	55.9
9	5.6	100	62.1
10	6.2	200	124.3

HEIGHT: METRES TO FEET

m	ft	m	ft
10	32.81	150	492.13
20	65.62	200	656.17
30	98.43	250	820.21
40	131.23	300	984.25
50	164.04	350	1,148.29
60	196.85	400	1,312.34
70	229.66	450	1,476.38
80	262.47	500	1,640.42
90	295.28	1,000	3,280.84
100	328.08		

AREA: HECTARES TO ACRES

ha	acres	ha	acres
1	2.47	6	14.83
2	4.94	7	17.30
3	7.41	8	19.77
4	9.88	9	22.24
5	12.36	10	24.71

AREA: SQUARE KILOMETRES TO SQUARE MILES

km^2	$miles^2$	km^2	$miles^2$
1	0.39	6	2.32
2	0.77	7	2.70
3	1.16	8	3.09
4	1.54	9	3.47
5	1.93	10	3.86

Short Guide to Further Reading

(English references only)

BOOKS

Armstrong, T.E. *The Russians in the Arctic.* Methuen, London, 1958.

Armstrong, T.E. *The Northern Sea Route.* Cambridge: Sp. Pub. SPRI, 1952.

Armstrong, T.E. *Russian Settlement in the North.* Cambridge UP, London, 1965.

Armstrong, T., Rogers, G., and Rowley, G. *The Circumpolar North.* Methuen, London, 1978.

Balzak, S.S., Vasyutin, V.F. and Feigin, Ya. G. *Economic Geography of the USSR.* Macmillan, New York, 1949. Translated from the Russian, originally published in 1940.

Baransky, N.N. *Economic Geography of the USSR.* Foreign Languages Publishing House, Moscow, 1956.

Barashkova, E.P., Gaevskiy, V.L., L'yanchenko, L.N., Lygina, K.M. and Pivovarova, Z.I. *Radiatsionnyy Rezhim Territorii SSSR* (Radiation regime on the territory of the USSR). Gidrometeoizdat, Leningrad, 1961.

Barr, B.M. *The Soviet Wood-Processing Industry.* University of Toronto Press, Toronto, 1970.

Berg, L.S. *The Natural Regions of the USSR.* Macmillan, New York, 1950. Translated from the Russian.

Borisov, A.A. *Climates of the USSR.* Oliver & Boyd, Edinburgh and London, 1965. Translated from the second Russian edition of 1959, by R.A. Ledward and edited by Cyril A. Halstead.

Central Intelligence Agency. *Soviet Economic Plans for 1976-80. A first look (Research Aid).* Washington DC, 1976.

Cohen, S.B. *Geography and Politics in a Divided World.* Methuen, London, 1963.

Cole, J.P. *Geography of the USSR.* Penguin Books, Harmondsworth, 1967.

Cole, J.P. and German, F.C. *A Geography of the USSR: The Background to a Planned Economy.* Butterworth, London, 1961.

Cole, J.P. and German, F.C. *A Geography of the USSR: The Background to a Planned Economy.* 2nd edn. Butterworths, London, 1970.

Conolly, V. *Beyond the Urals — Economic Developments in Soviet Asia.* Oxford UP, London, 1967.

Conolly, V. *Siberia Today and Tomorrow.* Collins, London, 1975.

Council of Ministers of the USSR: Central Statistical Board. *The USSR in Figures for 1977. Statistical Handbook.* Statistika Publishers, Moscow, 1978.

Crankshaw, Edward. *Kruschev's Russia* (rev. edn.). Penguin Books, London, 1962.

Cressey, George B. *Soviet Potentials: A Geographical Appraisal.* Syracuse UP, NY, 1962.

Davies, R.W. (ed.). *The Soviet Union.* Allen & Unwin, London, 1978.

Dewdney, J.C. *Patterns and problems of regionalisation in the USSR.* Dept. Geog., Research Paper No. 8, Univ. of Durham, 1967.

Dewdney, J.C. *A Geography of the Soviet Union,* 2nd edn. Pergamon, Oxford, 1970.

Dewdney, J.C. *The USSR.* Hutchinson, London, 1978.

East, W. Gordon. *The Soviet Union.* Searchlight Book, No. 15. D. Van Nostrand, New Jersey, 1963.

East, W. Gordon and Moodie, Arthur E. (eds.). *The Changing World.* Harrap & Co., 1956. (Chapters on the USSR by W. Gordon East and Theodore Shabad.)

East, W. Gordon and Spate, O.H.K. (eds.). *The Changing Map of Asia: A Political Geography,* 4th edn. Dutton, New York; Methuen, London, 1961. (Chapter 6 deals with the Asiatic USSR.)

East, W.G., Spate, O.H.K. and Fisher, C.A. (eds.). *The Changing Map of Asia.* Methuen, London, 1971.

Elliot, I.F. *The Soviet Energy Balance.* Praeger, New York, 1974.

European Communities (Statistical Office). *Eurostat. Basic Statistics of the Community,* Luxembourg, 1978.

French, R.A. and Hamilton, F.E.I. (eds.). *The Socialist City: spatial structure and urban policy,* and *The Individuality of the Soviet City.* Wiley, Chichester (England), 1979.

Fullard, H. (ed.). *The Geographical Digest, 1982.* Geo. Philip, London, 1982.

Gerasimov, I.P., *et al. Natural Resources of the Soviet Union: Their Use and Renewal.* Freeman, San Francisco, 1971.

Ginsberg, N. (ed.). *The Pattern of Asia.* Prentice-Hall, London, 1958. (Chapters 38 and 39.)

Goldhagen, E. (ed.). *Ethnic Minorities in the Soviet Union.* Praeger, New York, 1968.

Gregory, J.S. *Russian Land, Soviet People.* Harrap, London, 1968.

Hall, P. *The World Cities* (second edition). Weidenfeld and Nicolson, London, 1977. (Chapter on Moscow pp. 150-177.)

Hamilton, F.E.I. *The Moscow City Region.* In *Problem Regions of Europe* (ed. D.I. Scargill). Oxford UP, London, 1976.

Harris, C.D. (ed.). *Soviet Geography: Accomplishments and Tasks.* Amer. Geog. Soc., New York, 1962.

Harris, C.D. *Cities of the Soviet Union. Studies in their functions, size, density and growth.* Assoc. Amer. Geogr. Monograph Series. No. 5, Rand McNally, 1970.

Harris, C.D. *Cities of the Soviet Union.* Assoc. Amer. Geogr., Washington DC, 1972.

Hemy, G.W. *The Soviet Chemical Industry.* Hill, London, 1971.

Hodgkins, J.A. *Soviet Power: Energy Resources, Production and Potentials.* Prentice-Hall International, London, 1961.

Hoffman, G.W. (ed.). *A Geography of Europe, including the Asiatic USSR.* Ronald Press, New York, 1961. (Chapter 9 by T. Shabad.)

Hooson, David J.M. *A New Soviet Heartland.* Searchlight Book, No. 21. D. Van Nostrand, New Jersey, 1964.

Hooson, David J.M. *The Soviet Union.* Univ. of London Press, London, 1966.

Howe, G.M. *The USSR.* Hutton Educ. Pubs., Amersham (England), 1972.

Hutchings, R. *Soviet Economic Development.* Blackwell, Oxford, 1971.

Jorre, G. *The Soviet Union: The Land and its People.* 3rd edn. Longmans, London, 1967. (Translated by E.D. Laborde; revised by C.A. Halstead.)

Kirby, E.S. *The Soviet Far East.* St. Martin's Press, London, 1971.

Lascelles, D. *Comecon to 1980.* Financial Times, London, 1976.

Lascelles, D. *Comecon Mid-Plan Report.* Financial Times, London, 1978.

Lavrischev, A. *Economic Geography of the USSR.* Progress Publishers, Moscow, 1969.

Lloyds Bank. *Union of Soviet Socialist Republics.* Report prepared by Overseas Dept. 1978.

Lydolph, P.E. *Climates of the Soviet Union.* Vol. 7. In *World Survey of Climatology* (ed. H.E. Landsberg). Elsevier Sc. Pub. Co., Oxford, 1977.

Lydolph, P.E. *Geography of the USSR.* John Wiley & Sons, London, 1977 (3rd edn.).

Mackinder, H.J., *Democratic Ideals and Reality.* Constable, London, 1919.

Mathieson, R.S. *The Soviet Union: an economic geography.* Heinemann Educational Books, London, 1975.

Mellor, Roy E.H. *Geography of the USSR.* Macmillan, London, 1964.

Mirov, N.T. *Geography of Russia.* Wiley, New York, 1951.

Muir, R. *Modern political geography.* Macmillan, London, 1975.

Narodnoye Khozyaystvo SSSR (The economy of the USSR), *Statistical Yearbook.* Moscow, 1978, 1979, 1980.

Nove, A. *The Soviet Economy.* Allen & Unwin, London, 1968.

Nove, A. *An economic history of the USSR.* Revised edn. Allen & Unwin, London, 1976.

Parker, W.H. *An Historical Geography of Russia.* London Univ. Press, London, 1968.

Parker, W.H. *The Super-Powers: The United States and the Soviet Union compared.* Macmillan, London, 1977.

Paxton, J. *The Statesman's Year-book, 1978-79.* Macmillan, 1978.

Pokshishevsky, V. *Geography of the Soviet Union.* Progress Publishers, Moscow, 1974.

Price, L.W. *The periglacial environment, permafrost and man.* Ass. Amer. Geogr., Washington DC, 1972.

Pryde, P.R. *Conservation in the Soviet Union.* Cambridge UP, London, 1972.

Research Associates. *Bibliographical guide to the political economy of oil and natural gas in the Soviet Union and Eastern Europe.* Research Associates, Stone (England), 1978.

Robinson, H. *The USSR.* Univ. Tutorial Press, London, 1975.

Seatrack Publications. *Soviet Shipping.* Seatrack Pub., Colchester (England), 1976.

Shabad, T. *Geography of the USSR.* Columbia UP, New York, 1951.

Shabad, T. *The administrative territorial patterns of the Soviet Union.* In *The Changing World* (eds. W.G. East and E.A. Moodie). Harrap, London, 1956.

Shabad, T. *Basic industrial resources of the USSR.* Columbia UP, New York, 1969.

Shabad, T. and Mote, V.L. *Gateway to Siberian Resources* (The BAM), Scripton Publ. Co., Washington DC, 1977.

Slavin, S.V. *The Soviet North. Present development and prospects.* Progress Publishers, Moscow, 1972.

Smith, H. *The Russians.* Quadrangle Press, New York, 1976.

Solzhenitsyn, A. *The Gulag Archipelago.* Harper & Row, New York, 1975.

Suslov, S.P. *Physical Geography of Asiatic Russia.* W.H. Freeman, San Francisco, 1961. (Translated from the Russian.)

Symons, L.J. (ed.). *Geography of the USSR. (The Evolution of the State,* L.J. Symons; *Population,* J.C. Dewdney; *Transport,* R.E.H. Mellor; *Soils and Vegetation,* W.W. Newey; *Collectivised Agriculture,* L.J. Symons; Industrial Development,
Industrial Development, R.E.H. Mellor; *Physiography,* J.C. Dewdney; *Mineral Resources,* W.W. Newey; *Water,* W.W. Newey; *Climate and Man,* D.J.M. Hooson; *Cities and Villages,* R.E.H. Mellor; *The Regions,* J.C. Dewdney), Hicks Smith, Wellington, N.Z., 1969-70.

Symons, L.J. *Russian Agriculture: a geographical survey.* Bell, London, 1972.

Symons, L. and White, C. *Russian Transport: an historical and geographical survey.* Bell, London, 1975.

Sysoev, N.P. *Economics of the Soviet Fishing Industry.* (Translated from the Russian.) Program for Scientific Translations, US Dept. of Commerce and the National Science Foundation, Washington DC, 1974.

Thiel, E. *The Soviet Far East: A survey of its Physical and Economic Geography.* Methuen, London, 1957. (Translated by A. and B.M. Rookwood.)

Tikhomirov, M. *The Towns of Ancient Russia.* Foreign Languages Publishing House, Moscow, 1959.

Tseplyaev, V.P. *The Forests of the USSR.* (Trans. Gourevitch.) Daniel Davies & Co., NewYork, 1966.

Utechin, S.V. *Everyman's Concise Guide to Russia.* London, 1961.

Westwood, J.N. *Forestry.* Sector Policy Paper, Washington DC, Feb., 1978.

Young, O. *Resource Management at the International Level.* F. Pinter, London, 1977.

ATLASES

Kish, G. and Arbor, A. *Economic Atlas of the Soviet Union.* University of Michigan Press, Michigan, 1960.

Oxford Regional Economic Atlas: The USSR and Eastern Europe. Oxford UP, Oxford, 1956. (Rev. edn. 1969.)

Taaffe, R.N., and Kingsbury, R.C. *An Atlas of Soviet Affairs.* 2nd edn. Methuen, London, 1976.

Times Atlas of the World, Fifth Comprehensive Edition. Times Publishing Co. Ltd., London, 1975.

ARTICLES

Adams, R.B. "The Soviet metropolitan hierarchy: rationalization and comparison with the United States". *Sov. Geog.,* **XVIII** (9), 313-27, 1977.

Agranat, G.A. "Exploiting and conserving the rich Soviet North". *Geog. Mag.,* **XLVIII**, (10), 618-22, 1976.

Aleksandrov, Yu. K., Kistanov, V.V. and Ephshteyn, A.S. "A quantitative approach to designing a system of economic regions of the USSR". *Sov. Geog.,* **XV** (9), 543-54, 1974.

Armstrong, T. "The Soviet Northern Sea Route". *Geog. J.*, **120**, 136-48, 1955.

Armstrong, T. "The population of the north of the USSR". *Polar Record*, **II**, 172-8, 1962.

Armstrong, T. "The Baykal-Amur Railway". *Polar Record*, **17** (111), 677-81, 1975.

Ball, B. and Demko, G.J. "Internal migration in the Soviet Union", *Econ. Geog.*, **54** (2), 95-113, 1978.

Barr, B.M. "Regional variations in Soviet pulp and paper production". *Ann. Assoc. Amer. Geogr.*, **61** (1), 45-64, 1971.

Biryukov, V. "The Baykal-Amur Mainline: a major national construction project". *Sov. Geog.*, **XVI** (4), 225-30, 1975.

Bone, R.M. "The Soviet Forest Resources". *Canadian Geog.*, **10** (2), 94-116, 1966.

Brook, S.I. "Population of the USSR — Changes in the demographic, social and ethnic structure". *Geoforum*, **9**, 7-21, 1978.

Conolly, V. "The second Trans-Siberian railway", *Asian Affairs*, **2**, (Feb. 1975), 23-9.

Derbinova, M. "Industry located by plan". *Geog. Mag.*, **XLVIII** (6), 336-41, 1976.

Dewdney, J.C. "Population changes in the Soviet Union, 1959-70". *Geography*, **56** (4), 325-30, 1971.

Dienes, L. "Soviet energy resources and prospects". *Current History*, Sept. 1976.

Feshback, M. and Rapawy, S. "Soviet population and manpower trends and politics". In *Soviet Economy in a New Perspective*. Joint Economic Committee, US Congress, Washington, 112-54, 1976.

French, R.A. "Drainage and economic development of Poles'ye, USSR". *Econ. Geog.*, **35**, 172-80, 1959.

Harris, C.D. "Urbanisation and population growth in the Soviet Union, 1959-1970". *Amer. Geog. Rev.*, **LXI** (1), 102-24, 1971.

Holowacz, J. "Soviet forest resources analysed". *World Wood*, **15** (13), 13-15, 1974.

Khruschev, A.T. "Industrial nodes of the USSR and principles for a typology". *Sov. Geog.*, **XXII** (2), 91-102, 1971.

Konstantinov, O.A., Dzhaoshvili, V.Sh., Ata-Mirzayey, O. and Raimov, T. "Urbanisation in the USSR (Fifty Years of Experience)". In *Urbanisation in Developing Countries.* (eds.) S. Manzoor Alam and V.V. Pokshishevsky. Hyderabad, A.P. Osmania Univ., 1976.

Kristof, L.K.D. "The Russian image of Russia: an applied study in geopolitical methodology." In *Essays in Political Geography.* (ed. C.A. Fisher), Methuen, London, 1968.

Listengurt, F. "Soviets seek the city lights".*Geog. Mag.*, **XLVIII** (8), 492-6, 1976.

Lonsdale, R.E. and Thompson, H. "A map of the USSR's manufacturing". *Econ. Geog.* **36**, 36-52, 1960.

Lydolph, P.E. "The Russian sukhovey". *Ann. Ass. Amer. Geog.*, 291-309, 1964.

Lydolph, P.E., Johnson, R., Mintz, J. and Mill, M. "Recent population trends in the USSR". *Sov. Geog.*, **XIX** (8), 505-39, 1978.

Matrusov, N. "Western Siberia offers energy". *Geog. Mag.*, **XLVIII** (9), 548-52, 1976.

Mellor, R. "Some influence of physical environment upon transport problems in the Soviet Union." *Adv. Science*, **20**, 564-71, 1964.

Moshkin, A.M. "A typology of regional territorial production complexes". *Sov. Geog.*, **XVIII** (1), 60-7, 1977.

Mackinder, H.J. "The geographical pivot of history". *Geog. J.*, **23**, 421-4, 1904.

Popova, Ye. I. "The transport industry in the western and eastern zones of the USSR." *Sov. Geog.*, **XV** (4), 187-243, 1974.

Probst, A. Ye. "Territorial production complexes". *Sov. Geog.*, **XVIII** (3), 195-203, 1977.

Ratnieks, H. "Power reserve beyond the Caucasus". *Geog. Mag.*, **XLVIII** (7), 397-8, 1976.

Ratnieks, H. "Soviet nuclear energy without restraint". *Geog. Mag.*, **LII** (1), 1-6, 1979.

Reteyum, A. "Transformation scene in Central Asia", *Geog. Mag.*, **XLVIII** (11), 682-6, 1976.

Rikhter, G., Preobrazhenskiy, V. and Nefed'yeva, V. "The Soviet land revealed". *Geog. Mag.*, **XLVIII** (5), 266-72, 1976.

Rodgers, A. "The locational dynamics of Soviet industry". *Ann. Assoc. Amer. Geogr.*, **64**, 226-40, 1974.

Runova, T.G. "A natural resource regionalisation of the USSR". *Sov. Geog.*, **XIV** (8), 506-18, 1973.

Sallnow, J. "The population of Siberian and the Soviet Far East (1965-76)". *Sov. Geog.*, **XVIII** (9), 689-97, 1977.

Shabad, T. "News Notes." In *Soviet Geography. Review Translation.* Published monthly (except July and August), *Amer. Geog. Soc.*, Washington DC, since 1960.

Shabad, T. "Soviet migration patterns based on the 1970 census data". In *Demographic Developments in Eastern Europe.* Praeger, New York, 1977.

Sopko, R. "The USSR's paper industry." *Paper and Pulp International*, **15** (9), 25-7, and 43, 1973.

Soviet News. "Baykal-Amur Railway will speed development of Soviet Far East. 16 July, 1974.

Soviet News. "Big deposit of phosphorites has been found in Yakutia". 3 June 1975.

Soviet News. "Container route". 29 July 1975.

Sutton, W.R.J. "The forest resources of the USSR: their exploitation and their potential". *Commonwealth Forestry Review*, **54** (2), 160, 1975.

Symons, L.J. "Soviet civil air services". *Geography*, **58** (4), 328-30, 1973.

Thomas, C. "Population trends in the Soviet Union, 1959-64". *Geography*, **52**, 193-7, 1967.

Thomas, C. "Urbanisation and population change in European Russia, 1959-1969", *Scot. Geog. Mag.*, **88** (3), 196-207, 1972.

Turnock, D. "Transportation in the Soviet Union and Eastern Europe". In Schöpflin, G. (ed.) *The Soviet Union and Eastern Europe.* A. Blond, London, 1970.

Vasilev, P.V. "Forest resources and forest economy". In *Natural Resources of the Soviet Union: their Use and Renewal* (eds. Gerasimov, I.P., Armand, D.L. and Yefron, K.M.) (English edn. ed. W.A.D. Jackson). W.H. Freeman, San Francisco, 1971.

Index

References to maps and tables are distinguished by italic type. No distinction is made in the Index between administrative units and towns and cities of the same name.

Note: Rendering of Russian words in Latin presents some problems differently solved by various authors. No system of transliteration is fully satisfactory: when perfect, it must be rather complicated and difficult; when simple, it is not perfect. It seems, however, more important to have a transliteration system that can be consistent and generally used than a perfect one. Therefore in this Index when the geographical names used in the text are in their "traditional" form, transliteration rendered in Standard British System (BS 2979:1958), generally accepted also in most scientific American publications, is always added in square brackets.

This system cannot dispose of diacritical signs, which in the text are mostly omitted for technical typographic reasons. These signs mark the sound

soft *o* as ё (in text e)
hard *i* as ȳ (in text y)
hard *e* as é (in text e)
half consonant *i* as ĭ (in text y)
and the sign of palatalised consonants as ′ after the corresponding letter (in text omitted).

483

DATE DUE
